Race and Regionalism in the Politics of Taxation in Brazil and South Africa

Nationally specific definitions of citizenship proved decisive for the development of the Tax State in Brazil and South Africa in the 20th century. Although both countries had been divided along racial and regional lines in the late 19th century, watershed constitutions addressed these political problems in very different ways. South Africa's institutionalized white supremacy created a level of political solidarity that contributed to the development of a highly progressive and efficient tax system. In Brazil, federalism and official non-racialism proved more divisive, making the enactment and collection of progressive taxes much more difficult. The legacy of these divergent state-building processes remains evident at the beginning of the 21st century. Lieberman extends this analysis to a wider group of country cases and finds similar patterns and causal relationships between the politics of race, region, and taxation. The findings are based on extensive field research, large-scale national surveys, macroeconomic data, and various archival and secondary sources.

Evan S. Lieberman is Assistant Professor of Politics at Princeton University. He has published several articles in the field of comparative politics in scholarly journals, including *Comparative Political Studies*, *Politics and Society*, *Studies in Comparative International Development*, and *Journal of Development Studies*.

Cambridge Studies in Comparative Politics

General Editor
Margaret Levi   *University of Washington, Seattle*

Assistant General Editor
Stephen Hanson   *University of Washington, Seattle*

Associate Editors
Robert H. Bates   *Harvard University*
Peter Hall   *Harvard University*
Peter Lange   *Duke University*
Helen Milner   *Columbia University*
Frances Rosenbluth   *Yale University*
Susan Stokes   *University of Chicago*
Sidney Tarrow   *Cornell University*

Other Books in the Series

Stefano Bartolini, *The Political Mobilization of the European Left, 1860–1980: The Class Cleavage*
Mark Beissinger, *Nationalist Mobilization and the Collapse of the Soviet State*
Carles Boix, *Political Parties, Growth and Equality: Conservative and Social Democratic Economic Strategies in the World Economy*
Catherine Boone, *Merchant Capital and the Roots of State Power in Senegal, 1930–1985*
Michael Bratton and Nicolas van de Walle, *Democratic Experiments in Africa: Regime Transitions in Comparative Perspective*
Valerie Bunce, *Leaving Socialism and Leaving the State: The End of Yugoslavia, the Soviet Union, and Czechoslovakia*
Ruth Berins Collier, *Paths Toward Democracy: The Working Class and Elites in Western Europe and South America*
Donatella della Porta, *Social Movements, Political Violence, and the State*

Continues after the Index

For Amy

Race and Regionalism in the Politics of Taxation in Brazil and South Africa

EVAN S. LIEBERMAN

Princeton University

CAMBRIDGE
UNIVERSITY PRESS

PUBLISHED BY THE PRESS SYNDICATE OF THE UNIVERSITY OF CAMBRIDGE
The Pitt Building, Trumpington Street, Cambridge, United Kingdom

CAMBRIDGE UNIVERSITY PRESS
The Edinburgh Building, Cambridge CB2 2RU, UK
40 West 20th Street, New York, NY 10011-4211, USA
477 Williamstown Road, Port Melbourne, VIC 3207, Australia
Ruiz de Alarcón 13, 28014 Madrid, Spain
Dock House, The Waterfront, Cape Town 8001, South Africa

http://www.cambridge.org

First published 2003

Printed in the United States of America

Typeface Janson Text Roman 10/13 pt.   *System* LaTeX 2_ε [TB]

A catalog record for this book is available from the British Library.

Library of Congress Cataloging in Publication data
Lieberman, Evan S.
Race and regionalism in the politics of taxation in Brazil and South Africa / Evan S. Lieberman.
    p.   cm. – (Cambridge studies in comparative politics)
Includes bibliographical references and index.
ISBN 0-521-81678-5 – ISBN 0-521-01698-3 (pb.)
1. Taxation – Brazil.   2. Taxation – South Africa.   3. Taxation – Comparative studies.
I. Title.   II. Series.
HJ2525 .L54   2003
336.2′00968–dc21   2002041246

ISBN 0 521 81678 5 hardback
ISBN 0 521 01698 3 paperback

Contents

List of Figures and Tables		*page* ix
Acknowledgments		xiii
Abbreviations		xvii
1	THE POLITICS OF TAXATION	1
	The Problem in Perspective	5
	The Argument	9
	Alternative Explanations	23
	Plan of the Book: A "Nested" Approach to Comparative Analysis	32
2	THE TAX STATE IN COMPARATIVE PERSPECTIVE	38
	The Tax State Defined	39
	Toward a Typology of the Tax State	43
	Measurement and Classification	60
	Conclusion	67
3	CRITICAL JUNCTURE: DEFINING NATIONAL POLITICAL COMMUNITY	68
	Cleavages: Race and Region	70
	Two Definitions of National Political Community	78
	Influence on Class Relations	89
	Conclusion	104
4	THE RISE OF THE MODERN TAX STATE IN BRAZIL AND SOUTH AFRICA	106
	Legacies of Pre-Modern Taxation	107
	The Context of 20th-Century State-Building	113

Patterns of Taxation and State Development (1900–1975)   117
Three Episodes of Politics and Taxation   122
Implications: Weathering Economic and Political
   Crises (1975–1990)   167
Conclusion   171

5   SHADOWS OF THE PAST: TAX REFORM
   IN AN ERA OF GLOBALIZATION AND
   DEMOCRATIZATION   173
Pressures for Tax Reform from Home and Abroad   177
The Reconstruction of Racial and Regional Identities   185
Class Relations and Political Strategies   195
Patterns of Tax Reform Compared   213
Conclusion   235

6   POLITICAL COMMUNITY AND TAXATION
   BEYOND BRAZIL AND SOUTH AFRICA   237
Case Selection   238
Estimating the Impact of National Political Community
   on Taxation   239
Alternative Explanations   264
Conclusion   269

7   CONCLUSION   271
The Influence of Identity Politics and Political Community   274
Implications for Brazil and South Africa in the 21st Century   277

APPENDIX   COMPARATIVE-HISTORICAL ANALYSIS   284

References   291

Index   309

Figures and Tables

Figures

1.1   National income and property tax collections as a
        function of GDP/capita, 1990–1994   *page* 11
1.2   The political community model of tax state development   13
2.1   Hypothetical tax policy framework   47
2.2   The process of tax administration   51
3.1   Party strength in Brazil and South Africa, 1910–1962   92
3.2   White tolerance of other groups in South Africa, 1937   94
4.1   Real GDP/capita in Brazil and South Africa, chain index
        1911–1990   114
4.2   Trade revenues in Brazil and South Africa, 1900–1960   117
4.3   Income and property tax collections in Brazil and South
        Africa, 1900–1975   118
4.4   Social security and "hand-to-mouth" taxes in Brazil and
        South Africa, 1900–1975   120
4.5   Consumption taxes in Brazil and South Africa, 1900–1975   137
4.6   Cost of tax administration in South Africa, 1952–1990   157
4.7   Total domestic tax revenues in Brazil and
        South Africa, 1975–1990   168
4.8   Interest payments in Brazil and South Africa, 1980–1993   169
4.9   Annual inflation in Brazil and South Africa, 1960–1990   170
5.1   International economic growth rates, 1967–1996   180
5.2   World trade, 1980–1996   181
5.3   Racial composition of party support in Brazil (1995) and
        South Africa (1997)   189

5.4   Party representation in the lower house of the legislature in
      Brazil and South Africa, 1999   200
5.5   Union density in upper-middle income countries, c. 1994   208
5.6   Monthly inflation in Brazil, 1985–1996   217
5.7   Income redistribution through taxation, c. 1994   221
5.8   Income tax collections in Brazil and South Africa, 1973–1997   233

Tables

2.1   Typology of the tax state   56
2.2   Income and property tax collections as share of GDP,
      descriptive statistics, average 1990–1994   63
2.3   Tax collections around the world, 1990–1994   64
3.1   Constitutional definitions of National Political Community
      (NPC) in Brazil and South Africa   79
4.1   Late 19th-century tax states in Brazil and Southern Africa   108
4.2   Generalized Least Squares (GLS) estimate for regression
      of annual tax collections in South Africa, 1912–1990   121
4.3   Paths to the general income tax in Brazil and South Africa,
      1888–1930   124
4.4   The tax state in Brazil and South Africa during the Second
      World War, 1939–1945   139
4.5   Average annual GDP growth in Brazil and South Africa,
      1960–1975   154
4.6   Tax state reforms under modernizing authoritarian regimes
      in Brazil and South Africa, 1960–1975   156
4.7   Average annual GDP growth in Brazil and South Africa,
      1975–1990   167
5.1   Selected economic indicators for Brazil and South Africa,
      c. 1994   177
5.2   Racial and regional identities in Brazil and South Africa,
      1990s   186
5.3   Collective actors, strategies, and bargaining power in Brazil
      and South Africa in the 1990s   196
5.4   Tax state reforms during periods of democratization and
      globalization in Brazil and South Africa, 1985–1999   214
5.5   Government receipts in Brazil and South Africa, 1998   232
6.1   Classification of countries according to early definitions of
      National Political Community   242

Figures and Tables

6.2 OLS estimates of the determinants of tax collections by
level of government, 1990–1994   258
6.3 OLS estimates of the determinants of income and
property tax collections for all levels of government,
1990–1994   265
A.1 Summary of in-depth interviews conducted   287

Acknowledgments

Many individuals and organizations were exceptionally generous to me and to this project over several years of research and writing.

The U.S. Fulbright Commission, the Social Science Research Council, the National Science Foundation (award 9724055), the MacArthur Foundation, and the Latin American Studies and African Studies Centers at the University of California, Berkeley, all provided funding. I am extremely grateful for this generous financial support, which allowed me to conduct field research in Brazil and South Africa.

The book grew out of a doctoral dissertation completed while in the department of political science at the University of California, Berkeley. My dissertation advisors, Ruth Berins Collier, Robert Price, and David Leonard, provided a constant stream of support and intellectual inspiration since my first semester of graduate school. Each offered careful and extensive feedback, both in person and electronically, to the various corners of the globe. I truly enjoyed working with them on this project.

Within Brazil and South Africa, so many individuals were kind and helpful that it is not possible to identify them all by name, but I will try. Several people at the Institute for Democracy in South Africa (IDASA), including Warren Krafchik, Robert Mattes, Albert Van Zyl, Luvuyo Msimango, Laura Walker, Shirley Robinson, Juliana Veloen, Alta Fölscher, and Helen Taylor Macdonald, contributed to an especially engaging and collegial environment for carrying out research. Nicoli Nattrass challenged me with incisive comments in several discussions and in response to several drafts presented in South Africa and coincidentally in New Haven, when we were both at Yale as I was finishing this manuscript. I would also like to thank Iraj Abedian, Andrew Feinstein, Paula Gumede, Hennie Kotze,

Jeremy Seekings, and Marius Van Blerck in South Africa; and Maria Hermínia Tavares de Almeida, Luiz Cattapan, Renata Cattapan, David Fleischer, Christina Markman, Issac Markman, Luiz Carlos Bresser Pereira, Carlos Pio, Fernando Rezende, Maria Helena de Castro Santos, Lourdes Sola, and Ricardo Varsano in Brazil. Scores of individuals in both countries took time out of their busy days to be interviewed, often for several hours, to share their thoughts and experiences with no reward except to be helpful to a foreign scholar trying to learn about their country. The librarians at UC Berkeley, the South African National Library, the University of Cape Town, the Pontifícia Universidade Católica do Rio de Janeiro, and the Instituto de Pesquisa Econômica Aplicada were extremely helpful and I am grateful that these wonderful human resources were available to identify valuable materials that no electronic search engine would have found. I am grateful to Sarah Chartock, Anel Powell, and Ryan Sheely for excellent research assistance.

I have had the opportunity to present parts of this work in various settings, one of which proved particularly fortuitous. In May 2000, Ivan Szelenyi hosted an engaging workshop for young scholars at Yale University under the auspices of the Society for Comparative Research. In attendance at my seminar was Margaret Levi, whose book, *Of Rule and Revenue*, profoundly influenced my thinking about taxation, politics, and state-building. She encouraged me to develop the project as a book manuscript, and it has been a treat to work with her on this project along with Lewis Bateman at Cambridge University Press. Two anonymous reviewers from the Press provided extremely thoughtful comments, which helped to improve every chapter of the manuscript.

Several friends and colleagues were kind enough to read chapters, and/or to provide helpful suggestions and feedback, including Ana-Maria Bejarano, Henry Brady, David Collier, Larry Diamond, John Gerring, Jeffrey Herbst, Gregory Huber, Courtney Jung, Ira Katznelson, Robert Kaufman, Peter Kingstone, Atul Kohli, Julia Lynch, Lauren Morris Maclean, Eric Oliver, John Quigley, Aaron Schneider, Ian Shapiro, Rogers Smith, Sven Steinmo, Richard Turits, and Deborah Yashar. I am particularly grateful to Anthony Marx, who was so generous with his time while I was living in New York and shuttling back and forth to Brazil between 1998 and 2000. Kimberly Morgan read the penultimate draft in its entirety and offered important suggestions just at the point when it was virtually impossible for me to look at the manuscript with anything approximating a "fresh" eye. Mark Morjé Howard read, commented on, and discussed every chapter of the

Acknowledgments

dissertation, often several times, and his friendship and intellectual guidance have been invaluable ever since we were office mates at Berkeley.

Family members tolerated physical and mental absences and provided needed encouragement along the way. My parents, Janice Lieberman and Alvin Lieberman, each inspired me with their passion for travel, writing, and teaching, and I am grateful that their loving guidance has led me to such rewarding endeavors. My brother, Mark Lieberman, provided family and friendship during several years of traveling into and out of the Bay area, and my in-laws, Margot and Norman Freedman, were also steadfastly supportive. Finally, Amy Lieberman was an incredible source of energy throughout the marathon process of producing the research and writing of this book. She assisted me technically, emotionally, and intellectually in more ways than I can list here, and while I think she enjoyed some of our travels through South Africa and Brazil, perhaps no one will be more delighted to see this manuscript go to press than she. I dedicate this book to Amy.

Abbreviations

AHI	Afrikaanse Handelsinstituut
ANC	African National Congress
ASSOCOM	Association of Chambers of Commerce
BNDES	Banco Nacional de Desenvolvimento Econômico e Social
BSA	Business South Africa
CGT	Confederação Geral dos Trabalhadores
CNI	Confederação Nacional da Indústria
CONFAZ	Conselho de Política Fazendária
COSATU	Congress of South African Trade Unions
CUT	Central Única dos Trabalhadores
DP	Democratic Party
FF	Freedom Front
FIESP	Federação das Indústrias do Estado de São Paulo
FGV	Fundação Getúlio Vargas
FIRJAN	Federação das Indústrias do Estado do Rio de Janeiro
GST	General Sales Tax
IADB	Inter-American Development Bank
IBGE	Instituto Brasileiro de Geografia e Estatística
IFP	Inkatha Freedom Party
IMF	International Monetary Fund
IPEA	Instituto de Pesquisa Econômica Aplicada
MAR	Minorities at Risk Dataset
NAAMSA	National Association of Automobile Manufacturers in South Africa
NAFCOC	National African Federated Chamber of Commerce
NEDLAC	National Economic Development and Labour Council
NNP	New National Party
NP	National Party
NPC	National Political Community (analytic term used throughout the book, defined in Chapter 1)
PAC	Pan Africanist Congress
PDS	Partido Democrático Social

PDT	Partido Democrático Trabalhista
PFL	Partido da Frente Liberal
PMDB	Partido do Movimento Democrático Brasileiro
PSDB	Partido da Social Democracia Brasileira
PT	Partido dos Trabalhadores
SACOB	South African Chamber of Business
SACP	South African Communist Party
SAFCOC	South African Federated Chamber of Commerce
SAP	South African Party
SARS	South African Revenue Service
SRF	Secretaria da Receita Federal
TRC	Truth and Reconciliation Commission
VAT	Value Added Tax

1

The Politics of Taxation

The spirit of a people, its cultural level, its social structure, the deeds its policy may prepare – all this and more is written in its fiscal history, stripped of all phrases . . . The public finances are one of the best starting points for an investigation of society, especially though not exclusively of its political life.

— Joseph Schumpeter[1]

When former exiles Nelson Mandela and Fernando Henrique Cardoso were elected as presidents of South Africa and Brazil in 1994, the poor and largely black majorities in both countries had good reason to be hopeful. Both men had been outspoken critics of prior authoritarian regimes, socio-economic inequality, and persistent racial discrimination in their respective countries. Democratic transitions, which paved the way for these men to take the helm of government, provided unique opportunities to steer state policy on a new course. It finally appeared as though the plight of the poor and previously disenfranchised could be improved in what had become the first and second most unequal societies on Earth.[2]

Yet, these new presidents soon discovered that they had inherited very different *states*, with different capacities to govern, and in particular, to collect taxes. The South African state emerged as one of the most effective collectors of income tax in the world, and was able to collect approximately 15 percent of its gross domestic product (GDP) in the form of progressive, direct income taxes. Meanwhile, the Brazilian state could barely collect

---

[1] Schumpeter 1954: 7.
[2] As measured by the GINI coefficient, according to World Bank (1996): 197 rankings. Brazil's GINI coefficient was 63.4 in 1989 and South Africa's was 58.4 in 1993.

1

5 percent of GDP of such revenues. Instead, Brazilians were paying a wide range of complicated, hidden, and typically regressive taxes, levies, and other charges that are largely not present in South Africa. Moreover, it cost the Brazilian bureaucracy approximately three times as much as its South African counterpart to collect revenues.[3] The wealthy minority in South Africa was largely complying with the state's demands for taxes, while the wealthy minority in Brazil deployed a vast set of tools to avoid and to evade payment. Given the extraordinary concentration of income in these two countries, the associated impact of these different patterns of compliance on the fiscal health of the state has been dramatic: In the wake of the Asian currency crisis of 1997, the Brazilian government announced a multibillion-dollar bailout from the International Monetary Fund (IMF) while the South African government reported better-than-expected collections of taxes, and did not require interventions from any international organizations. In an essay relating class struggle to democratization and state power, Rudolph Goldscheid prophesized, "The masses which eventually acquired greater power in the State saw themselves cheated of their prize when they got not the rich State but the poor one."[4] Indeed, this was the case for Brazil, but not South Africa.

Important differences in the tax systems and tax structures of these two transitional societies were largely legacies from the countries' respective predemocratic pasts. Yet, such outcomes are surprising when one considers the reputation of the South African state as historically allocating resources in a *regressive* manner, and the reputation of the Brazilian central state as exceptionally large and influential over significant levels of resources. Ironically, the tax burden was much heavier on the poor and on blacks in Brazil than it was in South Africa, where the wealthy, white population continued to pay most of the tax bill. Mandela's government, with one of the most progressive tax systems in the world, enjoyed greater effective authority with respect to the privileged minority than Cardoso's government in Brazil. This book attempts to explain this conundrum.

Questions about the determinants of national tax structures, and of state capacity more generally, are longstanding questions, but standard social scientific explanations do not provide an obvious answer for why the Brazilian and South African states extract tax revenue in such different ways. Purely structural explanations – which relate the influence of economic and/or

---

[3] Cost of collections as share of total collections.
[4] Goldscheid 1964: 205.

international influences to the development of taxation systems – are clearly incomplete, as these factors have been extremely similar across the two countries during the course of the 20th century. Both countries pursued similar development strategies in the 20th century, mainly through protected industrialization, and both enjoyed periods of extremely rapid economic growth in the post-War period. Levels of economic development have been very similar, and by the mid-1990s, per capita income was $2,970 in Brazil and $3,040 in South Africa.[5] In both countries, the state is relatively large, and total government expenditure is about the same (about 32 percent of GDP in the 1990s). Explanations emphasizing the role of political regimes are not very helpful because both countries share histories of long authoritarian pasts with recent democratic transitions. Cultural explanations have tended to be largely tautological, "explaining" varied tax outcomes in terms of different tax "cultures." Moreover, both societies are comprised of a wide mix of racial and ethnic groups; both were colonies of European countries; they share legacies of European immigration and slavery; and in both, racial characteristics continue to be highly correlated with income and wealth. Even more technical arguments, relating tax structures to levels of professionalism in the tax administration, do not stand up to careful empirical analysis – there is no evidence to suggest that the South African bureaucracy is either better trained or more technologically sophisticated than the Brazilian bureaucracy.

As an alternative, this book provides a political-institutional explanation highlighting the importance of foundational moments when notions of "us" and "them" get socially constructed, shaping the logic and trajectory of political competition for long periods of time. It argues that patterns of inter- and intra-class cohesion are critical to the ways in which the free rider problem of taxation gets resolved. Although such class relations get put in place during the process of economic change, economic factors alone do not determine those relations. An explanation must include the historically constructed definitions of National Political Community (NPC) – the group of people officially entitled to the rights and responsibilities of citizenship. Definitions vary in terms of how racial, ethnic, and regional identities get configured, and in what ways certain groups are included or excluded (i.e., with racial or nonracial definitions of citizenship; as federations or as unitary states). Such definitions have an important influence on

---

[5] World Bank 1998.

the strength of class unity and cross-class relations. In turn, such relations shape the context and strategies of citizen behavior, which ultimately affects the types of tax policies that get adopted and the ways in which they are implemented.

Different definitions of NPC are responsible for the divergent legacies of state revenue production evident in the South African and Brazilian states during the contemporary period of democratic transition. Looking back to the turn of the 20th century, this book argues that the construction of a racial union in South Africa led to high levels of inter- and intra-class solidarity, which in turn motivated upper groups to pay, whereas an officially nonracial federation in Brazil led to inter-class polarization, intra-class fragmentation, and, ultimately, resistance to tax payment.

The political glue of race, or "whiteness," helped the South African state to solve the collective action problem of taxation among the upper groups controlling private economic resources by providing a clear idiom that emphasized strategic and normative obligations to one another and to "poor whites" within that society. During key historical moments during the 20th century, the political salience of race in South Africa implied that social and economic policy should help to uplift all whites in ways that they would not "sink" to the level of blacks or "natives." By contrast, in Brazil, a different strategy was implemented to address the race question. *Official* discrimination was made illegal, and poor whites have been treated simply as "poor," rather than as "white." Nevertheless, racial stereotyping and prejudice were perpetuated in Brazil with the government's deliberate attempts to "whiten" the population through racial mixing, immigration, and other policies.[6] In such a political environment, race-based class solidarity was unavailable, and inequalities within and between race groups were tolerated as part of a more "acceptable" socioeconomic hierarchy.

Moreover, the political salience of regions, stemming from Brazilian federalism, exacerbated the problem of taxation, dividing upper groups from one another and impeding the ability of the poor majority to make national, class-based demands for progressive taxation. The flame of regional competition in Brazil gained fuel from an underlying perception of different racial demographics between North and South that could not be articulated explicitly within the discourse of race politics. By contrast, in South Africa, the formation of a union – as opposed to the federation that most

---

[6] Skidmore 1995.

had expected – helped to smooth over regional divides within the white polity. The physical boundaries of the country were defined in racial terms – in which a small portion of the land was reserved for the black majority – strengthening the sense of solidarity and willingness to pay among the white minority. White workers organized themselves on a national scale, unfettered by the regional divisions found in Brazil, and acted to maintain political pressure for the expansion of progressive taxation.

In short, definitions of NPC shaped the development of tax policies and administrative patterns – a combination of outcomes that I refer to as the *tax state*[7] – and the legacy of the respective state-building processes continues to account for wide cross-national differences in levels and structures of tax collection. The remainder of this and the following chapters provide a more general theoretical framework and substantial evidence to support this argument. This analysis begins by discussing why the question of explaining variation in taxation systems is worth asking in the first place. Second, it specifies a relatively general, institutional argument, the *Political Community Model* of tax state development. Third, it identifies a set of possible alternative explanations for variation in the state's ability to tax. Finally, it provides an overview of the methodology for assessing the explanatory power of these models, and it describes the organization of the book.

The Problem in Perspective

This study of the politics of taxation in Brazil and South Africa addresses questions relevant to students of comparative politics, economic development, state-building, and identity politics. In fact, this book is likely to be of *least* interest to those interested in the minute details of tax policy and tax administration, because such details are not the focus here. Rather, the central objective is to take up Joseph Schumpeter's charge to use taxation as a lens onto broader social and political problems. For readers already familiar with the political and economic histories of Brazil or South Africa – and even the tax systems of the respective countries – this book provides a framework for understanding each of these cases in a comparative context. However, the book does not assume that readers are familiar with the political or economic histories of either of these two countries, particularly of their tax systems. By investigating the politics of taxation in Brazil and

---

[7] A term generally associated with Schumpeter's work. In Chapter 2, I provide a more precise analytic definition.

South Africa, this text sheds light on many of the poorly understood dynamics of politics and policy-making relevant to other countries, including the United States.

Why a Study of Taxation?

A comparative study of the history of taxation provides insights into the development of modern state capacities to wield their authority over individuals and groups within society. The ability to tax is virtually a prerequisite for governance. Douglass North goes so far as to include taxation as central in his definition of the state: "... an organization with a comparative advantage in violence, extending over a geographic area whose boundaries are determined by its power to tax constituents."[8]

The power of states to tax varies widely across countries. Since the earliest times, collection has always provided a difficult challenge for political leaders. Throughout the history of modern governments, citizens have complained about the burden of taxation. Yet, despite the similarity of their words and claims – that taxes are "too high" or "unfair" – citizens have responded in quite different ways to demands for payment. In some societies, including those in which public rancor over taxes seems constant, many individuals not only pay more than half their annual income to the state in the form of taxes, but they spend substantial amounts of time keeping records of their income and expenses in order to comply relatively faithfully with various tax laws and policies.[9] In other societies, the state's demand for tax payment falls on deaf ears. Even individuals with substantial means manage to resist payment of virtually any tax. Either they influence the writing of the tax laws in such ways that they are able to legally escape tax liabilities, or citizens actively find ways to evade their legal burdens. In the wake of such differing citizen responses to the demand for taxes, levels and structures of collections vary widely across countries.

As will be discussed in greater detail in Chapter 2, we can observe qualitative and quantitative differences in national patterns of taxation. States that regularly collect from a wide range of societal actors are generally also able to govern effectively in a range of other areas, while the inability of a state to generate significant revenue through taxation is often a precursor to state failure or even collapse. As new states seem to be sprouting up

---

[8] North 1981: 21.
[9] Peters 1991.

around the globe on a regular basis, the need to understand the process of state development – and the development of capacities to collect taxes in particular – could not be more pressing.

By focusing on the development of modern state capacities to tax economically "privileged" groups within society, this book attempts to understand the origins of varied taxation regimes and to resolve longstanding questions about the relationship between state and capital. During the 20th century, leaders of most modern states paid lip service to the notion that tax systems should be fair, advocating that those with greater economic means ought to pay a relatively larger share of the tax burden. Particularly in societies in which income and wealth are concentrated in the hands of a relatively small minority of people, the state's ability to tax this group is particularly relevant. Although a wide range of scholars, from Karl Marx to Charles Lindblom, have noted that upper groups tend to occupy a privileged position with respect to state authority, the law-like characterization of this relationship is at odds with the observation that the relationship between these two groups varies so widely across countries such as Brazil and South Africa.[10] While the state does collect quite a bit of tax revenue in both countries, the relationship between the state and upper groups in Brazil is *adversarial*, whereas the analogous relationships embedded in the South African "tax state" are *cooperative*.

An investigation of taxation must be central for students interested in the political economy of development, poverty, and inequality. In the contemporary world of declining foreign aid, tight credit, and a policy orthodoxy against state ownership of enterprises, modern states largely depend upon tax revenues to finance security and welfare functions. Clean water, education, roads, health care, police, national defense, and all of the other goods and services states provide are largely financed through taxation systems. Moreover, the operations of a national tax system influence the distribution of income, the functioning of markets, and the nature of investment. As a result, the question of taxation is particularly relevant for developing countries, in which taxation capacities tend to be quite fragile. The implications of differences in capacities to collect taxes has serious multiplier effects on the ability of those states to finance their expenditures, because creditworthiness on international financial markets is often determined by such collections and their relationship to the size of national budget deficits.

---

[10] For a review of these arguments, see Przeworski and Wallerstein 1988.

Despite the substantive and theoretical relevance of such concerns, the politics and practice of taxation in this set of countries have been remarkably understudied.

Finally, a study of the development of the tax state provides an opportunity to investigate the roots of collective action and cooperation. The central dilemmas of collective life are embodied in the question of taxation. The state's demand for such revenues from society implies the thorny questions of *who* should pay, and *how much?* Because the demands for public goods and the incentive to free ride on the payment of others are both great, "taxation inherently implies politics."[11] Nonetheless, a surprising amount of revenue is collected by states in the form of taxes, amounting to more than one-fifth of global economic production in recent years. In 1994, middle-income countries collected $630 billion in tax revenues.[12] Few people would disagree that politics and taxation are intimately related, but the task of specifying the relationship between the two – particularly when considering broad patterns of cross-national variation – remains incomplete.

Why Brazil and South Africa?

This book is concerned with general questions pertaining to the development of national tax systems, but it is focused on taxation in Brazil and South Africa. Both substantive and analytic concerns motivate this two-country comparison.[13] The vast array of social, political, and economic similarities between the two countries described above provides something of a "natural experiment" which is rare in cross-national social science research. In order to explore the argument that variations in the salience of particular identities influence the development of tax policy and tax administration, it is most useful to compare countries in which there is significant *variation* on this score. Brazil and South Africa, as will be argued much more fully below, developed extremely different approaches to racial and regional cleavages, and it is this high degree of variation that allows us to assess the impact of

---

[11] Bates 1989: 479.
[12] World Bank 1998.
[13] Others have usefully made quite explicit comparisons between Brazil and South Africa, reinforcing the notion that these are comparable cases. See, for example, Marx 1998; Seidman 1994; and Friedman and de Villiers 1996. Moreover, studies of Brazilian race relations have tended to employ the South African example as a point of reference. See, for example, Andrews 1991.

this factor on other outcomes, particularly in the wake of various analytical controls. A single country study would provide far less analytic leverage.

Second, although Brazil and particularly South Africa often appear unique in terms of certain aspects of their political and economic histories, these cases generate a series of insights about the political economy of state development. In grappling with questions about nationhood and the problems of racial and regional heterogeneity, these societies have many analogs, including, but not limited to, the United States. Indeed, these are extreme cases in terms of how definitions of NPC have been specified, but in a paired comparison, such contrast provides the most analytic leverage for assessing the impact of definitions of NPC on taxation outcomes. The book draws on broad cross-national comparisons in order to make inferences to a much broader population of country cases. Where variation in definitions of NPC is less extreme, we should expect less extreme variation on the outcome, but the same causal forces may be at work.

Finally, because of the great inequalities in both societies, and because of the fragile nature of these new democracies, the factors that influence tax collections and the development of state authority are materially relevant in the near term. If the clear and transparent operation of a taxation system is important for economic growth and development, as most development analysts argue, then the stability of these fragile democracies is at least partially dependent upon the outcome of the questions considered here. In an increasingly integrated international economy, the fiscal health of these two economies – the largest in the sub-Saharan African and Latin American regions – affects financial conditions around the world.

The Argument

Having established the puzzle of variation in the types of tax states developed in Brazil and South Africa, and having justified why this puzzle should be of interest, the remainder of this chapter develops more fully an explanation of these outcomes. Three key factors – economic structure, the international environment, and historically rooted institutions that define the NPC – provide the basis for a robust explanation of cross-national variation in taxation structures, particularly in terms of the state's ability to tax upper groups within society. This book focuses on measuring the impact of institutional definitions of NPC, demonstrating the limits of the other two factors on their own to account for important variations across time and space. While changes in the mode of production; variations in the

9

timing of development; and international ideas, conflicts, and structures all affect taxation outcomes, historically rooted institutions, which give political salience to certain group identities and not others, mediate those pressures into specific sets of class configurations and coalitions that lead to distinctive types of tax states.

Economic and International Influences

As scholars from a range of theoretical perspectives have argued, the processes of economic development and modernization have been central to the development of taxation systems.[14] Depending upon the theoretical orientation, the hypothesized relationship between these factors varies widely across these studies, but they commonly recognize the correlation between the process of modernization and the development of taxation systems within and across countries. Economic development is generally associated with the concentration and specialization of production, which leads to increased demands for publicly provided goods and services, in turn making tax collection easier because citizens can be convinced of the state's need for financial resources. More industrialized economies have tended to generate not just more tax revenue in an absolute sense, but even relative to the size of their economies. Moreover, the state's reliance on direct income taxation has also tended to increase with level of economic development. Such observations led earlier analysts, enchanted with the tenets of modernization theory, to predict that countries would follow a common path of development of taxation capacity, and would eventually collect a greater share of income tax revenues.[15]

In particular, during the process of economic development, business leaders and high-income individuals tend to enjoy increased economic returns on investment, and they become more willing to pay taxes to a government that will act to protect their property. Of course, one would imagine that there are certainly upper bounds to the extent to which levels of economic development positively influences the relationship between the state and upper groups, but when comparing wealthy countries to poor ones, it is relatively easy to understand the increased willingness of privileged groups in wealthier societies to cooperate with the state's efforts

---

[14] Tanzi 1987; Peters 1991; and Levi 1988.
[15] Hinrichs 1966.

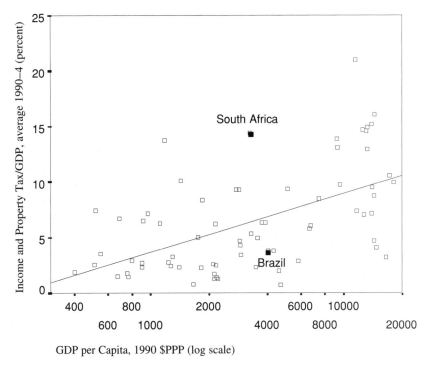

Figure 1.1 National income and property tax collections as a function of GDP/capita, 1990–1994. *Source:* World Bank 1998.

to collect taxes. Within poorer economies, not only will upper groups with private sources of income and wealth have less to protect, but they will have less reason to believe that the state will be able to serve their needs.

Indeed, cross-national comparisons reveal a strong correlation between level of economic development and tax collections. For example, looking at income and property tax collections for the period 1990–94, it is clear that there is a strong and statistically significant (Pearson's $R = .56$) relationship between collections and GDP per capita (in purchasing power parity units), as demonstrated in Figure 1.1. Nonetheless, the scattering of countries both above and below the best-fit line implies that there is room for other explanations and that other factors may affect levels of collections. The contrast between Brazil and South Africa is particularly striking – as South Africa is way above the best-fit line and Brazil is significantly below.

Beyond domestic economic factors, scholars have also emphasized the role of international influences on the development of tax systems.[16] Wars, foreign models of policy and/or administration, participation in the state system and international organizations, and new trade regimes are among the many factors that influence domestic policies and practices. Specifically, major wars have tended to inspire upper groups to see beyond narrow self-interests and to cooperate with the state by consenting to heavier tax burdens. In the absence of threatening events such as wars, upper groups are more likely to challenge demands for revenue. Moreover, international trends in the degree to which the state collects from upper groups tend to influence the development of any given tax state by providing important political and technical ammunition for actors within society to advocate for prevailing norms.

It is relatively easy to show that national patterns of tax policy and tax collection are strongly influenced by a set of common factors, including demonstration effects, and that international trends are temporally marked by particular years and/or events, demonstrating the importance of factors that transcend national borders. As will be discussed more below, shocks tend to have a long-term ratchet effect on tax collection. Yet again, we find that even countries such as Brazil and South Africa, which have played broadly similar roles in the international political economy, and have been influenced by relatively similar international factors, have developed very different types of tax states, suggesting the need for a fuller account.

National Political Community

While it is true that both economic and international factors have influenced the development of tax systems, the impact has been far from uniform. In fact, in the face of similar albeit changing international and economic pressures, state capacities to govern and to collect taxes have not converged but have diverged during the past century. Many scholars have been puzzled by the great variations in policy instruments and administrative practices employed across countries, and have relegated important "residual" variation to a political "black box." As one economist explained in an essay on taxation systems in developing countries, "Although political constraints are clearly important, most economists feel uneasy about taking them into account.

---

[16] See, for example, Weber 1968; Goldscheid 1964; Tilly 1975; Steinmo 1993; Levi 1988; and Kiser and Linton 2001. For a discussion of the influence of "emergencies" on the development of the American tax system, see Brownlee 1996.

The Argument

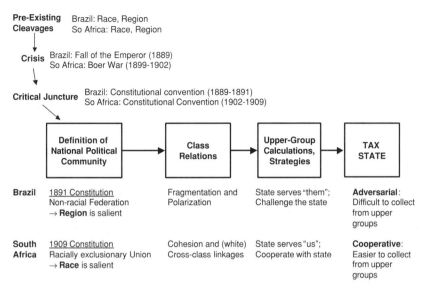

Pre-Existing Cleavages Brazil: Race, Region
So Africa: Race, Region

Crisis Brazil: Fall of the Emperor (1889)
So Africa: Boer War (1899-1902)

Critical Juncture Brazil: Constitutional convention (1889-1891)
So Africa: Constitutional Convention (1902-1909)

Definition of National Political Community	→	Class Relations	→	Upper-Group Calculations, Strategies	→	TAX STATE

Brazil 1891 Constitution
Non-racial Federation
→ **Region** is salient

Fragmentation and Polarization

State serves "them"; Challenge the state

Adversarial: Difficult to collect from upper groups

South Africa 1909 Constitution
Racially exclusionary Union
→ **Race** is salient

Cohesion and (white) Cross-class linkages

State serves "us"; Cooperate with state

Cooperative: Easier to collect from upper groups

Figure 1.2 The political community model of tax state development.

Part of the reason is that they are not well understood – by economists, at least."[17]

The political community model of tax state development (see Figure 1.2) highlights the transformative role of mobilized political identities in shaping the development of the state. It is a *critical junctures* model that relates the definition of the NPC, or the formal criteria for citizenship, to the development of the tax state. The most prominent characteristics of the NPC are defined during a comparable "period of significant change, which occurs in distinct ways in different countries . . . and which is hypothesized to produce distinct legacies."[18] These critical junctures follow crisis periods of major social, political, and economic upheaval, such as social revolutions, wars, and other serious breakdowns of the normal political order. In response to such crises, political elites may debate and negotiate for their preferred specification of who should be included and who excluded from membership. In this model, the critical juncture of interest is the historical period during which a wide range of possible definitions of NPC are considered as serious alternatives and possibilities by national political

[17] Newbery 1987: 198.
[18] Collier and Collier 1991: 29.

13

elites, and concludes when a definition is ultimately specified in crucial legal documents, typically including the constitution, various laws, and national policies. In particular, this book focuses on two sets of alternatives in specifying the definition of the NPC in response to pre-existing racial and regional cleavages: whether or not to adopt federalism, and whether or not to continue excluding blacks from full and equal citizenship. The definition of the NPC tends to be reinforced through other important documents and symbols, including the media, museums, the census, and maps.[19]

Subsequently, the distinguishing characteristics of the critical juncture – that is, the different ways in which the NPC gets defined – tend to cast a long shadow on the future, even once the initial conditions have changed.[20] The institutions that remain and endure set in motion path-dependent processes of state development.[21] Depending upon how the NPC gets defined, certain identities, including racial, religious, ethnic, or regional identities, are more likely to become politically salient than others.[22] When the definition of NPC explicitly provides special protections or powers for certain groups, it is much more likely that such groups will become politically salient. The specification of group rights in the form of official state documents and policies provides a strong set of incentives for political entrepreneurs to make claims based on such identities. Alternatively, when particular identities or cleavages are ignored in the definition of the NPC, they are much less likely to be mobilized in the political arena. While the state's influence on identity formation is neither determinative nor exclusive (other factors may shape which groups mobilize and on what basis), it is certainly powerful. Federalism, for example, tends to give important political salience to regional identities, and official racial exclusion tends to give much greater salience to racial identities than in other countries characterized by racial heterogeneity, but with more liberal policies toward race.

---

[19] For discussions of the concept of the nation, and how national identities are articulated within societies, see especially Anderson 1996; and Haas 1986. These ideas are elaborated more fully in Chapter 3.

[20] Goldstone 1998: 842–3.

[21] See Thelen 1999; Pierson and Skocpol 1999; Pierson 2000; Skocpol 1984; and Mahoney 1999, for discussions and examples of path dependency. The paradigmatic example of this work is Moore 1966.

[22] As Laitin (1986: 19) points out, a society may contain multiple cultural or other identities, but only certain identities emerge as relevant for *politics*.

The Argument

Class Relations

The mobilization of group identities structures the quality of inter- and intra-class relations, which are central to the strategic environment in which societal actors make decisions about cooperation and compliance with the state's demand for tax payment. Because I do not assume that identities are merely reflections of economic resources within society, upper-income groups will either be *cohesive* because they share common political identities or they will be *fragmented* because they are divided by particular political identities. Moreover, upper groups may share group identities with lower-income groups that can be the strong basis for cross-class linkages. If they do not share such identities, they are more likely to be polarized, separated by differences in material interests *and* group identity.

A critical manifestation of these class relations develops in the form of organizations, which serve as actors in political interactions with the state. That is, upper groups may become either united or divided by the main business organizations, political parties, and government institutions that tend to aggregate interests within a society.[23] Their relationship to lower groups is largely influenced by the quality of labor organizations and the ways in which labor gets incorporated into broader political organizations. The definition of the NPC tends to structure the qualities of these organizations because, depending upon which identities get mobilized, some groups are likely to join certain organizations and not others. Some organizational bases are commonly accepted as salient and important, while others are dismissed as irrelevant and without meaning. For example, regional organizations are less likely to form when regions have little salience in a constitution and have never formed part of the national imagination. Racial organization is similarly unlikely when that category has no political salience. Leaders of particular groups – whether they be political parties; religious, ethnic, or racial groups; trade or employer associations; or issue-oriented groups – are likely to be politically influential depending upon the degree to which they are recognized within a particular political order.

Group identities – and again, the cohesion or fragmentation of economic groups or classes – are also mobilized through the creation of social norms and through the creation of idioms and rhetoric about who and what matters. Such institutions provide information both to the state and to societal actors about which groups can be understood to be having common

---

[23] North 1990: 7.

interests and which are understood to be in conflict. These less formal institutions provide frameworks for making sense of the political world in which people live.

Upper-Group Calculations and Strategies

The structure of class relations, including the strength of broad coalitions among upper groups, and between upper and lower groups, strongly influences the political calculations and strategies of upper-group actors. Although the political community model takes into account the political influence of lower groups, I focus on the political calculations and strategies of the economically privileged sectors of society. Upper groups – comprised of high-income individuals, firms, and organizations – are critical to the development of the tax state because they control the lion's share of taxable resources, particularly in highly unequal societies such as Brazil and South Africa. The incentives for all individuals and groups to free ride on the tax payments of others are high, and wealthier actors within society generally possess extensive capabilities to influence the development of tax policy, and to avoid and/or to evade the tax burden when they are so inclined. In the absence of cooperation, or "quasi-voluntary compliance"[24] from upper groups, the state will seek out other forms of revenue that may be less reliable, more complex, and may exacerbate inequalities within society. At least initially, the state's authority over upper groups depends upon the willingness of those actors to cooperate and to comply with state initiatives.

When upper groups within a society come to *share* a common and meaningful political identity, this is likely to lead to high levels of class cohesion, and the state executive will find it much easier to provide bargains and credible commitments that will actually appeal to those upper-group interests than if there is significant political fragmentation. In turn, willingness to comply is a function of perceptions of normative obligations and calculations about the *collective* benefits of tax payment. Group identity and a sense of where the "other" lies are important determinants of such sentiment. Within the public economy, individuals are more willing to pay when they are confident that the benefits will be restricted to "our" group. If there is a perception that the state will transfer benefits to "them," or some other group, or if the barriers to in-group membership are permeable, citizens

[24] Levi 1988: 48–70.

are less likely to perceive tax payment as a beneficial or rational move. People are more willing to pay if the state can make credible promises that the money will go to "us," either in the near term, or as an intertemporal or intergenerational transfer. The central state attempts to negotiate its desire to collect revenue, calculated against the costs of anticipated resistance, including monitoring and enforcement costs. It may adjust its proposals and desire to impose uniform authority, in line with the realities of varied levels of political support within society.

To the extent that the state makes appeals to this sense of common identity, upper groups will more likely be willing to pay taxes, as they will be motivated by a sense of normative or ethical group obligation *as well as* self-interest. They are also more likely to believe that others, sharing a common, collective identity, will perceive the situation in a similar manner, and will comply with the state's demands for payment. Within-class cohesiveness also provides opportunities to strike *cross*-class bargains, in which upper groups are willing to bear the weight of a progressive tax burden as a financial inducement for lower groups. Alternatively, when upper groups are more politically fragmented, cross-class bargains are much less likely to be implemented.

When responding to state demands for tax payment, upper groups make calculations and develop strategies based on the objective circumstances in front of them. However, the political community model emphasizes that the salience of group identities, and the ways in which those identities overlap with the allocation of economic resources, affect the degree to which individuals and groups with common economic means will view their long-term political and economic interests either as shared or as competing. Because individual and collective actors have little information about the future, and particularly little information about how the state's actions are likely to benefit them as *individuals*, they can use political identity to make group-based calculations, assessing the degree to which state action is likely to serve "us" or "them."

When upper-income actors see their collective political identity as shared with that of lower groups within society, particularly in ways that clearly differentiate them collectively from a relevant "other," the prospects for collecting progressive taxes are further increased, as upper groups are more likely to accept some of the tax burden away from those with less ability to pay. A shared identity connotes some degree of horizontal camaraderie and suggests that future returns for the entire group will depend, at least to an extent, upon the well-being of its economically least-well-off members.

17

When upper groups are willing to make collective sacrifices, they are less likely to make taxation a highly partisan issue and more likely to allow technical experts within the state to make decisions about the structure of the tax code. Cooperating upper groups may even serve as partners with the state, assisting in the writing of extractive and efficient tax codes, and in the administration of the tax system.

Alternatively, when salient political identities *fragment* economic classes – that is, when groups with similar economic means do not share common political identities – upper-income actors will more likely interpret state expenditures in terms of how they serve "other" groups, implying that tax payment would be a bad or irrational investment in the future. Under such circumstances, groups are much more likely to mobilize against state demands for tax payment based upon equity grounds – that is, that the "other" group ought to pay more relative to the status quo. In other words, upper groups with identity A will compete with upper groups with identity B regarding who should bear more of the tax burden, ultimately making the state's goal of taxing both groups more difficult. The executive may be forced to make more narrow bargains to secure support. When the support of multiple, conflicting groups is necessary to write a set of tax policies, such codes are more likely to be ridden with loopholes. Competing claims regarding fairness impede the taxation of upper groups, forcing the state to write tax codes with greater levels of complexity and fiscal *illusion* (the use of multiple, often hidden, tax instruments that obfuscate the true tax burden paid by citizens to the state). Within such a dynamic, upper groups may also step up their efforts to avoid and/or evade their obligations, hindering the tax bureaucracy in its efforts. The relationship with the state winds up being more adversarial.

The Political Community Model Applied to Brazil and South Africa

When applied to the cases of Brazil and South Africa, this model is used to investigate the impact of racial and regional identities on class relations and the politics of taxation. In both countries, skin color has been largely, but not perfectly, correlated with income and wealth, to the extent that almost all upper groups have been light skinned, and most people of color have been poor and working class, though many whites have also been poor and working class. Despite these similarities, varying definitions of NPC have produced contrasting patterns of identity formation and class politics. The political mobilization of race in an exclusionary manner in

South Africa helped upper groups to see their interests as more shared than competing. "Whiteness" or "Europeanness" framed the collective interests of upper-class actors spanning a wide range of economic sectors and diverse regions within the country. Although lower groups in South Africa have been largely dark skinned, the definition of a white NPC also facilitated strong cross-class linkages between the white lower groups in that country and the virtually all-white upper groups. Despite important social, economic, and cultural differences across regions, the choice to develop a unitary state implied that regional claims for special treatment would fall on deaf ears in the political arena. By contrast, in Brazil, where race was not made salient, class relations unfolded in almost the exactly opposite manner. The salience of regional identities born out of Brazilian federalism created deep-seated divisions among people even with largely similar economic means. In that country, the virtually all-white upper groups came to see their interests as more competing than shared, and Brazilian federalism further exacerbated the distance *between* economic classes by providing idioms for mobilizing a sense of difference. As a result, the politics of taxation in South Africa has been characterized more by cooperation, and in Brazil, more by conflict.

Mechanisms of Reproduction

Although the explanatory variables identified in the political community model may all take on a wide range of values over time, trajectories of state development tend to be reproduced through nationally distinctive political logics. In recognizing the stickiness of political patterns and the national structures of taxation, this book draws insights from several strands of institutional analysis, especially an emerging stream of historical institutional analysis that shares a concern for explaining enduring, national patterns of variation in policies and outcomes. The most relevant example is Sven Steinmo's *Taxation and Democracy* (1993), which investigates the political institutions of Sweden, the United Kingdom, and the United States, and their impact on the development of modern tax policy.[25] As others have found, even in the wake of potentially homogenizing external shocks, nationally distinctive patterns or paths are not easily changed. The exact idioms used for politics or the proper names of political organizations may change, but

[25] Other prominent examples of historical institutional analysis include Pierson 1994; Ertman 1997; Immergut 1992; Zysman 1994.

the ideas and myths that hold some groups together and keep others apart may be reinvented and adapted to new circumstances over time. Indeed, some of the mechanisms through which institutions shape identities and politics are part of a more general phenomenon that many describe as *political culture*. It is important to note, however, that such cultural attitudes, norms, and beliefs have specific institutional origins, and are mutable within the context of institutional change.

Because the costs of inventing new bases for political mobilization are likely to be high, political entrepreneurs typically have strong incentives to preserve existing patterns of political organization, and institutional stickiness maintains a consistent rhythm to politics over long periods. The idea that some people are insiders and some outsiders, that some groups are allies and others adversaries, becomes a natural part of political life in a given society, shaping reactions and counter-reactions to particular political orders. It is simply easier and less expensive to re-apply old political idioms and organizations than to re-invent new ones, and past experiences provide an important guide for making decisions about the future. Of course, the degree of institutionalization of the NPC may vary across societies, but this generally increases as particular identities, rules, and common-sense frameworks are taken for granted as the perceived reality of politics. Even when there is consensus that a particular form of political organization is generally detrimental to the well-being of a society, political entrepreneurs may find it difficult to agree upon rules that would fundamentally change the institutional foundations of politics.[26] Because the rules defining the NPC affect tax policy and administration, the resilience of these rules implies an associated dynamic for the politics of taxation.

Further influencing the tendency toward pathway development, patterns of taxation tend to reproduce themselves independent of the other exogenous factors identified in the political community model.[27] As a result, the timing and sequencing of critical junctures and of state development prove to be extremely important. Early divergences set states on quite different trajectories, making subsequent convergence enormously difficult even when other circumstances and other factors are highly similar. That is not to say that politics or external economic factors become unimportant. Rather,

---

[26] For a discussion of this problem with respect to the obvious need for political reform in Southern Italy, see Putnam 1993.

[27] Others have observed the stickiness of tax regimes. See, for example, Ames and Rapp 1977.

as societies become accustomed to particular sets of policies, compliance patterns, and administrative capacities, change is much more likely to be marginal than wholesale. Because taxation is such a central aspect of national life, patterns of taxation are likely to reinforce the material and organizational bases of the political arena, which shaped the tax state in the first place. In other words, "actors adapt their strategies in ways that reflect but also reinforce the 'logic' of the system."[28] Moreover, once certain policies are codified into law, or patterns of collection are regularized, through computerized or other mechanisms, the costs of change increase, generating a technological form of path dependency.[29] Bureaucracies that benefited from good citizen compliance in earlier periods gain the information and skills to enforce compliance in later periods. The institutions through which tax policy gets evaluated and shaped tend to be highly resilient, even once initial conditions are no longer recognizable. Together, these factors serve as powerful mechanisms of reproduction even under radically changed circumstances. Such observations imply that purely cross-sectional attempts to understand variations in taxation outputs, and state authority more generally, are likely to be highly limited.

Among political scientists, economists, and sociologists, observations about the powerful influence of institutions have become increasingly prevalent. In recent years, a common *theoretical core*[30] has emerged, and there is significant evidence of cross-fertilization of approaches to the role of institutions in political life.[31] Nevertheless, it is useful to try to be clear about real scholarly disagreement. For example, according to the rational choice institutionalists, "institutions ... induce choices that are regularized because they are made in equilibrium. In equilibrium, no actor would unilaterally choose to alter his or her behavior, given the options, the payoffs, and expectations regarding the choices of others."[32] Although I do not challenge this observation (and it would be difficult to refute empirically), I do not find the rational choice/game theoretic treatment of politics to provide significant added value for understanding the role of institutions for the problems and cases I consider. As in the rational choice approach, I agree that actors make calculations and strategies in order to pursue their

[28] Thelen 1999: 392.
[29] Thelen 1999: 384; Pierson 2000.
[30] Immergut 1998: 5–34.
[31] Thelen 1999.
[32] Bates et al. 1998: 8.

best interests. Rather than starting with actors and a given set of costs and benefits, however, I find that institutions *define* which collective actors get to "play" the game of politics, and they help to define the preferences of those actors. For example, should we assume that a light-skinned person will always value "white rule," as was the case in South Africa? Only if being white appears to matter, and if blacks are seen as the relevant "other," which the Brazilian case demonstrates is not a foregone conclusion. It would be reasonable to assume that all upper groups will pursue strategies that help them to stay wealthy, but their allies in this political game vary depending upon how institutions structure the political landscape. Similarly, the normative claims made by political leaders that motivate strategies and actions are likely to vary according to institutional environment. The benefit of the historical institutional (HI) approach is that such aggregation of actors and preference functions are made problematic, and not assumed.

Moreover, as compared with rational choice analysis, and its stated commitment to individual-based analysis,[33] this HI analysis does not focus on individual behavior and choices. Particularly when it comes to taxation, individual-based information about costs and benefits is so imperfect that it is simply beyond comprehension that any actor could make an accurate assessment of how these compare. Rather, a macro-level logic, in which individuals perceive themselves to be members of groups, and political leaders help them to evaluate how they are benefiting and how they ought to contribute as *members of the group*, appears a much more accurate representation of the reality in which people live. The HI approach focuses on how those groups develop and gain power within the political arena, and assumes that most members of society will pursue their interests in line with those of the most politically relevant groups to which they belong. Principals and agents act within particular institutional frameworks, and when trying to understand macro-level variation across countries, it seems more pressing to focus on understanding key similarities and differences in those institutions and the political logic they engender rather than to evaluate the calculus of individual action at the margins – which is the analytic value added of a microeconomic approach such as rational choice theory. The HI approach is more useful for understanding big differences across countries, particularly when the institutional environments are not well understood.

---

[33] However, in practice most rational choice work analyzes aggregated actors.

The rational choice institutional approach is more useful for understanding particular decisions within well-specified institutions.[34]

Alternative Explanations

In order to evaluate the plausibility and value of the political community model, rival explanations of the determinants of taxation outcomes must be examined. As has been discussed above, explanations emphasizing the role of economic and international factors need to be considered. In addition, this book evaluates the insights derived from explanations emphasizing bargaining power, the trustworthiness of the state, regime type, bureaucratic capacity, and culture. In certain cases, I point out that the political community model provides a better specified, but not necessarily contradictory, argument. In other cases, truly alternative and testable hypotheses can be derived, which are explored in later chapters of the book. When examining the Brazilian and South African histories, I also consider country-specific arguments that highlight the causal role of noted historical events and developments. I demonstrate the limits of these accounts when seen in broader comparative perspective.

Bargaining with the State

In many important ways, the political community model presented above reflects an attempt to build upon Margaret Levi's model of predatory rule.[35] She argues that the emergence of revenue systems can be modeled as the product of a bargain or contract between a ruler and the ruled, or state and

---

[34] Increasingly, rational choice scholars have begun to loosen the assumptions under which they analyze politics, employing more interpretive methods, abandoning the individual as the unit of analysis, and conceding that preferences can be shaped by institutions. In these cases, I find little difference between their enterprise and that of the historical institutionalists. See, for example, Bates, de Figueiredo, and Weingast 1998: 603–42. Similarly, with respect to the new institutionalism in economics, a wide variety of assumptions are employed. Many New Institutional Economists believe that competitive markets produce efficient outcomes in well-specified settings, that outcomes can always be explained in terms of individual utility-maximizing behavior, and that preference formation is unproblematic. In these respects, the political community model shares little common ground. However, in considering more recent scholarship from this school, such as Douglass North's work, in which he abandons an efficiency view of institutions (North 1990: 7), it is again difficult to draw sharp distinctions between the various institutionalist approaches.

[35] Levi 1988.

citizen in more modern times, and she highlights the importance of quasi-voluntary compliance on the part of citizens, as an ultimately determining influence on the structure of state revenue. In order to generate significant amounts of tax revenue, the state must provide a contract or bargain that is fair.[36]

What accounts for differences in the ways in which revenue contracts emerge across time and space? For Levi, structural factors, such as changes in the mode of production and the international environment, as well as changes in forms of government, affect the relative bargaining power of states and citizens, their time horizons or discount rates, and the transaction costs of negotiating and implementing tax policies. She hypothesizes that revenue-maximizing rulers will be able to increase revenue when their bargaining power is greater relative to subjects or citizens, and when the transaction costs of negotiating and enforcing a tax contract are lower. Further, she argues that when rulers discount the future more heavily, they will attempt to extract much higher levels of revenue, even to the detriment of long-term productivity within the economy. Using this model, she attempts to account for differences in the development of revenue systems across time and space. For example, she argues that as military technology changed – becoming more expensive and requiring greater centralization – the bargaining power of rulers to impose war-based taxes increased. "Monarchs needed more funds to win battles and were the obvious persons to organize war. These facts gave them considerable ammunition in the claim that taxpayers gained from contributing."[37] Looking comparatively at royal taxation, she concludes that, because of "the relatively greater bargaining power of French than English monarchs in relation to nobles, French monarchs would be able to impose a greater range of lay taxes than English monarchs."[38]

Despite the powerful insights of the argument, including its emphasis on the role of structural and strategic factors on state development, and on the importance of citizen compliance and voluntarism in the production of revenue, the model fails to capture the various ways in which the political environment can be affected by socially constructed factors, such as the mobilization of group identities, or rhetorical appeals to normative concerns. In emphasizing the centrality of the state, Levi's study does not

[36] Levi 1988: 48–70.
[37] Levi 1988: 106.
[38] Levi 1988: 96.

adequately address the influence of the varied political configurations of society.[39] Indeed, the mode of production and the international context cannot account for key differences in the operation of politics or taxation outcomes across Brazil and South Africa, suggesting the need for a more nuanced explanation. A better specified model would incorporate the prior factors that affect the bargaining power of actors, their discount rates, and associated transaction costs of making and enforcing bargains with the state. Without such additions, it becomes all too easy to make claims about the sources of these rather general analytical variables in a post hoc manner.

The political community model adds an important degree of specificity to Levi's argument by focusing on upper groups in society and by recognizing definitions of NPC as a key determinant of actor preferences, aggregation, and strategies. It argues that such definitions, which give political salience to certain identities and not others, influence inter- and intra-class relations, in turn affecting the actions of key political actors, ultimately shaping tax policies and tax administration. In highlighting the role of quasi-voluntary compliance and the strategic interactions between state and society, this model very much builds on Levi's. However, a key difference is that Levi's analytic variables – bargaining power, transaction costs, discount rates, time horizons, and notions of fairness – are made endogenous. The potential drawback of this move is that the scope of application of the model is more limited, while the advantage is that the predictive power is greater, as the relevant explanatory variables are more thoroughly and restrictively specified. The political community model is more vulnerable to falsification through empirical investigation because we can establish a greater proportion of the relevant contextual factors ex ante.

Trustworthiness of the State

One prominent alternative account of variations in revenue collections and structures, and of citizen compliance more generally, focuses on the trustworthiness and credibility of the state executive and the bureaucracy.[40]

---

[39] In a later work on military conscription, Levi (1997) develops an argument about the determinants of "contingent consent." The argument in this book is more explicit about the role of norms of fairness and the possibilities for ethical reciprocity within ethnic and racial groups.

[40] This argument is also associated with Levi's (1988, 1997) work. For a review of this literature, see Levi and Stoker 2000. Levi's 1988 study of taxation conceptualizes and measures

Specifically, one could hypothesize that the problems of corruption and of the failure to gain the trust of upper-income citizens have been more acute in Brazil than in South Africa, and that this variation explains important differences in the amount of direct income tax revenues collected. To be sure, there is far more bribery of tax collectors and deceptive reporting of financial accounts in Brazil, particularly among the business elite, but the question is, why?

Although perceptions of corruption, credibility, and trustworthiness in-fluence taxation outcomes, we gain more analytic leverage if we consider these factors as part of the puzzle that needs to be explained, rather than as exogenous determinants of tax compliance and levels of collection. Cor-ruption on the part of tax collectors – in particular, the deliberate underval-uation of the tax liabilities of a firm or individual in return for a bribe – is simply one aspect of the outcome under investigation. I assume that most tax collectors are vulnerable to graft, but it is only when citizens actively attempt to evade their tax liabilities that tax collectors engage in such behav-ior as a regular practice. Tax fraud, whether carried out in partnership with the state's agents or not, is a phenomenon that is conceptually so proximate to the outcome of measured levels of collection that it is hardly useful to say that the former "explains" the latter.

An important argument emphasizing the role of trust concerns the types of *social capital* that Putnam (1993, 2000) has identified in his vari-ous works on the functioning of civil society. In his study (1993) comparing the varied functioning of Italian regional governments, Putnam argues that the *horizontal* networks of trust within Northern Italy have facilitated more efficient government than the *vertical* networks of Southern Italy, because citizens are more likely to trust the actions and behavior of their fellow citi-zens and elected leaders in the former case than in the latter. Building on this argument, Joel Slemrod (1998) proposes – though he does not empirically examine – that this hypothesis is likely to apply to the realm of national tax-ation systems. Similarly, Scholz and Pinney (1995) explain voluntary com-pliance as at least partially due to a sense of duty. I do not contest that duty, trust, and social capital are analytical constructs that capture aspects of the societal relationships necessary for cooperation and collective action that

the outcome somewhat differently than I do, in that she explores types of revenue systems, whereas I consider the extent to which the state can effectively collect certain types of taxes, as discussed in more detail in Chapter 2. Levi's 1997 work is concerned with military conscription – a related but clearly distinctive outcome.

are central to the process of taxation and of governance more generally.[41] Yet again, these concepts remain so intertwined with patterns of compliant behavior that we cannot easily distinguish between cause and effect.

At a deeper level, in order to assess the arguments posed by Levi and by others who emphasize the influence of credible commitments made by government leaders, it is necessary to explore the hypothesis that citizens are less likely to meet their tax obligations quasi-voluntarily if they believe that the national treasury is being pilfered for private, narrow gains, or if they believe that state revenues are not being spent fairly. In both Brazil and South Africa, and certainly in many other societies, the citizens who challenge the state's demands for tax payment in the policy arena or through aggressive avoidance and evasion strategies typically justify their resistance to taxation with the claim that they are not getting a fair deal, and that the money is being wasted on bad policies, poor implementation, or through outright stealing by individuals in government. Perceptions of corruption or perceptions that one's interests are not being considered are likely to make the government seem less trustworthy, and as a result, citizens can justify their challenges to the state's demands for tax payments. At the extreme, when state executives and their agents demonstrate a wanton disregard for public interests, and when virtually no government services are provided, it would be reasonable to predict that citizens will resist tax payments.

An important problem with hypotheses concerned with credibility and trustworthiness is that it is very difficult to define and to measure such influences. What is a well-intentioned redistributive project for some may be interpreted as evidence of corrupt patronage for others. By its very nature, "actual" corruption is virtually impossible to measure at a macro-level scale because the very concept implies a relativistic understanding of what is legal and acceptable behavior. Ironically, transparent democratic institutions, such as a free press, may lead the average citizen to *perceive* higher levels of corruption, and/or lower levels of trustworthy and credible behavior, simply because such information is made available to an extent that is not true in less transparent but potentially more corrupt polities. Certainly, in the cases of Brazil and South Africa, for most of the 20th century, the respective governments have demonstrated through substantial expenditure

---

[41] See, for example, the various contributions in Braithwaite and Levi 1998 and the review of the literature on political trust and trustworthiness in Levi and Stoker 2000.

projects that the treasury has not been used *exclusively* for the personal gains of government leaders. Massive modernizing development projects were carried out in both societies,[42] major infrastructure projects were completed, and in both cases, these largely served the (upper-income) citizens who were liable for the payment of income taxes. In both countries, there exist documented accounts of illegal and corrupt behavior on the part of state leaders as well as of low-level bureaucrats, but such anecdotes provide little clue as to the extent to which *actual* corruption has varied across the two countries. Neither country has had a profligate dictator such as the former Zaire's Sese Seko Mobutu, and particularly during more authoritarian periods, the respective states have been governed by regimes committed, at least to a degree, to the development of professional, legal-rational bureaucracies. In short, there is little empirical evidence that can lead us to conclude that a more corrupt or untrustworthy state is to blame for Brazil's relatively weaker record of income tax collections, despite over a century of attempts to increase collections.

If not *actual* state corruption or trustworthiness, what can account for cross-national variation in *perceptions* of credibility? As Levi points out, "political and cultural organizations can also affect perceptions of the trustworthiness of government and of the extent of ethical reciprocity."[43] This suggests the need to look more closely at such factors in comparative perspective. Perceptions of state action on the part of individual[44] and collective actors may be largely determined by political context, independent of the goods and services the state actually provides. The political community model provides a framework for understanding how citizens interpret state action.

Culture

A conventional explanation advanced by scholars and others for cross-national differences in tax policy and tax administration is a theoretical black box often labeled *culture*. As discussed earlier, there is a cultural aspect to the

---

[42] Though in both cases, with tragic consequences for human development. See the discussions of these projects as described by Scott 1998.

[43] Levi 1997: 27.

[44] As I have shown elsewhere (Lieberman 2002), individual perceptions of getting a fair deal, and of their inclinations to comply with tax obligations, are strongly influenced by their level of agreement with the definition of NPC.

political community model, but it is contained within a theory of political institutions. Alternatively, culture is frequently identified as an autonomous causal influence on key political and policy outcomes. Cultural factors potentially provide the most powerful alternative hypothesis because they are often difficult to disprove. Indeed, as a last resort, many analysts of taxation identify cultural differences as the basis for unexplained variations that tend to be sustained across countries over time. Of course, this is a large category with quite varying notions of how to define the concepts, let alone the specification of the causal mechanisms involved. Thus, in order to seriously consider the impact of culture, both theoretical and empirical investigation is necessary.

Again, it is critical to separate cause and effect. If patterns of taxation or patterns of compliance are described as tax cultures, then culture cannot be said to explain patterns of variation. This would be true by definition. Scholars have observed that across time and space, different norms and practices of taxation develop in particular places. In other words, they argue that the very policies and practices that comprise the tax state constitute their own nationally distinctive cultures. Webber and Wildavsky's (1986) discussion of tax systems around the world is an important contribution in its identification of differences in budgetary systems across places and history, but this presentation lacks a true theory of why such patterns emerge in the ways they do. As a result, no testable hypothesis can be derived when culture is defined as the *outcome*.

More sophisticated conceptions of culture advanced by analysts such as Weber (1991); Almond and Verba (1963); Inglehart (1990); Inglehart and Carballo (1997); and Swank (1996) have described culture independently, as a set of shared norms, values, and beliefs that tend to structure politics and particular outcomes. Although an institutional theory of identity is certainly a close cousin of many cultural approaches, the institutional argument of the political community model differs from the cultural one in that material interests still ultimately motivate politics, whereas in the cultural theory, cross-national variations are explained by variations in norms and values per se. To a limited extent, we can adjudicate among these arguments through empirical analysis. A standard refrain in this regard is that taxation is easier in Protestant, Anglo-Saxon cultures, whereas in Catholic, Latin, or Iberian cultures, states have a difficult time collecting taxes. For example, Haycraft argues that the high level of tax evasion of direct taxes in France and Italy relative to other European countries is the product of Latin suspicions of the state on the part of French and Italian citizens, and that such values ultimately generate a greater reliance on indirect taxation in those countries.[45]

An important challenge in adjudicating among cultural and institutional hypotheses is the potentially spurious correlation between what is observed as culture and the outcome under examination. If they are both caused by the same set of factors, culture will tend to covary with taxation systems even if the causal relationship between the two is weak or nonexistent. In particular, the notion of *colonial legacies* – the social and/or political inheritance of empires – is an example of this form of relationship. Former colonies have tended to inherit both institutional and cultural qualities from the imperial state. Many English-speaking societies (particularly former British colonies) may share similar political dynamics and similar taxation capacities, but the institutional argument will suggest that this stems from similarities in institutional constructions rather than from Anglo-Saxon or Protestant values. Similarly, the resistance to taxation on the part of citizens in Latin societies has more to do with a commonality of political institutions, including the ways in which the NPC is configured, than with a more deep-seated set of values inherently opposed to the welfare state or the civic realm. The political community model is explicitly an alternative to such arguments. Most importantly, the model predicts that the definition of NPC will produce a distinctive legacy for the outcome under investigation independent of that produced by constant causes or antecedent conditions existing within countries prior to the critical juncture.[46]

Undoubtedly, the explanatory power of cultural factors is difficult to assess both on theoretical and empirical grounds, but through process tracing and careful observation, it is possible to assess the degree to which one or another set of influences shapes tax policy and administration. In particular, the nature of change over time within countries often provides clues about the relative influence of culture when compared with other factors. Broader cross-national comparisons provide additional insights. This book evaluates the hypothesized effects of colonial legacies and religious orientations as potential cultural influences, and ultimately, does not find support for such explanations.

---

[45] Haycraft 1985, as cited in Peters 1991: 5.
[46] Collier and Collier 1991: 30.

Regime Types

A central task for students of comparative politics has been to characterize the relationship between the nature of the political regime – democracy or dictatorship – and the quality of state authority. This analysis helps shed light on this question by measuring state authority in terms of operational measures of taxation. Theories about the relationship between regime type and extractive capacity suggest conflicting hypotheses. On the one hand, democracies may legitimize the state's authority by providing real and perceived recognition of taxpayer interests, following the logic of "no taxation without representation." On the other hand, authoritarian governments may be better at limiting the numbers of demands and conflicting interests articulated within a society, and they may be more willing to use coercive and invasive tactics to collect revenue. For example, they may severely fine or jail tax cheats, or use search and seizure methods of investigation in a manner or to an extent generally not practiced or acceptable in democracies with strong protections for civil liberties and potentially long and expensive legal procedures. While Cheibub's (1998) multicountry statistical study finds that on average, democracies collect more (total) taxation than do dictatorships, many of the causal factors found to be associated with regime types are themselves strong influences on taxation, leading to the conclusion that regime type probably has no independent effect. Since this study uses different measures of the tax state (see Chapter 2), and employs different methods of analysis, it is possible to re-assess the alternative hypothesis that regime type affects state performance. This hypothesis can be evaluated from a static perspective – comparing countries at a particular moment in time, or from a dynamic perspective – investigating the influence of regime changes within each country over time.

Bureaucratic Performance: Leadership and Professionalism

In a practical sense, tax collection is a form of public administration, and the quality of the bureaucracy likely provides a strong proximate explanation of the relative success of different states in collecting taxes.[47] Indeed, much of the public finance literature written by the taxation specialists of the major international financial organizations identifies the poor technical quality of administration in developing countries as the root of high levels of evasion

---

[47] The notion of the legal-rational bureaucracy is generally associated with Weber 1968.

31

and low levels of collection. Authors of multiple prominent case studies on the development of tax systems and tax reform around the world have pointed to the importance of a well-functioning, well-trained bureaucracy on tax collection.[48] The implication of such arguments is that it is possible to improve the performance of collections by reforming the technical skills of the state bureaucracy, independent of other concerns.

As it turns out, technical skills are a necessary but far from sufficient basis for collection. In an environment in which evasion and false reporting are the norm, the most skilled administrators will find it difficult to effect significant change. Society plays at least as important a role as the state in the collection of taxes, and the efficacy of the state is not likely to be high without the cooperation of citizens. We can evaluate a narrower aspect of the rival explanation which has direct implications for policy makers: If we separate the concept of professionalism (training, technical skills, numbers and types of employees, promotional criteria) from performance (success in collecting taxes) and use available measures of bureaucratic professionalism, it is possible to measure the strength of this relationship.

Plan of the Book: A "Nested" Approach to Comparative Analysis

The central objectives of this book are to explain why Brazil and South Africa have such different tax systems, and to provide a more general accounting of the factors that influence cross-national variation in the state's ability to extract revenue from economically privileged groups in society. The book investigates the explanatory power of the political community model, and the various alternative frameworks discussed above, through a "nested" research design that draws inferences from comparative case study and cross-national statistical analyses.

Primarily, the argument is developed and explored with a comparative historical analysis of the development of the tax state in Brazil and South Africa. Focused, comparative analysis provides a remarkably powerful basis for making causal inferences about historical institutional theories. Comparative, cross-period analyses within the historical record provide multiple opportunities to measure the causal effects of institutional and other explanatory variables. Establishing chronologies and sequences is vital in a discussion of relationships in which the plausibility of the causal arrow pointing in the opposite direction is quite high. Understanding

---

[48] Boskin and McLure 1990; Gillis 1989; Newbery and Stern 1987.

contemporary patterns of variation demands an analytical excursion backwards to the various forks in the historical road, constantly questioning the extent to which "it could have been." Moving forward through history, we can observe the extent to which options become opened or closed off because of prior actions and outcomes. By analyzing the treatment of similar policy proposals at similar moments in time, it is possible to consider the influence of other factors on outcomes. In particular, the analysis of primary documents and interview transcripts reveals how differently the calculus of action has been in these different contexts.[49]

That analysis is embedded within a statistical analysis of a multicountry dataset with valid data from the period 1970–94.[50] Such a mixed approach compensates for the inferential limitations generally associated with standard research strategies in comparative politics: On the one hand, two-country studies often suffer from limited analytic leverage, whereas large-N studies may suffer from problems of poor measurement, conceptual stretching, or spurious correlation. The shortcomings of the respective analyses are largely addressed through this analytical marriage. Together, the findings from the comparative-historical and the statistical analyses provide strong support for the central arguments associated with the political community model.

Within the comparative historical analysis, both cross-sectional and over-time analyses generated many degrees of freedom beyond the two country cases central to the investigation, providing yet a further solution to the problem of small-N. This flexible, mixed strategy provides solutions to many of the theoretical and data constraints typically associated with the types of problems raised by HI analysts, including a concern for simultaneously understanding the particularities of specific country cases while attempting to advance more general propositions about the mechanics

---

[49] For a fuller discussion of these strategies, see Lieberman 2001a.

[50] The data requirements of the project are diverse and far-reaching. See Chapters 2 and 6 for fuller explication of the sources of the statistical data. The comparative historical analysis is based upon extensive field research, supplemented by archival research in the United States and extensive consideration of secondary source materials. Extensive archival materials were gathered in both countries, including government and nongovernment reports on the tax system, newspaper coverage of tax politics, and various publications from business, labor, and political organizations. Over 150 structured, open-ended elite interviews were conducted with tax bureaucrats, political party leaders, tax lawyers, accountants, consultants, relevant analysts of the tax system inside and out of government, top business leaders, and representatives from international financial institutions.

of political life. As a result, the conclusions can be accepted with a high level of confidence.

Although the findings of the research are presented separately in terms of the comparative historical research on the one hand and the statistical analysis on the other, such presentation belies the iterative discovery process that was central to the research and analysis. Moving back and forth between small-N and large-N analyses provided opportunities to sharpen the analysis and to verify hypotheses generated at one level with data from the other level. The paired comparison was critical for developing and illuminating central concepts and causal relations within the analysis, particularly for identifying difficult-to-measure factors, including political discourse and interpretation. Longitudinal analyses within country cases provided opportunities to explore rival explanations, causal order, and the operation of legacies. The cross-national statistical analysis was useful for framing the paired comparison, measuring the influence of rival explanatory factors, and for testing the broader explanatory power of the central model. Early in the research, such statistical analysis helped to confirm the value of the paired study. For example, the simple scatter plot and correlational analysis presented in Figure 1.2 help to make clear that varied levels of income tax collections between Brazil and South Africa are truly puzzling when seen from a broader comparative perspective. I decided to pursue a more nuanced political-historical explanation after finding that I simply could not account for this variance despite attempts to specify several multivariate models incorporating a range of standard social, economic, and political factors. Such strategies represent a significant advance over the use of Mill's method of difference in which there are important limits to the number of controls that can be identified with only a small number of cases.

Before turning to causal inference, however, it is necessary to paint a better portrait of the problem of taxation, and to provide a tool for comparison and measurement. The question of variation in national patterns of taxation is more fully articulated in Chapter 2, which presents a framework for comparative analysis of the development of national taxation systems, or *tax states*. It explains why taxation provides a useful focus for the comparative investigation of state-society relations, building upon the subfield of fiscal sociology. It highlights key differences between the contemporary Brazilian and South African cases by identifying variation in tax policy and tax administration within a larger typology.

Chapters 3 through 5 present the comparative historical analysis of tax state development in Brazil and South Africa. Although the countries are situated in different world regions, different languages are spoken there, and some other obvious differences exist, the selection of South Africa and Brazil as the foundation for this analysis is due largely to their great similarities in social, economic, and geopolitical terms. That analysis draws on the political, economic, and social histories of the two countries in order to make causal inferences about the determinants of tax policy and tax administration in the 20th century.

Chapter 3 provides an analysis of the cleavages, crises, and critical junctures in the two countries. A central task in specifying a critical junctures model is to establish analytical equivalence in the timing or characteristics of the hypothesized critical juncture, demonstrating that contrasts are actually "different values on the same variable."[51] It describes the common problems and challenges of national integration that faced constitutional planners following the onset of industrialization in the late 19th century, and the different ways in which NPC got defined. In particular, the two countries had been divided along the lines of *race* and *region*. That is, perceptions of racial heterogeneity combined with racial prejudice, along with competing ethnic and ethno-regional claims to power, contradicted the unity implied by the notion of shared nationhood. After major political conflicts and upheavals in the respective countries, periods of indeterminacy ensued, and political elites gathered in formal bargaining processes to negotiate new constitutions and to develop new definitions of NPC. Following the conclusion of the Boer War in 1902, constitutional architects in South Africa eventually agreed upon an explicitly racially exclusionary, white union for their 1909 constitution. By contrast, their Brazilian counterparts, prompted to the negotiating table by the overthrow of the emperor in 1889, created an officially nonracial federation in their 1891 constitution. As a result, in South Africa, race became the dominant political idiom for politics while in Brazil, regionalism emerged as the dominant idiom, with important implications for the emergence of class relations in these countries.

Using comparative historical analysis of the development of the tax state in Brazil and South Africa in the 19th and 20th centuries, Chapter 4 explores the power of the political community model to provide useful insights into the unfolding of cross-national variation. It traces the link between the process of industrialization and new pressures from the international

---

[51] Collier and Collier 1991: 32.

environment on the one hand, and the political dynamics associated with the NPC on the other, and the joint effect of these causal factors on the development of the tax state. Overall, South Africa's racial coordination is found to have provided the political glue necessary for the state executive to command high levels of sacrifice from upper groups. Meanwhile, Brazil's regional fragmentation generated intra-elite competition, producing a zero-sum political game and high levels of private resistance to such taxes. In Brazil, no analogous political "glue" to that found in South Africa could generate a sense of common identity and purpose among upper economic groups. As a result, the Brazilian state executive has consistently found it difficult to tax upper groups. Both from the perspective of policy and administration, South Africa's tax state developed in a much more efficient and progressive manner than the Brazilian one.

Chapter 5 provides a more temporally focused analysis of the politics of taxation at the end of the 20th century. It considers taxation in an era of globalization, democratization, economic liberalization, and the historic collapse of apartheid, a period during which all major domestic and international trends would lead one to predict increased convergence in national tax policies and administrative practices. Yet, the chapter finds that far from converging, patterns of taxation have remained nationally distinctive during this period: South Africa's tax state remains extremely efficient and progressive – if somewhat less so than in previous years – while Brazil's remains highly inefficient, complex, and regressive. The chapter demonstrates the powerful and almost always unintended ways in which the institutional variation first identified in Chapter 3 has cast a long shadow onto the future, reproducing patterns of class cohesion in South Africa and fragmentation in Brazil, as well as pre-existing patterns of engagement with the state.

Returning to the multicountry component of the study, Chapter 6 presents the findings of statistical analyses designed to increase our confidence in the findings from the comparative historical analysis. Regression analysis is used to assess the influence of varied definitions of NPC on the performance measure of the tax state, while controlling for levels of economic development. Robust statistical results confirm that varied configurations of race and region have affected the central state's ability to collect taxes from upper groups in a much larger sample of country cases. Although South Africa and Brazil may be "extreme" cases in terms of the respective salience of race and region, the influence of such institutional variation in the definition of NPC is clearly evident elsewhere. The chapter also demonstrates that several other rival explanatory factors do *not* have an independent influence on cross-national variation. Such findings complement the comparative historical analysis, which could not rule out several rival hypotheses because of its weak statistical power.

Chapter 7 concludes the book by discussing the broader implications of the findings for questions about equitable development, and the future of the tax state, and by identifying avenues for further research. It demonstrates that the legacy of state-building in these two countries has provided South Africa with a tax state far better equipped to redistribute resources in favor of poor blacks than is the case in Brazil. The finding is particularly ironic given that the raison d'être of the South African state for most of the 20th century was the explicit advancement of the white population, to the *detriment* of blacks. Because so much work in the field of taxation has been dedicated to the task of identifying "optimal" models and policy prescriptions, it is worth re-iterating that this is *not* the task of *this* project. The South African political path to the development of its tax state should not be regarded as the preferred one, because a host of other factors not considered here would obviously weigh heavily against such a ridiculous policy prescription. Nevertheless, it is important to be clear that the research does generate a somewhat dismal conclusion – that explicit exclusion seems to provide some of the political "glue" that can help overcome key collective action and coordination problems associated with taxation.[52] Of course, this does not imply that exclusion is the *only* mechanism for generating such political dynamics, but as was true during the processes of war-making and nation-building in Western Europe, the socially constructed notion of solidarity and cohesion that was produced through processes of explicit exclusion in South Africa proved remarkably powerful, particularly when compared with other countries at similar levels of development, such as Brazil.

---

[52] As Russell Hardin (1995) points out, solutions to collective action problems often lead to socially undesirable outcomes.

2

The Tax State in Comparative Perspective

For the means needed for common purposes and aims, the public economy appeals to the citizens' spirit of sacrifice and demands their property and life without reward. Given the unequal measure of people's communal spirit, the voluntary principle is not enough. The contributions and obligations must be legally determined and laid down. In fundamental contrast to the exchange society and market economy, community and public economy rest on compulsory military service and taxation.

— Hans Ritschl[1]

The successes and failures of governments in their attempts to collect taxes are a critical source of variation in the types of relationships that exist between states and societies around the world.[2] Although there are other political arenas in which the authority and efficacy of the national state can be examined, it is in the realm of taxation that we have relatively good, comparable data, useful for cross-national analysis.[3] Which data to look at and how to interpret those data are not so obvious, however, and it is necessary to justify how taxation outcomes reflect more broadly on political life and the development of the modern state.

This chapter provides a framework for understanding the basic building blocks of a national tax system and develops a set of tools for cross-national

---

[1] Ritschl 1964: 240.

[2] Seminal essays by Schumpeter (1954) and Goldscheid (1964) provided strong scholarly foundations for studying taxation as a central institution in social and political life, and helped spawn the still nascent field. More recent contributions include Webber and Wildavsky 1986; Steinmo 1993; Peters 1991; Levi 1988; Brownlee 1996. For a review of fiscal sociological studies, see Campbell 1993.

[3] Lieberman 2001c.

comparison. It reveals how the dynamic process of taxation can vary in terms of patterns of cooperation and conflict between state actors and the economically privileged groups within society who control the lion's share of taxable resources. Particularly in late developing countries, in which the distribution of resources tends to be highly unequal, the direct taxation of upper groups – largely through income taxes – is a high-stakes endeavor for the financial solvency of the state, and for the after-tax distribution of resources within society. Studying how taxes are levied on this group is a uniquely powerful strategy for understanding patterns of political authority and collective action that are central to the very process of state development. The chapter identifies the multiple stages during which actors may challenge the size and allocation of the tax burden, revealing the ubiquitous nature of the political arena.

A central goal of the chapter is to situate the contemporary Brazilian and South African cases in broader comparative perspective in order to make clear the magnitudes of similarity and difference within this paired comparison. Specifically, it describes modern Brazil as a case of an adversarial tax state, in which upper groups are consistently at odds with one another and with the state over the allocation of the tax burden. That case is contrasted with South Africa's cooperative tax state, characterized by more productive patterns of engagement between the tax collector and high-income taxpayers. Tax state variation is measured quantitatively, by comparing income tax collections as share of GDP, and qualitatively, by comparing the tax policy mixes and patterns of administration and compliance within countries.

The Tax State Defined

In this book, the outcome under investigation is a set of institutions, which I refer to as the *tax state*. The tax state is defined as the aggregate of a set of relationships between the state executive and state bureaucracy on the one hand, and citizens or taxpayers on the other, manifest in a set of national tax policies and administrative practices. In comparing taxation across countries, it is possible to imagine multiple possible foci, but I emphasize the taxation of upper-income groups. While the taxation of workers and of the poor are considered in this study, such forms of taxation are presented as *alternatives* to the taxation of business owners, high-income individuals, and other segments in society with significant economic resources. Although there are normative implications stemming from this conceptualization, my main goal is to provide a positive analysis of the origins of differing relationships between the state and economically privileged groups.

The conceptualization of the tax state builds from the neo-Weberian state-in-society approach outlined by Joel Migdal and his collaborators.[4] The state-in-society framework makes room for a political explanation of cross-national variation in taxation systems by identifying the different ways in which the state's attempts to impose a uniform authority may be challenged, shaped, and reconfigured by various actors within society. The process of state development is an iterative one that responds to relationships forged within society. Indeed, taxation provides a very concrete area for empirical analysis that highlights many of the central tensions in the development of state capacity and state-society relations in general.

The process of raising taxes embodies the central tension of modern political authority in its juxtaposition of the state as tax collector and society as tax payer. Like others, I assume that states attempt to maximize revenue, but are subject to serious political and economic constraints.[5] Even as modern states claim to collect taxes for the benefit of society, perhaps no demand presents greater incentives for free riding: Members of society desire collectively provided goods, while preferring someone else pay for them. In order to generate significant tax revenues, the state and/or groups within society must find ways to solve this dilemma, coordinating policy and administration with the economic activities contained within society. Although the state's use of coercive forces generally plays some role in the process of tax collection, coercion is a particularly expensive form of authority, and is relatively ineffective in the wake of extensive avoidance and evasion schemes. To raise significant amounts of revenue, in the most efficient manner possible, the state must enlist society as a group of cooperative partners engaged in a joint project, rather than as a set of subjects with opposing interests. The challenge of developing such a relationship becomes evident as we consider these two sets of actors and their interests.

The State as Tax Collector

The state is the bureaucracy and leadership associated with the central government of a territory that claims a monopoly over the legitimate use of

---

[4] Migdal 1994, 2001.
[5] Levi 1988; Bates and Lien 1985; North 1981.

force and is widely recognized by international organizations such as the
United Nations as the state authority.[6] It is a group of political actors and
bureaucrats with interest in sustaining power and shaping the social and
economic relations of people within its borders.[7] The administrative staff
of the state is almost always organized into a pyramidal power structure:
At the top are the policy-making and law-granting bodies, including executive political leadership and the cabinet. In the case of taxation, a minister
of finance or an individual holding a similar position is likely to be the
key leader, in addition to the president or prime minister, focused on raising taxes. Next is the central administration of the taxation bureaucracy,
generally located in the national capital. Third, there are the regional and
functional offices of the bureaucracy. Finally, at the bottom of the pyra-
mid are the field posts, which constitute the most local-level offices of the
bureaucracy, and are often known simply as local tax offices or local re-
ceivers of revenue.[8] Various policies and informal practices tend to guide
the division of labor across these spheres of the state in the collective goal
of raising revenue.

The puzzle of explaining variation in the tax state merely reflects one
aspect of a larger question of explaining the degree to which particular states
are successful in their attempts to impose uniform authority over groups
within society. As Migdal points out:

What makes the modern state modern? Serving both the ideals of the enlightenment
and the needs of modern capitalism, the modern state has been constructed to create
a uniformity or universality to life within its borders. . . . Unlike most premodern political structures, the state has aimed to impose uniform and ultimate conformity on
social life within far-reaching (but still circumscribed) boundaries. . . . Compliance
to these sorts of social norms was not new, but the claims of a single centralized organization to enforce such norms over huge territorial expanses were novel almost
everywhere they were made. (Migdal 1997: 209)

The executives of modern states in the 20th century have tended to share
similar goals: They have attempted to establish centralized bureaucracies
that carry out a uniform set of functions throughout their territories, and
they have attempted to advance a collective transformation of society by
establishing rules requiring conformity and compliance. In particular, they

---

[6] Bendix 1964.
[7] See, for example, Evans, Rueschemeyer, and Skocpol 1985; Young and Turner 1985;
Levi 1988, 1997; O'Donnell 1994.
[8] The outline for this pyramidal structure is provided by Migdal, Kohli, and Shue 1994: 16.

have asked citizens to relinquish sizeable shares of their income and wealth in the form of tax payments.

Upper Groups as (Potential) Tax Payers

Upper groups are the individuals in society who control the majority of a nation's wealth and income. "Upper" groups include *capitalists* – in other words, investors and company heads – as well as professionals and other high-income groups, that elsewhere might be labeled *middle class*. In modern economies, they are likely to have a range of diverse economic interests and needs and are likely to be located across a range of geographic regions. Although they tend to lack the highly organized, pyramidal structure of the state, such groups often organize themselves into business organizations, or political parties – sometimes in a coordinated manner, and sometimes along competing lines. They may attempt to exert influence over the government collectively or on a more individualized basis. In a two-class model of society, they are distinctive from *lower groups*, which include organized labor as well as nonorganized workers, the unemployed, and the destitute.

At least initially, the collection of taxes is problematic because compliance and conformity are rarely the primary instincts of the materially well endowed upper groups when asked to forego income and/or wealth. At various levels of its pyramidal structure, the state must forge relationships with private firms, high-income individuals (business owners, executives, professionals), taxation intermediaries (accountants and lawyers), employer organizations, organized political groups and parties, and other organizations within society. Meanwhile, these upper groups have interests of their own, including the desire for protection and the coordinated development of infrastructure for facilitating economic and other transactions. They are likely to compete with one another over the question of who ought to bear the largest tax burden.

Upper groups within capitalist societies deploy very different strategies with respect to the state's initiatives to exert uniform authority – complying with state demands in some cases, and challenging them in others. Indeed, the control of capital and taxable resources makes this group intrinsically important, and as Przeworski and Wallerstein point out, Marxist political theory has concluded that "capitalists are endowed with public power, power which no formal institution can overcome."[9] Nonetheless, through a formal

---

[9] Przeworski and Wallerstein 1988: 11.

theoretical analysis of the behavior of owners of capital, they conclude that a wide range of tax policies are compatible with investment, implying that governments are not limited by the "structural dependence of capital," to the extent Marxist and neoclassical scholars had previously argued.[10] Such a conclusion reveals what can be seen clearly in practice – that the relationship between the state and upper groups, or between the state and capital, is not basically uniform across capitalist society, but that it varies widely across contexts.[11]

Toward a Typology of the Tax State

In the finest detail, no two tax systems are alike, and from a microscopic perspective, meaningful comparison would be impossible if the goal were to make inferences about national-level politics. Instead, I take a more system-level approach in order to characterize the institutions that guide the relationship between states and societies. I identify five ideal-type tax states that reflect qualitative differences in the state's ability to tax upper groups within society. Before presenting this typology, however, I outline the basic building blocks of a tax system – tax policy and tax administration – in order to establish a common language for further discussion.

A Restrictive Definition of Taxation

The political and logistical challenges associated with raising tax revenues are quite different from those associated with other forms of government finance, and as a result, it is necessary to introduce a strict definition and to specify what types of revenues should and should not be included under this heading. Taxes are "unrequited compulsory payments collected primarily by the central government."[12] They are levied on a particular base and paid to the government to provide certain public goods or services or to redistribute income or purchasing power within society – but without provision or promise of any *specific* good or service in return for payment. Indeed, tax

[10] Przeworski and Wallerstein 1988: 11–29.
[11] Although not concerned with taxation, Peter Evans' (1995) comparative analysis of the state's role in the information technology sector in Brazil, Korea, and India further reveals the different types of relationships that are possible between states and capitalist sectors of the economy within societies at middle levels of economic development.
[12] World Bank 1988: 79.

revenues represent only one of several forms of financing the national budget, including debt, entrepreneurial (parastatal) income, or user fees. Yet, it is the unique qualities of taxation that provide such great insights into state-society relations. As Lorenz Von Stein explains in his classic work on taxation:

Taxes are conceptually entirely different from all other public revenue. . . . Taxes can be said to represent the nation's entire civic sense on the economic plane. . . . In administering public property, the State is an independent economic agent with its own capital; fees and regalia represent a payment to the State in return for services rendered to individuals for the satisfaction of their individual needs. Taxation, by contrast, represents a field in national economic life where, by virtue of the State's constitution and administration, part of the individuals' economic income is withdrawn from them and becomes the community's economic income.[13]

Taxation is the process of converting private income and wealth into public resources; collections from society are used and allocated by the state. A theoretical interest in taxation as a way of looking at state-society relations is premised on the idea that levels and mixes of tax revenues reflect the state's ability to exercise authority over different groups within society.

Many other forms of finance, while important for virtually all states, have different administrative and political implications. Monies raised through provision of specific government services, such as postage stamps, school fees, or road tolls, cannot be considered taxes because, as Von Stein suggests, such revenue is hardly distinguishable from ordinary market transactions. Because such revenues are collected with explicit reference to individual benefits even if some of the profits generated from such services may be used for other government services, there is seldom a free rider problem associated with such revenues. Similarly, when a state generates surpluses from its ownership over certain productive firms this cannot be considered taxation, except when the firm is run along business principles and income and/or production are taxed in the same manner as private firms.

Certain forms of finance are completely divorced from society, and also have no place in the definition of taxation. Financing the state through monetary instruments – using inflation or money printing to generate additional resources for the state (modern forms of *seigneurage*[14]) – requires no participation on the part of society. For example, the use of selective

---

[13] Von Stein 1964: 28.
[14] See Ardant 1975: 191.

credit or subsidies particularly within inflationary environments may wind up placing an indirect burden on particular groups, but no payment is made to the state, and thus such burdens cannot be usefully described as taxation. While opportunities for financing the state in these ways may influence tax systems, and vice versa, tax revenue remains a unique source of revenue with respect to the challenge it presents for distributing the burden within society and coordinating payment with the state.

Although duties and tariffs on trade *are* forms of taxation, I also differentiate such revenue sources from the domestic taxes that are at the heart of this study because the state's ability to collect taxes on foreign revenues does not provide relevant insights into the quality of the relationship between the state and upper groups within society. Strategies for developing domestic industries often motivate the imposition of such trade taxes to a much greater degree than the need for revenue, particularly for semi-industrialized and advanced industrialized countries. The fact that most state bureaucracies make a clear distinction between inland revenue and customs further reveals the extent to which these are really different processes. Levels of trade revenues may be related to domestic taxation, and this relationship will be considered, but the problem of domestic taxation remains the central question of this research. The relationship between taxation and the state's ability to utilize other forms of finance is an ongoing tension discussed in the study, but it is critical to maintain these important analytical distinctions in order to stay focused on the investigation of state authority.

Employing this restricted definition of taxation, it is possible to elaborate on the practical problems and challenges of tax collection. There exist multiple sites for political competition in which the state attempts to levy taxes, and individuals and groups within society may have opportunities to resist payment. Taxation involves two main sets of tasks: the establishment of a set of tax policies that codify what the state is entitled to collect, and the implementation of those policies in the form of administration. Both the enactment and administration of tax policy provide multiple opportunities for political competition within society, and between state and society.

Tax Policy

The tax policy framework of a given country at a given moment in time is comprised of a set of laws and/or codes that ultimately define the potential tax revenues that may be collected by the state from the economy. As shown in Figure 2.1, a national economy can be regarded as having a set of potential tax *handles*, or resources that can be defined in concrete ways either as *stocks* or *flows*. Economic stocks include property or wealth accumulated by individuals or firms such as land, capital equipment, or buildings. Economic flows are transactions, including income, consumption, production, and the sale or transfer of property. The tax policy framework creates the legal basis for the state's collection of taxes with respect to economic stocks and flows, and is defined in terms of the tax base, rates, exemptions, and specification of the taxpayer, all of which are described below. The construction of each aspect of the framework affects the nature of the tax burden, and each provides a focus for political competition.

Tax policy is determined in a variety of places and forums, including in the offices of the state executive and/or the minister of finance; in the legislature; in the offices of tax bureaucrats; and in joint commissions between the government and the private sector. The set of codes and rules that are in place in a given year are intended to provide answers to the questions of who is responsible for paying, and how much. While all governments attempt to make their tax system "fair," such an outcome is highly political and contextualized, subject to the forces of political competition in each of its component parts.

The *tax base* is the set of economic stocks and flows, or tax handles, that will ultimately generate a tax liability for taxpayers. The tax base is generally specified with rules or guidelines for measurement. For example, the very concept of income may vary widely, including different definitions of how to calculate revenues and expenditures for a particular industry or type of firm, or what types of remuneration constitute income for an individual, and the time frame around which such bases may be calculated. Individuals themselves may constitute a tax base – often referred to as a *head tax* – but in modern economies, it is generally economic units that constitute the base.

The specification of the tax base helps to codify the relationship between the state and upper groups in two important ways. First, the tax policy framework actually identifies the extent to which the total tax base makes upper groups liable for payment. Generally speaking, this varies in terms of the degree to which income and property are important tax bases, defined in broad enough terms that those with significant resources will be assessed for tax payment. Other types of taxes, such as consumption taxes, tend to place a far greater relative burden on lower groups and are likely to constitute an

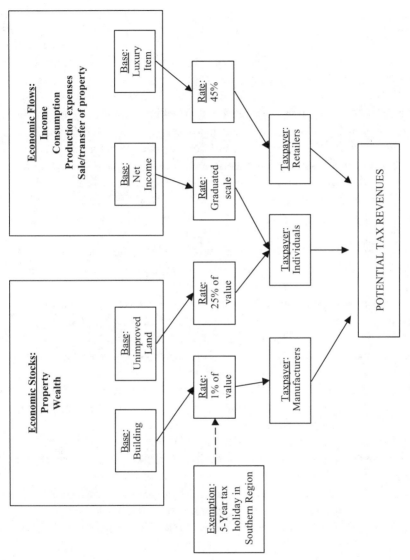

Figure 2.1 Hypothetical tax policy framework

47

insignificant share of the total income and wealth of a wealthier member of society. A key exception is when luxury items consumed by upper groups are taxed more heavily and/or when items consumed by lower groups are taxed more lightly in order to target income groups in a progressive manner.

Second, it is possible to compare the relative transparency of the total tax base. On the one hand, the state may levy only a few key taxes in which the tax base is defined in such a way that individuals and firms are likely to be well aware of the extent to which they are liable for tax payment, particularly because they must *declare* their liability for such taxes, and the individual or firm that bears the burden of the tax also pays the tax – what is referred to as *direct* taxation. Again, income and property taxes tend to be highly transparent in this manner. On the other hand, governments may engage in *fiscal illusion*,[15] by levying multiple, hidden taxes that are difficult for taxpayers to identify. Typically, such taxes are understood to be *indirect* because they are not formally declared by those who ultimately bear the burden of the tax. Taxes on worker payrolls, taxes on financial transactions, "stamp" taxes, licenses, and social security contributions are the least visible forms of taxation – in the sense that taxpayers are often unaware that they are paying or they believe that their own individual benefits are tied to payment – minimizing the free rider problem. While some policy-makers are likely to propose such taxes exactly because they *are* so hidden, such taxes do tend to be regressive, and from a normative perspective, the hiding of taxes is not necessarily a favorable quality in terms of the accountability that tax payment may generate with respect to the actions of public officials. The collection of social security contributions creates a political obligation, which may or may not be fulfilled, to pay benefits to the contributors, limiting the flexibility of the state to spend as it pleases.

A central assumption of this study is that taxes levied on income are largely progressive, and taxes on consumption are largely regressive. In practice, the question of measuring actual tax incidence is fraught with difficulties,[16] and many analysts have argued that the burden of corporate income taxes may be shifted to consumers through the price of goods. Even

---

[15] Oates 1988.

[16] Shah and Whalley (1991) question several of the assumptions of standard theories of tax incidence. In particular, they argue that because certain country characteristics may distort policy to a high degree, standard assumptions that individual income tax is progressive and

if this were the case, in this study, the degree to which the state collects such income taxes is still relevant because the ease with which such taxes are collected, and ultimately the amount extracted, are largely dependent upon the willingness of upper groups to comply with state needs and demands. Moreover, as Webber and Wildavsky point out in a discussion of how to categorize different forms of revenue, the taxation of all forms of income provides a *sense* of greater vertical equity within society, and both individual and company income taxes "have the political appeal of at least appearing to redistribute wealth by taxing high incomes more heavily than low incomes."[17] Particularly in more open economies, company taxation is at least partially borne by upper groups when it is effectively collected, and it is almost always firms and high-income individuals, not organized workers or lower groups, that challenge the levying of taxes on companies. Although property and wealth taxes also tend to be progressive and fall almost exclusively on upper groups, they are such an insignificant source of revenue for modern states around the world that these are not investigated thoroughly here.

Because consumption reflects a greater share of income for the poor than for the wealthy, reliance on consumption taxes generally implies a more regressive distribution of the tax burden. The only significant exception in this respect is when consumption taxes are differentiated between luxury goods and basic goods consumed disproportionately by the poor.

For other taxes, the implications of incidence are far less clear. Generally speaking, they are probably neutral or flat, although social security withholdings tend to have a regressive effect.[18] Particularly for this broad category, however, such assumptions are difficult to make on a sweeping basis without knowledge of the distribution of resources within society and the specific ways in which the tax is enacted.

Once the tax bases are established, *tax rates* must be specified, determining the share of the base that will constitute the tax burden. Rates may be differentiated within a group of taxes – for example, higher rates for income beyond a certain threshold. Rates may be expressed either as a share of the

VAT is regressive must be called into question. These observations are considered in the detailed country analyses in this book.

[17] Webber and Wildavsky 1986: 522. Bates and Lien (1985) make a similar point, suggesting that because tax incidence is so difficult to determine, a more revealing piece of information is how taxpayers actually perceive tax policies.

[18] Shah and Whalley 1991.

determined value of the tax base, or as a fixed sum for a given quantity of the taxable base. Although tax rates are highly visible to taxpayers, they are not directly comparable across countries or over time unless other aspects of tax policy are also taken into account.

The tax policy framework may identify certain sets of *tax exemptions*, incentives, or tax expenditures. Such policies identify certain types of taxpayers or tax bases that are afforded special treatment with respect to their tax liability. Typically, such policies are employed to create incentives for certain types of investments, to promote certain social goals, or simply to favor some groups over others. For example, investors in certain regions may receive tax holidays, those who provide job training may enjoy reduced tax rates, those who make charitable donations may be able to deduct such transfers in the calculation of their tax liability, those with dependents may receive special deductions, or those with outstanding tax liabilities and penalties may receive amnesty. The effect of such exemptions, holding all other policies constant, is to reduce the overall tax burden within society. The impact on the taxation of upper groups depends on the application and duration of such exemptions.

Tax policy also designates who is ultimately responsible for paying over the money to the state agent by specifying the *taxpayer*. In the case of income tax, for example, individuals may pay this tax on their own, or their employer may withhold part or all of the tax from their wages. When consumers pay taxes on products, this tax is typically paid to the government by the retailer. Whoever is designated as a taxpayer becomes the target of government attempts to collect the tax through a process of bureaucratic engagement.

Tax Administration

The execution of tax policy is rarely the subject of major policy debate in the office of the national executive or even the legislature, and the nuts and bolts of tax administration tend to be decided and executed by the tax bureaucracy. Nonetheless, politics pervades this process in the form of action and inaction in response to the state's demands. As depicted in Figure 2.2, the central goal of tax administration is to convert *potential* tax revenues into *actual* tax revenues, a process that can be defined in terms of several additional active steps on the part of state executives and the bureaucracy, and potential areas for negotiation, conflict, and resistance from groups within society. In particular, the registration of taxpayers, calculation of

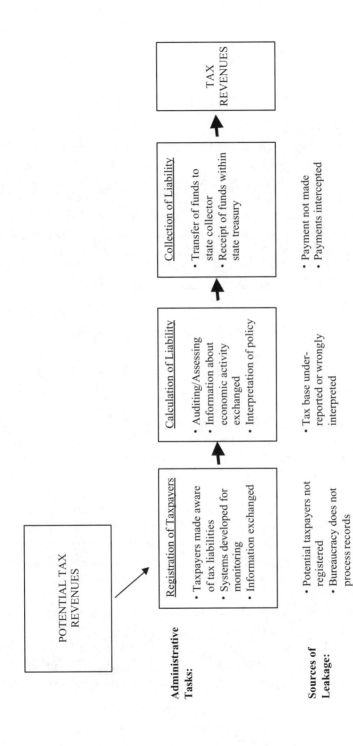

Figure 2.2 The process of tax administration

liabilities, and actual collection of taxes are the most significant steps in the administrative process. Each step presents a potential source of leakage in the state's attempts to convert private resources into public ones based on its legal authority derived from the tax policy framework described above.

The first task of administration involves the *registration of taxpayers*. At this stage, the state executives and bureaucracy must make citizens aware of their obligations while gathering information about their whereabouts and economic activities, and maintaining such information through various information management systems. Rarely is it necessary for the state to register every citizen for its tax rolls, because only a certain portion of the population will be responsible for paying taxes. For example, only individuals earning above a certain threshold must be registered for income tax, and only certain retailers, distributors, and manufacturers must be registered for consumption tax – as most final consumers do not directly pay the tax over to the state. The first obvious source of leakage is that the state may not manage to register all of the taxpayers liable for the tax. Citizens or firms may hide their existence from the state, and escape any registration process whatsoever. Given the concentration of income and wealth among upper groups within some societies, the failure to register any individuals or firms can represent an important loss of tax revenue.

A second key task involves *calculating the tax liability* for specific taxpayers. This involves measuring the size of the taxable base associated with each taxpayer, and identifying appropriate rates and exemptions as defined in the tax policy framework. Such calculation or assessment may take place either on an annual or more regular basis. Tax liabilities are calculated by individuals, firms, and/or tax intermediaries (accountants, lawyers, etc.) and submitted to the bureaucracy, or the necessary information for making such calculations is submitted directly to the bureaucracy for assessment. In both cases, tax auditors employed by the state may review the assessments and the underlying information supporting the calculations to determine the accuracy of the assessment.

Sources of leakage are both willful and accidental. On the one hand, taxpayers may purposefully under-report or fail to declare certain transactions or property that would incur a tax liability. They may engage in corrupt collusion with the tax authorities to maintain a loose or false interpretation of the taxable base in order to minimize the liability. Alternatively, the sheer complexity of tax legislation and/or the level of education and effort on the part of taxpayers is likely to affect how the tax liability gets calculated. Of course, in the wake of complex legislation, individuals, firms, and tax intermediaries may make heroic interpretations in order to minimize tax liabilities. Because upper-income individuals and firms tend to be aware of the potentially high cost of tax liabilities, these groups are often well aware of common practice regarding how assessments are made, the degree to which they get audited, and what level of honest compliance is necessary to stay out of jail. Norms and standard practices of interpretation strongly influence how potential tax revenues get converted into actual revenues.

Finally, states will attempt to *collect* the tax liabilities. Again, even if a tax liability is assessed, the money owed to the state may or may not be paid. Such payment involves action on the part of the citizen as well as the state. The tax policy framework is likely to specify particular penalties for delinquent or nonpayment of taxes, including legal authority for the state to forcibly extract payment through confiscation of property or income. Those citizens inclined to not pay may take extraordinary measures to resist, by hiding their resources and/or bribing tax officials. They may also challenge the legality of such collections through personal appeals or by contesting the very legislation or interpretations that made them liable for the tax in the first place. The degree to which they resist payment – or the bureaucracy fails to collect – has a significant influence on the tax revenues ultimately collected by the state.

The political and administrative challenges of tax collection tend to vary across tax bases, implying distinctive political problems. For example, the administration of income and wealth taxes is particularly difficult, and as many analysts point out, such taxes have been virtually impossible to collect in many countries.[19] When attempting to collect from large firms or high-income individuals, the amount of information required to adequately assess the tax liability may be enormous. Moreover, those who control the greatest amount of taxable resources may be the ones who are most politically powerful within society, making enforcement difficult. The scope for hiding income and wealth tends to be much greater than for other tax bases. At least initially, such taxes are generally the most difficult to collect

[19] World Bank 1988: 92.

because they are the most visible, require the greatest transfer of information between the taxpayer and the bureaucracy, and are the easiest to avoid and to evade. As a result, payment of such taxes is almost always experienced as the most burdensome form of taxation, implying that the challenge to the state to gain compliance with this tax is almost always the most difficult.

By contrast, the administration of consumption taxes, while still complex, tends to be less information-intensive than the administration of income taxes because valuations of the taxable base are considerably less complex and the timing of payment is far more straightforward. Moreover, these taxes are paid *indirectly*. For example, when consumers purchase a good, they pay a marked-up price to a retailer who then pays over the taxes collected to the state. Actual payment is much less visible – often the tax is included in the purchase price of a particular good, and accumulates over multiple daily purchases as opposed to as a large lump sum with respect to income. (When rates become particularly high, however, these taxes can hardly be said to be invisible.) Finally, because these taxes tend to be paid for by sellers, collections are more concentrated than in the case of income and wealth taxes, generally making registration, calculation, and collection of tax liabilities easier.

Likely because of this ease of administration, consumption taxes have become an important source of revenue in many countries, and the advent of the Value Added Tax (VAT) has made it a particularly important form of revenue, particularly in Western Europe. Those liable for paying over consumption taxes to the state certainly have significant opportunities to cheat, and the state's ability to gain widespread compliance is clearly a major logistical challenge. Nonetheless, for the reasons described above, collection of consumption taxes implies less about the strength of the relationship between state and upper groups in society than does collection of direct taxation on income and wealth.

A Typology of the Tax State

Meaningful cross-national comparison requires a synthetic approach incorporating these various aspects of tax policy and administration. By describing a series of ideal-types defined in terms of patterns of conflict and cooperation between the state and upper groups, it is possible to characterize certain tax states as similar to or different from one another, both across space and time. Table 2.1 defines five ideal-type tax states in terms of varied tax policies and administrative practices: the Skeletal state, the Rentier state, the Communist state, the Adversarial state, and the Cooperative state. When working with ideal-types, few states are pure cases of any one, and some may reflect a mix of different elements of the various types. On the other hand, the primary goal of specifying this limited number of ideal-type states is to suggest major qualitative differences in state-society relations, providing a strong sense of system-level variation.

The *Skeletal state* is characterized primarily by a lack of bureaucratic capacity. Various types of tax policies designed to collect from upper groups may be legislated in such states, but such policies are rendered meaningless when they are not effectively administered. The bureaucracy has little information about the private sector, and neither calculates liabilities nor collects significant domestic taxation from such bases. Individuals may occupy offices and buildings designated for the revenue bureaucracy, and may manage to generate some revenue from aid or arbitrary collections, but in such cases, the state is only a very small skeleton of an organization with extremely limited engagement with society. In order to secure revenues, the state may arbitrarily confiscate property or resources, but not in a legally prescribed manner as is the case with ordinary taxation. Countries with minimal bureaucracies such as Ghana or Mali, or at the extreme, virtually stateless societies such as Somalia or Liberia, all may be described as skeletal tax states.[20] Newly constructed states that do not inherit pre-existing tax policies or administrative capacities typically begin as skeletal states, and leaders attempt to put flesh and skin on the tax system through attempts to extend their authority within society.

By contrast, in the case of the *Communist state*, the state's role in the economy is so large that it virtually eliminates the private sphere of the economy. There is effectively no taxation in such cases as the state controls the means of production and need not gain cooperation from nonstate actors in order to obtain resources. Because society is defined in this analysis as a *private* sphere, there is no point of tangency between state and society when the state engulfs the entire private sphere. Indeed, this was the case with most Leninist regimes.[21] As Migdal points out, such states were never *completely*

---

[20] Widner 1995. Sub-Saharan Africa has a disproportionate share of states with limited authority. See Herbst 2000.
[21] See Jowitt 1991.

Table 2.1 *Typology of the tax state*

	Ideal-Type:	Skeletal	Rentier	Communist	Adversarial	Cooperative
Overall		Little-to-no bureaucracy; state is largely unable to tax those with significant resources	State taxes and/or controls a major natural resource; other sectors largely untaxed	State controls means of production, so no need for taxation	State attempts to tax widely, but with uneven results; upper groups challenge state authority	State successfully taxes upper groups in most sectors and regions
Policy	*Bases*	Varied	Concentrated on particular sectors	N/A	Direct tax bases tend to be highly diluted; many bases used; constantly challenged; "fiscal illusion"	Generally significant reliance on income and property taxation; transparent; challenged at the margins
	Exemptions	Varied	Not likely for target industry	N/A	Many; significant loopholes	Highly targeted, limited
	Rates	Varied	Varied	N/A	Varied	Varied
Admin.	*Registration/ monitoring of private sector*	Little information collected	Information only on leading sectors	N/A	Significant information collected, but of mixed quality	Significant, high-quality information collected

Calculation of liability	Limited to bureaucracy's ability to calculate with limited information	Transparent for select sectors; typically easy to measure	N/A	Nontransparent; citizens take extreme measures to reduce liability	Transparent; citizens may attempt to minimize tax payment, but largely within spirit of law
Final payment/ Collection	Little payment of liability	Targeted sectors pay liability	N/A	Upper groups attempt to challenge liability	Upper groups pay liability
Cost of admin.	Varied	Low–none	N/A	High	Low-medium
Examples	Ghana Mali Somalia New states	Saudi Arabia Kuwait Venezuela	Soviet Union North Korea Cuba	Greece **Brazil** India	Denmark **South Africa** U.K.

successful in their attempts to stamp out society,[22] and black markets clearly emerged outside the control of the state, but the nature of the relationship in such contexts is one in which the state attempts to take control of all production and exchange. The former Soviet Union was an example of such a state, as are the contemporary cases of Cuba and North Korea.

A special type of tax state defined by cases in which the state is engaged in a tax relationship with only a single – typically extractive – sector of the economy is the *Rentier state*.[23] In such cases, the high value of a particular mineral or other natural resource obviates the need to tax other sectors of the economy to a significant degree. In such cases, the state may either formally nationalize such industries (eliminating the need for taxation) or it may allow domestic or foreign companies to carry out the production and/or marketing of such resources, while taxing such output rather heavily. Because the extraction and/or refinement of such resources tends to take place in fairly well concentrated areas, and the pricing and cost structures of such industries are well known and/or heavily regulated, the collection of taxation is a relatively easy affair when compared with attempts to tax other sectors. Although the set of tax policies may extend to other sectors, administration is effectively limited to collections from the leading sector. Most of the oil exporting countries would be described as rentier states, including Saudi Arabia and Kuwait. Venezuela would also fit within this category, but more extensive attempts to tax other sectors within its more diversified economy suggest that it is less of an exemplar of the ideal-type than the others.

Both the Communist state and the Rentier state are special categories of state-society relations that have been the focus of much scholarship, but will not be considered in the comparative empirical analyses in the chapters that follow. Instead, the main focus of this study concerns contrasts between *Adversarial* and *Cooperative* tax states. On the one hand, the ideal-types share certain important similarities. They are characterized by significant state engagement with upper groups across a wide range of sectors – unlike the skeletal and rentier states. And yet, the private sector manages to maintain a significant degree of autonomy from the state – unlike the Communist state. Both types possess significant tax

[22] Migdal 1997: 228.
[23] For discussions of other characteristics of the Rentier state, see Karl 1997: 16, 49; Barkey and Parikh 1991; and Chaudhry 1997.

bureaucracies, as taxation is a central component of the functioning of the economy.

Nonetheless, there are very important differences between the two types in terms of how the state executive and bureaucracy interact with taxpayers as defined by the policy framework and its implementation through the tax administration. When the executive and bureaucracy actively attempt to tax upper economic groups across sectors and regions, the cooperative state is defined by higher levels of success and uniform authority, whereas the adversarial state produces more uneven results given significant challenges from many or all upper groups.

The cooperative tax state tends to have a much greater reliance on a few key tax bases, typically more direct taxes, because it can count on the support of upper groups liable for such taxes, while the adversarial tax state relies on a multiplicity of tax bases, engaging in higher levels of "fiscal illusion." Because the adversarial state is characterized by higher levels of resistance to state authority, particularly from upper groups, fewer declaratory taxes are collected, in favor of more indirect (and generally regressive) taxes. In modern economies, tax policy must, virtually by necessity, be complex, but in cooperative tax states, the incidence of the tax burden is far more clear, and less contested, than in adversarial ones. Exemptions and incentives proliferate in adversarial tax states as various upper groups secure special treatment, whereas in the cooperative tax state, special treatment tends to be highly targeted and limited.

The two ideal-types can also be distinguished from one another in terms of very different administrative relationships between states and upper groups. The cooperative state implements tax policy much more effectively and efficiently – minimizing leakage in the conversion of potential tax revenues into actual revenues. Although individuals and firms may attempt to minimize tax payment, the reporting of information and execution of responsibilities tends to be carried out much more closely to both the letter and spirit of the tax laws than in the case of the adversarial state. The private sector effectively acts as a partner to the revenue bureaucracy through high levels of quasi-voluntary compliance. Upper groups are much more likely to pay what they owe the state in cooperative states when compared with their counterparts in adversarial states, leading to much lower administrative costs as a share of total collections. By contrast, the adversarial tax state is defined in terms of significant challenges on the part of individuals and firms to the bureaucracy's attempts to collect. Upper groups within society may resist being registered as taxpayers, they may take extreme measures to hide information that would affect their tax liabilities, and/or they may take extreme license in interpreting the tax policy framework to minimize payment.

As will be discussed in subsequent chapters, Brazil is a prototypical case of an adversarial tax state, and South Africa a case of a cooperative tax state. Identifying which other country cases should be classified as one or the other of the two types requires more extensive research and analysis. Nonetheless, initial analyses would suggest that India, Argentina, and potentially France are also examples of adversarial tax states, while Denmark, Sweden, and the United Kingdom are cases of cooperative tax states. In recent years many cooperative tax states, particularly in Western Europe, have levied indirect taxes to a much greater extent than they did previously. However, because these states still effectively collect from upper groups who engage and cooperate with the executive and the bureaucracy, they should still be classified as cooperative states. Indeed, the distinction between adversarial and cooperative tax states is not particularly useful for making sense of differences among the advanced industrialized countries, most of which would be classified as cooperative.

Measurement and Classification

In order to test hypotheses about the determinants of the development of the tax state, it is necessary to develop an instrument for comparing tax systems across countries and over time. This book uses two sets of measurement strategies: in-depth investigation of cases through historical research and interviews, and quantitative comparisons using tax collection data. Each strategy has advantages and disadvantages, and both are used to improve the accuracy of measurement and classification.

For the comparative analysis of Brazil and South Africa, I draw upon a wide range of sources. In-depth historical investigations of national accounts, printed reports of political leaders and bureaucrats, journalistic accounts, and interviews with individuals involved in the tax system – including bureaucrats at all levels of administration, taxpayers, and taxation intermediaries – all provided insights into the actual functioning of the national tax systems in a highly contextualized manner. In the process of gathering historical information about the policies and administration of a national tax system, patterns emerged, and it was possible to identify a coherent characterization of the national tax system for particular periods of time. The classification of cases required gathering sufficient evidence to convincingly demonstrate that in sum, the component parts of the tax state resemble one or another of the various ideal-types. While not every single fact gathered about the country's tax policy framework or its administration always fits into a single, coherent portrait, the challenge of comparative historical measurement is to honestly assess all of the relevant materials, and to justify classification in as transparent a manner as possible.

While such in-depth investigation sheds light on how things really work within countries, it is impossible to compare more than just a few tax states in any single framework in this manner. As a result, it is difficult to know exactly how a particular country or set of countries compares to other cases more broadly. Since we are interested in the state's ability to extract taxes from society, the most straightforward strategy is to compare the amount of taxes actually collected by governments. And yet, as implied by the earlier discussions of the varying political challenges of alternative types of taxation, it is not immediately obvious what type of tax revenues ought to be compared.

In particular, the ratio of income tax to GDP is a good measure of the state's taxation of upper-income groups for which fairly reliable cross-national data can be assembled for comparison.[24] While other cross-national taxation studies have tended to employ aggregated measures of total tax collections – incorporating all tax bases, foreign and domestic – as share of GDP,[25] this study relies much more heavily on income tax collections as an estimator of the performance of tax states. This choice is justified given the theoretical focus on the relationship between the state and upper

---

[24] Like virtually all measures of social scientific concepts, however, problems of reliability and validity cannot be ignored. National accounts data, particularly in economically less advanced countries, suffer from inaccuracies. As reported by the World Bank (1988), "Data on government revenues and expenditures are collected by the IMF through questionnaires distributed to member governments and by the Organisation for Economic Co-operation and Development (OECD). Despite the IMF's efforts to systematize and standardize the collection of public finance data, statistics on public finance are often incomplete, untimely, and noncomparable." Measuring the size of the economy, for example, is extremely difficult with a very large informal sector, and the methods used to approximate economic activity vary across countries. Revenues that accrue directly to the government are easier to measure, and IMF and UN guidelines for national accounts have helped to promote a reasonable level of consistency in reporting. Nonetheless, slightly different interpretations of tax instruments create some additional measurement error. I do not take up the task of trying to approximate the magnitude or direction of possible errors in any of the cases. On balance, these data provide relatively useful and valid measures for the comparison presented here.

[25] See, for example, Hinrichs 1966; Cheibub 1998; Steinmo and Tolbert 1998.

groups. As discussed above, income taxes tend to be the most progressive, and the most difficult to collect. As a result, significant collections of such taxes tend to reflect more cooperative relations between the state and upper groups.

Obviously, governments collect such revenues in local currencies, and in order to compare across states, it is necessary to standardize the measure in a meaningful way. Looking at income taxes as share of *total revenues* would not be a valid measure because countries that were poor at collecting *all* sources of tax revenue might score high on such a measure, and countries that collect significant revenues from several sources might score low, and neither case would adequately reflect the central concept under investigation. By looking at income tax collections as share of *GDP*, the measure controls for the relative size of the economy, but assumes that the challenge of collecting direct taxes from any economy is basically the *same* problem.

There are limitations for using this performance measure to adjudicate among the process-oriented ideal-types described above. First, it is not possible to measure income tax collections for *Communist* states because, as discussed above, there is no "real" taxation in those economies. Even in former Communist countries, tax collections are much less likely to reflect on the quality of state authority because the legacy of state ownership of firms has so strongly affected contemporary tax structures. In these countries, reported tax collections tend to over-represent the authority of the state over upper groups. Moreover, in *Rentier* states, income tax collections are not very good measures of state authority over (private) upper groups because the vast majority of revenues tend to come from a single, easy-to-tax industry, which is likely to be largely controlled or even owned by the government.

The measure is useful for evaluating the degree to which countries are likely to approximate the other ideal types. Skeletal, adversarial, and co-operative states are expected to have low, medium, and high collections of income taxes/GDP respectively. Even among these groups of states, the measure is not perfectly valid, as historical factors may have caused certain countries to collect less in income taxes than is *possible* given the level of engagement between state and society, but on balance, this measure is a fairly good indicator of the type of relationship being explored here. Triangulation with the more qualitative and descriptive measures highlighted above help to assess the characterization of any given case.

Table 2.2 *Income and property tax collections as share of GDP, descriptive statistics, average 1990–1994*

	Mean	Median	Min.	Max.	Std. Dev.	Brazil	South Africa
Central state only	6.3	5.8	0	21.0	4.4	3.8	14.4
All levels of government	7.3	6.2	0	29.4	5.6	3.8	14.4

Note: N = 107
Sources: World Bank 1998; IMF 1999.

In order to conduct a cross-national analysis of the performance of the tax state, the ratio of income tax collections to GDP for each country has been averaged for five-year periods.[26] This was done to minimize the risk that collections in any single year were the product of unique circumstances, rather than the structural foundations of the tax policy framework and tax administration. Descriptive statistics are presented in Table 2.2, and case summaries are presented in Table 2.3.

These analyses reveal key contrasts between the two central country cases when seen in comparative perspective. Between 1990 and 1994, the average income and property tax collection for 107 states was 6.3 percent of GDP, when considering only the collections of the central state, and 7.3 percent of GDP when such revenues from provincial and local governments are also included. During this period, South Africa collected 14.4 percent of GDP, and Brazil collected 3.8 percent of GDP – in both cases all income taxes are collected exclusively by the central state. Within the world distribution, South Africa ranked 11th in terms of collections, toward the top of the top third of countries when ranked in order of income tax collections, while Brazil ranked 71st, at the bottom of the middle third of countries. If these measures of taxation are relatively good indicators of state authority, we have good reason to believe that the quality of state authority is very different in these two otherwise very similar countries.

[26] Central state collections of property taxes are included in these statistics, but such revenues are extremely low in virtually all countries, and as a result, these are not discussed in this book. However, because such revenues do tend to be paid by upper groups, particularly when paid over to the central state, their inclusion actually provides a better estimator of state authority.

Table 2.3 *Tax collections around the world, 1990–1994. Ranked by income and property tax collections. All collections expressed as percent of GDP*

Rank	Country	Income and property taxes	Income and property taxes	Consumption taxes	Social security taxes	Other taxes
		(All levels of govt)	(Central govt only)	(Central govt only)	(Central govt only)	(Central govt only)
1	Denmark	29.4	15.2	15.9	1.6	1.4
2	Sweden	26.3	4.1	12.8	13.5	3.2
3	Finland	22.5	9.5	14.4	3.5	1.0
4	New Zealand	21.0	21.0	10.0	0.0	0.9
5	Canada	17.0	10.5	3.8	3.7	0.0
6	Belgium	16.5	14.9	10.8	15.5	1.2
7	Botswana	16.1	16.1	1.4	0.0	0.1
8	Australia	16.0	16.0	5.1	0.0	0.4
9	Italy	16.0	14.7	11.5	11.7	1.0
10	Netherlands	14.5	14.5	10.5	18.2	1.5
11	South Africa	14.4	14.4	9.4	0.5	0.2
12	Norway	14.3	6.6	14.8	9.8	0.4
13	Ireland	13.8	13.8	11.2	5.3	1.3
14	Luxembourg	13.8	13.8	10.9	11.5	3.8
15	Zimbabwe	13.8	13.8	7.0	0.0	0.3
16	Japan	13.2	8.8	2.9	4.1	1.1
17	Israel	13.1	13.1	12.6	2.6	1.4
18	United Kingdom	12.9	12.9	11.4	6.0	2.6
19	Switzerland	12.7	3.2	3.5	11.5	0.6
20	United States	12.3	9.9	0.7	6.8	0.2
21	Germany	11.8	4.7	7.9	14.5	0.0
22	Trinidad and Tobago	11.6	11.6	8.0	0.7	0.5
23	Poland	11.5	11.5	11.6	10.1	0.6
24	Venezuela	11.1	11.1	1.7	1.1	.
25	Austria	11.1	7.0	8.8	13.3	2.9
26	Spain	10.5	9.8	6.9	12.1	0.1
27	Papua New Guinea	10.1	10.1	2.7	0.0	0.5
28	Romania	10.0	10.0	8.3	9.5	1.7
29	Indonesia	9.6	9.6	4.8	0.1	0.4
30	Hungary	9.5	9.5	16.6	15.5	0.1
31	Malaysia	9.4	9.4	5.9	0.3	1.0
32	Namibia	9.3	9.3	8.7	0.0	0.3
33	Ecuador	9.3	9.3	3.9	0.0	0.3
34	Bulgaria	9.1	9.1	7.4	9.7	1.4
35	Portugal	8.7	8.5	12.2	8.7	1.1

Rank	Country	Income and property taxes (All levels of govt)	Income and property taxes (Central govt only)	Consumption taxes (Central govt only)	Social security taxes (Central govt only)	Other taxes (Central govt only)
36	Fiji	8.4	8.4	6.0	0.0	0.4
37	Malta	8.4	8.4	2.5	5.4	1.1
38	Mongolia	8.4	8.4	5.8	2.3	0.0
39	France	7.7	7.1	11.1	17.8	1.5
40	Malawi	7.4	7.4	6.6	0.0	0.1
41	Singapore	7.3	7.3	4.6	0.0	4.0
42	Czech Republic	7.3	7.3	13.2	15.3	1.1
43	Lithuania	7.2	7.2	11.4	9.3	0.6
44	Lesotho	7.1	7.1	8.3	0.0	0.1
45	Oman	6.8	6.8	0.3	0.0	0.3
46	Solomon Islands	6.7	6.7	0.8	0.0	0.2
47	Greece	6.7	6.0	12.9	1.8	2.1
48	Zambia	6.7	6.7	6.1	0.0	0.0
49	Kenya	6.5	6.5	10.6	0.0	0.2
50	Gabon	6.5	6.5	5.8	0.2	0.4
51	Syrian Arab Republic	6.3	6.3	7.6	0.0	1.6
52	Turkey	6.3	6.3	5.5	0.0	0.6
53	Egypt, Arab Rep.	6.3	6.3	4.1	3.4	3.1
54	Morocco	6.2	6.2	10.6	1.0	1.0
55	Iceland	6.1	6.1	13.6	2.1	1.9
56	Estonia	5.8	5.8	11.0	9.5	0.2
57	Korea, Rep.	5.8	5.8	6.1	1.1	1.3
58	Seychelles	5.6	5.6	2.8	7.9	0.4
59	Belize	5.5	5.5	2.6	0.0	0.7
60	Colombia	5.3	5.3	5.1	0.0	0.1
61	Mexico	5.1	5.1	7.8	2.1	0.3
62	Philippines	5.0	5.0	4.7	0.0	0.6
63	Thailand	5.0	5.0	7.6	0.2	0.6
64	Grenada	4.9	4.9	11.4	0.0	1.1
65	Panama	4.7	4.7	4.4	5.3	0.8
66	Yemen, Rep.	4.7	4.7	2.0	0.0	0.8
67	Tunisia	4.3	4.3	6.3	3.8	1.5
68	Latvia	4.0	4.0	10.0	8.8	0.0
69	Croatia	4.0	4.0	13.8	13.9	0.2
70	Chile	3.8	3.8	9.8	1.6	0.7
71	Brazil	3.8	3.8	2.3	8.6	2.0
72	Belarus	3.7	3.7	12.5	10.1	3.0

(continued)

Table 2.3 *(continued)*

Rank	Country	Income and property taxes (All levels of govt)	Income and property taxes (Central govt only)	Consumption taxes (Central govt only)	Social security taxes (Central govt only)	Other taxes (Central govt only)
73	Ethiopia	3.7	3.7	3.3	0.0	0.3
74	Burundi	3.5	3.5	6.7	1.2	0.3
75	Jordan	3.4	3.4	5.8	0.0	2.6
76	Argentina	3.3	0.7	3.5	5.1	0.8
77	Nicaragua	3.2	3.2	10.6	2.7	1.6
78	Gambia, The	2.9	2.9	8.3	0.0	0.1
79	Mauritius	2.9	2.9	5.1	1.1	1.4
80	Russian Federation	2.8	2.8	6.0	7.4	.
81	Cameroon	2.7	2.7	2.9	0.4	0.5
82	Ghana	2.7	2.7	5.0	0.0	0.0
83	Sri Lanka	2.6	2.6	9.7	0.0	0.8
84	Burkina Faso	2.5	2.5	.	0.0	0.7
85	Dominican Republic	2.5	2.5	3.9	0.6	0.1
86	India	2.4	2.4	4.5	0.0	0.1
87	Costa Rica	2.3	2.3	7.6	6.9	0.3
88	Sierra Leone	2.3	2.3	3.2	0.0	0.0
89	Pakistan	2.3	2.3	5.5	0.0	0.1
90	El Salvador	2.2	2.2	5.1	0.0	0.6
91	Iran, Islamic Rep.	2.1	2.1	0.8	1.5	0.8
92	Uruguay	2.0	2.0	9.8	8.7	4.0
93	Chad	1.9	1.9	3.3	0.0	0.8
94	Rwanda	1.7	1.7	3.9	0.5	0.4
95	Guatemala	1.7	1.7	3.6	0.0	0.4
96	China	1.5	1.5	1.5	0.0	0.0
97	Lebanon	1.5	1.5	1.0	0.0	2.4
98	Madagascar	1.5	1.5	2.2	0.0	0.2
99	Guinea	1.4	1.4	3.1	0.0	0.1
100	Myanmar	1.4	1.4	2.6	0.0	0.0
101	Peru	1.4	1.4	6.2	1.3	1.3
102	Paraguay	1.3	1.3	3.5	0.0	2.5
103	Congo, Dem. Rep.	1.3	1.3	1.1	0.1	0.2
104	Bolivia	0.8	0.8	6.0	1.3	1.5
105	Nepal	0.8	0.8	3.3	0.0	0.5
106	United Arab Emirates	0.0	0.0	0.6	0.0	0.0
107	Bahamas, The	0.0	0.0	2.0	.	2.6

Sources: World Bank 1998; IMF 1999; Author calculations.

Conclusion

The State, variously conceptualized, has long been at the center of comparative research within political science. In order to theorize about the determinants of varied patterns of state development, we need to know what those different patterns are. And in order to assess such hypotheses empirically, we need to be able to recognize cases of various patterns when we see them. This chapter has provided a framework for both of these problems, identifying the different ways in which the national state may interact with upper groups during the process of enacting and implementing tax policy. A focus on taxation provides an excellent opportunity for systematic, comparative analysis because relatively good data do exist, and there is good reason to believe that such data are highly suggestive of the quality of state authority more generally. The chapter has also discussed some of the limitations of using taxation data as indicators of state-society relations and the need to employ alternative measures when possible.

The political problems of taxation are now clear, and it is evident that when high-income citizens want to avoid payment, there are multiple avenues for resistance. Ultimately, tax collection reflects the degree to which the state can manage to gets its citizens to overcome instincts toward noncompliance. From this perspective, it is clear that by the end of the 20th century, the Brazilian and South African tax states had very different types of relationships with upper groups in their respective societies. The next chapter begins the task of explaining how and why these differences emerged.

3

Critical Juncture

DEFINING NATIONAL POLITICAL COMMUNITY

In order to demonstrate how and why the political community model can be used to account for variance in patterns of state development, this chapter takes an historical turn, and describes the critical junctures during which definitions of National Political Community (NPC) were codified in Brazil and South Africa. To gain analytic leverage from a critical junctures framework, it is necessary show that a significant change occurred in each case, and that the changes took place in distinct ways in different cases.[1] This implies that the initial conditions under which the two countries operated prior to the critical juncture must have been similar enough that neither the critical junctures themselves, nor the outcomes that would follow, should appear to have been pre-determined. In addition, to the extent that other periods have been widely noted as "very important" in the respective national histories, it is helpful to explain why such periods were not identified as the relevant critical juncture for the question being studied.

With respect to the cases of Brazil and South Africa, and to the political community model, this chapter demonstrates that although both societies had been divided by similar social and political cleavages in the late 19th century, different constitutional definitions of citizenship articulated around the turn of the 20th century produced contrasting patterns of inter- and intra-class relations. Subsequent chapters relate these varied political dynamics to the development of tax policy and tax administration during the century to follow. The focus of the analysis is on constitutional choices because in most countries, the constitution is the central institution that defines the membership of the NPC – the population of people entitled to the rights and responsibilities of citizenship, as defined by the state.

---

[1] Collier and Collier 1991: 30.

Constitutions get written during moments of great political change, when the very foundations of political life have been shaken. During such periods, which often follow violent conflicts that render certain groups more powerful than others, political elites negotiate the definition of the NPC. Rules concerning who should be included and who excluded, and on what basis, are contested because there is no "natural" or genetic basis for nationhood. As Benedict Anderson points out, these are "imagined communities."[2] Of course, the definitions of NPC may be revised to adapt to new ideas and/or circumstances, but at certain critical moments, truly novel definitions are advanced and accepted in the form of political settlements that become accepted as basic rules of the game, or institutions, within society.

Political crises largely associated with the process of modernization and developments in the state system paved the way for new constitutions in both countries. In late 19th century Brazil, a Republican movement of modernizing urban and military groups increasingly viewed the imperial form of government as an anachronism that stood in the way of social and economic progress. Following the end of the Paraguayan War (1865–70), these groups made a final decisive push toward a Republican model and overthrew the emperor on November 15, 1889. Meanwhile, in Southern Africa, multiple political tensions between various groups escalated into the bloody Anglo-Boer War (1899–1902). Conflict finally ended with a surprisingly difficult British victory, marked by the May 31, 1902 signing of the Treaty of *Vereeniging*.

In both cases, these events led to periods of constitutional negotiation: between 1889 and 1891 in Brazil, and between 1902 and 1909 in South Africa. These periods were the critical junctures during which Brazilian and South African political elites engaged in the process of specifying definitions of NPC. Constitution writing was an elite-level process of political negotiation in both countries. In Southern Africa, representatives from varying provincial, ethnic, sectoral, and racial groups expressed views and opinions during this process – though their opportunities for participation were far from equal. Among the key decision-making moments were the several inter-colonial conferences held around the region; parliamentary and plebiscitary votes in the four colonies; and submission of a proposed constitution to the British legislature and crown. The South Africa Act was given Royal Assent on September 20, 1909. In Brazil, the constitution was also the product of elite deliberation and conflict, and largely

---

[2] Anderson 1996.

written by small committees appointed by the provisional government. In November 1890, each of the twenty states and the federal district were represented in a constituent congress to discuss the draft constitution. As in South Africa, representatives with varying regional, sectoral, and racial interests expressed their views about the content of that constitution, but again with varied levels of bargaining power and influence within those negotiations. Finally, on February 24, 1891, the first Republican constitution was promulgated in Brazil.

The remainder of this chapter compares the different ways in which similar constitutional questions about how to define the NPC were resolved in the two countries during these negotiations. First, it describes the similar racial and regional cleavages that had divided these societies in the late 19th century. Second, the chapter shows how these similar cleavages got addressed in very different ways in the respective constitutions. It contrasts the South African strategy of defining NPC as a racially exclusionary union with the Brazilian strategy of defining it as an officially nonracial federation. Finally, it describes the implications of these different solutions for the relative cohesion and fragmentation of economic interests in organizational and discursive terms.[3] Racial exclusion created strong upper-group cohesion and strong cross-class alliances in South Africa, while in Brazil, strong regional political divides created class fragmentation and polarization.

Cleavages: Race and Region

As in many other late developing countries, the challenge of establishing a workable definition of citizenship was highly problematic in Brazil and South Africa around the turn of the 20th century. Various pre-existing political cleavages and differentiated bases of political support obscured any obvious set of terms and criteria for membership in the NPC. Comparative historical analysis reveals that there was nothing pre-ordained about how the NPC would be defined in either country. If a nation is "conceived as a

---

[3] Many prominent contributions to the literature on the formation of welfare states and/or modern political regimes in the advanced industrialized countries have identified the critical role of class coalitions during earlier critical junctures or defining periods. In this book, I develop such an argument, but consider one prior step, by identifying the *determinants* of such coalitions. Moreover, the argument adds political identity as a causal factor guiding the logic of politics and helps to explain the reproduction of class cohesions and class coalitions over time. For examples of this literature, see Moore 1966; Luebbert 1991; Esping-Andersen 1990.

deep, horizontal comradeship," and constitutes a bounded, political identity tantamount to the notion of a "people,"[4] there were many "peoples" living in these two land areas. Legacies of immigration from Europe, Asia, and Africa; slavery; miscegenation; and centuries of internal conflict created important political cleavages that obscured any obvious basis for nationhood in Brazil and in Southern Africa.[5] In particular, *racial* and *regional* cleavages created political fault lines that threatened national cohesion, and it would become apparent to political elites that political solutions would be necessary.

The Problem of Race

In the 19th century, race constituted a central social and political cleavage in both societies. I employ an analytical definition that recognizes the socially constructed and yet politically powerful logic of racial identity and associated discourse. The category of race may be defined as

a legacy of stereotypes developed by Europeans in the age of expansion of Europe to world dominion. It is based above all on conspicuous physical differentiation, especially skin pigmentation and facial characteristics, which facilitate the stereotyping process which is so valuable in the maintenance of prejudice.[6]

The racial categories employed in political discourse may have no scientific basis, but the power of racial identity has often stemmed from the imputation of scientific "fact" relating real or perceived physical differences (phenotype) to a host of mental and psychological differences across groups.[7] Even when debunked, the legacy of such myths has provided a shared experience in politics, society, and economy, making race highly salient in societies where physical differences vary to a sufficient degree that they are recognizable as categorical distinctions for most people.

The very idea of race as a way of classifying humans was constructed within the processes of imperialism. "Race was the emergency explanation of human beings who no European or civilized man could understand and whose humanity so frightened and humiliated the immigrants that they no longer cared to belong to the same human species."[8] For societies in which

---

[4] Anderson 1996: 7.
[5] Louis Hartz (1964) describes both Brazil and South Africa as "European fragment" societies.
[6] Young 1976: 49.
[7] See Banton 1992 for an overview of how scientific theories about race have developed over time.
[8] Arendt 1979: 185.

an oppressive colonial political authority was maintained on the basis of a racial *hierarchy*, even the end of imperial rule still left intact the salience of race as an important category for social differentiation and political control.

Racial differentiation became important in both South Africa and Brazil from the beginning of European contact with the indigenous populations in those countries. As is well known, in the case of South Africa, white supremacy was mobilized as the basis for social and political organization almost from the day the Dutch East India Company representative Jan Van Riebeeck landed at the Cape of Good Hope in 1652.[9] The conquering of various African populations as part of ongoing European territorial expansion in Southern Africa was legitimized with racial prejudice. Soon after European arrival, the institution of slavery was established at the Cape with slaves taken from Angola, Madagascar, and Mozambique. Although slavery was abolished in 1834, the institution of white supremacy permeated virtually all aspects of interaction across the color bar in that country.[10]

Similarly, the Brazilian racial experience began when Portuguese immigrants arrived on the South American continent in the 16th century and encountered a sizeable indigenous population. European settlers differentiated themselves in racial terms. Moreover, approximately 3.5 million people were brought to Brazil through the African slave trade, an institution rooted in racial prejudice.[11] Similar to the case of South Africa, in Brazil, "the relationship between race and politics in that country has been a close and integral one. Portuguese state policy made black slavery the very foundation of Brazil's social and economic order during three centuries of colonial rule. That foundation remained in place even after independence."[12] Immigration and miscegenation produced phenotypically heterogeneous societies in both countries. And yet, "scientific" ideas about race reinforced prejudice and provided a workable political strategy for maintaining social hierarchies.

[9] See, for example, Elphick and Giliomee 1989, and Fredrickson 1982, for two of the best historical accounts of the early manifestations of white supremacy in Southern Africa.
[10] Four racial categories have been salient in South Africa during the 20th century, with multiple labels: Black/African/Native, White/European, Indian/Asian, and Coloured. At varying times in South African history, individuals have alternatively embraced and rejected these labels, with many individuals embracing different labels during different stages of their personal histories. See Jung 2000.
[11] Marx 1998: 49.
[12] Andrews 1992.

The combination of such racial legacies, and the prevalence of enormous racial prejudice in the two countries, did not augur well for easy consolidation of a national political community at the end of the 19th century. In both countries, efforts on the part of (mainly white) political elites to consolidate national sentiment had to confront the fact that whites were clear minorities: The 1911 South African census reported that 21 percent of the population was white,[13] while the 1872 Brazilian census cited 38 percent white.[14] Indeed, a much higher degree of mixing had taken place in Brazil, producing a relatively much larger mulatto population. Only one-third of the nonwhite population in Brazil was counted as "pure" black, while more than 80 percent of the nonwhite population in South Africa was considered "black" or "African."

Widely accepted notions of white supremacy imported from Europe overlapped with sharp differences in terms of income, education, and work and precluded a feeling of deep horizontal comradeship in either country. Moreover, whites in the countries were divided over what to do about the racial question, caught between conflicting moral and economic interests in the future legal status of people of color, and well aware of the conflicts associated with the race question in the United States.

Although neither Brazil nor South Africa witnessed *major* black revolts in the late 19th century, this group and their sympathizers applied political pressure and resistance in both countries. Both international and domestic currents gave blacks significant basis for hope that conditions would improve and that they would increasingly receive more equal treatment. Slaves who participated in the Brazilian military in the Paraguayan War were emancipated following the conflict. Similarly, many Africans who fought on the side of the British in the Anglo-Boer War had been promised that victory would bring greater political equality. While scientific racism remained prevalent in the 19th century, a series of foreign events, including

---

[13] Bureau of Census and Statistics South Africa 1960.

[14] These statistics are from IBGE 1990. In fact, the phenotypical demographics may have been more similar than censuses suggest. Further revealing the socially constructed nature of race, many analysts have pointed out that the specification of racial categories in Brazil is different from what is found in either the United States or South Africa. Of course, since all of these categories are socially constructed without any clear scientific divide, the maintenance of a color bar in all of these societies was fraught with the problem of establishing arbitrary criteria for racial group membership. The employment of a multitude of labels for racial categories – literally dozens of labels – suggests the difficulty of establishing consistent or useful measures. See Andrews 1992, and Turra and Venturi 1995, for a discussion of these labels.

the ban on the slave trade and the end of slavery in the United States and other countries, amounted to foreign pressure on these countries to respond with new political dispensations. Segments of the political elite in both countries recognized the contradictions between unequal treatment for people on the basis of color and their desire to develop more "modern" societies.

The Problem of Region

A parallel set of critical questions for defining NPC in Brazil and South Africa stemmed from the legacies of regional and/or ethnic political fault lines also associated with the colonial past. Analytically, it makes sense to discuss region and ethnicity together because in the context of Brazil and South Africa, both were very much about political conflicts over claims to autonomy. Ethnicity is a collective identity rooted in beliefs about shared culture and ancestry, that is often mobilized around a territory – or homeland – as an important, politically symbolic resource. Regionally based political claims are often advanced in a similar manner by political leaders who mobilize a sense of difference from other neighboring regions, proposing special claims for group rights, often including a degree of political sovereignty. National unity and feelings of commonality are clearly jeopardized by ethnic and/or regional distinctions, particularly when they are associated with claims to autonomy over particular physical and political spaces. In Brazil and South Africa, such identities overlapped with real economic differences providing a basis for serious political competition in the second half of the 19th century.

The fundamental problem of reconciling these subnational cleavages was analogous in Brazil and South Africa. In both countries, pre-existing boundaries and multiple European groups challenged planners to devise solutions that would maintain national unity and not foster discontent. Nothing as violent as the bloody three-year Anglo-Boer War (1899–1902) in Southern Africa took place in Brazil, but strong regional identities and a model of state fragmentation from the former Spanish empire (occupying much of the rest of the South American continent) posed stark concerns for unity. Nor were ethnic tensions in Brazil as high as those that existed between Afrikaners and Englishmen, but language, culture, and mode of production did overlap with European origins among Brazilian immigrants, again posing an important question about how to integrate these important groups into a single horizontally conceived nation.

The Problem of Ethno-Regionalism in Southern Africa. By the late 19th century, the European population in Southern Africa was physically divided across four distinct political entities (the Cape Colony, Natal, the Transvaal Republic, and the Orange Free State) that had been constructed through the interactive process of territorial expansion, black-white conflict, and intra-white conflict. Dutch settlers arrived in the southwestern corner of the African continent in the mid-17th century, but the Cape settlement fell into British hands during the Napoleonic Wars. British rule was generally found to be repugnant to most of the Dutch descendants, many of whom called for a federal solution within the Cape Colony – with the idea of devolving power to provincial administrations.[15] Many others found the situation so unbearable that they began to head eastward, developing along the way a heightened sense of Afrikaner ethnic solidarity. Yet, the British would eventually follow these frontiersman to the various corners of Southern Africa, struggling for political authority in their path, and creating in the wake of this conflict four separate states. The original settlement at the Cape would remain as the Cape Colony. The Afrikaner settlement in Natal (in the southeastern part of the region), which originally restricted citizenship only to those Dutch-speaking people who had rebuked the British government in the Cape, was eventually claimed as a second British colony in 1842.[16] Disenchanted Afrikaners would continue their trek into the interior of the country, forming two Afrikaner states that were guaranteed independence by Britain under the Sand River Convention of 1852 and the Bloemfontein Convention of 1854.[17] Ethnic and regional identities, though far from neatly divided across the territories, would begin to overlap: Two sovereign states were recognized as Afrikaner states and two as British colonies, and no central state held them together, even in confederation.

The salience of such regional boundaries was at the heart of very concrete political dilemmas regarding levels of autonomy and integration. Previously, federation, let alone unification, had proved to be impossible. Multiple British administrations during the second half of the 20th century attempted to federate the Southern African colonies and republics together under the British crown – as was eventually done in Australia and Canada – but these efforts failed.[18] The demographics of a British settler minority

---

[15] Wilson and Thompson 1969: 319.
[16] Thompson 1990: 92.
[17] Pakenham 1988: 17.
[18] Thompson 1960: 2–3.

within the white population and a white minority within the larger population suggested a different set of political constraints from the otherwise analogous Canadian situation.[19] This generated a conundrum for the effective establishment of authority under the British crown. Making matters more complicated, the discovery of diamonds in 1867 and gold in 1886 – both in the Afrikaner states – raised Britain's interest to an unprecedented degree, and some form of political control appeared strategically desirable. Pakenham argues that even more problematic than federating the Boer (Afrikaner) Republics was the heightened level of "colonial nationalism at the Cape that had been stimulated both by responsible government and the diamond boom."[20]

The Anglo-Boer War brought to a head the question of a decisive political settlement in Southern Africa. Both sides had been humiliated by a bitterly fought war, and when South Africans spoke of the "race question" in the early part of the century, it was generally accepted that they were referring to the division between Dutch or Afrikaners on the one hand and British or English-speakers on the other. The greatest fear of political elites – both leading Afrikaner generals as well as British emissaries – in the early years of the first decade of the 20th century was how to deal with this quite threatening cleavage, which cut across regional lines.

The Problem of Regionalism in Brazil. By the end of the 19th century, region was also a politically meaningful category within Brazil. It is true, as Anthony Marx points out, that compared with South Africa "Brazil experienced much less violent regional and no ethnic conflict..."[21] However, long-established state and regional identities had been politically important and divisive in that country since the early days of Portuguese colonization. The crown's over-extension in other world areas necessitated a more decentralized strategy for colonization. Beginning in 1534, João III created fifteen capitanias (concessions of land) as a strategy for administration, but he initially recognized most of these authorities as administrative failures. He developed a centralized administration,

---

[19] Thompson 1990: 56.
[20] Pakenham 1988: 18.
[21] Marx 1998: 165. Marx further argues that the American North–South divide was analogous to the Afrikaner–English divide of South Africa, differentiating those two cases from the Brazilian one, which had no such deep-seated tension.

purchasing the captaincy of Bahia to be the seat of a general Brazilian government, and unified these rudimentary provinces under a general government under Tomé de Souza.[22] The captaincy system remained in place, and maintained a relatively comfortable system of regional autonomy for local elites. This proved to be a strong impediment to the formation of a strong class consciousness among the notables leading the respective captaincies, and this group did not develop any sense of mutual interest or identity.[23]

Instead, the captaincy system served to produce important political fault lines. Although the level of conflict never approached the bloody warfare of Southern Africa, the consolidation of the Brazilian empire was a constant concern, and the territorial integrity of Brazil was often challenged. In 1621, the area between Ceará and Amazonas detached under the independent state of Maranhão, and the Dutch empire threatened Portuguese control with its 1624 invasion of the North, but that incursion was eventually fought off by 1654.[24] These tensions were mostly manifest between regions and the center rather than among the regions themselves. For example, five major provincial revolts between 1832 and 1838 reflected dissatisfaction with regional leadership dispatched from the capital.[25] The process of forming a Brazilian national identity was constantly tied up with regional political movements, which for the entire period of the monarchy, "waved implicitly or explicitly the flag of separatism."[26] Although the Northern parts of Brazil were originally the wealthiest, by the last decades of the 19th century, the balance of wealth and power clearly shifted to the South. The discovery of gold in Minas Gerais in the 1690s and the subsequent development of the coffee industry in the region[27] helped initiate a process of industrial development and income and wealth concentration in the Southern and Southeastern regions of the country which exacerbated regional jealousies and tensions.

These regional differences came to overlap with, and helped to define, ethnic differences. By 1900, approximately 90 percent of foreign-born people living in Brazil were in the Southern and Eastern regions of the country,

[22] Burns 1993: 29–30.
[23] Barman 1988: 30.
[24] Marx: 1998: 31.
[25] Burns 1993: 136.
[26] Moraes 1991: 170.
[27] Baer 1995: 14–16.

predominantly in São Paulo. By 1890, the state of São Paulo alone was absorbing more than 50 percent of all immigrants, most of whom were of Italian descent.[28] São Paulo newspapers from the early 20th century often referred to the city as a tower of Babel because of the multiplicity of European languages heard in the factories and cafes. Meanwhile, the North and Northeast, whose European-descended population was largely Portuguese – soon came to be considered poor, providing an economic basis for further political tension.

Almost nothing held together the ranchers on the rolling pasturelands of Rio Grande do Sul in the far South, the miners grubbing for gold in the cold streams of Minas Gerais, the black slaves working in the humid cane fields of Pernambuco in the northeast, the mulattoes and mestizos herding cattle through the thornbush and cacti of Piaui in the Northern interior, and the Amerindians forced to gather the forest products of the unending Amazon basin.[29]

Today, regional divisions in Brazil are not ordinarily described by citizens or by analysts as a manifestation of ethnic politics. Yet, as early as the late 19th century, the overlapping of cultural and ancestral differences, with political and economic variations between various states and regions, and a general awareness of these differences, certainly constituted an ethno-regional political cleavage analogous to that existing in Southern Africa between Afrikaners and English-speakers. Patterns of prejudice continue to reflect these fault lines in contemporary Brazil.

Two Definitions of National Political Community

During the period 1889–91 in Brazil and 1902–9 in South Africa, constitutional planners faced the problem of having to address these racial and regional cleavages. As Reinhard Bendix points out, "A core element of nation-building is the codification of the rights and duties of all adults who are classified as citizens. The question is how exclusively or inclusively citizenship is defined."[30] Despite the availability of a host of similar constitutional questions and options, elites ultimately constructed very different solutions for defining NPC (as summarized in Table 3.1). The South Africa Act of 1909 codified the existing racial hierarchy and limited

---

[28] IBGE 1990; Villela and Suzigan 1977.
[29] Barman 1988: 40–41.
[30] Bendix 1964: 90.

Definitions of National Political Community

Table 3.1 *Constitutional definitions of National Political Community (NPC) in Brazil and South Africa*

		Approach to race cleavage	
		Nonracialism	Racial exclusion
Approach to regional cleavage	Unitary state		South African constitution (1909)
	Federalism	Brazilian constitution (1891)	

the salience of regional political claims with a unitary political system. By contrast, in Brazil, race was not identified as a relevant category in the eyes of the state, while the primacy of regional identities was established firmly in a federal constitution. Thus, with respect to the problem of race, the South Africans opted for an explicitly exclusionary strategy, while the Brazilians did not, opting to maintain a socioeconomic hierarchy with more subtle devices. The Brazilians made regional identity the most important dimension of political life, while the South Africans made it quite secondary to questions of race. The remainder of this section attempts to elaborate these constitutional choices in the respective countries, and it identifies the ways in which they were reinforced with other strategies and ancillary institutions.

The South African Definition of NPC

The South African definition of National Political Community made racial identities politically much more important than ethnic or regional identities, defining full citizenship as a privilege essentially reserved for whites only, and providing little opportunity for different regions to express group interests. Despite the emotive quality of territorial autonomy that had been evident prior to the Anglo-Boer War, and the fierce tension between Afrikaners and Englishmen, much more attention was paid to the division between "Europeans" – which included both British and Afrikaners as an undifferentiated group – on the one hand, and "Africans" or "Natives" on the other. Although the formal system of *apartheid*, which codified a host of draconian legislation for separating the race groups, was not put in place until four to six decades after the 1909 constitution was signed, that strategy is the ultimate extension of original decisions made around the turn of the century.

To argue that race became a politically important aspect of political life in South Africa in the 20th century may seem like a lesson in the obvious. Yet, an historical analysis of when, how, and why race became so important in that country highlights that such an outcome was a contingent path – not a predetermined one. Prior legacies of racial thinking and racial politics provided necessary but not sufficient conditions to institutionalize race in the manner that occurred in South Africa. Many inhabitants of Southern Africa and observers from abroad had good reason to believe that the sur- render of the Afrikaner generals meant that blacks would gain significant new political rights in the region. The decision to pursue a strategy of racial exclusion was not necessarily predictable from the start – particularly given British claims to improve the lot of blacks in Southern Africa, and evidence that the British were enforcing the ban on the slave trade elsewhere and pur- suing more liberal race policies elsewhere. Various interests pressured for greater racial equality. An organization representing "coloureds" requested that the franchise be based not on race, but on level of "civilization." Many Africans protested that the rights afforded to Cape Africans should be ex- tended throughout the region. And, most influential, several white states- men pushed for near or full parity for Africans – though sometimes with a universal property or literacy qualification. In other words, a very wide range of proposals was mooted quite seriously during the years of drafting the constitution.[31]

Nonetheless, the 1902 signing of the Treaty of Vereeniging, ending three years of bloody warfare, marked the beginning of a critical period of smoothing British-Afrikaner antagonism through the idiom of white na- tional unity in what would become the Union of South Africa.[32] The South Africa Act of 1909 and several critical acts of parliament that followed iden- tified race as the primary basis for membership in the South African NPC. "The price of trying to reconcile the whites was paid by the blacks and browns."[33] Afrikaner generals Louis Botha (who would be the first Prime Minister) and Jan Smuts (who would be the second and fourth Prime Min- ister) pursued conciliation within a divided antebellum polity.[34] The British crown had come to respect the surprising political resources and military might of the Afrikaners who formed a majority of the white population in

---

[31] Thompson 1960: 214–16.
[32] Thompson 1960, 1990; Marx 1998.
[33] Pakenham 1988: 576.
[34] Wilson and Thompson 1969: 341.

this country – and which possessed such great deposits of mineral wealth. Moreover, while many British leaders found the legacy of white supremacy to be unacceptably extreme, racial thinking continued to pervade the consciousness of Europeans in Southern Africa. It was British Lord Milner who in this decade of negotiation proclaimed, "A political equality of white and black is impossible. . . . The white man must rule, because he is elevated by many, many steps above the black man; steps which it will take the latter centuries to climb, and which it is quite possible that the vast bulk of the black population may never be able to climb at all."[35]

In England, the Liberal party won the 1905 by-elections and Sir Henry Campbell-Bannerman pursued the new standard British policy for colonies: "a united, self-governing, pro-British South Africa." Rejecting what he saw as the alienating, coercive policy of the Unionist party, Campbell-Bannerman sought Afrikaner cooperation through sharing and trust.[36] The two sides believed this could be achieved with agreement upon a national political community bounded by skin color, or race. In this sense, the racial strategies pursued for South Africa were similar to the group of British settler colonies such as the United States, Canada, Australia, and New Zealand.[37] Agreement soon after the war to postpone the question of the native franchise until after the introduction of self-government paved the way for a long series of laws and agreements that would make race the idiom through which other questions would be resolved. Various African, coloured, and Indian political groups protested this fateful initiative.[38] Nonetheless, "racial prejudice came together with strategic advantage in encouraging an Afrikaner-English alliance and the further exclusion of 'natives.'"[39]

The 1909 South Africa Act was highly explicit in its racial codification of citizenship, reserving the privileges and responsibilities of voting and leadership only to those of "European" descent. Only in the Cape Province, where blacks previously had been allowed to vote, was the franchise initially afforded on a nonracial basis. Article 35 of the constitution that made this provision for the Cape franchise was specially protected by a clause that required at least two-thirds of a joint sitting of the Parliament to vote

---

[35] As quoted by Thompson 1960: 5–6.
[36] Wilson and Thompson 1969: 333–4.
[37] Thompson 1990: 146. These similarities are revisited in Chapter 6.
[38] Davenport 1991: 209–11, 226–8.
[39] Marx 1998: 91.

to disqualify voters from that Province on the basis of race. Moreover, provincial representation in the Parliament was based on the numbers of "European males" counted in the census within each region. Race became the central criterion for citizenship – as well as a central question to be addressed – in the new Union of South Africa.

In the years following the promulgation of the constitution, several acts complemented and deepened the original ideas established in the constitution. The 1927 Immorality Act made it illegal to have sexual intercourse across the color line. In the 1930s, a series of laws progressively removed the very small number of black and Indian voters from the rolls. Of course, the development of the apartheid state following the 1948 election was a "logical" extension of these early policies institutionalizing white supremacy. From the birth of Union, the constitution made racial subordination a core aspect of the definition of the NPC, and bureaucratic mechanisms were put in place to enforce the color bar.

Strategies for dealing with land were more concerned with the larger racial strategy than with intra-white regional divides. The 1913 Native Land Act restricted the purchase and lease of land by Africans to the reserves, which constituted a mere 7 percent of the land – while they represented more than 60 percent of the population living in the country at the time. In practice, this law, when combined with subsequent legislation, meant that Africans could reside only on reserves except when "the interests and convenience of the whites required them to be elsewhere."[40] Throughout the 20th century, physical space was demarcated according to racial classification in South Africa, making nonracial regional divisions of secondary political importance.

Meanwhile, the South African "solution" to (white) ethno-regional cleavages was to create a unitary political system in the constitution and to postpone the question of ethnic rivalries through a constitutional clause reserving discussion of the language issue. In retrospect, this outcome was rather surprising: Recognition of overlapping cultural and political borders in Southern Africa suggested to most actors and observers of the second half of the 19th century that any future political linkage in the region would be carried out along federal lines, with a relatively weak central state.[41]

[40] Fredrickson 1982: 241.
[41] Davenport 1991: 221.

While the policies that excluded blacks from the NPC was one aspect of the strategy to ease the ethno-regional tensions that helped ignite the Boer War, British as well as Afrikaner political elites feared racial policy alone would be insufficient to maintain national unity, and additional measures were taken. First, political authority in the country was centralized, and this afforded little autonomy to the old states that became the new provinces. Parliamentary sovereignty was made explicit and few avenues were left open for the expression of *regional* interests. As in Great Britain, the executive was responsible to a majority in the House of Assembly and the Senate. In order to appease Natal, the constitution provided for the Senate as a weak second chamber meant to reflect the interests of the Provinces, opting against the more federal solution that Natalians had earlier promoted.[42] It was agreed that the "Native question ... needed to be confronted as a whole by a centralized state capable of pooling all available ideas and implementing them rapidly."[43] The Senate did provide equal representation for provinces of unequal size, but was indirectly elected and weaker in many critical ways.[44] Perhaps most important, money bills (those appropriating or raising revenue) would originate in the House of Assembly and were immune to amendment (but not rejection) from the Senate.[45] Provinces would have councils and governors to manage certain internal affairs, but they would be clearly subordinate to national government. Their status was completely unprotected in the constitution, and in all ways, parliamentary sovereignty was made clear.

The other sticking point addressed in the constitution was how language differences would be handled. The British victory could have quite plausibly meant a single language policy, with a deliberate strategy to anglicize the defeated Afrikaner population. Common language provides a very strong basis for political community, but the attractiveness of a single language for the new nation had to be balanced against the cultural claims of the defeated Afrikaners. The language section of the constitution was heavily contested, but ultimately, the two languages (English and Dutch)

---

[42] Wilson and Thompson 1969: 351–2.
[43] Cell 1982: 64.
[44] In administrative terms, the Union of South Africa had three tiers of government (and a parallel native administration), which allowed for some devolution of administrative functions. In political terms, however, it was still a unitary state because subnational tiers were afforded very little say in decision making and virtually no autonomy.
[45] Thompson 1960: 243.

were both made official languages of the Union and were to be "treated on a footing of equality." Like the Cape franchise for blacks, this clause was specifically shielded with a clause requiring the approval of two-thirds of the Parliament. In 1925, the constitution was amended to replace Dutch with Afrikaans, the language it had become in South Africa.[46]

The Brazilian Definition of NPC

In the Brazilian constitution of 1891, racial and regional identities were recognized in almost exactly the opposite manner as in the 1909 South African constitution. First, state and/or regional identity was central for locating one's place within the polity, as a federal constitution was adopted. The NPC was defined as an agglomeration of semi-autonomous territories. Second, race was not explicitly discussed in that document, and as a result, no individual was excluded from citizenship *on the basis* of race. A more subtly expressed race chauvinism combined with the legacy of slavery certainly acted to maintain a racial hierarchy in terms of economic opportunity and achievement in Brazil, but without a rigid color line. In the absence of a clear racial "other," racial categories became largely meaningless as the basis for collective political identities in Brazil.

Unlike in South Africa, where provincial powers were carefully enumerated and restricted, in the 1891 Brazilian constitution, the provincial states (*estados*) gained the power "to exercise in general any and every power or right not denied them by express provision of the constitution or contained by implication in such express provision." States could form their own military forces, directly elect their own governors, and were responsible for carrying out the fundamental functions of government. Indeed, a few important limitations were placed upon state powers, particularly where federal powers were concerned, but this *estado* sphere of government was identified as the one deserving of all residual powers, essentially making state-level government the authority of last resort. Unlike the parliamentary sovereignty accorded in South Africa, in Brazil, the federal government was highly restricted in its ability to intervene in state affairs and all central state powers were enumerated in the constitution. In addition to this autonomy, states gained significant voice within the structure of national decision making. Like in South Africa, the Parliament was bicameral, but

---

[46] Thompson 1990: 160.

the Senate had much greater powers – as all bills could originate in and could be amended or rejected by either house.

The decision to opt for a federal solution marked a reversal from the political and administrative centralization that took place during the final decades of the Brazilian empire. In the late 19th century, wealthy landowners of the Southeast, including the coffee *fazendeiros* of Rio de Janeiro, helped to topple the empire in search of greater autonomy over their own affairs.[47] Constitutional planners believed that serious conflict could be avoided by affording greater autonomy. A driving idea that helped secure this outcome was that decentralization would defuse regional separatist movements. As in South Africa, the American federal constitution was used as model for discussion – but its impact was interpreted differently. In South Africa, the federal solution was interpreted as the factor that triggered civil war in the United States, while in Brazil, American-style federalism was interpreted in terms of liberty and progress. However, as Abrucio points out, highlighting the reflections of early statesman and scholar of American federalism, Rui Barbosa, the Brazilian federation was formed in the opposite manner as the American one: The United States of America came together because separate entities *wanted* to share some form of political authority. The federal inclinations of the United States of Brazil (as it was called in the 1891 constitution) reflected a desire to gain autonomy from an already established central state.[48] Despite a sizeable opposition, which included many former slaves who viewed federalism as a strategy for increasing the power of a sometimes cruel "master," a well-orchestrated campaign on the part of the federalists successfully entrenched the federal model within the constitution.

While many provisions were made for regionally based political representation and autonomy in the Brazilian constitution of 1891, there was no mention of race, and Brazil's racial hierarchy would be reproduced through more subtle mechanisms.[49] When the constitutional convention began in

---

[47] Fausto 1986: 787–9.

[48] Abrucio 1998: 32. A similar point is made in Stepan 1999.

[49] Thomas Skidmore (1995: xi) identified a powerful current in Brazilian intellectual life when he observed, "In the fourteen years since this book was first published, relatively little new research has been done on the themes defined here, especially the link between race and nationality. This can perhaps best be explained by the fact that Brazilian scholars, especially from the established academic institutions, continue for the most part to avoid the subject of race, in virtually all its aspects, at least for the 20th century. Indeed, Brazilians often regard non-Brazilians who pursue the subject as having misunderstood it. They

1889, it had been less than two years since Princess Isabella signed the Golden Law abolishing slavery. That institution had come under severe pressure throughout the 19th century, and it was the last bastion of chattel slavery of African-descended people. European colonizers brought slaves to Brazil and indoctrinated local elites with racist theories for three centuries, until the 19th century, when the pressures to end slavery in Brazil could no longer be resisted. After 1850, Brazil did end its participation in the slave trade (sixteen years *after* South Africa had abolished slavery completely), gradually enacting various forms of emancipation, eventually culminating in the complete abolition of slavery in 1888. High degrees of racial prejudice when combined with a racially stratified economic structure provided the necessary ingredients for the discriminatory codification of race. And yet, the constitution made absolutely no mention of either race or the particular race groups themselves, let alone the recently abolished institution of slavery. It has been a longstanding political tradition in Brazil to point to the lack of race-based legislation and absence of racial distinctions in the constitution as part of a deliberate attempt to construct a nonracial society – what Brazilian national thinkers have mythically referred to as a *racial democracy*. And yet, as more recent scholarship has pointed out, such decisions, in the wake of the high political, social, and economic salience of race during this period in Brazil, cannot be interpreted as the result of purely benevolent or egalitarian motives. Rather, this was a different strategy for securing a privileged position for elites of the day.

In fact, Brazilian elites – well versed in the scientific racism developed on the continent – reconciled the heterogeneous character of its population and a desire to construct a strong Brazilian nation with a very different type of strategy. Like their South African counterparts, many dominant (and white) Brazilian intellectuals and political and economic leaders sought the development of a white nation as they also subscribed to the notion of a racial hierarchy. They attempted to carry out a policy of *whitening*, that is,

---

are sometimes inclined to dismiss U.S. scholars, in particular, as being unable to avoid projecting onto Brazil assumptions about U.S. society." Similarly, in my own research, I have confronted similar resistance from Brazilian scholars who rejected the mere question of the impact of race politics on state development as invalid and a comparison with South Africa as misplaced. As I argue, there *are* important variations in the ways in which race has been configured into politics and society in these countries, but it is the subtleties of that variation that are explored here. The comparative project helps to unearth the burying of an understanding of race in Brazil, a project that only began receiving serious scholarly attention in the final years of the 20th century.

those Brazilians with Indian and/or African blood were to be integrated into a single Brazilian race through mixing of the races. The premise of this strategy was that over the course of 50–100 years, the combination of European immigration and miscegenation would produce offspring that were increasingly "whiter" and as a result, "better."[50] Rooted in a scientific doctrine that suggested the benefits of cross-breeding, the philosophy was easily welcomed in a country that had been mixing for generations. As in South Africa at the turn of the century, political leaders argued that the imagining of a homogeneous nation required a racial basis, and Brazilian elites also opted for a white Brazil. Given demographic patterns, intellectual traditions, and a set of contingent ideas and inclinations, the Brazilians developed an alternative to the immediate racial exclusions of South Africa in favor of a more gradual integration. This was a melting pot strategy taken to its most extreme conclusion, with the assumption – a seemingly blind one with 20–20 hindsight – that mixing would result in a lighter, more Europeanized population.

Although this strategy was more informally developed, and was not reflected in the constitution, certain policies and acts of state made clear that the racial aspect of the NPC would be dealt with through whitening. Immigration policy was one clear tactic: A June 28, 1890 decree encouraged the immigration of healthy, able-bodied workers, "except natives of Asia or Africa, who can be admitted only by authorization of the National Congress and in accordance with the stipulated conditions." These immigrants served to displace Afro-Brazilian workers from the labor market in the Southeast, creating poverty and forcing internal migration patterns, but in an indirect manner.[51] European immigration simultaneously provided an important pillar for a whitening strategy with the effect of bringing a highly racist European population to the Southeast: 80 percent of the 3.7 million immigrants who arrived before 1930 settled around São Paulo. In its official diplomatic channels, the state furthered the strategy by promoting the idea of a white Brazil to the rest of the world. Foreign Minister Rio Branco (1902–12) filled the diplomatic service with whites only, "to reinforce the image of a Europeanized country growing whiter and whiter."[52] Finally, in its use of the census, the Brazilian state managed to promote the image of

---

[50] Skidmore 1995: 65.
[51] Andrews 1991: 54.
[52] Skidmore 1995: 133–7.

a fluid and increasingly whiter society.[53] Unlike in South Africa, where the racial strategy required very rigid and fixed lines, in Brazil, the boundaries of race were more flexible. For example, one analyst argues that the rapid increase in the number of whites in the country reported in the census was the result of the inclination of census takers to "classify whiter."[54] Although the census counted only a limited number of racial categories, in practice Brazilians came to use dozens of different labels to describe mixtures of race groups along a single continuum, as opposed to the rigid racial categories employed in South Africa.

In the 1891 constitution, blacks were not directly excluded from the NPC. Largely as the result of the legacy of slavery and discrimination, however, most blacks were not actively incorporated into mainstream politics either. For the slaves who had been denied citizenship, it was now theoretically possible for these and other black Brazilians to enjoy the same legal opportunities and rights to vote and to serve in public office as white Brazilians. Indeed, restrictive requirements for suffrage and representation based on literacy requirements effectively excluded most blacks from active participation. In the most powerful set of rules in the land – the constitution – race was not even mentioned, while at the same time, racism and a deliberate racial strategy were at work within society.

Many blacks recognized the prospects for more subtle forms of subordination even in a post-emancipation political environment, and attempted, unsuccessfully, to block the political transition that would decentralize political power along regional lines. As Andrews points out, many Afro-Brazilians were highly suspicious of the oligarchic-led Republican movement. From the perspective of many ex-slaves, the monarchy had freed them and they did not believe that former masters would ever have their interests at heart. Immediately following abolition, the journalist José do Patrocínio enlisted former slaves in a paramilitary organization – the Black Guard – to disrupt Republican meetings, sometimes in a highly violent manner.[55] While some Afro-Brazilians saluted the Republican movement, others perceptively feared for their future. Many recognized that the legacy of slavery left them poor, illiterate, and jobless – the very criteria for exclusion from

[53] Marx 1998: 166.
[54] Wagley 1971: 128. Particularly in Brazil, individuals were more likely to classify themselves as white at higher levels of income and socioeconomic status. For a discussion of the relationship between race and the census in Brazil, see Nobles 2000.
[55] Andrews 1991: 44.

the vote, and from political power. On the other hand, it is quite conceivable that the outcome could have been far more overtly repressive: In the first two decades of the Republic, a proposal to establish a formal color bar was debated in the Parliament and ultimately rejected.[56]

Influence on Class Relations

The political community model links the definition of NPC to the development of the tax state through the intervening effects of inter- and intra-class relations. By structuring the organization of unions, employer organizations, political parties, and political discourse more generally, definitions of NPC help give meaning to economic interests, which could otherwise aggregate in multiple forms and configurations. Politically salient labels provide a basis for discussions about fairness and equity that become central within the process of political competition. In a world of highly imperfect information about future economic returns, definitions of NPC provide a starting point for individual and collective actors to evaluate the likely benefits of various government policies and particular responses. Moreover, a shared collective identity provides a basis for justifying self-interest in a way that naked economic reasoning does not.

In the 20th century, rapid industrialization gave way to new class cleavages in Brazil and South Africa, and the particular definitions of NPC crafted in founding constitutions in those countries strongly influenced how political relations would develop within and across classes. Economic inequalities largely overlapped with racial and regional boundaries in both countries, but the actual *political mobilization* of classes was rather different. Definitions of NPC, which gave meaning to particular labels and categories, framed the dynamics of political competition during the process of modernization. As described above, race became politically meaningful in South Africa, and region became politically meaningful in Brazil.

In turn, the relations among and between upper and lower groups unfolded along opposite trajectories in Brazil and South Africa during the course of 20th-century industrial development. In South Africa, the political salience of race cemented together upper economic groups into a coherent national class, while in Brazil, the political salience of region or territory created strong divisions within that economic stratum. Similarly, race bonded

[56] Marx 1998: 166.

together South Africa's white workers into national organizations, while regionalism, and Brazil's ambiguous approach toward race, divided the labor movement in that country. Finally, whiteness served as a link between classes within South Africa, whereas in Brazil, no particular political idiom joined these groups together.

South Africa: Centripetal Tendencies within the White Polity

The explicit exclusion of blacks from the South African NPC following the signing of the 1909 South Africa Act set in motion a pattern of centripetal political dynamics within the white community that led to relatively high levels of class cohesion, and ultimately, a strong cross-class coalition between upper- and lower-income whites. By the end of the first half of the 20th century, three key changes had been wrought on the South African polity: Regional identities became increasingly less salient, racial identities became increasingly more salient, and white ethnic political conflict, while still important and divisive, had been greatly tempered. Institutionalized white supremacy helped to placate intra-ethnic competition within the white minority, and co-existed quite easily with the process of capitalist development.[57] In such an environment, key decisions were made authoritatively at the national level, as the Parliament, central state, and nationally organized associations cooperated and partnered in a process of mutual transformation. The interests of the (white) nation were consistently placed above more narrow subdivisions of economic interests, particularly when seen in light of the Brazilian case.

The South African political party system was a key source of white political cohesion: The parties were virtually all white, nationally organized, and to an extent, differentiated along white ethnic lines – but not regional ones. The history of white politics in South Africa (1910–94) has been dominated by strong political parties with one or two parties in power and only one or two strong parties in opposition. For example, in every election between

---

[57] Similar arguments are made by Esman 1994; Marx 1998; and Greenberg 1980. I am well aware that my contention that race trumped intra-white competition will be met with some skepticism and disagreement, particularly among some South African observers of South African history. While cultural prejudice and outright conflict have certainly characterized aspects of the relationship between these two groups, since the end of the Anglo-Boer War, such tensions have truly been of a different order of magnitude when compared with the white–black cleavage, in which the latter group has been excluded from ordinary social, political, and economic life in South African society.

1910 and 1961, the top two parties secured more than 63 percent of the seats in the Parliament, and on average, the top two parties secured a full 88 percent of the seats[58] (see Figure 3.1). Rather than forming coalitions, smaller parties tended to be absorbed into larger ones – a trajectory of party system development characterized by strong centripetal forces as opposed to fragmentation.

Upper-Group Organization. Representatives from the business community organized themselves in exclusively white, highly national terms. Strong organizations such as the Chamber of Mines and the Association of Chambers of Commerce (ASSOCOM) integrated the business community from various city and regional organizations into a strong national voice that cut across sectoral lines. Although the mining sector was regionally concentrated in the interior of the country, it made no claims for regional privilege or differentiation. This body limited its political interactions and demands almost exclusively to national government – virtually ignoring the provincial administration as an important authority.[59] Representatives of South Africa's economic elite clearly viewed white nation-building as critical to its own successes, and as W. Ehrlich, president of the Associated Chambers of Commerce, proclaimed,

The old trade barriers have been removed, and to-day we are no longer Transvaalers, Natalians, Free Staters or Cape Colonists – we are South Africans in nationality and territory. . . . All South Africa goes into the melting pot, and the new nation arising therefrom will be a powerful factor in the great forward movement which the future has before us. (Proceedings of 15th Annual Congress of the Associated Chambers of Commerce, Bloemfontein July 12–14, 1910)

The idioms of whiteness and Europeanness helped upper groups to frame their fortunes in South Africa as tied up in a collective fate. Of course, this strategy was not simply fantasy, but provided concrete material gains across sectors. "The alliance of gold and maize" – the cooperative arrangements between mining magnates and commercial farmers – helped to maintain institutions that provided a steady stream of cheap labor: the large black population living in the region, yet deprived of the rights of citizenship.[60]

[58] Author analysis of election returns from Davenport 1991: 564–5.
[59] Barely any references are made to provincial administration or provincial leaders in the annual reports of the Transvaal Chamber of Mines.
[60] Cell 1982: 63.

Votes received by top two parties in elections to the Câmara Federal in Brazil

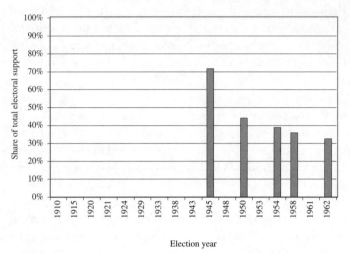

Seats held by top two parties in the National Assembly in South Africa

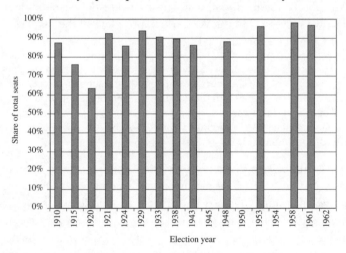

Figure 3.1   Party strength in Brazil and South Africa, 1910–1962. *Sources:* IBGE 1990; Davenport 1991.

The South African definition of NPC was intended to promote white cohesion through shared anti-black sentiment, and there is significant evidence to suggest that this strategy worked. For example, in a study of the race attitudes of white university students in South Africa, published in

1937, MacCrone found that among this elite group, intra-ethnic tensions were minimal when compared with the fundamental race cleavage in the country. The results of MacCrone's study are reproduced in Figure 3.2. They show that while English-speaking and Afrikaans-speaking South Africans tolerated or preferred their own group to the other, both groups shared a strong lack of tolerance of the various black groups in the country, including "Coloureds," "Indians," and "Natives."

Lower-Group Organization. In a similar manner, organized labor in South Africa would develop in response to, and further contribute to the development of, national political institutions defined in terms of the new NPC. Despite potentially shared economic interests and the lure of strength in numbers, black labor was forbidden from collective bargaining and white labor articulated its demands in direct opposition to blacks. White workers, under the banner, "Workers of the world unite and fight for a White South Africa," cast the problems of unemployment, poor working conditions, and low wages in racial terms. They organized a highly disruptive political challenge in the early decades of the 20th century, including important strikes in 1913 and 1914, which "demonstrated conclusively that quarrels between employers and unionized employees on the gold mines were national issues that could not be ignored by the rest of South African society."[61] Strike activity culminated with the exceptionally violent Rand Revolt of 1922 – which amounted to a small-scale civil war, in which over 1.3 million man-days were lost to strike activity.[62] In short, whiteness provided very strong "glue" for organized labor, which created a source of political power through sharp confrontations and helped to force concessions from upper groups in that society.

Blacks did not complacently accept their exclusion from the NPC and the associated loss of political and economic opportunities. In a society in which race mattered so much, lower groups did not organize as "the poor" or see their interests as common. Rather, blacks – who were also largely poor – organized and resisted *as* blacks, gaining no solidarity from poor whites – who were, in fact, among their fiercest adversaries. In the first decade of the 20th century, middle-class and educated black South Africans organized against these emerging strategies: Black leaders made

[61] Yudelman 1983: 124.
[62] Bureau of Census and Statistics South Africa 1960.

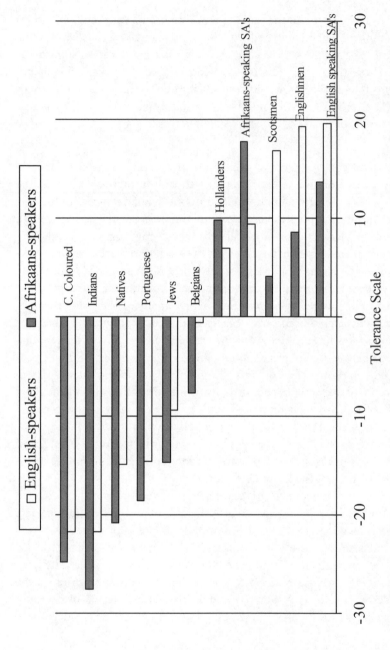

Figure 3.2 White tolerance of other groups in South Africa, 1937. Study of first-year college students at the University of the Witwatersrand, Johannesburg. *Source:* MacCrone 1937.

contact with Mohandas Gandhi and organized a delegation to England to address these problems.[63] In 1912, the South African Native National Congress was formed – the precursor to the African National Congress (ANC) – to challenge the proposed Lands Act. Without significant financial or organizational resources, let alone significant international support, this effort initially failed to make any serious advances for blacks. Rather, the formation of such resistance probably aided white political elites in translating beliefs of racial supremacy into political solidarity. Ultimately, the strength of race-based resistance would undo institutionalized white supremacy, but it would be more than eight decades before this struggle was successful.

Cross-Class Coalition.   State leaders in South Africa, as in most industrializing Latin American countries and in other countries, came to realize that the threatening potential of organized labor needed to be addressed, and that the labor movement would need to be incorporated into the political arena in a more coherent and secure manner. Indeed, the challenge of organized labor was posed within the dominant idiom of race, and this provided an opportunity to defuse labor-capital tensions with a shared identity. In both 1914 and 1922, employers promoted the incorporation of white labor through industrial conciliation councils with broad national scope.[64] In turn, the white unions supported the state as they were incorporated within political parties, including one that would run the government (in coalition) in 1924.[65] After taking control of government, the color bar was extended in the form of the 1924 civilized labor policy, which provided job incentives and reservations for whites. Also, beginning in 1924, white unions began to play an even more important role in industrial councils, and businesses allowed them to participate in decision making.[66]

While the period 1909–24 witnessed significant conflict between employers and organized labor, these events should be viewed in light of the

---

[63] Davenport 1991: 226–7.

[64] Yudelman 1983: 200.

[65] In this sense, the South African case resembles the "Party incorporation" strategy summarized in Collier and Collier 1991: 166–7. For a discussion of the role of white trade unions in the organization of South African political parties, see Bunting 1986; O'Meara 1978, 1983, 1996.

[66] Yudelman (1983) goes to great lengths to prove that 1924 was not a turning point in South African history because of the relative continuity in outcomes, but this downplays the important role that the election of a labor party and new labor relations legislation would have in truly defusing the labor challenge.

fact that the political solutions contained in the 1909 constitution did not necessarily suit the immediate interests of all white South Africans. In particular, many South African employers still objected to a job color bar for economic reasons, and despite the agreements in the 1909 South Africa Act, they had incentives to try to renege on the spirit of that document. When their privileged position was challenged, white labor struck back with work-stopping violence. Certainly, the development of the industrial relations system after this period marked an important change in state-business-labor relations among whites, but this set of patterns, which established a privileged position for white workers, represented a *continuity* from the ideas articulated and agreed upon between 1902 and 1909, not a completely new paradigm.

The incorporation of white labor helped upper groups induce union leaders to acquiesce to their point of view.[67] Although, as Yudelman notes, repression was initially used to confront violent strike activity, white organized labor was ultimately incorporated largely through support and negotiation, not repression or control. By recognizing workers as *whites*, rather than in terms of their economic position, state and capital helped to ease inter-class tensions, de-mobilizing the political challenge they posed and harmonizing their interests. This political settlement was decisive in placating the challenge from labor. In particular, relations improved dramatically following the 1924 election, which gave labor a place in government. As a long-term solution to class conflict, strikes would be permitted as long as industrial conciliation was pursued first.

The idiom of whiteness – and the existence of a proximate "black other" – was used repeatedly to bring together a polity with multiple potential bases for division. Given the contentions of some neo-Marxist scholars[68] that the racial schism in South Africa was merely *reflective* of class conflict, what is striking about the South African case is that race shaped the formation of class interests, and served as an idiom for cross-class rhetoric during the early decades of Union. Most notably, sympathy for the "poor White" problem, and fears about what might happen if it were not solved, proved to be powerful political emotions that helped to gain acceptance of progressive policies on the part of upper groups in South Africa. The

---

[67] Seidman 1994: 24–5.

[68] See, for example, Davies 1973, and Davies et al. 1976, for Marxist interpretations of state-labor-capital relations in South Africa. A variant of this argument is that there has never been a real white working class. See Simson 1974.

Report of the Carnegie Commission (1932) on "The Poor White Problem in South Africa" gave international legitimacy to a definition of political community that clearly excluded blacks, suggesting that whites *should* help themselves as a coherent group.

Examination of South African company and industry association annual reports revealed significant attention to the demands of organized labor leaders within the European Labor sector, and the English-speaking newspapers were riddled with the discourse of the "poor white problem."[69] As Arendt observes, "The poor whites in South Africa...demanded and were granted charity as the right of a white skin; having lost all consciousness that normally men do not earn a living by the color of their skin."[70]

Brazil: Class Fragmentation and Polarization

Among scholars studying Brazil, there has been widespread agreement that economic classes have been relatively fragmented and polarized.[71] There is less clear consensus, however, about the factors that shaped such fragmentation. In order to understand the roots of class fragmentation and polarization in Brazil, it is necessary to identify the factors that actively inhibited the formation of more encompassing organizations and movements during the process of industrialization, and to consider which factors were *not* present that might have led to higher levels of political cohesion. Weyland (1996: 40) points to the (presumably racially and ethnically) heterogeneous populations, regional differences in economic development, large informal sectors, and the lack of serious military challenges, as impediments to political organization with broad national scope, particularly when compared with the experiences of Western Europe.[72] While these factors surely posed important constraints on broad-based political unity, such factors were also characteristic of South Africa, where class cohesion has been much stronger. Moreover, although clientelism and particularistic politics have been longstanding traits of Brazil, and of much of

---

[69] In particular, the reports of the Transvaal Chamber of Mines, and the Association of Chambers of Commerce of South Africa.

[70] Arendt 1979: 194.

[71] Schmitter 1971; Abrucio 1998; Collier and Collier 1991; Weyland 1996; various contributions in Durand and Silva 1998.

[72] See also Durand and Silva 1998: 1–50, and Weyland 1998a.

Latin America, these characteristics were also present in pre-modern Europe, where such practices were eventually replaced with more encompassing political organizations and movements. Our understanding of the roots of political fragmentation in Brazil remains incomplete.[73]

What appears to differentiate Brazil from South Africa is that very different configurations of race and region in the definition of the NPC established very different trajectories for organizing otherwise analogous economic interests. Federalism reinforced a sense of regional identity and provided incentives to organize politically along *estado* and regional lines. Meanwhile, the Brazilian approach to race provided no opportunities for race-based political organization – as was the case in South Africa – but allowed racial and ethnic chauvinism to persist, proving to have a divisive influence within and across classes. As a result, the process of industrialization proceeded in Brazil with a political logic that impeded political organization with a broad, national scope.

The definition of NPC tended to create political instability in Brazil through the manifestation of irreconcilable differences among states and regions, and between these entities and the federal government. Anthony Marx argues that national cohesion was relatively well established in Brazil, as epitomized by the Brazilian flag – which had no marks of internal division.[74] Other currents in Brazilian scholarship, however, point to a more tenuous federative pact.[75] Only by looking at the national flag, one would not see the great emotive significance of *state* flags, which President Gétulio Vargas would order to be burned decades after the first Republican constitution. "In some state capitals, the state flag flew from every mast, while one searched in vain to locate the Brazilian colors."[76] Efforts to crush meaningful regional identities would provide the spark for flames of resistance in future generations. "As the system

---

[73] I should be clear here that my understanding of political fragmentation in Brazil does not necessarily contradict what others have argued. However, my analysis focuses the long list of state and organizational sources of political fragmentation as being the product of Brazil's definition of NPC in light of that society's particular social and economic characteristics.

[74] Marx 1998: 81–2.

[75] For discussions of the history of regionalism and federalism in Brazil, and their relationship to race and nation, see Leite 1992; Abrucio 1998; and Moraes 1991. The various works of Gilberto Freyre (Freyre 1986; Freyre and Putnam 1946; Freyre and Horton 1986) deal explicitly with these questions, but because Freyre was so clearly concerned with the task of *inventing* a Brazilian national identity, his work must be read with closer scrutiny, differentiating what *was*, from what he would have *liked*.

[76] Burns 1993: 342.

functioned in practice, federalism became regionalism and national interests were sacrificed to regional ones."[77]

Various terms have been used to describe the regional character and diffuse sources of political power in the Old Republic of the period 1891–1930. *Coronelismo*, the politics of the governors, and the Barons of Federation, are widely used descriptions reflecting the fact that political power in Brazil did not rest in the national capital with the Parliament, but in the hands of state leaders. During these early years, state governors from the Southern states of São Paulo and Minas Gerais enjoyed the greatest political clout in the new legislature. After 1909, these two states established an unwritten agreement – Café com Leite – in which they agreed to alternate the presidency and share regional control of the presidency, to the dismay of the Northern, Northeastern, and Southern regions. State political machines, and in particular the state governors, gained enormous power during this period.[78] The structure of this particular political arrangement sowed the seeds of its own destruction, however, as even more narrowly defined state interests prevailed over regional ones in the 1920s.[79] As states grew wary of one another and of the federal government, governors raised their own national guards to the strength of the national army, and in the case of São Paulo, the military was made even stronger. Eventually, these armies were appeased and were integrated into the national military, but this only served to introduce an additional line of political contestation – that between the states on the one hand and the federal government on the other. Ambiguities in the constitution over which spheres of government contained which authorities set off a series of early intergovernmental conflicts that would be replayed for many years.[80] Over the course of the century, this tension would manifest itself in both violence and multiple new constitutions.

Inter-state political hostility across regions gained additional momentum from underlying racial prejudices that persisted in Brazilian society.[81] Racial discrimination was not codified in the South African manner, but in subtle ways, race chauvinism, migration patterns, and the legacies of racial discrimination reinforced Brazil's regional political divides and general political

---

[77] Burns 1993: 266.
[78] Abrucio 1998: 35.
[79] Fausto 1986.
[80] James 1923: 181.
[81] Leite (1992: 325) argues that rampant racism was used to justify the economic superiority of some regional groups over others within Brazil during the period 1880–1950.

fragmentation. As late as 1951, an IBOPE report stated that a full 65 percent of Rio de Janeiro residents surveyed responded that they would *not* marry a black person.[82] On the other hand, 72.5 percent said they would be happy to have a black as a neighbor.[83] Although comparable survey data are not available for that period in South Africa, it is literally inconceivable that such a large share of white South Africans would have accepted blacks as neighbors. Although white Brazilians did not view dark-skinned Brazilians as equals in more general terms, blacks were not constituted as a proximate "other" such that white identity would have any significant political salience.

As compared with South Africa's more blatant policies of racial exclusion, Brazil's more subtle whitening strategy reinforced the logic of regional politics – a whiter South versus a darker North[84] – a sentiment that would be expressed by many European immigrants taking residence in the Southern region of the country.[85] Just as South Africans employed cultural stereotypes to reinforce divisions across race and ethnic groups, in Brazil, racial differences were used to reinforce divisions across regional groups. However, unlike in South Africa, where political elites trumpeted the racial issue as one that needed to be addressed in a coordinated, national manner, no such issue captured the imagination of political elites in Brazil.[86] Within the loosely articulated whitening strategy, state governors, most notably from the government of São Paulo, encouraged European immigration. Important Brazilian writers framing the myths of national identity and regionalist discourse, such as Alfredo Ellis, made clear their beliefs that São Paulo was a suitable home for Europeans, and not well suited for the black and Indian races. During various secessionist attempts in the South, many white Brazilians fingered the "deficiencies of Brazil" as the fault of the mestizo.[87]

The Brazilian configurations of race and region did not augur well for the integration of national class interests through organizations. For example, Brazilian political parties maintained a distinctively local flavor, with extremely little national organization or sense of national purpose. The relatively greater political importance of state-level politics was reflected in their internal organizations. A mass-based, political party system would not

---

[82] A public opinion service similar to the American Gallup organization.
[83] IBOPE 1951.
[84] Skidmore 1995: 61.
[85] Ribeiro 1995: 242.
[86] Marx 1998: 161.
[87] Leite 1992: 237–8.

develop until after the 1946 constitution, but even the extension of suffrage did not transform the party system into a more nationally based institution. The practice of making demands along state or regional lines was already in the repertoire of political organization, and tended to be reinforced during the Vargas presidency (1930–45).[88] Moreover, those parties took on an increasingly fragmented quality as a small number of sanctioned parties would eventually splinter into multiple, weak parties with little coherence across regions or sectors. As shown in Figure 3.1, during the 1945–62 period, individual parties increasingly lost their command over the national polity, and the top two parties secured only about 30 percent of the vote in 1962. Multiple factors surely contributed to the development of the respective party systems, but the political parties themselves, which consistently employed territorial idioms, formed part of the national political institutions that would shape the patterns of politics in the country. As a result, during periods in which the congress was operating as a legislative body, more narrow, as opposed to national, interests were represented.[89]

Upper-Group Organization. In a reinforcing manner, employer organizations have fragmented class interests along state and regional lines throughout the century. For example, in various studies of Brazilian business sectors throughout the 20th century, the National Confederation of Industries has been found to be a weak organization, unable to articulate a clear national vision.[90] In particular, ethnic heterogeneity, and the often unwelcome amalgamation of various immigrant business groups, have been sources of division among upper groups in Brazil. As Nathaniel Leff describes them:

Descendants of immigrants from a variety of countries and native Brazilians of very diverse socioeconomic backgrounds, the industrialists do not share a common tradition.... Indeed, instead of acting together under the leadership of the Confederation of Industries, individual industrialists and rival "groups" usually compete with each other for political access. Their competition is all the more fierce because the political role allocated to the class as a whole is limited.[91]

[88] See Chapter 4 for further discussion.
[89] Leff 1968.
[90] Schmitter 1971; Leff 1968; Payne 1994. My own interviews with business and political leaders in Brazil point to similar conclusions.
[91] Leff 1968: 116.

Lower-Group Organization. Labor solidarity has also been impeded by the salience of regionalism, and quite opposite to the South African case, racial heterogeneity actually undermined the cohesion of the working classes. Federalism provided unique opportunities for the state to structure a corporatist framework of labor organization divided along state and local lines. This strategy served to promote a much greater salience for local-level identities among unionized workers, impeding national-level collective action or solidarity.

Meanwhile, the Brazilian approach to race reinforced political fragmentation among workers. Although European workers did displace Afro-Brazilians from jobs, and came to Brazil with racist views, just as in South Africa, in the political context of post-abolition Brazil, ideas of white or European supremacy were not used explicitly as a basis for solidarity. In fact, the strategy was quite the opposite: "Acutely aware of the tactical opportunities which an ethnically and racially divided working class offered to employers and the state, and inspired by the egalitarian doctrines of socialism, anarchism, and anarchosyndicalism, labor organizers repeatedly invoked the goal of eliminating such divisions."[92] Blacks and mulattos participated in the labor movement, sometimes even as leaders, but their acceptance by whites varied across regions, and was noticeably lower in São Paulo, the industrial center. Moreover, racial fault lines remained apparent as preferred jobs went to white immigrants over blacks. In the 1920s and 1930s, just as the South Africans were implementing policies of job reservation, the Brazilians shrugged their shoulders and cautiously nodded their heads that the racial problem was being "solved" through whitening.[93] In practice, racial prejudice led to employers seeking whites only for certain jobs, but this was not enforced by government policy, which was otherwise color-blind. Nonetheless, particularly in São Paulo, the "agrarian-mercantile bourgeoisie preferred immigrant, especially Italian, workers to alternative sources of labor," notably the black population remaining in São Paulo after abolition.[94] Regionally varied racial attitudes further impeded solidarity across regions, contributing to the weakness of organized labor evident by the 1920s, at a time when South African organized labor was particularly strong. Thus, labor unity could be built neither on racial exclusion,

[92] Andrews 1991: 61.
[93] Skidmore 1995: 173.
[94] Fausto 1986: 781.

nor on racial inclusion – the product of the Brazilian strategy to erase racial categories as a basis for national politics.

Cross-Class Relations. During an analogous period to the South African case, in which organized labor was integrated into a strong, national political party, Brazilian organized labor came to be controlled more explicitly by the state. Because of the political weakness of Brazilian organized labor, it posed much less of a threat to the state and to capitalist development in general, and control strategies were employed to a much greater degree than inducement and cooptation strategies. Rather than encouraging participation in decision making, as was the case in South Africa after 1924, in Brazil, "the government severely constrained the new legalized and legitimated unions in the sphere of labor-capital relations and conceived of unions more centrally as organizations through which the state could paternalistically grant social welfare benefits."[95] This mode of labor incorporation, which Collier and Collier label "State incorporation," was built upon far more repressive tactics, including police raids and the jailing of union leaders.[96] There was no legally sanctioned color bar, but Brazilian labor law was highly constraining in other ways – which affected both blacks and whites. The state laid down the terms of how unions could organize, and the extent to which unions were provided opportunities to participate in decision making. State and regional lines provided a key lever of organizational control: Under Vargas, the new corporatist arrangements divided unions along sectoral lines, creating federations at the state level and confederations at the national level. Even within sectors, the confederations have not been unifying organizations, the manifestation of a blueprint designed to divide the working class. If South Africa's national integration strategy excluded blacks from full citizenship, while providing full citizenship to white laborers, in Brazil, the lines were more blurred: Workers of all races were politically divided and afforded fewer rights and privileges and less political clout.

Unlike in South Africa, where race suggested some solidarity between upper- and lower-income whites, in Brazil, the existence of poor whites has had much less emotive connotations for the white elite. The less essential approach to race has meant that (generally white) elite Brazilians

[95] Collier and Collier 1991: 169.
[96] Collier and Collier 1991: 186.

have viewed poor whites as more similar to poor blacks than to themselves. This approach, which became common-sense in Brazil, has served to divide upper and lower groups, even within the same racial category. In retrospect, the final acceptance of abolition on the part of large rural landowners depended upon a calculation – which turned out to be correct – "that abolition need not endanger their social and economic dominance."[97]

Judging from more recent statistics and analyses, it is clear that Afro-Brazilians benefited least from and suffered most in the process of industrialization and modernization.[98] The Brazilian approach to the racial cleavage, articulated in the 1891 constitution and expanded in the decades to follow, undermined the bases for mobilization along racial lines both from the perspective of white support or black resistance. As Carl Degler and others have pointed out, the social mobility of small numbers of mulattoes and Africans has served to defuse potential bases for race-based resistance.[99] The first serious black political movement did not emerge until more than three decades after abolition, when the Frente Negra Brasileira was founded in 1931.[100] Like other short-lived racially organized movements that would follow, the movement actually embraced the state's strategies and tactics for addressing racial inequities rather than challenging them.[101] The fluidity of racial categories has certainly worked to mollify potential political conflict in that country. The Brazilian saying, "money whitens," reflects a viable – if limited – social mobility for darker skinned individuals. Because they could gain some acceptance from an established white elite, socially and economically accomplished blacks or mulattos have had little basis for political solidarity with poorer members of society with a similar skin color.

Conclusion

While few would dispute the importance of constitutions and periods of constitution-writing in the development of national histories, some scholars have identified other periods as being of crucial importance or as constituting a critical juncture in the respective histories of Brazil and South Africa. For example, in their studies of labor incorporation, Collier and

[97] Skidmore 1995: 39.
[98] Hasenbalg 1977; Fontaine 1985.
[99] Degler 1971.
[100] Marx 1998: 255.
[101] See also Andrews 1992.

Conclusion

Collier (1991) identify the period 1930–45 for Brazil, and Yudelman (1983) identifies the period 1902–39 for South Africa, as decisive periods for institutionalizing systems of labor relations. In the political community model, these patterns of labor incorporation play an intermediate role between definitions of NPC and the development of national taxation systems. I maintain that for the purposes of understanding the politics of taxation in these two countries during the 20th century, a focus on the challenges of organized labor, and the subsequent incorporation of this group, would not, on its own, explain such wide differences in the politics of taxation.

Rather, patterns of political cooperation and conflict in 20th-century Brazil and South Africa can be largely understood from the perspective of a single, well-defined period during which critical decisions about how to "invent" the respective nations were made. Through deliberate constitutional and other policy provisions around the turn of the century, racial identities were made politically important in South Africa and physical space, or regions, were made politically important in Brazil. If citizenship had *not* been defined in racial terms in South Africa, or if Brazil had *not* opted for a federal constitution, it is highly unlikely that these political patterns would have emerged in the ways that they did, suggesting the critical importance of these initial decisions. Despite a series of reactions and counter-reactions to these constitutional choices, the salience of those respective identities persists until this day. Path-dependent processes were set in motion, creating radically different institutional foundations for political life in the two countries. A key implication of this difference was much higher levels of both inter- and intra-class cohesion in South Africa than in Brazil. The following chapters turn to an investigation of the impact of these different definitions of NPC, and the associated class relations on the development of the modern tax state.

4

The Rise of the Modern Tax State in Brazil and South Africa

In the previous chapter, I showed that despite similar sets of political cleavages in Brazil and South Africa, very different definitions of National Political Community (NPC) were specified in key constitutions written around the turn of the 20th century. Chapter 2 revealed that the modern tax structures of these two countries are extremely different, particularly when seen in light of other countries around the world. This chapter develops causal links between these seemingly unrelated outcomes, while assessing the plausibility of a host of rival explanations.[1] I attempt to make sense of divergent patterns of tax state development through a comparative historical analysis that is analytically guided by the political community model.

Even when considering only these two countries, the use of within-country comparisons, comparisons of the two countries at single moments in time, and comparisons of trajectories of development all provide significant analytic leverage. In detailing sequences of events, and the words and deeds of various actors in the respective countries, it is possible to provide a window onto causal processes and to highlight the manner in which early divergences established the basis for enduring patterns of state development.

The analysis proceeds through a series of deliberate steps.[2] It begins by considering the respective colonial legacies of taxation, demonstrating that these inheritances cannot account for important differences in the trajectories of state development. This finding helps to establish that the critical junctures identified in the previous chapter indeed marked a break from the

---

[1] Much of the analysis presented in this chapter draws from Lieberman 2001b.

[2] For a more general description of these analytical strategies, see Lieberman 2001a; and Collier and Collier 1991.

past for the outcome under investigation. Second, it describes the context of state development, including the similar patterns of economic development and sets of international pressures that faced the two countries during the 20th century. Although these influences provide important contextual background for the expansion of the size and scope of the respective states, the *similarity* of the timing and patterns of these influences reveals that such factors cannot account for the variations in taxation outcomes. Third, the chapter describes these patterns of taxation, identifying both similarities and differences in collections. Fourth, the chapter examines three key policy episodes during which similar demands for new taxes were made by the state executives in the respective countries. Those analyses reveal how definitions of NPC were associated with very different responses from societal actors, and different outcomes in terms of tax policy and administration. Finally, the chapter briefly describes how the Brazilian and South African states weathered the challenges of financing state expenditures during periods of significant political and economic crisis during the 1970s and 1980s, highlighting the important legacy of the tax state in meeting new expenditure demands, and political crises more generally.

Legacies of Pre-Modern Taxation

In order to assess the influence of the critical juncture described in the previous chapter, it is necessary to gain some understanding of the nature of the respective tax states during prior periods. Such analysis allows us to evaluate whether alternative factors, such as legacies of colonial tax policy and administration or longstanding cultural patterns, may have been important influences on the trajectory of tax state development in the 20th century. If patterns of taxation prior to the hypothesized critical juncture were found to be similar to patterns of taxation following the critical juncture, we would have grounds to be skeptical that the "critical juncture" had any influence at all.

Nevertheless, comparative historical analysis reveals that there is an unambiguous disjuncture in the patterns of taxation on either side of the turn of the 20th century, when foundational constitutions were written in the two countries. Both Brazil and the four political entities that would later become the Union of South Africa were essentially skeletal tax states in the late 19th century (see Table 4.1). Moreover, the observed patterns of cross-national difference that characterize much of the 20th century were not present in the 19th century – and if anything, prior patterns of state

Table 4.1 *Late 19th-century tax states in Brazil and Southern Africa*

	Brazil	Southern Africa
Policy	Multiple, mostly failed attempts to enact general income tax	Multiple, mostly failed attempts to enact general income tax in various colonies
	High reliance on trade duties, user fees, excise taxes	High reliance on trade duties, user fees, excise taxes
Administration	Relatively greater development than South Africa	Nascent, uncoordinated tax administrations
		No central state
	Low–medium levels of compliance	Low levels of compliance
	Various tax protests, revolts	Various tax protests, revolts
Tax state	SKELETAL	SKELETAL

development would have suggested very different outcomes than the patterns described above.

Colonial Tax Administration

State authority was much more centralized and consolidated in Brazil than in Southern Africa, where a central state did not even exist prior to the 20th century, and there was no coordinated bureaucracy to speak of prior to the formation of the Union. During the political negotiations to create the Union of South Africa, the government finances of the Cape Colony, Natal, the Orange River Colony, and the Transvaal remained basically autonomous. Just as the idea of a central state was taking root, all public finances were still effectively managed at a subnational level. Early forms of joint financial administration following the 1902 Treaty of Vereeniging included the uniting of the Transvaal and Orange River Railways into the Central South African Railways and the establishment of a South African Customs Union of all British colonies south of the Zambesi River.[3] Yet, with separate accounts, this arrangement had a largely divisive effect and hardly constituted a coordinated public economy. Between 1902 and 1910, the combination of railway receipts and customs duties comprised over

[3] Thompson 1960: 13.

70 percent of total revenues in the four colonies. Even during these years of transition, the establishment of a common financial framework was not foreseeable. Between 1902 and 1908, the dire financial situation of the coastal colonies coupled with the loss of railway revenues due to the diversion of Transvaal trade to the Mozambican port of Lourenço Marquez provoked significant tension between the colonies.[4] The seeds of intergovernmental fiscal competition could surely have taken root during this period, particularly when one considers the increasingly stern stance of Natal with respect to the customs union and its desire for a tariff increase on Mozambique.[5] Based on economic considerations alone, the potential for division was strong, particularly as the coastal colonies became dependent on the Transvaal, while the Transvaal could be independent using the port at Delagoa Bay in Mozambique.[6]

Although the Brazilian central state under the empire was not the highly interventionist state that would develop in the modern era, at the very least, government authority was much more consolidated by the late 19th century when compared to South Africa. Since 1500, colonial Brazil faced various challenges to centralized authority, but in 1850, the emperor crushed the last serious regionalist threat to the centralized monarchy. This provided almost forty years to develop various administrative mechanisms of a centralized tax state prior to the negotiations for the Republican constitution.[7] The administration of taxation had evolved according to needs and possibilities over the prior four centuries, as monarchies experimented with tax farming, decentralized collections, and finally, more centralized forms of administration.[8] In the late 18th century, the Pombal government initiated important steps toward uniform control of Brazil, including incorporating the state of Maranhão in 1772.[9] Intent on centralization and standardization, Pombal also conducted an inquiry into the financial systems, and decided to devise a new organization and system of accounting staffed by bookkeepers and accountants familiar with advanced practices (such as the double-entry system). Two comptrollers-general from Portugal would become responsible for Brazil, and new treasury boards (*juntas da fazenda*) were formed in each

---

[4] Thompson 1960: 54.
[5] Thompson 1960: 58.
[6] Wilson and Thompson 1969: 344.
[7] Skidmore 1999: 47.
[8] Alden 1968.
[9] Burns 1993: 90.

captaincy-general of Brazil.[10] In 1808, the arriving royal family in Brazil took over the more centralized Royal Treasury, originally created in 1770, paving the way for the Brazilian bureaucracy under a newly independent monarchy. In 1831, the independent Brazilian monarch created a Tribunal of the National Treasury and under this body emerged the Director General of Public Income, a forerunner to the modern tax bureaucracy.[11] As of 1850, all treasury postings were subject to competitive examinations.[12] By 1886, 76 percent of all government revenue was collected by the central state.[13] In other words, the Brazilian state hardly had to start from scratch to develop a tax administration for the new Republican government.

Early Tax Structures

Neither in Brazil nor in Southern Africa were tax collectors particularly successful in extracting direct taxes on income prior to the 20th century. Instead, the various colonies and nascent states of Southern Africa and the Brazilian emperor had relied heavily on trade duties, various indirect taxes, and user fees to fund government expenditures. In both countries, several attempts to levy broad-based income and other consumption taxes had been rebuked in the face of societal resistance.

In Brazil, although some direct taxes had been collected prior to the 20th century, these were largely resisted both during the rule of the Portuguese crown and after independence in 1822. As early as 1641, the Portuguese crown attempted to levy some direct taxes – the *décima secular direta* – but this generated very little revenue.[14] Various attempts to collect tax on gold, including the imposition of a "royal fifth" on production, were resisted, and led to both dodging and a series of minor revolts.[15] Other attempts at direct taxation brought about regionally based uprisings including a revolt in Pernambuco in 1817.

While it is easy to understand resistance to the tax efforts of a foreign ruler, the record of collections in independent Brazil was not radically

[10] Alden 1968: 280.
[11] *Ministério da Fazenda* Website, www.fazenda.gov.br
[12] Lambert 1969: 167–88, 170.
[13] Skidmore 1999: 105.
[14] Canto 1949: 75.
[15] The *Inconfidência Mineira* of 1789 is remembered today as an important resistance movement against the imperial tax on gold, which helped form future ideas about Brazilian nationalism.

different. The new Brazilian emperor, Dom Pedro I, wanting to win the sympathies of a potentially critical Brazilian economic elite, actually abolished some taxes, such as import duties on salt, and lowered taxes on exports. The implications of such largesse were soon felt in the balancing of the treasury accounts: Every year between 1823 and 1831, the government ran a deficit, which ranged from 10 percent to more than 50 percent of total expenditures. Attempts to address these shortfalls through direct taxation met with mixed success. Beginning in the 1840s, taxation on the salaries of public servants were continually enacted and repealed.[16] The empire's Council of State rejected a proposal to levy an income tax in 1822, and again in 1843, despite a constitution that proclaimed, "no one shall be exempt from contributing to the expenses of the state in proportion to his assets." Finally, in 1867, despite divisions within the Council of State about the appropriateness of the tax, a short-lived set of direct taxes including a 1.5 percent tax on annual benefits distributed by corporations, a mildly progressive personal tax, and a tax on civil servant earnings were enacted.[17] Yet both were abolished prior to the signing of the 1891 constitution.

Acceptance of a general income tax was no more forthcoming in the pre-Union colonies of Southern Africa. Prior to Union, only two direct taxes were of any consequence to the revenue account. First, beginning in 1871, the government began generating revenues indirectly from the gold mines in the form of leases and other arrangements, but it was not until 1898 when the *Zuid Afrikaanse Republiek* – later to become the Transvaal Province – would levy a direct tax on gold mining profits, at a rate of 5 percent on net profits. Gold revenues subsequently funded virtually all the expenses of the Boer war effort to the tune of approximately £100,000 per month,[18] and the tax was taken over by the new British administration in 1902 at a rate of 10 percent on net profits.[19] Particularly in the early years of the Union, the role of gold as a source of capital and the basis for government revenue proved to be critical, but as will be discussed later, the collection of these taxes does *not* explain the significant collections of nonmineral taxes later in the century. Beyond gold, general income taxes were enacted and temporarily implemented in the provincial governments of the Cape Colony starting in 1904 and in Natal starting in 1908. These generated almost no revenue

---

[16] Ministério da Fazenda: 1982.
[17] Penna 1992: 21.
[18] Pakenham 1988: 298.
[19] Van Blerck 1992: C-2.

and were abolished with the start of the Union. In other words, the Union of South Africa would inherit almost no pre-existing capacity to collect direct taxes on nonmining income when it was formally born in 1910.

Even the collection of other forms of domestic taxation proved difficult in Southern Africa. After the Cape Colony was granted "representative" government in 1850, budgetary expenditures rose from £321K to £745K between 1854 and 1861 and nontax revenues, including loans, monies from the Imperial treasury, and sale of crown lands, were necessary to finance this ballooning bill. Also, the government relied on indirect forms of revenue, particularly on customs duties, as stamp and transfer duties generated almost no revenue. The result was a doubling of the public debt within two decades. Despite clear needs for new revenues, a host of tax proposals were continuously rejected: For example, wool producers fiercely opposed a wool tax which was debated between 1862 and 1869, and Governor-General Sir Philip Wodehouse's proposed income tax of 1.25 percent was rejected in 1869.[20]

The record of taxation elsewhere in Southern Africa was no better. For example, both Africans and white settlers resisted the efforts of various governments to collect taxation in Natal, which was intended to be a self-supporting colony.[21] A flat £1 poll tax was imposed in 1905 on most men, 60 percent of which was paid by Africans. Citing unequal treatment, Africans in Umgeni defied attempts to collect the tax on February 7, 1906, and this sparked a harsh military response and the deaths of over 3,000 Africans.[22] Similarly, when the British annexed the Transvaal under Lord Shepstone after a low-scale civil war broke out among divided Afrikaners, it was unable to collect taxes from the population. The refusal of a Transvaal farmer to pay taxes provided momentum for a serious armed uprising, and this brief war, which ended in 1881, led to the re-constitution of an autonomous Afrikaner Republic.[23]

Many Brazilians today point out that resistance to taxation is a cultural tradition that goes back to colonial times, but the comparative record suggests that such resistance was also very much present in Southern Africa. The implication for both cases is that the colonial and imperial legacies provided only minimal foundations for building the modern tax states,

[20] Wilson and Thompson 1969: 329–30.
[21] Thompson 1990: 95.
[22] Thompson 1960: 42–3.
[23] Thompson 1990: 134–5.

and if anything, the ground was much more solid in Brazil than in South Africa.

The Context of 20th-Century State-Building

Levels and patterns of economic development, and international influences such as wars and policy ideas, clearly are important determinants of the qualities of the tax state. In a comparative analysis of Brazil and South Africa, however, these factors serve as analytic controls because both the process of economic development and the countries' respective roles in the international political economy have been largely similar for most of the 20th century. In both cases, longer-term processes and more acute "shocks" associated with the process of modernization and with changes in the international system all provided the impetus for a series of government demands for new taxes.

Industrialization Strategies and Patterns of Growth

The low level of development of the Brazilian and South African tax states at the end of the 19th century can easily be explained by the structure of their respective economies: Up until that period, both had been largely rural, nonindustrialized economies, with few easily taxable bases, and without great needs for centrally provided public goods. The discovery of mineral wealth in South Africa and the development of a profitable coffee industry in Brazil at the end of the 19th century helped initiate rapid industrial development in the respective countries. Following Wagner's Law (1883), one would predict that growth in the size of government – both expenditure and revenue – should outpace national income, leading to an overall increase in taxation as share of GDP. Indeed, this relationship held for both countries during the course of the 20th century.

Both Brazil and South Africa implemented prototype examples of protected industrialization strategies – more commonly known as following patterns of import substitution industrialization (ISI).[24] Secondary "infant" industries were established with the protection of high tariffs, particularly beginning in the 1920s and 1930s. In this sense, the South African economy developed with a strategy that was much more like that followed in

[24] Cardoso and Faletto 1979: 1–2.

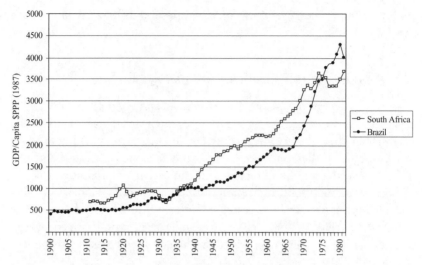

Figure 4.1   Real GDP/capita in Brazil and South Africa, Chain Index 1911–1990. Prior to 1950, extrapolated using real economic and population growth rates. *Sources:* Heston and Summers 2000; Central Statistical Service 1995; IBGE 1990.

the Brazilian and other Latin American economies than in the East Asian countries which largely followed export-led strategies.[25] Probably as a result of such similar strategies, the long-term patterns of economic growth and development were also remarkably similar. As shown in Figure 4.1, the two countries followed very similar paths of economic development as measured by levels of real per capita income over the course of the century. Other modernization indicators such as rates of urbanization and industrialization also developed along very similar lines in the two countries. Together, such factors help to explain increasing needs for public goods as well as expanded and increasingly concentrated tax bases.

International Factors

International factors also clearly shaped the context of state development. Even in the early 20th century, the emergent national states of South Africa and Brazil were highly connected to the polities and economies of Europe

---

[25] See, for example, Bulmer-Thomas 1994; and various contributions in Wyman and Gereffi 1990. For the South African case, see Jones and Muller 1992; and Nattrass and Ardington 1990.

and the United States. Not just through trade and investment, but through the transmission of policy ideas, participation in international organizations, and participation in global conflict, foreign actors influenced the politics and economic development of both countries. The tumultuous early decades of the 20th century, during which the relationship between states, markets, and societies was radically reconfigured around the globe, were also critically important for countries on the "semi-periphery."[26] War and welfare expenses created needs for new taxes, and periodic shocks in world demand and the trade cycle made it necessary for those taxes to be collected at home.

More than anything, it was war that proved decisive for state development. The needs implied by monumental military expenditure within increasingly modern and industrialized economies provided the basis for developing new capacities to tax. As Peters points out for the countries of Western Europe, the first three decades of the 20th century produced "rapid and momentous developments in taxation."[27] Income taxation became the revenue option of choice for most of the warring states, and led to an eightfold increase in the size of the United Kingdom's budget between 1914 and 1916. The Second World War provided an even greater impetus for greatly increased taxation, ushering in rates as high as 94 percent on personal income in the United States.[28] Although South Africa and Brazil were both situated outside the immediate theater of military conflict, the war was critically important for state expansion. European-descended groups in both countries expressed strong feelings about World War II, and both economies were deeply tied to the international economy, particularly through important trade and investment relationships with England. In both countries, national leaders committed troops and resources to the allied forces, even as groups within society were divided over the war. Brazil was the only Latin American power to sustain more than 1,000 battle deaths in the war; while South Africa was the only African power apart from Ethiopia with this distinction.[29] Following both wars, peace gave birth to new international organizations such as the League of Nations and eventually, the United Nations, which would provide a place for the demonstration

---

[26] For the most important statement of the crafting of national markets and states during this period, see Polanyi 1944. Also see Tilly 1992.

[27] Peters 1991: 231.

[28] Steinmo 1993: 102.

[29] Tilly 1992: 198.

of "stateness" and a reference group of state powers that might be emulated. This state system, of which Brazil and South Africa were members (as two of the original fifty-one signatories of the UN Charter in 1945), provided an epistemic community of leaders and bureaucrats to exchange ideas about a range of policy matters, including the crucial task of taxation. In subsequent decades, the United Nations and the Bretton Woods organizations – the World Bank and the International Monetary Fund – would play active roles in exchanging information and promoting common accounting standards for national accounts, including taxation.

In between the wars, the social dislocations generated by the market crash of 1929 suggested a rethinking of the relationship between states, markets, and societies. Keynesian economic theories about economic management implied a greater role for the state and provided a theoretical basis for increased levels of progressive taxation.[30] The need for a social safety net was articulated most prominently by increasingly strong labor-based parties around the globe, and in many cases variants of America's New Deal were established to dampen the potentially dislocating effects of modern capitalism. These new initiatives did not go unnoticed by political entrepreneurs in both Brazil and South Africa, who looked North for models of policy and practice. In the post-War era, both countries endeavored massive programs of social and economic development.

International trends away from trade taxes, stemming from changes in the nature of trade, as well as new policy ideas, forced international shifts toward more domestic tax bases. This pattern also held for Brazil and South Africa. As shown in Figure 4.2, trade revenues – once the most important source of income for governments in Brazil and Southern Africa – had been in steady decline in both countries since early in the century, and after 1960, neither country would ever collect more than 2 percent of GDP from such revenues.

Finally, large-scale pressures stemming from the politics of the Cold War were also at the root of tax state development in both countries. Communist parties had been formed in both countries early in the century (and later banned), and as U.S.–Soviet relations became increasingly tense, particularly in the 1960s, East–West standoffs became more frequent in these Third World centers. In both countries, repressive regimes would carry out violent campaigns to weed out Communist infiltrators, in order to secure greater internal security. Wealthy private interests in

[30] Peters 1991: 229–39; and Steinmo 1993.

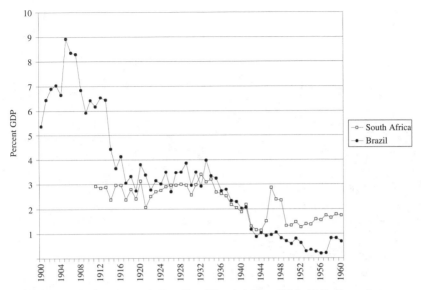

Figure 4.2   Trade revenues in Brazil and South Africa, 1900–1960. Central government only. *Sources:* Mitchell 1993; Villela and Suzigan 1977; Ludwig 1985; Bureau of Census and Statistics South Africa 1960.

both countries supported the respective governments in their efforts to stamp out threats to property rights and capitalist development. Expanded needs for security required more revenues, particularly in the form of tax payments.

Patterns of Taxation and State Development (1900–1975)

In the face of such economic change and international pressures, during the first three-quarters of the 20th century, both the size and scope of the central state were radically transformed in Brazil and in South Africa. From the chief executive down to the local field office, the state broadened its influence within society, developing additional capacities in the areas of national defense, policing, social policy, health care, and industrial development. The enormous expense of such tasks created increasing needs for revenue, and state executives demanded an array of new taxes. As a result, the Brazilian and South African tax states were *both* radically transformed during this period. The respective state executives and bureaucracies attempted to extend the reach of the state within the economy and society, gathering information, and most importantly, collecting revenues. State leaders

117

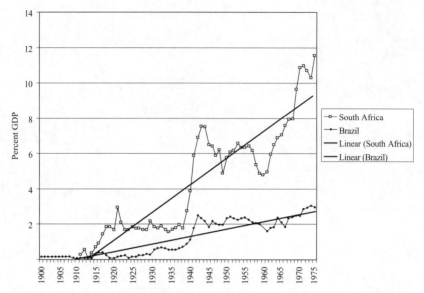

Figure 4.3 Income and property tax collection in Brazil and South Africa, 1900–1975. Does not include mining taxes; central government tax collections only. *Sources:* Commissioner for Inland Revenue, various; Bureau of Census and Statistics South Africa 1960; Wainer 1987; Department of Finance South Africa *Budget Review*, various; Mitchell 1993; Villela and Suzigan 1977; Ludwig 1985; IMF, various.

engaged upper groups in those societies decade after decade in an ongoing effort to secure tax revenue through new policies and administrative practices.

In both countries, collection of direct taxes on income and property rose from virtually nil at the beginning of the century to substantial shares of much larger economies by century's end. Figure 4.3 plots the central state's collection of income and property taxes in the two countries – from 1900 to 1975 in Brazil, and from 1911 to 1975 in South Africa, and reveals important patterns of similarity and difference in the timing and quality of state development.[31] In particular, collections of this source of revenue

---

[31] The South African collections do not include mining taxes which have been taxed at different rates. Because virtually all gold is exported, this revenue could be considered more akin to taxation on trade. At the very least, it is much easier to tax than other forms of income. By removing this source of revenue from the South African case, we can be more confident that income tax collections reflect the types of state-society relations described in

rose dramatically between approximately 1939 and 1945, and then was followed by slight declines in collections until the mid-1960s. After this period, collections rose fairly steadily in both countries until the mid-1970s. It is worth noting that in both cases, income tax revenue formed the overwhelming majority of all direct tax revenues collected. Only in one year did property taxes (specifically transfer and estate duties) amount to more than 1 percent of GDP in South Africa (1946–7), and such taxes have not been collected by the central state in Brazil. The similar patterns and timing of economic development and similar sets of international pressures described above help to account for important similarities in trends in tax collection. Increases in direct taxation during the 1914–17 period, the 1939–45 period, and following the 1960s were undoubtedly linked to the pressures and policy models stemming from various global conflicts. In broad structural terms, the "needs" implied by these developments were similar across the two countries, and help to account for aspects of the timing of peaks and valleys in collections of the various taxes.

Yet, comparative analysis of tax collections in the 20th century highlights important differences in the trajectory of tax state development across the two countries. The most prominent contrast in the two-country, over-time comparison is that the rate of increase in total collections of income and property taxes was more than three times greater in South Africa than in Brazil. In 1914, South African collections grew quickly to almost 2 percent of GDP, while in Brazil they remained at a fraction of 1 percent until the 1940s. During both subsequent periods of increased collections, the gains achieved in the South African case were much greater than those in Brazil. These divergent trends were fairly well established by the first half of the century, as demonstrated by a visual inspection comparing the best fitting trend lines to the actual collections data in the two time series. The slope of the South African trend is approximately three times steeper than in the case of Brazil.

An analysis of collections of other forms of taxation across the two countries provides additional insights into the respective patterns of state development, and helps to demonstrate the much greater reliance of the Brazilian federal government on more hidden forms of revenue when compared with South Africa. In particular, contemporary tax structures vary widely in

Chapter 2. If these revenues were included in measures of income taxation, cross-national differences in levels of collections would be even greater because Brazil has no significant collections of taxes on mines.

119

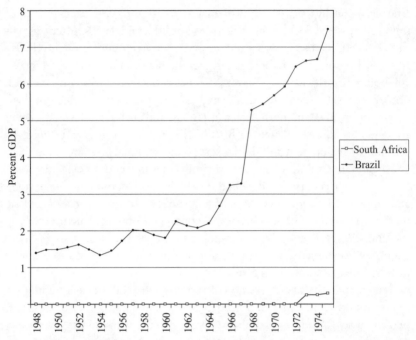

Figure 4.4 Social security and "hand-to-mouth" taxes in Brazil and South Africa, 1900–1975. Central government tax collections only. *Sources:* IBGE 1990; South African Reserve Bank 1994.

terms of their reliance on social security and "hand-to-mouth" (earmarked transfers) taxes. As shown in Figure 4.4, the cross-national contrasts that emerged in the post-War period are particularly stark: In Brazil, particularly after the mid-1960s, collections of this source of revenue increased sharply, and grew to almost 8 percent of GDP by 1975, whereas in South Africa, such revenues have never amounted to even 1 percent of GDP.

It is worth noting that an important and unique feature of the South African economy has been its mining sector. To adjust for this, the tax revenue statistics I present do *not* include mining revenues because these tend to be easier to collect, and would inflate the size of the South African collections in a way that might over-estimate the South African state's authority to collect from upper groups. Nonetheless, the question of mining revenues warrants some further exploration because of a common misperception – that South Africa's exceptional tax collections can be explained by its access to mining revenues.

Table 4.2 *Generalized Least Squares (GLS) estimate for regression of annual tax collections in South Africa, 1912–1990. Dependent Variable: Income and Property Tax Collections*[†]*/GDP*

	Unstandardized coefficient	Standard error
GDP/capita (Thousands $PPP, constant)	3.36**	0.17
WW2	0.96*	0.47
Mining revenues (Percent GDP)	−0.37**	0.11
Adjusted R-squared	.85	
SEE	.63	
N	79	
Durbin-Watson	1.60	
Rho	.80	.07

Note: constant suppressed
[†] Exclusive of mining revenues
** $p < .001$; * $p < .05$; two-tailed tests

In order to evaluate the impact of mining taxes, I carried out a time-series regression analysis of the determinants of income and property tax revenue in South Africa during the period 1912–1990 (see Table 4.2).[32] When controlling for the positive effects of level of economic development as measured by GDP per capita, and a dummy variable for the years during which South Africa participated in the Second World War, we can see that mining actually had a *negative* influence on the collection of other forms of direct taxation. The negative and statistically significant parameter estimate for mining revenues implies that the state eased off on income tax collections during years in which mining revenues surged – a finding that resonates with statements made by finance ministers during annual budget speeches analyzed during the first half of the 20th century. The prevalence of a lucrative mineral source has been the source of otherwise quite *weak* tax states (rentier states) in other parts of the world,[33] implying that the South African outcome is particularly remarkable in light of this important sector, which might have crowded out the political imperatives to build an extractive tax state with respect to other sectors of the economy.

---

[32] Following Kiser and Linton: 2001, fn15, I estimated this model using the Prais-Winsten method of the Generalized Least Squares (GLS) model using Stata 9.0.

[33] For examples of how mineral wealth can lead to the development of very weak tax capacities, and weak states more generally, see Young and Turner 1985; and Chaudhry 1997.

Three Episodes of Politics and Taxation

Having established the central differences in the patterns of 20th-century tax collection, and having demonstrated the inability of several alternative explanations to account for such differences, it becomes possible to explore the central hypothesis of this book: that definitions of National Political Community (NPC) affected the politics and ultimately the outcomes of tax collection. In order to make this causal link, this section looks more closely at the political contests associated with national government initiatives to collect taxes and provides proximate and contextually relevant historical evidence.

The development of tax policy, and particularly the income tax in Brazil and South Africa, involved a punctuated bargaining process between the state executive and upper-income groups. Although national executives made broadly similar demands for tax payment in response to similar exogenous pressures, upper-group responses to those demands were quite different across the two countries, both in terms of support for policies during the policy-making process and in terms of levels of quasi-voluntary compliance during the collections process. The behavior of upper groups was strongly influenced by their relations to one another – that is, by the extent to which they believed they shared collective interests and had good reason to believe others would also pay the tax burden; and by their relations to lower groups – that is, by the extent to which lower groups could pressure them to make payment using moral suasion and/or disruptive collective action such as strike activity.

Upper-group responses profoundly influenced the quality of tax policy, tax administration, and ultimately, tax collections. In Brazil, where class relations have been fragmented and polarized, upper groups, pitted against one another in defense of regionally narrow interests, have tended to challenge the government's demands during the policy-making process and during the process of collection. As a result, an adversarial tax state developed, in which the bureaucracy has not been able to uniformly collect taxes from individuals and firms who engaged in deliberate avoidance and evasion schemes and noncooperation in the formulation of policy.

By contrast, in South Africa, where a unitary and racially exclusionary definition of NPC produced more coherent class relations within the white polity, analogous upper groups have largely accepted the state's demand for progressive taxes. A cooperative tax state emerged, in which the tasks of bureaucrats and policy makers were largely facilitated by the free exchange of information and the minimization of challenges to the state's claim to authority. The minister of finance, the head of the revenue bureaucracy, and the managers of various regional and functional offices were freed to focus on efficiency strategies because a critical level of compliance was attained.

As is usually the case, individual actors are generally unaware of the institutional environment in which they operate because rules of the game become so well accepted that they appear as the natural order. As a result, we would not expect to find individuals proclaiming their willingness to comply with the state's demands for tax payment based on definitions of NPC. Rather, through comparative-historical analysis, we can observe how institutional differences created different political environments, leading to the development of different types of tax states. Three historical episodes reveal that even in the wake of similar structural conditions, different political logics, and patterns of engagement between state and society resulted in very different taxation outcomes. During each period, similar exogenous international and economic pressures generated revenue "needs" in both countries, leading the executive to make demands or initiatives for new taxes or major tax reforms. During the first decades of the 20th century, particularly around the First World War, executives acted to adopt a general income tax; during the Second World War, they were prompted to expand and to consolidate the tax in order to generate additional revenues; and during the 1960s, rapid industrialization and the politics of the Cold War inspired modernizing reforms of the respective tax systems. Even in the wake of these changing circumstances, the resilient definitions of NPC were re-interpreted and adapted to the new context, reproducing national patterns of class relations and distinctive responses to state demands. As a result, during each of these three episodes, the development of the tax state unfolded in increasingly distinctive ways, producing wide divergences in the quality of the central state's authority by the 1970s.

The Enactment of a General Income Tax

Both in Brazil and in South Africa, the first executives of the national governments in power following the writing of the constitutions of 1891 and 1909 sought to establish a firm footing for financing public expenditures by proposing the enactment of a general income tax. Yet, as summarized

Table 4.3 *Paths to the general income tax in Brazil and South Africa, 1888–1930*

	Brazil	South Africa
Policy		
Timing	First proposed in 1889 Not enacted until 1922	Proposed in 1914 Enacted in 1914
Loopholes/ exemptions	Complex legislation with multiple schedules and differences	Relatively uniform legislation with single progressive rate structure
Administration	Not implemented until four years after enactment (1926) Unevenly applied Significant resistance from upper groups	Implemented immediately after enactment (1914) More evenly applied High levels of cooperation from taxpayers
Collections of income and property tax (% GDP)*		
1910	0.1	0.0
1915	0.4	0.8
1920	0.1	1.7
1925	0.2	1.9
1930	0.3	2.2

* Does not include mining revenues.

in Table 4.3, similar proposals for a general income tax were met with very different policy, administration, and collections outcomes. The sluggishness of the Brazilian response to state demands reflected a much greater reluctance to pay than in the case of South Africa. Starting from the deliberations around the new federal constitution (1889), the Brazilian finance minister proposed a general tax, but found himself rebuffed in his attempts for more than three decades in the face of a regionally divided economic elite. By contrast, in South Africa, where high-income earners and business owners rallied around the notion of common cause, the tax was enacted and effectively implemented within a year after being proposed.

As in many countries around the world, the First World War prompted demands for this tax, and state executives invoked both mobilization needs as well as economic policy needs for the new tax. In defining themselves in racially exclusionary terms, white South Africans – particularly upper-income English-speakers – viewed themselves as constituting a virtually European country, with a sense of common, collective obligation, and the war efforts were interpreted as a collective responsibility.[34] When the state executive posed the demand of taxes to upper groups in this context, he met virtually no resistance. By contrast, in Brazil, a very different approach to race and regional political concerns provided little emotive or strategic inspiration for sacrifice. Though many Brazilians loosely identified themselves as Europeans in terms of socioeconomic status, the constitutional articulation of political community in that country provided little opportunity for white immigrants to express a collective sympathy for the war effort *as Europeans*. Upper groups resisted the tax, and when it was passed, business groups secured loopholes and various exemptions within further political battles over the equitable application of the tax. The result was that in South Africa, the passage of the income tax was smooth and swift, and was implemented with significant cooperation from taxpayers, whereas in Brazil, it was a highly contested and protracted struggle, which produced a more complex piece of legislation that was unevenly applied within society. By 1930, South Africa would collect approximately seven times more than Brazil in income and property taxes when measured as share of GDP.

South Africa. Although the income tax act of 1914 has been modified in some form almost every year since its passage, that single tax came to define the tax system for the remainder of the century. Its initial enactment and implementation continues to influence the structure of the contemporary tax system. The path to passage and acceptance was largely uncontested and paved the way for the rapid development of the nascent bureaucracy. The emerging patterns of inter- and intra-class cohesion within the white polity helped to overcome possible political conflict and inclinations toward free riderism.

The composition of the first government of the Union of South Africa fully represented the definition of the NPC as a racially exclusionary union: It was all-white, ethnically balanced between Englishmen and Afrikaners, and controlled from the center – by former military generals – rather than from the provinces. The South African Party of Louis Botha won the 1910 general election largely supported by an alliance of English-speaking commercial and mining interests and the wealthier core of Afrikaner farmers. In government, the party promoted nation-building as an all-white endeavor

---

[34] This is my interpretive assessment from reading scores of newspaper articles, and various business publications from the period.

and implemented various policies to "protect" whites from African labor.[35] The Minister of Finance, whose party carried the legitimating wave of optimism upon which the Union was formed, and 67 of the 121 seats in the National Assembly, did not meet significant political opposition when proposing new tax policies.

When major conflict erupted in Europe, and South Africa prepared to enter that war, the government in 1914 made critical new demands for taxation. The challenges of growing expenditures became evident, particularly as a provision to discontinue using the railways as a source of government finance became effective with the 1913 budget.[36] Although the Minister of Finance explained in his 1914 speech that the treasury was not in a crisis position, he pointed to the longer term financial health of the state as the basis for demanding income tax payments. Minister H. C. Hull explained in his April 24, 1914 speech:

The Government proposes to do the right and wise things, and to settle the economic policy of this country on a sound footing without delay, and I think the best and fairest thing to do would be to go in for an income tax. . . . No doubt these proposals will not be popular in every part of the country, because taxation proposals are never popular, and the form of taxation which is suggested will be very deeply scrutinised in certain quarters . . . but, there is no doubt we have come to a point when we must deal with the financial policy wholly and comprehensively, in this country, and I think the proper course is to see the thing through now – to start a taxing machine which will make revenue and expenditure balance, and to lay down a system which will mean a sound policy for the future of the country.[37]

Although the presentation of the income tax proposal did not go entirely unchallenged in parliamentary debates, no sustained appeal was made against the tax. Most arguments about the new tax base concerned more marginal issues about the level at which individuals should be exempted from the tax rather than questioning the very proposition of a progressive, direct tax. The idea that wealthier members of society should pay more was simultaneously consistent with the larger white nation-building strategy and with prevailing international norms. Extensions of the original income tax would come only a few years later, in 1916, in the form of an even more progressive supertax on top incomes.

---

[35] Nattrass and Ardington 1990: 7–8; Davenport 1991: 231–6.
[36] The South Africa Act (1909) specified that interest due on the Railway account would be used to finance general government expenditures only for four years.
[37] Budget Speech, April 24, 1914, as quoted in Surtees 1985: 64.

The economy was already sufficiently diversified that sectoral interests could have prevailed as the basis for politics, and vast differences in the tax bases of the four provinces could have been articulated as the basis for distributive conflict,[38] but these potential cleavages were not mobilized in political contests over taxation to any significant degree. Instead, the question of race often helped to unify discussions veering toward more narrowly defined group interests.[39] Parliamentary debates during these years were sometimes characterized by bitter and acrimonious conflicts over policies and priorities, but these were often resolved with the idiom of common racial interests, just as once-bloody conflicts between Afrikaners and those of British descent had been greatly softened during the formation of the Union. For example, the question of Native Policy was a recurring theme of business and political leaders within the chambers of Parliament and the congresses of organized business. When it came to financial matters, members continuously weighed the potential value of a particular program or initiative with respect to the challenge posed by nonwhites. For example, a 1917 debate over the extent to which revenues ought to be going to the war effort or communications infrastructure in rural towns populated by whites ended with consensus around the need to separate "Coloureds" on the trains.

Also important for understanding the enactment of the income tax was the push from white lower groups in South Africa. Following the 1913 strike on the Rand, in which white workers challenged the possibility of threats from black competition on the labor market, upper groups calculated the strategic advantages of progressive taxation, and the state recognized the need to create policies that would be seen as benefiting this group. In announcing the income tax, the Minister of Finance argued against the alternatives, explaining, "indirect taxation ... bears more heavily on the poor man than on the rich."[40] While tensions between organized labor and

---

[38] In 1920, the taxable incomes of the Cape and Transvaal Provinces were £26.9MM and £35.1MM, respectively, while in Natal, total taxable income amounted to just £9.0MM and in the Orange Free state, £6.0MM. Commissioner of Inland Revenue South Africa 1922.

[39] I did not find any specific examples of explicit racial rhetoric within specific debates about taxation. My argument, however, does not imply that individual-level behavior about taxation was specifically guided by a conscious awareness of the definition of NPC. Rather, the argument is that class cohesion more generally was influenced by race policy.

[40] Budget Speech. Union of South Africa. *House of Assembly Debates*, April 24, 1914: 1936.

employers were clearly strong during this period, particularly as they debated over issues such as job reservations for whites – which would prove costly for employers – the availability of the race issue helped to maintain unity among organized white workers and important bargaining power in negotiations with the state and employer organizations.

Posed as a necessary ingredient to the future success of the white nation within the British empire, the income tax was accepted by the upper groups who would pay. Indeed, many whites rejected South Africa's participation in the War on the Allied side, but these were mainly from Afrikaner segments of society that would not be liable for the income tax, and so they did not resist the tax. The challenges posed by Afrikaner nationalists opposed to the war were "most conveniently handled in the light of attempts by the Government to consolidate the foundations of white power."[41] For those upper groups supporting the war and who would have to pay the tax, a willingness to sacrifice was the prevailing sentiment. The 1917 Associated Chambers of Commerce (ASSOCOM) conference minutes reflected

... that as commercial men they were prepared to do their share in the great world war by placing the interests of the war before everything else. They had all been called upon to make personal sacrifice.... They had to pay additional taxation, but they had done nothing in that line compared with other parts of the British Empire, and ... if it was necessary to make even greater sacrifices they as commercial people were prepared to do their duty to the very utmost. (Hear, hear)...

Similarly supportive statements could be found within the minutes of the presidential speeches of the Chamber of Mines during these years. Meanwhile, as expenditure was also considered for social policy, such policies were evaluated with respect to the impact on the poor white, against the possibility that "this class of people would deteriorate to the level of the black population and become unreclaimable."[42] From such a perspective, progressive taxation emerged as a sound policy and strategy. While expenditure on blacks exceeded tax receipts from that group, such expenditure (and Native Taxation for that matter) was largely presented as a form of social control, and did not contradict the notion of a racially exclusionary distributive regime.

By the end of the First World War, the income tax surpassed customs duties as the single most important source of state revenue. In the first act

[41] Davenport 1991: 233.
[42] ASSOCOM Annual Report 1912.

of 1914, taxes were levied on incomes greater than £1,000 at a smoothly graduated rate of sixpence plus 1/2,000 of a penny per pound up to a total taxable amount of £24,000.[43] In other words, tax rates ranged from 2.5 to 7.5 percent of taxable income. By contemporary standards, such rates may not seem terribly high, but they must be seen in light of their novelty, the first time most citizens were paying direct income taxes to the state. By 1922, the supertax rate grew to 25 percent for upper-income brackets, already taxed at a rate of 10 percent under the normal income tax.

Total income tax collections grew rapidly during this period because of the new excess profits tax initiated in 1917. This tax was similarly accepted within the business community and was applied on a base of profits that was considered above the "normal" prewar profitability of a firm. It was generally agreed that no one should profit disproportionately from the war economy – in which supply was limited and the opportunity for price gouging was great – and that taxation would be the fairest way to redistribute the economic effects of the war within the white population. Today, it is difficult to imagine support for such a tax as the notion of excess profits is outside the realm of serious discussion in societies in the late 20th century. Although the excess profits tax was slated to be removed six months following the end of the war, in 1919, it was increased to 5 percent of excess profits for "meeting war expenditure." The ratcheting effect that fiscal historians have noted for other contexts certainly characterized this war-time adjustment. In the 1921–2 budget, the excess profits tax and special war levies *were* removed – but they were replaced with higher normal rates of tax on companies (7.5 percent instead of 5 percent) amounting to a slight overall increase in taxation. Although mining taxes continued to be an important component of direct taxation – and were incorporated within the income tax soon after its enactment – during this period, the combination of income taxes on individual incomes and on nonmining companies surpassed the sum collected from the mines.

These early proposals, and the expressed willingness of upper groups to pay, facilitated the development of the tax bureaucracy. By virtually all accounts, the South African state's efforts to collect the income tax were as successful as treasury officials could have hoped. In a report on the working of the income tax act in its first year, the Commissioner of Taxes reported that projections for numbers of taxpayers and revenues collected were met

---

[43] Surtees 1985: 66–7.

or surpassed.[44] Even in describing the details of building the bureaucracy, the Commissioner made clear the importance of taxpayer views of the tax as legitimate: "The public as a rule have recognized the need for fresh taxation, and have accepted their liability to contribute towards the country's requirement."[45] The tax roll rapidly increased from about 5,000 in 1914 to close to 100,000 in 1921, and among other things, provided information about individuals' residences, trades, expenses, and incomes. The highest income earners within the country were responsible for the lion's share of payments: In 1921, the 1,785 individual taxpayers earning over £2,500 in taxable income per year – less than 2 percent of those qualified and registered for income tax, were responsible for 52 percent of the combined normal and supertax on income.

The nascent tax system relied heavily on the honest intentions of taxpayers rather than on the withholding efforts of an employer, as tends to be the case in contemporary tax systems. Explaining how the tax state would be built, the Commissioner wrote:

There is bound to be leakage but this will be gradually reduced as the Department's organisation is extended and information is accumulated. It is of course futile to expect that every one liable to tax will be caught in the tax collector's net. All that can be hoped for is that the proportion escaping tax will be reduced from year to year.[46]

By 1917, the number of tax offices had expanded from five to thirteen, and local magistrates played a key role in the collections process, allowing the central state to utilize local government officials toward the fulfillment of national revenue objectives. The commissioner explained that Union revenue officers during these early years visited scores of local towns to speak with attorneys and accountants about the practice of taxation in order to ensure standardization and harmonization.[47] In other words, the strategy of eliciting standardization did not rely solely on the work of revenue bureaucrats but on those members from within society who would act as links to the state.

Although norms of compliance were not well established prior to the formation of the Union, the early legitimacy of the tax helped to

---

[44] Moffat 1915.
[45] Moffat 1915.
[46] Moffat 1915: 7.
[47] Commissioner of Inland Revenue South Africa 1919.

reproduce patterns of payment in subsequent generations. Very quickly, compliance became the normal response for white taxpayers, and evasion came to be viewed as deviant behavior. It would be an overstatement to suggest that payment was *entirely* due to the voluntary inclinations of taxpayers. As reported in the press, and in various government reports, many South Africans were attempting to avoid and/or evade payment even in these early years of the income tax. Undoubtedly, threat and coercion played a role, but a surprisingly minor one, as inland revenue authorities prosecuted violators only with minor fines.

Brazil. By comparison, early efforts to collect income taxes in Brazil met significant resistance from upper groups, and the state was far less successful in its attempts to extend its authority uniformly across the country. The Brazilian Republic had already been constituted for more than two decades when the Great War erupted, and national leaders renewed their efforts to increase revenues through a general income tax. As in South Africa, industrialization had proceeded apace since about 1870, and the growing concentration of capital in the urban areas of the coffee-producing Southeast region provided an attractive potential base for direct taxation by the central state, but the desire of state treasury officials to collect a general income tax was already mired in political struggle associated with regionalist politics.

On the eve of the First World War, the Brazilian tax structure was in many ways similar to the way it had been since the first Republican constitution of 1891.[48] During the first three decades of the republic, import taxes accounted for approximately two-thirds of all taxation levied by the central state. The constitution immediately provided new taxing powers to the lower spheres of government. The central state received exclusive control of the import tax, laws of entry, exit and stay of ships/vessels, stamp taxes and taxes on posts and telegraphs while the *estados* (states) were granted powers to tax exports, various forms of property, and a tax on certain industries and professions.

The ideals of the Republican government helped fuel a new drive to enact a general income tax, but these initiatives were unsuccessful. Rui Barbosa, a leading abolitionist from the Northeastern *estado* of Bahia, was the first finance minister of the new Republic, and epitomized a group of modernizing reformers who tried to transform the social relations of the

[48] Varsano 1996: 2.

131

Brazilian nation and to shape or construct a more modern state. As part of a broader strategy to craft a new model of citizenship and Brazilian nationhood, he hoped he could successfully reconfigure the fiscal relations between state and society. From the perspective of these modernizing reformers, imperial taxation had never been just: The very nature of a Royal monarchy was antithetical to the idea of taxation as a collective expression of society. The Republican model suggested a new opportunity to collect direct taxation, and reformers believed collective sacrifice would provide a more effective and less harmful basis for financing the state's budget than simple reliance on trade duties or money-printing. Direct taxation of income and capital could also serve another important social goal: By taxing the rich progressively more, the state would address the deep social inequality which stood in contradiction to the original ideals of the Republic. In proposing a general income tax to the Constituent Assembly of 1889–91, Barbosa espoused a set of ideals that were not particularly different from those of his South African counterparts. He called for an income tax that would be "progressive, exempt the poorest, distinguish earnings on occupations from earnings on capital, and be based on individual declarations where the taxer and the taxpayer would be one and the same," recognizing liberal ideals such as individualism, equality among men and protection of property rights.[49] Presumably, under the Republican model, with an articulate spokesman such as Barbosa making the demand for the state executive, the outcome *could have been* different. Moreover, Barbosa expressed fears that the federalist idea – largely based on the American model – had perhaps been taken too far, and he feared the disintegration of national unity.[50] However, both Barbosa (1889–91) and a finance minister who would succeed him, Francisco de Paula Rodrigues Alves (1891–2; 1894–6), were rebuked in their attempts to alter the balance of political authority in favor of the central state with the enactment of a general income tax.

Not surprisingly, the fiscal motivations for this tax persisted and intensified with the onset of the First World War. Plummeting export prices in 1913 brought down overall levels of trade, and led to a deficit that was exacerbated by the onset of war the following year. Meanwhile, industrial capital formation was proceeding rapidly, particularly in the period 1910–13.[51] As in South Africa, the need for other sources of revenue became clear, and

[49] Penna 1992: 27, 31.
[50] Canto 1949: 80.
[51] Villela and Suzigan 1977: 95.

domestic income was similarly available as a potentially productive base for taxation.

Yet, private resistance to the tax prevailed as the response to this demand, even during and after the war, when revenue was so critically needed. Upper-income groups interpreted central state demands for sacrifice through a set of political idioms and institutions that reinforced the inclination to free ride. While South African commercial agriculture and various industries found common ground in critical "native" policies, in Brazil, the *leitmotif* of early 20th century politics was competition between agricultural and industrial interests, and the articulation of industry-specific needs – which found expression in localist politics.[52] Moreover, particularly with the second generation of Brazilian industrialists – around the start of the First World War – business was increasingly organized along *estado* lines,[53] as compared with the encompassing business organizations found in South Africa. For example, the *Centro Industrial do Brasil*, transformed in 1904 from the *Associação Industrial* (1880), eventually became the *Federação Industrial do Rio de Janeiro* (1931), revealing how business interests were tending toward fragmentation rather than agglomeration at the national level, as was the case in South Africa.

Since the start of the Republic, industrialists challenged the imposition of state authority and protested the damage that such a tax would incur on their earnings and ability to accumulate capital. Without the ability to reach consensus on a general, uniformly applied policy, the beginnings of a general income tax emerged with various smaller policies; for example, in 1910, a tax on dividends and on industry and professions; in 1914, a tax on interest and public corporations; in 1916, a tax on credit interest; in 1919, a tax on the net profits and earnings of public corporation directors.[54] The Industrial Center of Brazil in 1919 vehemently protested the imposition of a 3 percent tax on profits and dividends on the manufacturing industry.[55]

While the First World War ultimately inspired a sense of common cause among South African upper groups, which led to acceptance of a general income tax among dominant economic actors in that country, this event simply exacerbated political divisions in Brazil. New pressures from labor, the urban middle sectors, and a core of modernizing army officers exposed

---

[52] Carone 1978: 8–9.
[53] Carone 1978: 6.
[54] Ferreira 1986: 74–5.
[55] Penna 1992: 40.

fault lines within the Brazilian oligarchy between and within regions.[56] The proliferation of interests impeded a collective solution to the problem of state finance, as each group demanded more, while insisting that others pay. Despite the persistence of several legislators in the Chamber of Deputies Budget Committee, sufficient consensus could not be built, with several others arguing – and correctly predicting – that collection would be difficult.[57]

Divisions *across* economic classes further impeded the acceptance of a progressive income tax among upper groups. While South Africa's strong, racially exclusive labor movement helped promote the idea of the need for greater social equality and improved conditions for (white) workers in the eyes of capitalists in that country, no analog existed in Brazil. Union organized labor remained largely confined within *estados* lines, and as pointed out in Chapter 3, racial differentiation was actually a source of labor *weakness* in Brazil. Moreover, ethnic differentiation among white workers wound up being divisive in the absence of a white organizational base. "The size of the work force gave rise to ethnic friction – between Brazilian and foreign immigrants, Portuguese and Italians, and even between Italians from different parts of Italy."[58] Ironically, the whitening strategy simultaneously restricted workers from organizing themselves separately, along racial lines, while exacerbating feelings of race chauvinism, and together, these factors undermined labor unity. Without a shared normative appeal to upper groups, and particularly without the collective muscle to back up their demands, organized labor in Brazil could not make a strong claim either to the state or to upper groups, that the burden of taxation ought to be carried according to ability to pay.

Only after decades of protracted struggle within legislative circles was the general income tax eventually passed in the Chamber of Deputies in 1922. Once enacted, the Brazilian legislation was slow to be implemented, and was specified in a complex manner. Despite the concentration of income in the industrial states of the South, these taxes raised surprisingly little revenue. The tax presented by Francisco Tito de Souza Reis – a technically oriented bureaucrat – was finally enacted in Law no. 4625 on December 31, 1922. It applied to the annual income of individuals and legal entities above 6,000 réis allowing deductions for various reasons, as long as not in

[56] Fausto 1986: 817.
[57] Penna 1992: 36.
[58] Fausto 1986: 809.

excess of 5 percent of income. Part of the tax was proportional (a flat rate), which differed according to the source of the income, and the other part was progressive on a calculated base of net income, with rates ranging from 0.5 percent to 8 percent beyond the exempt level. The initial law was ridden with exemptions, particularly on agricultural profits and any interest on loans associated with agriculture or extractive industries.[59] Reflecting various political squabbles over the particular details of the tax, including the strong objections of entrepreneurs, it was not even effectively implemented until 1926.[60] Moreover, several proposals to extend the calculation of taxable income were quickly revoked.[61] In creating the new general tax, an existing tax on corporate dividends was eliminated, resulting in a net decline in income tax revenue in 1924![62]

Once enacted, business leaders and other private interests expressed their resentment of the tax. The São Paulo newspaper *Folha* argued that the income tax was "absurd," and predicted, "The income tax is destined to fail. And all the country will profit from this..."[63] Oliveira Passos of the *Centro Industrial do Brasil* – the organization that would become the *Centro Industrial do Rio de Janeiro* – argued in a 1928 meeting of the organization that the income tax was a tax that should not have been introduced in Brazil, "a new country, an importer of foreign capital and labor... the tax repels capital and can only be properly introduced in countries with excess capital."[64] (Similar claims could have been made in South Africa, but were not.) Strong resistance to the tax from representatives of such business organizations as well as from (*estado*) state governors forced the national executive to grant a panoply of regional and sectoral privileges and exemptions.[65] Not surprisingly, amidst these challenges, collection proved difficult: In a dispatch to the American State Department, a representative from the American Embassy in Rio de Janeiro wrote, "The collection of income tax is very imperfect, and it is unlikely that a great

[59] ESAF 1994: 44.
[60] Ferreira 1986; Penna 1992: 40.
[61] ESAF 1994: 45.
[62] The general income tax was first collected in 1924. This made Brazil a relative latecomer to the tax on the world stage, along with other Latin American countries, including Mexico (1925) and Argentina (1932). A general income tax was introduced in the United States in 1913 (Newcomer 1942: 11a).
[63] *Folha de São Paulo*, October 19, 1926.
[64] Carone 1978: 97.
[65] Carone 1978: 97; Penna 1992: 41; Villela and Suzigan 1977: 285–6.

deal of profit will be shown, were the government to consider the amount spent in administration and the number of individuals and firms who evade payment."[66]

Upper-group resistance to the tax affected its codification and implementation. Eight different methods of computation were adopted for arriving at taxable income or profits, a complex and potentially leaky basis for calculation even in the early law. The so-called general income tax was rife with sectoral privileges and exemptions. Subject to such ambiguous interpretation, the application of tax rules could also provide an opening for favoritism and friends of state officials could expect leniency.[67] While South African industrialists pushed the government to apply the tax with increasing uniformity during the early years of its enactment, Brazilian industrialists did the opposite – pressuring for special exemptions. Penna points out that the Industrial Center of Brazil requested that their activities "be granted fiscal privileges as well as privileged financing."[68] Similarly, coal, cement, glass, cellulose, beer, sugar, steel, and other industries benefited from special concessions on various taxes – mostly on customs duties – and these were generally initially granted to individual firms, suggesting a completely nonuniform practice.[69]

The complex quality of the initial legislation embodied a sense that various sectors and regions needed to be treated separately because they were more different than similar. Not surprisingly, the tax was relatively ineffective. In 1928, when over 3 percent of GDP was collected in the form of income tax in South Africa, less than 0.3 percent of GDP was being collected in Brazil.

Brazilian finance ministers resorted to more inflationary and regressive means of securing revenue. Serious revenue needs during the war were met with increased taxes on consumption (see Figure 4.5). Both the rates as well as the number of goods that were taxed increased, and the share of total federal receipts generated through taxes on internal transactions grew from 13 percent to 32 percent between 1912 and 1918.[70] Still, expenditures outpaced budgeted amounts – the average budgetary deficit was 45 percent

---

[66] American Embassy, Rio de Janeiro. "Course of Legislation: Income Tax Law." Declassified letter May 29, 1926. Published on Microfilm Reel 31 of U.S. Department of State, *Records of the Department of State Relating to the Internal Affairs of Brazil.*
[67] Weyland 1996: 80.
[68] Penna 1992: 41.
[69] Villela and Suzigan 1977: 285–6.
[70] Villela and Suzigan 1977: 102.

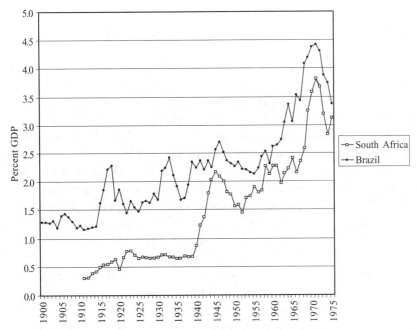

Figure 4.5 Consumption taxes in Brazil and South Africa, 1900–1975. Central government tax collections only. *Sources:* Commissioner for Inland Revenue, various; Bureau of Census and Statistics South Africa 1960; Wainer 1987; Department of Finance South Africa *Budget Review*, various; Mitchell 1993; Villela and Suzigan 1977; Ludwig 1985; IMF, various.

of receipts between 1913 and 1918 – which again led to the printing of money to meet revenue shortfalls. By 1928, the year before the stock market crash, the central government earned the lion's share of its revenue through import taxes, but consumption taxes had grown to a close second, with income taxes providing virtually no revenue at all.

Special Taxation for the Second World War

The next major moment of international tax reform was associated with the Second World War – a period that was critical for the development of the tax state in Brazil and South Africa as well. For both countries, the period was marked by dramatic increases in the amount of direct tax collected, and in the consolidation of the respective tax administrations. Both countries required revenue to finance their participation in the war effort, and finance ministers acted to protect the economies from the tide of inflation that could

137

result from price gauging amidst supply shortages. Such needs led to the proposal of higher tax rates on existing income taxes, and the enactment of special war taxes.

However, not only did the varied manifestations of identity politics affect how these new demands would be received within the respective societies during this period, but the effects of pre-existing differences in the tax state further structured the outcome of this reform episode. In South Africa, a relatively strongly knit group of employers and professionals, linked together through business organizations and political parties, supported the war efforts and did not exercise voice or exit options to push the burden onto others. Political differences in attitudes about the war that were divided along white ethnic lines were mollified through the idiom of race, and the institutions born out of policies of racial exclusion. As a result, the largely white, English-speaking population accepted the tax burden. For upper-income Brazilians, vague expressions of support were not matched with a sense of common cause. Demands for excess taxation inspired more narrowly defined battles across regional and sectoral lines, and effective increases in taxation were minimal by comparative standards. Although the period under investigation is generally noted for the vast expansion of the central state and for the consolidation of taxes in Brazil, the analysis discussed here reveals that the gains in tax revenues and in the very extension of the state within society were perhaps not as impressive as generally thought.

As summarized in Table 4.4, although both states expanded their income taxing authorities during this period, revenue and efficiency gains in South Africa were far more impressive than in Brazil. By the end of the war, South Africa was collecting more than three times what the Brazilian state was collecting in income taxes. Moreover, its ability to stem the tide of inflation was much greater, as the price index grew only 35 percent during the six-year period, compared with 120 percent in Brazil. Such performance outcomes reveal fundamentally different relationships between the state and upper groups in the respective countries. South Africa developed a cooperative tax state, as upper groups complied actively with state demands. By contrast, the Brazilian tax state could be characterized in terms of its adversarial relationship with analogous economic actors.

South Africa. The South African government garnered strong support for the war effort, and under the leadership of Afrikaner General Jan Smuts, the young state managed to mobilize significant financial and human resources.

Table 4.4 *The tax state in Brazil and South Africa during the Second World War,* *1939–1945*

	Brazil	South Africa
Policy		
New bases	Special war taxes on firms and individuals	Special war taxes on firms and individuals
Exemptions	Multiple	Few
Top company income tax rates (including special)	8 percent	30 percent
Top individual income tax rates (including special)	~30 percent	~70 percent
Administration		
Calculation of liability	Complex, significant avoidance	Straightforward/ transparent
Payment/compliance	High levels of resistance "Getting the taxpayer to pay is a struggle."	Significant cooperation "The citizens have accepted the tax."
Costs/technical skills	Significant investment in administrative reform	Highly efficient cost structure (0.3 percent of collections)
Collections of income and property tax (% GDP)*		
1939	0.75	1.77
1945	2.16	7.52
Inflation (1939–45)	120%	35%
Tax state	ADVERSARIAL	COOPERATIVE

* Does not include mining revenues; central state tax collections only.

Centripetal political forces help to account for this outcome. In 1938, the United party, along with its partners, won an overwhelming victory of the white electorate, claiming 111 of 153 seats in the National Assembly with a support base that was largely similar to that held by the SAP during the first parliamentary election. Although it lost some Afrikaner support in the 1943 election, the United party maintained a strong majority with 89 seats.[71] The most vehement proponents of racial exclusion sat on the opposition benches during these years, but the very constitution of the

[71] Davenport 1991: 564.

nation in European terms, exclusive of the local black population, facilitated collective action even among those with a more liberal stance on the race question. During this period, regional concerns were virtually absent from the national political arena, and the race question, which starkly drew lines between "us" and "them," helped national leaders to invoke calls for duty and a sense of obligation.

The state's demand for taxation from upper groups was cast as an appeal to national conscience. For supporters of the war, the Nazi regime threatened the future of freedom and capitalism, and the newspapers were covered with news of the war on a daily basis. Ironically, just as the government made claims to the noble humanitarian causes of the war, only whites were allowed to join combat units.[72] As upper groups largely viewed their fate as shared with that of the state and the larger war effort, the executive was empowered to make demands in broad, collective terms, and did not have to appeal to more narrowly defined interests. In a rousing speech to the Chamber of Commerce, State President Smuts appealed to this sentiment.

That great spirit has saved this country, and will also save the future of South Africa. . . . That is my appeal to commerce and to the nation: Let us not slacken, let us not weaken; let us not falter for a moment in the great task which we have set ourselves. Let us keep alive the spirit of sacrifice and never climb down from the high ideals in the cause to which we have dedicated ourselves. . . . You are called upon to bear many burdens, and are subject to controls of all sorts. . . . I wish to impress upon you that these things are not matters of choice. So far as the government are concerned we do not wish to inflict these evils upon you. They are dictated through the necessities of the situation in which we find ourselves.

We are fighting not only for victory at the front, but also for decent conditions at home. . . . As the burden falls heaviest on the poor, it is our duty to see that the cost of living is kept down . . . (J. C. Smuts, Nov 4, 1941, reported in the 1941 ASSOCOM minutes)

Smuts called for solidarity within the white polity. He pointed to the need to continue using income taxation, even if on a very narrow base of individuals, because this would be more just with respect to the economically less well off – at the time a clear euphemism for poor white Afrikaners. The poor white problem remained emotive, but altruism is probably not

[72] Many Africans and Coloureds participated in the war, as unarmed members of South African auxiliary units (Davenport 1991: 299). Of the approximately 5,500 South African battle deaths, approximately half were African (Thompson 1990: 177).

the most useful characterization of the motives for accepting progressive taxation on the part of upper-income whites. Instead, it was clear that poorer whites could organize themselves relatively effectively and that capital interests were best served through conciliation with this group, as was being demonstrated by labor peace and profitability in the mines and other industries. Business leaders could not easily forget the highly damaging Rand Revolt, and they closely monitored their relations with European labor in order to avoid any rekindling of old flames. Although English-speaking upper-income groups tended to hold more liberal views with respect to the race question, strategic conciliation with white labor required the perpetuation of racially exclusionary practices. Between 1939 and 1948, black workers challenged the state and industry with multiple protests and strikes, but ultimately, employers refused to recognize non-European trade unions, a move that further cemented the bonds of white workers, and their links with employers.[73]

During this period, revenues skyrocketed. With each successive war budget presented by the Minister of Finance, tax rates were increased. By 1941, when the Income Tax Act was rewritten to consolidate years of prior amendments and adjustments, and when one considers the additional wartime taxes and supertaxes levied on top income earners, the top marginal income tax rate for an individual earning over £100,000 was increased to 72.4 percent. (Wartime taxes included a set of surcharges on companies, mines, and individuals. The Personal and Savings Fund Levy imposed by the Special Taxation Act, No. 40 of 1942 include a basic surtax of 20 percent, and an additional surtax of 10 percent on all income liable for supertaxes.)[74] In fact, when compared with the United States, Canada, Australia, and Britain, South Africa's income tax system was considerably *more* progressive in its rate structure.[75] The Social and Economic Council reported that some individuals were liable for marginal rates of over 100 percent during the war years! Generally, the rate structure was highly progressive, with the exception of special African taxation, which was clearly regressive at the lowest income levels.[76]

[73] Thompson 1990: 179–80.
[74] Social and Economic Planning Council 1946.
[75] Social and Economic Planning Council 1946: 18.
[76] Because the focus of this book is on the taxation of upper groups, I do not pursue the question of various "Native Taxes" – largely "head" and "hut" taxes – which had more to do with efforts to force new workers into the cash economy than with revenue needs per se. The state proved far less successful at taxing Africans, and such taxes never represented

Such high rates did *not* induce massive corruption or evasion – a relationship many contemporary tax analysts argue is almost axiomatic. Rather, the response to demands for taxation was impressive: Income tax collections for individuals and nonmining companies increased during this period by a factor of three. Although consumption taxes increased slightly, as a share of GDP these taxes still only accounted for about 13 percent of total domestic taxation. The financial burden of the war effort was clearly taken on by those in the upper income categories, accepting that this was "their" war. In a response to the state's demands, P. M. Anderson of the Chamber of Mines in 1941 explained:

Shareholders in Gold Mining Companies of the Rand appreciate the difficult task confronting the Minister of Finance in deciding on ways and means for raising the necessary funds for the conduct of the business of the State. They are prepared to bear as cheerfully as any other section of the community their full share of the demands that have to be made by the Government to enable this country to maintain a maximum contribution to the common cause. The issues at stake, being what they are, require that all that can be done should and must be done. It is from that standpoint that we regard and accept taxation and other measures which, during this time of war, apply to and affect the Mining Industry.[77]

Reflecting the perceived legitimacy of the tax, in 1942, the *Rand Daily Mail* expressed the opinion that increased taxation, presumably upon its own readers and supporters (largely upper-income English-speakers), was simply unavoidable given the conditions of the day.

Most of Mr. Hofmeyr's taxation proposals will be accepted in the spirit of "grin and bear it" – the only honourable attitude in the present circumstances. Pipe and cigar smokers are justly made to come into line with cigarette smokers, and few people will object to the increase in the price of petrol, since they realize they are lucky in being able to use their cars at all. Nor are there likely to be any complaints about the increase in the admittedly low death duties. An increase in the incidence of normal income and super-tax was expected, and in this, Mr. Hofmeyr has not disappointed the public.[78]

There was no political space within which upper-income groups could publicly claim that their burden was truly *unfair*. At commercial and mining association meetings, as well as in Parliament, there were those who said they

---

a significant share of total revenues. Expenditure on Native administration was largely financed from the general revenue accounts of the state.

[77] Chamber of Mines, *Annual Report* 1941.

[78] *Rand Daily Mail*, February 26, 1942.

wished that agriculture would pay *more*, but by the time of the Second War, capitalists found themselves completely united around a series of idiomatic and organizational expressions. They were white, South African members of the British empire, members of a single, national political party, and participated in nationally unified business organizations. In these ways, their interests coalesced, and there was little political space to mobilize for particularistic exemptions.

Indeed, not all white South Africans shared such strong support for the war effort, but given the organization of politics, dissenting sentiments were effectively unimportant both for the decision to participate and to finance the war. There were clearly differences between those who supported Britain and those who did not, but fortunately from the perspective of the treasury, the correlation between war support and economic position was high, with the largely English-speaking business leaders and professionals, as well as some Dutch-speaking upper groups, strongly in favor of war.

Beyond the war, tax revenues were increasingly being used to support social welfare programs targeted at whites. The poor white problem became increasingly recognized with various studies between 1915 and 1932, and beginning in 1930, social welfare policies were increasingly influenced by developments abroad.[79] During the war years, the staff of the Department of Social Welfare increased by 250 percent, and of the total social assistance of £9,750,000 in 1943, a full £8,300,000 went to Europeans.[80] As a wide range of social programs were enacted, providing health, disability, and pension benefits, racial differentiation was a cornerstone of every policy. Although such programs were clearly targeted as policies to help those at the bottom of the socioeconomic ladder, those (white) citizens liable for income taxes could justify financing such programs through the idioms of social and political solidarity with whites who were struggling to make ends meet. Such sentiment would not be found in Brazil, where analogous social programs were being proposed at a similar period of time.

In turn, the strength of South Africa's taxing machine lay not with a coercive or technically sophisticated apparatus, but in its development of a relatively cooperative relationship with taxpayers. In fact, in 1945, the inland revenue service reported its most financially efficient year in its history – costing only 0.3 percent of total collections to run the

---

[79] Hellman 1949: 413.
[80] Hellman 1949: 415–16.

bureaucracy – a significant drop from 1915, when the cost was 2.0 percent. In 1917, the average inland revenue employee took in approximately £45,000 in domestic tax revenues (in constant 1938 pounds) while in 1945, those employees were collecting approximately £70,000 each – more than a 50 percent increase in productivity, even when adjusted for inflation.[81]

Brazil. Brazil also participated in the Second World War, and was also affected by the policy ideas and economic pressures of an international war economy, but the central state's ability to mobilize collective sacrifice among upper-income groups was comparatively much weaker than in South Africa. Students of Brazilian politics have long noted that the presidency of Getúlio Vargas (1930–45) and particularly the seven-year period (1937–45) known as the *Estado Novo* (New State) during which Vargas assumed dictatorial powers, were periods of remarkable centralization and consolidation of the central state.[82] Although this may be true from a purely historical perspective, from a cross-national perspective, the Brazilian central state still faced significant pressures from society in its attempt to uniformly impose centralized rule. Multiple intra-societal cleavages effectively carved out bargaining power for narrowly defined interests resisting the tax burden throughout Vargas's reign, even in the wake of war and national mobilization.

From the time of his 1930 installation in the presidency, Vargas sought to achieve a more modern state, less dependent upon local influences, and a key policy goal was to increase tax revenues destined for the national treasury. In fact, the very *tenentistas* (young, modernizing military officers) that helped bring Vargas to power in a 1930 coup d'etat argued that budgetary imbalances were evil, and quite clearly, increased taxation on income was a potential weapon against such deficits.[83] Following the charge from the chief executive, government bureaucrats at various levels were compelled to collect such taxes throughout the fifteen-year presidency.

Even under Vargas, who pushed hard for a more centralized government administration, the regional political idiom could not be erased from the political landscape. In the absence of a nationally unifying idiom for upper

---

[81] Figures from Inland Commissioner reports and South Africa. Bureau of Census and Statistics South Africa 1960.
[82] Weyland (1998b) argues that a developmental state was created during this period in Brazil.
[83] Fausto 1986: 815.

groups – such as a "black threat" – other political strategies were necessary for the new government to gain the acceptance of many economically and politically powerful actors who did not share the national visions of the urban middle sectors. In fact, the Vargas regime was consistently challenged in the name of regionalism. For example, the president raised the ire of the Paulista elite when he dispatched João Alberto, a *tenente* from the Northeast, to replace an elected governor in São Paulo. In 1932, the Paulistas struck back with a revolt of their own.[84] Vargas crushed the revolt but did not punish the dissenting factions, and instead made compromises with these groups to try to quell future regionalist uprisings.[85] Vargas made political pacts necessary to maintain political stability, but these were a model of the state accommodating interests, of compromise between sectors and social classes. As a result, the Revolution of 1930 brought to Brazil a more prominent role for the central government, but more as an agglomeration of regional powers than as a truly supreme authority over society. Vargas negotiated a political balance by accommodating multiple interests in the federal bureaucracy, leaving unaltered a set of political institutions that gave significant power to the *estados*.

These political dynamics were reflected in struggles over the allocation of the tax burden. During the constituent assembly, which led to the 1934 constitution, the question of who should collect the income tax re-emerged.[86] Those conversations were characterized by a high level of technical understanding of taxation matters, with an enormous amount of data and analysis presented by advisors within and outside the bureaucracy.[87] And yet, as is the case today, idealized notions of efficiency advanced by technocrats within the government could not trump the more fundamental political concerns of who should pay, and how much. The assembly itself was comprised of various parties, with wildly different positions, and quite opposite from the South African elections of 1933, local elites demonstrated their popularity and relevance in political life.[88] A draft law split the income tax, transferring a proportional base to the provincial states and the progressive tax to the federal government. Such political battles served to de-legitimize federal taxation, by allowing for the articulation of competing interests among the

[84] Burns 1993: 351.
[85] Abrucio 1998: 42–4.
[86] Penna 1992: 40.
[87] Costa 1995: 38–9.
[88] Fausto 1999: 207.

upper sectors of Brazilian politics and society. Paulista officials, in particular, voiced these concerns during the constituent assembly, "visibly discontent" with their role in the fiscal arrangement.[89] Ultimately, heroic efforts at tax reform in the constitutional negotiations produced only a minor increase in income tax collections, from 0.3 percent of GDP to 0.6 percent of GDP between 1930 and 1937.[90] This still paled in comparison with other sources of federal revenue in 1937 such as import taxes (2.8 percent of GDP) and consumption taxes (1.6 percent of GDP).

After seven years in office, the proliferation of competing interests became unmanageable for Vargas, and despite earlier efforts to consolidate and to centralize state power during his first term, he initiated a period of more extreme political change, arguing that the country must forego the threatening aspects of competitive politics. With the support of the military, he pre-empted the scheduled elections of 1938 and initiated a coup d'etat in 1937 to retain power, in the defense of national unity and security.[91] He implemented a dictatorial regime, introducing a new constitution that was centralizing in spirit, and made investments in education and transportation infrastructure in order to develop a much stronger national identity. Since the legislative process was fully vested in the executive, the options for watering down legislation within a chamber of politicians with their own constituencies was eliminated.

Under the new regime, the federal government made the collections of direct taxation a high priority, and the structural conditions were favorable for realizing this objective. Although the pace of economic growth slowed somewhat from the prior period, the economy was still growing and industrializing, and improved terms of trade actually meant a tangible increase in living conditions between 1939 and 1945.[92] Industrial production grew at a rate of 5.4 percent during 1939–45,[93] and several key industries, in particular textiles, expanded during these years because of shortages in world production.[94] These favorable circumstances, including extremely high coffee prices, led to consistent exchange surpluses, and industrial firms made large profits and accumulated significant reserves.[95] With the advent

[89] Hagopian 1996: 41–2.
[90] By 1936, the top marginal rate on individual income tax was 18 percent.
[91] Skidmore 1967: 30.
[92] Villela and Suzigan 1977: 174.
[93] Baer 1995: 38–40.
[94] Villela and Suzigan 1977: 167.
[95] Villela and Suzigan 1977: 181.

of Keynesian notions of fiscal policy, direct taxation was clearly becoming a popular tool around the world in the 1940s, and during Vargas's presidency, the Brazilian finance minister, Octâvio Gouvêa de Bulhões, sought to replace import duties with income tax as a source of revenue during the Second World War. Reading newspapers and administrative journals of the day, there is no doubt that the technocracy at that time was well aware of the increasing use of the income tax by other countries and its progressive impact on the distribution of income.[96] This tax was also viewed as particularly critical for controlling inflation.

And yet, the groups expected to pay the tax remained organizationally and ideologically divided. Despite the peak-level integration of employer and labor organizations into confederations, these national organizations remained extremely weak when compared with the *estado*-level federations, such as FIRJAN and FIESP, the industrial associations of Rio de Janeiro and São Paulo. Similarly, the urban middle class appeared heterogeneous – "divided in terms of income, social mobility, racial origin and degree of dependence on the regional ruling class."[97] They also varied in terms of their alignment with the working classes – more so in Rio de Janeiro and less so in São Paulo.[98] Moreover, Vargas had not eliminated the power of state political leaders, he had merely accommodated them into the framework of the federal bureaucracy.[99] The prevailing logic of regionalism suggested to Southeastern elites that compliance with central state demands would benefit their Northern counterparts – not benefiting "us," but "them." Cooperation and support for fresh taxation would have to be generated out of compromise rather than consensus.

As in South Africa, war was an important part of the political discourse during this period, and national government demands for tax revenue were couched in such terms during the 1940s. Brazil was unique in Latin America in terms of its commitment to go to war on the allied side. Already, under Vargas's leadership, the military doubled from 38,000 in 1927 to 75,000 in 1937,[100] and when Brazil formally entered the war in 1942, the cost in lives and real outlays to the cause were substantial. Moreover, the demonstration effect of warring nations paying special taxes was a powerful motivation

---

[96] Comissão de Finanças e Orçamento: 1936.
[97] Fausto 1986: 807.
[98] Fausto 1986: 808.
[99] Abrucio 1998: 48.
[100] Burns 1993: 357.

for the fiscal demands of national executives. New taxes were ultimately declared by the executive in the form of decree-laws, justified by the "need to establish a new source of income to face war-accruing necessities and the purpose of counterarresting the effects of inflation."[101] As in many of the belligerent nations, the notion of a special tax was critical to justify the fairness of the new demands, and as in South Africa, a specific excess profits tax was proposed to combat wartime inflation.[102]

Yet again, the response to such demands was shaped by the organization and perception of interests that had been structured by much earlier definitions of the NPC. Just as the government attempted to widen the tax base and to increase rates, the perceived need to accommodate various economic interests again produced a series of important gaps in the tax policy framework. Employer representatives repeatedly traveled to Rio de Janeiro to negotiate compromises that effectively diluted the overall burden on firms and high-income individuals. In a telegram to the Ministry of Finance, the Acting President of the Federation of Commerce of the State of São Paulo complained that the "interested classes" were "overloaded" with taxes. João Daudt D'Oliveira, president of the Federation of Brazilian Business Associations, affirmed that "The news of the recent creation of the tax on extraordinary profits is the source of profound apprehension on the part of the productive classes of São Paulo."[103] The discussions in Rio stumbled on acceptable definitions of extraordinary profits, and a complex piece of legislation was negotiated, with highly arbitrary rules and extremely high thresholds for assessing excess profits, and ultimately, relatively little additional revenue was collected. Moreover, industrialists secured the option to avoid war taxes by purchasing equipment certificates to import capital equipment when international conditions would allow it.

From the perspective of conventional wisdom about Vargas's powers during this time, it is surprising to observe just how difficult it was to negotiate with divided and polarized class actors. "The decree law recently signed, taxing the highest levels of commerce and business profits, is not, evidently, what the government of the Republic intended," *Folha* reported, pointing out that the ultimate policy outcome was an unequivocal victory for employers and entrepreneurs, as the tax would only affect truly astronomical

---

[101] Canto 1948: 70.
[102] ESAF 1994: 49.
[103] Associaçao Comercial de São Paulo: 1944.

profits. The newspaper pointed out that because the calculation was so complex, the government would have to accept the calculations of propertied classes, intimating that such groups were not likely to be honest reporters of their profits and losses.[104] Even under a dictatorship, the state executive still had to bargain with the leaders of organized business, and in fact, the president apparently lost the negotiations, possessing insufficient bargaining power to force taxation upon the diverse business interests of the various Brazilian regions.[105] On the other hand, it may be fair to suggest that in the absence of the political leverage gained by the executive through dictatorial control, the tax may never have been enacted at all.

During the Second World War, income tax rates were only slightly increased, the excess profits tax was imposed, and other taxes were slightly increased. The decree law 5.844 of September 23, 1943 included some income tax consolidation and some minor increases in rates. The rate changes could hardly be called radical – top rates for taxable incomes over Cr$500,000 increased from 15 percent to 20 percent; and for individuals with incomes over Cr$200,000, a surtax ranging from 2–10 percent was applicable. For companies, liable for rates ranging from 3–6 percent, the additional income taxes did not apply. It was only during the years of 1944–6 that additional taxes of 1 percent and 2 percent were added to these firms. The lower rates for company taxes provided incentives for individuals to retain income in legal entities in order to lower their tax burden. Through aggressive and often illicit reporting of expenditure, the tax burden could be minimized or eliminated. Moreover, although an excess profits duty was levied, industrialists had the option of avoiding that tax by purchasing equipment certificates or guaranteed deposits in order to import capital equipment when international conditions would allow it. Once again, business interests in Brazil found an avenue to avoid sacrifice in favor of individual gain.

Just as in South Africa, the period of the 1930s and early 1940s was one in which a variety of social policies offering benefits to workers were enacted and implemented. Under the Vargas regime, retirement and pension plans, benefits to mothers, training programs, and health policies were created, and as in South Africa, these benefits were guaranteed only to a privileged section of the lower segments of society. However, unlike in South Africa, where that group was defined in terms of race, in Brazil, these benefits

---

[104] *Folha de São Paulo*, January 29, 1944.
[105] See Abrucio 1998: 46–7, for a discussion of the corporatist-federative arrangements of the *Estado Novo*.

were largely reserved for workers in large industries in the major cities.[106] Without a political or emotive link to lower groups, there is little evidence to suggest that upper-income actors in Brazil felt compelled to carry the burden of financing such programs.

Beyond the bona fide exemptions and special treatment of certain taxpayers which narrowed the tax base, collection proved to be particularly ineffective in Brazil. The incentive to free ride on the tax payment of others exists in any tax system, but the divided nature of the Brazilian polity impeded the very legitimacy of the demand by simultaneously devaluing the perceived benefits of the public goods provided while reducing the confidence on the part of any taxpayer that others were complying with state demands, reinforcing norms of nonpayment. Under the *Estado Novo*, citizens had fewer opportunities to resist *policies* that demanded increased income taxes, but even with a relatively competent administration, they took advantage of opportunities to not pay. Writing in 1946, a high-ranking tax official characterized the process of getting taxpayers to pay as a "struggle."[107]

Moreover, the confusion of a multiplicity of taxes coming from all three levels of government, combined with a reluctance to pay on the part of the taxpayer, resulted in a "surge of animosity between the fisc and the contributor."[108] This marked a critical difference from the South African case in which most provincial taxes were collected by the central state anyway – perhaps technically difficult for the bureaucracy, but probably less burdensome to the taxpayer, who likely believed that all of the taxes (and expenditures) were associated with the national government. In Brazil, not only did each sphere of government collect its own taxes, but the bureaucracies saw themselves in conflict, not cooperation, despite the potential to share information and duties. As a result, taxes were not implemented in similar ways across the country. Such early practices, which differed from the more uniform treatments in the South African system, would institutionalize patterns of uneven state authority.

Total income tax collection peaked at only about 2.5 percent of GDP in 1943 – a year in which the South African central state collected 7.5 percent of GDP from such taxes (not including an additional 3 percent of GDP collected from mining taxes) – and by the end of the *Estado Novo*, indirect forms of taxation still comprised more than two-thirds of the central state's

---

[106] Burns 1993: 363.
[107] Bouças 1946: 4–6.
[108] Bouças 1946: 4–6.

domestic tax collections. Additional currency was put into circulation in order to finance deficits, fueling the flame of inflation.

The Tax State and the Post-War Period

Following the end of the Second World War, national patterns of taxation appeared largely frozen for more than a decade. In both countries, the immediate post-War years marked a shift toward inward development, as national executives identified new plans to guide the process of industrial development and to engineer social outcomes with distinctive visions of "modern utopias." In the case of South Africa, 1948 marked the election of the National Party, a turning point that would lead to the implementation of the *apartheid* project, the ultimate realization of institutionalized white supremacy in that country. Meanwhile, 1946 introduced mass politics to Brazil, leading to the election of Juscelino Kubitschek in 1955, and his plans for "developmentalism" under the banner of "fifty years of development in five." During his presidency, massive projects of capital development and human relocation were carried out to advance national goals of rapid modernization. The human costs of both projects continue to be felt in the respective countries to this day.

Despite these radical new initiatives, there were no serious initiatives to expand or to reform the tax state in the immediate post-War years. Rather, new leaders found they could spend revenues generated from the policies and administrative capacities built during the war years and before. While many of the special taxes raised for the Second World War lapsed within a few years of the cessation of hostilities, a ratchet effect was evident in both countries, and revenues did not fall to pre-War levels. Between 1946 and the late 1950s, patterns of taxation largely persisted in the two countries, characterized by slight declines in both consumption and income taxes relative to overall economic growth. Ironically, this implied that in South Africa, the Afrikaners who supported the National Party would benefit from the development of the tax state that took place during the war, which many of them so opposed. While a large proportion of the English-speaking population may have opposed apartheid, most members of this group, and particularly its business leaders, did not question the legitimacy of the state itself, and continued to cooperate with the laws and practices developed under their own rule. In the case of Brazil, relatively weak tax policy and leaky administration were reproduced, and deficit finance continued, resulting in high rates of inflation.

Taxation for the "War" on Communism

A mix of Cold War politics and rapid economic development implied a host of new administrative and revenue needs that would lead finance ministers and other national leaders to initiate a new round of tax reform in the 1960s. During this period, the scope of the respective tax states was vastly expanded, and collections increased dramatically in both countries. Yet, the nature of tax policy and administrative change remained nationally distinctive, and tax outputs diverged even more widely than in previous generations. South Africa continued to develop as a cooperative state, and Brazil as an adversarial one. The reproduction of such differences is surprising in light of the very similar political and economic pressures and influences that faced these two late developing countries during the period 1960–75. Drawing on the political community model, however, it is possible to account for these differences in terms of how racial and regional identities influenced class cohesion and the state's ability to elicit collective sacrifice, and in terms of how pre-existing patterns of taxation shaped the possibilities for reform.

Again, the context of reform was similar: Just as the two World Wars had been highly influential on the development of the Brazilian and South African tax states, the Cold War also provided the idea of a significant threat, which compelled state executives to articulate national interests and new demands for sacrifice. In the 1960s, the combination of rapid modernization amidst growing political conflict at home and abroad was threatening to upper groups in both countries, and paved the way for the development of highly repressive political regimes. The Cold War created both real and imagined challenges to capitalist orders within these late developing, highly unequal societies. National leaders highlighted the need to maintain order and internal security, and proposed that the government should take a more direct and active role in the process of economic development.

During this period, Cold War tensions, high levels of socioeconomic inequality, and rapid urbanization and industrialization processes sowed the seeds of political challenges from below in both countries. In South Africa, in 1952, the ANC helped launch a large passive resistance campaign, and in 1955, approximately 3,000 people gathered to adopt the Freedom Charter, asserting, "South Africa belongs to all who live in it, black and white ... no government can justly claim authority unless it is based on the will of the people."[109] In Brazil, political polarization in the early 1960s

---

[109] Thompson 1990: 208.

emerged between the more conservative congress on the one hand, and workers and peasants with the support of President João Goulart on the other. In March 1964, Goulart led a Rio de Janeiro rally of working-class people, calling for "basic reforms," effectively threatening the privileges enjoyed by the Brazilian business community.[110]

Such challenges to the social and economic organization of the respective societies sparked reactions on the right, initiating periods of massive repression and state-sponsored violence. Specifically, in 1960, the South African state responded violently to a peaceful protest against the *pass laws* in the township of Sharpeville, and sixty-nine Africans were killed.[111] That action set off a wave of further protests and challenges, and violent counter-responses from the state. In Brazil, the military seized the reigns of government in a 1964 coup, installing a military leadership that would remain for more than two decades. Thus, in both countries, the early 1960s marked turning points at which the state would go to new lengths to impose its authority in the name of anti-Communist rhetoric, adopting new powers such as the censoring of information and the capacity to detain suspects without trial. Both states deployed their respective militaries, traditionally used for external affairs, to detain suspected Communists and terrorists. Each developed new tools for maintaining internal security.

Alongside these violent campaigns, government leaders called for greater bureaucratization and more modern models of political and economic development.[112] These men sought to show the world that they were not simply ruthless or arbitrary dictators, but forward thinking modernizers who would help propel their economies into the ranks of the advanced countries, avoiding the socialist path being followed elsewhere in Latin America and Sub-Saharan Africa. In both countries they espoused the ideals of modernization, order, and economic nationalism, and tax reform was an important initiative that would give concrete expression to all of these objectives. They sought to reform the tax policy frameworks and the administrative

---

[110] Burns 1993: 400.
[111] A key pillar of apartheid legislation, the pass laws were used to regulate the flow of people into and out of various areas within Southern Africa based upon identity documents and racial classification. The purpose of these laws was to exclude black Africans from areas designated for whites, except when working for an employer.
[112] See Cardoso 1979, for a discussion of the 'Bureaucratic-Authoritarian' model in Latin America. The South African state was characterized by many of the features central to the BA model, although it was not led by the military. For discussions of the apartheid state, see Price 1991.

Table 4.5 *Average annual GDP growth in Brazil and South Africa, 1960–1975*

Period	Brazil	South Africa
1960–65	4.3	5.5
1965–70	8.1	5.6
1970–75	10.1	4.6

Sources: FGV (Website), South African Reserve Bank (Website).

systems that had developed and in many ways deteriorated in the post-War decades with the advent of increasingly generous allowances for deducting capital expenditures, and of selective exemptions for various types of organizations deemed to be in the public interest. By the late 1950s and early 1960s, policy makers in both countries were expressing increased desires to reform the respective tax systems, and to modernize them with new technologies. In fact, study commissions from as early as the mid-1940s presented arguments for long-term tax reform.[113] The accumulation of reform needs, combined with concrete political challenges, provided national executives specific opportunities to make new demands for sacrifice. Specifically, they attempted to achieve greater revenue yields, more efficiently, with fewer exemptions and loopholes, and with more modern technologies.

Such demands were made against a backdrop of strong economic growth during this period. Brazil's economic miracle included rates of economic growth among the highest in the world, with sustained periods of double-digit growth (see Table 4.5). Depending upon which source for data is used, the picture for South Africa is less clear, but at the very least, between 1960 and 1970, economic growth appears to have been above 5 percent.[114] In both countries, businesses and economic elites gained tremendously in

---

[113] For example, the study reports issued by Special Commission of the Tributary Code (1950s and 1960s) and the joint Fundação Getulio Vargas/ Inter-American Development Bank commission (1960s) in Brazil; and the Social and Economic Planning Council (1940s), and the Holloway (1946), Diederichs (1954), Steyn (1954), and Schumann Commissions (1966) in South Africa.

[114] According to O'Meara (1983: 247), between 1963 and 1972, South Africa's rate of return on invested capital was the highest in the world, and of the capitalist economies, only Japan expanded more rapidly than South Africa. Moll (1991) refutes this argument with substantial economic data, arguing that South African growth during this period was much less impressive than commonly thought. I am grateful to Nicoli Nattrass for pointing out these discrepancies.

material terms from the labor-repressive regimes of the mid-1960s and 1970s, and patterns of socioeconomic privilege were reproduced and re-inforced. Although Brazil's pattern of economic growth clearly was more robust during this period, this would lead us to expect relatively *greater* increases in income tax collections in that country.

Despite the broad similarity of political and economic context, how-ever, upper groups responded in very different ways to otherwise similar state demands for tax payment. The political idioms of race and region, and their organizational and discursive manifestations, structured the po-litical interchange between strong executives and economic elites. While the Cold War provided a series of its own political labels and cleavages – particularly the divide between Communists and Anti-Communists – such generic categories were re-interpreted within the context of national politics in different ways. Executives of these authoritarian regimes pursued their missions while re-articulating and re-interpreting definitions of NPC that had been inherited from prior periods. In Brazil, even as the military gov-ernment attempted to centralize government authority, the legacy of fed-eralism continued to shape politics. Regional and local identities remained integral to the decision-making process, and exacerbated the collective ac-tion problem of taxation among upper groups in society. By contrast, in the South African case, the post-1960 period was characterized by increasingly centripetal forces within the white polity, as the structures of black exclu-sion were erected to new heights. Class cohesion was further cemented, particularly as many Afrikaners entered the economically privileged social strata, mollifying lingering intra-white ethnic tensions in that country.

Owing to these different upper-group responses, national patterns of tax-ation diverged even further during the period 1960–75 (Table 4.6). While administrative and policy reform initiatives in South Africa were success-ful in increasing tax collections from upper groups, in Brazil, the unifor-mity of the system was challenged extensively by more narrowly defined groups. In South Africa, collections of income tax as share of GDP more than doubled during this fifteen-year period, from 4.9 percent of GDP to 11.5 percent of GDP. In Brazil, the rate of increase was much slower, and from a much lower base during the same period, and collections rose from just 2.0 to 3.0 percent of GDP. For all of the discussion of reforms to the income tax system during the military period in Brazil, income taxes never amounted to more than 6 percent of GDP. South Africa's policies were far more contained in terms of exemptions and incentives, while Brazil's indi-vidual and corporate income tax bases were quickly eroded with a plethora

Table 4.6 *Tax state reforms under modernizing authoritarian regimes in Brazil and South Africa, 1960–1975*

Reform area	Trends	
	Brazil	South Africa
Policy		
Bases	Significant simplification of income tax achieved in 1966–7 reforms Enactment of the Value Added Tax (VAT) Significant increase in reliance on social security and other social contributions	Consolidation of the Income Tax Act (1962) Consolidation of provincial income taxes as national responsibility Other bases still insignificant
Exemptions	Regional and sectoral incentives creep in during the early 1970s	Minimal
Administration	PAYE system	PAYE system
Automation and computerization of tasks	implemented Computerization implemented	implemented Computerization implemented
Compliance from upper groups	Initially improved with threats of coercion Quickly reverted to high levels of avoidance and evasion	Very high levels of cooperation
Collections costs	Medium–high (1.0–2.0 percent of total collections)	Low (0.3–0.5 percent of total collections)
Collections of income and property tax (% GDP)*		
1960	2.0	4.9
1965	2.4	6.9
1970	2.5	9.7
1975	3.0	11.5
Tax state	ADVERSARIAL	COOPERATIVE

* Does not include mining revenues; central state tax collections only.

of narrowly defined loopholes. The Brazilian state looked increasingly to consumption taxes and other hidden taxes such as social contributions and nontax revenue sources to finance the budget, while the South African state continued to rely mainly on direct taxes to finance expenditures.

Compliance and cooperation from upper groups was also extremely high in South Africa, while avoidance and evasion became normal again in Brazil after an initial period during which the military government used coercion and threat of coercion to collect the revenues that were due. Consequentially, the gains in efficiency and reduction of costs were much greater in the South African case than in the Brazilian case. Indeed, both states adopted new collections systems, implementing computer technologies and withholding systems. As shown in Figure 4.6, efficiency gains in South Africa from modernizing reforms implemented in the early 1960s led to sharp declines in the costs of administration relative to revenue collected. By contrast, in the Brazilian case, although costs of collection did drop as a share of total revenues from approximately 1.4 percent to 1.0 percent between 1970 and 1974, such costs were still three to four times higher

Figure 4.6 Cost of tax administration in South Africa, 1952–1990. *Sources:* Department of Finance, RSA, various; Commissioner for Inland Revenue South Africa, various.

157

than the collection costs in South Africa. Collection costs would continue to decline in South Africa into the 1980s, while they rose in Brazil during the same period.

South Africa. What is most noteworthy about taxation in South Africa during the period 1960–75 is the relative ease with which the state was able to deepen its level of extraction from upper groups. There is no evidence to suggest that white South Africans ever challenged the tax burden through boycotts, major protests, or public demonstrations to any significant degree. Given the prevalence of such challenges in other contexts, such cooperative behavior reflected tacit acceptance or a willingness to pay. High levels of cooperation in terms of timely and efficient payment indicate a combination of the perceived legitimacy of the state on the part of upper groups during that period and the increasing efficacy of the state developed during early periods.

Such collective sacrifice in South Africa was aided by the re-interpretation of Cold War ideology and conflict into racial terms. Apartheid state leaders managed to convince the citizenry that white South Africa was an anti-Communist bastion within black Africa. Such a frame helped to cement white interests. Although many business leaders (particularly within the manufacturing and commercial sectors) espoused a mix of pragmatic and truly empathic disdain for the degree to which racial legislation had been codified in South Africa, they did this while accommodating this order, often arguing that they were simply too politically weak to challenge the government policy. "Liberal" white South Africans did not argue that the basic premise of racial difference was flawed, but disagreed about the extent to which strict racial barriers needed to be legislated in all walks of life. Powerful whites opposing *apartheid* still equivocated on radical political reform, and enjoyed the profits that could be reaped while the state maintained a labor-repressive system of racial exclusion.[115] Although some whites in contemporary post-apartheid South Africa have boycotted tax payment due to declines in services, there is no evidence of a tax boycott or even a threat of one based on disenchantment with the apartheid regime.

White South Africans found themselves more unified than ever before, particularly as the poor white problem was being stamped out, and the state found it could count on business leaders to share the responsibility

[115] Thompson 1990: 206–7.

of defending the country against Communism. The glue of racial identity helped weld together potentially conflicting ethnic, regional, and economic interests.[116] The war on Communism, nation-building, and the goal of state preservation increasingly resonated with the white population. In a 1977 military white paper, P. W. Botha proclaimed, "... the principle of the right of self-determination of the White nation must not be regarded as being negotiable. Military strategy forms part of a broader national strategy to ensure this."

Apartheid legislation and strategies reinforced the degree to which the physical space of Southern Africa became politically meaningful in racial terms. The regulation of the movement of black people into and out of "white" areas, and the creation of a homeland system, further widened the gap between white and black, and depoliticized any economic or other regional differences within white areas. Although there was disagreement within the business community concerning its commitment to apartheid, such schisms were not manifest in more narrow sectoral or regional interests that might make the functioning of the tax system a highly politicized affair among whites. As Greenberg points out, soon after Sharpeville, even commercial interests began to engage the National Party government with words such as accommodation, trusted partners, and cooperation.[117] Though it is difficult to measure the degree to which upper groups actively supported the state with any precision, it is clear from newspaper accounts, oral histories, and secondary sources that a large share of the nation's upper-income individuals and leading firms believed that the state was advancing common class interests, particularly with its war on Communism. For example, the chief economist of one of the country's leading industrial holding companies explained in an interview, "We were fighting a war in those days and we had to pay for this war to keep the Communists out, and the good citizens didn't mind paying for that. It was a sort of conscience money to a certain extent."[118]

In each area of tax reform, such support was critical for the state's success. For example, initiatives to centralize revenues went largely unchallenged. Despite conflicting recommendations about the technical merits

---

[116] Marx 1998; Thompson 1990. In particular, see the discussion of Verwoerd's conciliatory stance toward the English-speaking population following the declaration of the South African Republic in Davenport 1991: 360–2.

[117] *The Manufacturer*, January 1966, p. 14, as Cited by Greenberg 1980: 205.

[118] Interview with chief economist of leading industrial firm in Johannesburg, South Africa (June 1, 1998).

of various models of intergovernmental fiscal relations, the apartheid state leaders simply mandated that virtually all taxation be collected by the national government, making the provinces absolutely dependent upon the center for financial resources. In 1971, the Minister of Finance withdrew the capacity of the provinces to levy surcharges on personal income taxes, explaining that this would improve the overall efficiency of collections. Moreover, because the central state wanted to use fiscal policy within a broader macroeconomic strategy, the Minister of Finance determined that centralization would avert the potential conflict that might arise if provincial governments pursued contradictory goals. As a result, between 1960 and 1975, the central state's share of total tax collections (excluding local government revenues) increased from 79 percent to 95 percent. Such consolidation elicited only minor protest from business sectors within society, who had no reason to believe that the relative loss of autonomy to their own province would have a meaningful impact on their future. Given the diminished salience of regional identities, most whites viewed the central state as far and away the critical source of political authority.

Support from upper groups was also clearly critical in terms of the national state's ability to raise the tax burden through increased rates, and the elimination of incentives in the tax code. Top marginal tax rates on individual income increased from 50 percent in 1960 to 60 percent in 1972, and on normal (nonmining) companies, went from 30 percent in 1960 to 40 percent in 1967. Moreover, although various tax incentives or tax expenditures were added to the tax code from year to year, the South African Minister of Finance had an unusually strong ability to stamp these out at will when they were found to cause too great a loss of revenue. For example, in the 1973–4 Budget Speech, he identified a loophole being used by wealthy individuals to lower their tax burden with a deduction that had been afforded with respect to the payment of insurance premiums, and he described efforts that would be taken to address this source of revenue leakage.[119] In both cases, within the context of a Parliament in which the National Party was in strong control, there was no need to bargain out the provisions of new policies. Rather, the Minister of Finance immediately delegated the task of raising rates, and/or removing such loopholes to the tax bureaucracy, without significant fear of narrowly based political challenges.

---

[119] Budget Speech, House of Assembly (Republic of South Africa), August 14, September 18, and September 3, 1974, 12–13.

Finally, the willingness of upper groups to pay aided the successful reform of the tax administration, which was perhaps the most critical factor leading to the sharp rise in income tax collections between 1960 and 1975, and beyond. Beginning in April 1962, the Data Processing Section of the Department of Inland Revenue installed a computer system to calculate and issue assessments, to record payments, and maintain controls. Government reports of the 1960s and the 1980s both reflected upon the enormous efficiencies gained from the installation of such equipment.[120] Moreover, in 1963, a withholding pay-as-you-earn system (PAYE) of tax collection was implemented, whereby employers became responsible for withholding taxes on a regular basis from employee paychecks, and were required to pay over such withholdings directly to the state. Such a system, which is today used in most modern tax systems, aids the state in securing collections in a timelier manner and in combating tax evasion by providing additional records of income generated. In both cases, white South African companies accepted the extra administrative burdens associated with such reforms, reflecting a longstanding pattern of recognizing the national state's initiatives as ultimately serving the collective interest. For example, the Commissioner of Inland Revenue wrote in his March 1964 report, "The PAYE scheme, which has been under way now for some months, has had its inevitable crop of teething troubles but the indications are that it has been well received on all sides and has the full support of the overwhelming majority of taxpayers."

Brazil. The comparison with Brazil's experiences with tax reform in the mid-1960s further reveals the influence of definitions of NPC on the dynamic of politics and upper-group support for the national state through the tax system. Despite strong pressures for reform, and the presence of highly skilled technocrats and advisors – arguably far more skilled and better trained than in the South African case – Brazil's national leaders were not nearly as successful as South Africa's in accomplishing their reform goals, and the adversarial relationship between the national state and upper groups was further institutionalized. The much greater political salience of regionalism and the very different influence of racial politics undermined the class cohesion necessary for successful reform, particularly a reform that would call upon upper groups to make greater sacrifices for the national,

---

[120] See the Report of the Secretary for Inland Revenue for the year 1965–6; and Margo Report 1987.

collective benefit. After an initial moment of national cohesion under the strong arm of the military, regional conflict re-emerged, producing bitter distributive conflicts within society over the longer term. Ultimately, the adversarial pattern of tax state development would be reproduced, as the resistance to payment on the part of upper groups forced the state executive and bureaucracy to allocate the burden downward, through more hidden means.

Undoubtedly, the abrupt installation of the military government provided an important opening to re-structure the tax system. Middle and upper sectors clearly benefited from the "Revolution of 1964," which articulated a goal of stamping out Communist threats, and business leaders initially supported the military government's call for tax reform. In fact, it initially seemed possible that a centralizing, military government such as the one that came to power in 1964 following a coup d'etat could stamp out sectional political pressures using coercion and a military nationalism that would appeal to the political right and the economic elite. And indeed, certain reforms that could be completed without the cooperation or significant sacrifice from upper groups were successfully implemented. The Minister of Finance during that period, Delfim Netto, argued that the initial tax reforms completed by the government were largely responsible for the "Brazilian miracle" of rapid economic growth in the late 1960s and early 1970s.[121]

The military government initially sought to consolidate its political authority by directly challenging the autonomy of the lower tiers of government, making centralization a primary goal of the major tax reforms of 1966 and 1967. Netto had argued for a much greater level of centralization and more uniform application of the tax system throughout the country, explaining that "The Revolution of March 31 ... was an expression of the collective national consensus," and that it would be impossible to direct economic policies with three competing and uncoordinated spheres of government directing their own tax systems.[122] As a result, the central government took over several tax bases from the state and municipal governments.[123] The central state's share of total tax revenues (excluding local taxes) grew from 62 percent in 1960 to 76 percent in 1975.

---

[121] Interview Delfim Netto, Brasilía, April 15, 1999.

[122] Revista de Finanças Públicas, September 1968, 2.

[123] For a detailed specification of which tax bases were assigned to the various spheres of government in the 1967 constitution, see IBGE 1990: 605.

Second, the Brazilian government also initiated multiple reforms to modernize its tax administration. Most importantly, this involved cracking down on tax fraud. During the Castello Branco regime, the tax authorities automated record keeping and prosecuted delinquents with much tougher inflation-adjusted fines. Such measures helped to increase the real yield of taxes by 34 percent between 1963 and 1966.[124] The old tax revenue administration was reformed as the *Secretaria da Receita Federal* (SRF) in 1968, and began to employ more modern organizational structures and more sophisticated information technologies. As part of these reforms, between 1967 and 1969, the number of individual federal income tax payers rose from 470,000 to over 4 million.[125]

Third, the consumption tax was restructured in 1964 from a cascading turnover tax into a Value Added Tax. Such a tax reduced inefficiencies in the tax system, and ultimately generated higher levels of revenue.

Nevertheless, the trajectory of modernization and efficiency embodied in the initial reforms was in many ways short-lived. Like in South Africa, the war on Communism was also advanced in Brazil as a way of legitimizing the state and its repressive policies, but internal political cleavages that had divided the economic elite in previous years were re-articulated. A parochial logic soon crept in to the politics of taxation, as old business organizations and regional idioms remained important, and intra-elite conflicts of interest re-emerged. As Abrucio and Hagopian have both argued, the centralizing military government still relied heavily upon state governors and other state elites to carry out their policies.[126]

Moreover, racial inequalities and race chauvinism played a very different role than in South Africa as these factors served to further undermine collective solidarity in Brazil. Officially, Brazilians sought to build on the idea of racial tolerance. Gilberto Freyre, a leading sociologist and social commentator who became closely tied to the Brazilian federal government, argued that *anyone who challenged the notion of a racial democracy was Communist and anti-Brazilian.* In this vein, the military government went on to declare as subversive the research of several scholars exposing racial inequality and discrimination in the country.[127] Nevertheless, survey research and anthropological research have identified the existence of pervasive race chauvinism

---

[124] Ellis 1969: 182.
[125] Skidmore 1973: 22.
[126] Abrucio 1998; Hagopian 1996.
[127] Andrews 1991: 7.

and racial inequalities pervading Brazil during this period.[128] Together, the state's definition of the NPC and pervasive race chauvinism emerged as forces impeding collective solidarity among the economic elite. In a society that prided itself in being a racial democracy, the only acceptable channel for expressing prejudices and feelings of difference continued to be the regionalist discourse that pitted the wealthy South and Southeast against the poorer North and Northeastern states.

The salience of regional identities impeded the collective mobilization of economic interests and structured a bargaining dynamic in which local government expenditures were valued more highly than national ones, delegitimizing the central state's demands for tax revenues. The center required the support of these powerful leaders, and was unable to wrest political control from state leaders still referred to as "oligarchs" or "colonels." Regionalist divides and battles over an equitable burden reinforced old political lines in which the central state was viewed as delivering benefits to "them," rather than serving "us." The political lines between "ins" and "outs" that were so clear in the eyes of white South African citizens were much more blurred in Brazil. Particularly after 1974, with the more moderate political approach of President Ernesto Geisel, it became evident that without a clearly defined Communist "other," Brazilian business did not have anything analogous to the racial "glue" that bound together upper groups in South Africa, and support for the authoritarian regime was more pragmatic than ideological.[129] Although a highly repressive military regime had the ability to make certain changes by fiat, on the other hand, the longer-term effectiveness of the tax system still relied upon quasi-voluntary compliance, and *estado*-level elites gained increasing bargaining power relative to the more soft-line military government of the 1970s, which was loosening its control on electoral outcomes.[130]

Within such a context, initially successful reforms were soon challenged, and the adversarial fiscal relationship between the state and upper groups would become manifest in greater policy complexity and regressivity, and more extensive leakage during the process of collection. For example, Netto, the same Minister of Finance who had orchestrated the centralizing project of the military period, explained that early successes in achieving national tax reform were quickly derailed with regional political idioms

---

[128] Hasenbalg 1977; Ribeiro 1995.
[129] Payne 1994: 51.
[130] Abrucio 1998: 82–90.

that undercut the military's claim to embody the goals of the entire nation: "Under the military system, there was the centralization idea. But, it was quite clear by 1973–4 that we would begin again with decentralization. (This) increased in 1979–80. There were lots of political pressures for decentralization. . . . Historically, you know, we were the United States of Brazil."[131]

In the late 1970s and 1980s, even in a tightly controlled congress, various representatives voiced concerns for the need for greater devolution of resources and tax capacities. Such concerns were also raised directly with members of the bureaucracy, as well as through public opinion. Such challenges served to weaken the central state's authority to exert uniform authority within society. While the military regime *did* manage to consolidate much of overall revenue collection in the federal government's hands, it did this to a lesser extent than in the South African case, where the central state was already a relatively more important collector of taxes. Moreover, as a large share of these taxes was designated for expenditure at the level of the states and the municipalities, with highly differentiated expenditure across regions, additional opportunities arose for economic elites to challenge the fairness of the fiscal system.[132]

The bargaining power of the executive diminished and various tax and expenditure handouts were necessary to maintain support. Such a dynamic fueled inter-regional competition, which was evident on the pages of the Brazilian newspapers of the 1970s. Various articles and editorials debated the fairness of the tax reforms in the country – specifically in terms of the loss of *estado* autonomy and regional disparities. For example, in 1974, the *Jornal do Brasil* questioned the fairness of a policy framework in which workers from the Northeast were paying the same taxes as workers from São Paulo.[133] The initiatives for centralization sparked reactions on the part of Southern and Southeastern elites who complained of a loss of autonomy, which could also be interpreted as a desire to maintain higher levels of economic resources in their own regions.[134] Sectoral and regional resistance to tax increases clearly trumped broadly based class responses to needed tax reform.[135] The resulting proliferation of regional and sectoral incentives

[131] Interview Delfim Netto, Brasília, April 15, 1999.
[132] Varsano 1984: 327–65.
[133] *Jornal do Brasil,* June 10, 1974.
[134] Hagopian 1996: 120.
[135] Weyland 1998b: 61.

provided during this period reduced the efficiency and progressivity of the income tax as well as other tax bases, and ultimately reduced the tax burden on upper-income groups.[136]

In the wake of these multiple conflicts over how the burden should be allocated, low levels of compliance among upper groups remained problematic, and the income tax reform ended up being successful mostly in terms of increasing collections from urban wage labor.[137] Collections of personal income taxes doubled between 1964 and 1970, but neither ideal of horizontal or vertical equity was successfully advanced, even with high top marginal rates of income and corporate taxation.[138] Given the breaks received by corporate taxpayers and the numerous exemptions that could be claimed by high-income earners, let alone the evasion of self-employed professionals, the income tax fell mainly on the middle class and sectors of better-off workers.[139]

As an alternative to the direct taxation of upper groups, as well as the losses of revenue that followed the devolution of consumption taxing powers to the *estados*, the central state relied increasingly on mandatory social contributions from employees and employers. These revenues effectively provided liquidity for new capital expenditures, even as they were earmarked for other uses. As shown in Figure 4.4, between 1960 and 1975, these revenues skyrocketed, growing from 1.8 percent of GDP to 7.5 percent of GDP. Most analysts of Brazil's tax system have noted that such contributions, for example to the Program for Social Integration (PIS), are largely regressive and cascading, ultimately flying in the face of the original goals of the 1964–7 reforms, which were to achieve greater equity and efficiency in the tax system. It is not possible to say that these revenues are *purely* regressive, as they often entail significant redistribution from urban to rural workers, but they are collected through a high degree of fiscal illusion.[140] In any case, Brazilian tax reform during this period largely got derailed from its original goals, and wound up back on a trajectory of greater complexity, higher regressivity, and lower revenue yields than what the modernizing national executive had hoped for.

[136] Varsano 1984: 338; Mahar 1975: 149.
[137] Ferreira 1986: 139.
[138] Rezende 1975: 142–3.
[139] Weyland 1996: 81–2.
[140] Weyland 1996: 90–91.

Table 4.7 *Average annual GDP growth in Brazil and South Africa, 1975–1990*

Period	Brazil	South Africa
1975–80	7.2	3.0
1980–85	1.4	1.4
1985–90	2.0	1.5

Source: FGV (Website), South African Reserve Bank 1994.

Implications: Weathering Economic and Political Crises (1975–1990)

The respective trajectories of tax state building that had developed during the first three-quarters of the century proved to be highly consequential for the continued operations of the national state more generally during subsequent periods of social, political, and economic stress. When multiple crises emerged in Brazil and South Africa in the 1970s and 1980s, the legacy of the tax state was evident in the respective abilities of economic planners to carry out adjustment programs in the respective countries. The tax system in Brazil left that economy far more vulnerable to new pressures and crises than was the case in South Africa. By all measures, these were turbulent times in both countries, as repressive authoritarian regimes gave way to massive challenges from below, and protected industrialization models stalled out. Oil shocks and international recession contributed to a significant deterioration in the rates of economic growth (see Table 4.7), when compared with earlier periods. The 1980s are generally regarded as a lost decade of development for both countries, and between 1980 and 1993, GDP per capita declined, on average, by 1 percent every year in both Brazil and South Africa.[141] As Seidman argues, the similarity of industrialization strategies helped to produce similar forms of labor and popular protest, including massive strike waves and pro-democracy social movements.[142]

In the wake of such pressures, both states were faced with increasing expenditure needs, but had very different capacities to finance those needs with tax revenue. By the early 1980s, the Brazilian state was basically unwilling and/or unable to collect more in taxes (see Figure 4.7), leading

---

[141] Simple average of year-to-year change in GDP/capita ($PPP) in constant 1987 prices. World Bank Data.
[142] Seidman 1994; See also Price 1991.

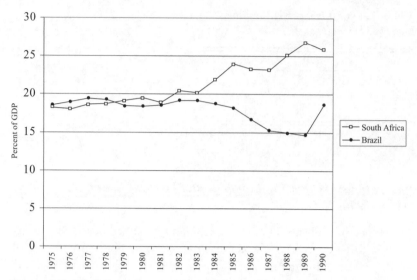

Figure 4.7 Total domestic tax revenues in Brazil and South Africa, 1975–1990. Central government collections only. *Source:* World Bank 1998.

to high levels of indebtedness. Its complex mix of revenue sources was not buoyant during this period of crisis, and the state conceded that it could not look to upper groups for additional sacrifice. Macroeconomic policy in Brazil proceeded in the 1980s as a troubled mix of heterodox solutions, including price and asset freezes, as decision making required compromise from fragmented and divergent actors within society.

While the South African state may not have had exactly the same options to borrow that were available to Brazil during this period, international lines of credit were still largely available until the mid-1980s. Nevertheless, the South African Minister of Finance was able to use the tax system to ratchet up revenues, and less foreign financing was necessary. During the period 1975–90, the South African state had effectively reached its limits in terms of its ability to tax from the very top of the income ladder, and in order to promote capital investments, the state began to offer new investment allowances, ultimately causing a downturn in company tax revenues.[143] To make up this revenue shortfall, the government enlisted the aid of major retailers to draw upon the untapped resource of consumption taxes, enacting a general sales tax, and steadily increasing revenues from between 2–4 percent

[143] Nattrass and Ardington 1990: 16.

of GDP in the 1970s to approximately 10 percent of GDP in the late 1980s. Meanwhile, on the income tax side, an effective and efficient tax system provided easy money in a mildly inflationary environment. By not correcting for inflation within the tax policy, lower-income salary-earners were pushed into increasingly higher tax brackets, allowing the state to extract higher levels of revenue without any need for significant policy change. Such a tactic was a relatively easy way to increase revenues without making additional demands during a period of political crisis, and had a regressive effect on the distribution of the tax burden. However, it is important to realize that such a strategy could only be effective in an environment in which taxes were being collected regularly and in which businesses and upper-income individuals liable for the taxes were already highly cooperative with the state's extractive bureaucracy.

Better able to finance expenditure needs through taxation, and better able to command authority over upper groups in that society, the South African economy was much less vulnerable to political and economic crisis than was the case in Brazil. One important implication of these differences was that Brazil would find itself wracked with massive interest payment obligations, particularly when compared with South Africa. As shown in Figure 4.8,

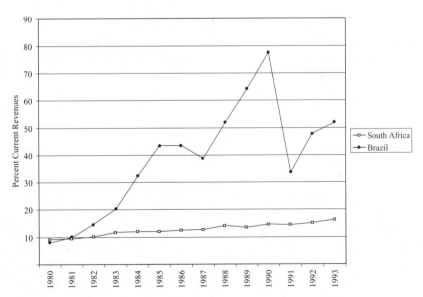

Figure 4.8 Interest payments in Brazil and South Africa, 1980–1993. *Source:* World Bank 1998.

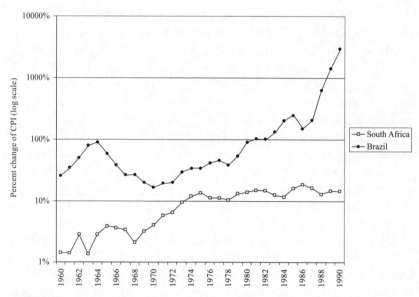

Figure 4.9 Annual inflation in Brazil and South Africa, 1960–1990. *Source:* Central Statistical Service 1995; IBGE 1990; World Bank 1998.

interest payments grew to a staggering 120 percent of current revenues in 1990 in Brazil, while in South Africa, such obligations remained under 20 percent of current revenues until the early 1990s, when they jumped slightly above that mark. A second key implication was with respect to infla-tion (see Figure 4.9). Although South Africans were extremely concerned with the high inflation of the 1980s, when seen in comparative perspec-tive with the Brazilian record, the inflationary problems were clearly not in the same league. Brazilian hyperinflation led to the collapse of several currencies, while throughout this period, the South African Rand remained relatively resilient.

Undoubtedly, the relationship between the quality of the tax state and economic performance is not unidirectional. For example, poor Brazilian tax collections were also *caused by* the *Tanzi effect* – the inducement of de-layed tax payment under highly inflationary conditions, producing real de-clines in revenue. Nevertheless, there is sufficient evidence to conclude that macroeconomic performance in these two countries was highly dependent upon the state's control over fiscal policy, which in turn was a function of how the tax state had developed during the first three-quarters of the century.[144] South Africa's cooperative tax state provided a relatively much stronger basis for weathering the economic storms of political and economic change than Brazil's adversarial tax state.

Conclusion

The comparative analysis of tax state building in Brazil and South Africa presented in this chapter has yielded multiple insights for making causal assessments. The analysis demonstrated that both economic and international factors created needs for tax revenue, leading national executives to make similar demands for new taxation. However, these factors were not determinative of tax outcomes, as similar economic and international influences were associated with wide differences in the development of the tax state.

The analysis also revealed the inability of several rival explanations to shed light on the problem of tax state development. Colonial legacies proved relatively unimportant as influences on 20th-century taxation because, if anything, such legacies would have led us to predict the development of a more centralized and extractive tax state in Brazil than in South Africa. The notion of different tax paying cultures – as a prior explanatory factor – could not account for differences because even in South Africa, prior to the formation of the Union, both whites and blacks resisted efforts to collect, suggesting that norms of tax payment are endogenous to larger political processes. An explanation emphasizing the technical or professional qualities of the respective tax administrations did not provide great insights into the outcomes because most historical evidence pointed to the existence of at least as much technical competency in the Brazilian tax administration as in the South African one. Regime type could not provide a particularly powerful explanation of difference because even during the period of similarly repressive, bureaucratic regimes, tax outcomes diverged widely across Brazil and South Africa. Moreover, the Brazilian state's ability to collect from upper groups was not markedly different throughout the period of bureaucratic authoritarian rule than it was during the prior democratic period.

The findings also shed new light on several important political-historical accounts of Brazil and South Africa. For example, Yudelman's analysis of

---

[144] The influence of fiscal imbalance in Brazil, particularly poor tax collections, on macroeconomic performance is discussed elsewhere. See Macedo and Barbosa 1997.

171

South African political and economic history pointed to the "incorporation of labor" as the most important determinant of government-business labor relations in the 20th century.[145] And yet, as the comparison with Brazil demonstrated, it was not the incorporation of labor per se, but a particular type of racially exclusionary and nationally unified incorporation of labor that gave rise to a national state with significant authority and highly cooperative relations with upper groups. Meanwhile, Weyland's historical analyses of the Brazilian state echo a characterization found elsewhere in the literature on Brazil – namely, that a highly effective developmental state was constructed during the Vargas era and later dismantled.[146] The comparison with South Africa, while not contradicting the assessment of over-time change, does suggest that even during the Vargas period, the authority of the Brazilian central state was still relatively weak for a country at its level of economic development.

Most importantly, the chapter demonstrated the plausibility of the central argument of this book – that critical junctures during which definitions of National Political Community get specified have a powerful and measurable influence on the development of the tax state. During three key episodes of tax policy reform in the 20th century, the varied salience of race and regionalism in the politics of taxation, and associated differences in inter- and intra-class relations, structured very different bargaining processes between the state and upper groups in Brazil and South Africa. During each of these three moments, nationally distinctive patterns of tax state formation were reinforced. These legacies of tax state building, and the continued salience of racial and regional identities in the two countries, also proved highly influential over the further development of the tax state during simultaneous transitions at the end of the 20th century – the period that will be considered in the next chapter.

[145] Yudelman 1983.
[146] Weyland 1998b.

5

Shadows of the Past

TAX REFORM IN AN ERA
OF GLOBALIZATION AND
DEMOCRATIZATION

Even when the most basic terms of social, political, and economic life are shaken up, certain old patterns die hard. Indeed, if ever there was a time when domestic and international conditions would have seemed capable of producing *convergence* in the trajectory of tax state building in Brazil and South Africa, the last two decades of the 20th century were such a period. First, the two countries continued to be characterized by similar levels of economic and industrial development, and given the generally strong relationship between modernization factors and patterns of tax collection, there would have been good reason to predict that their tax policies and administrative practices would increasingly resemble those of one another. Second, in an era of globalization, the international economy has provided strong incentives for countries to conform to global norms of tax policy and administration. Given the prospect of the flight of skills and capital, policy makers have been bombarded with demands for lower taxes on mobile capital and for the simplification of complex tax systems. Finally, democratic transitions in both countries have provided openings for significant tax reform. For the first time, poor majorities have had the opportunity to express political opinions on questions of taxation in both countries. Although the conventional wisdom about the impact of democratization on taxation outcomes is less clear, at the very least one could certainly have predicted that *similar* political openings should have led to *similar* types of tax reforms in the two countries.

Despite these strong domestic and international pressures, the nationally distinctive qualities of the respective tax states have been reproduced. In fact, in many critical ways, the tax policies and administrative practices in force in the two countries at the end of the 20th century were *more* different from one another than they were at any other time during the century.

173

The Brazilian tax state was a complex, inefficient, and highly regressive set of institutions, which was relatively less dominant with respect to subnational government authorities, while the South African one operated much more efficiently, with a set of rules that were more progressive, and carried out in a more transparent way. How do we account for the reproduction of such patterns in the wake of such substantial, homogenizing pressures?

The political community model provides useful insights for understanding this puzzle, relating definitions of NPC to the reform of tax policies and administrative practices. Despite similar initial conditions in the two countries approximately a century ago, historically contingent choices about who to include and who to exclude as full citizens in those countries shaped the paths of state development. More recent political struggles in these two transitional societies need to be understood from the perspective of historical choices that would subsequently constrain the range of options available to political actors, policy makers, and ordinary citizens. Indeed, the shadow of the past is very much evident in the organization of politics, society, and taxation in contemporary Brazil and South Africa. Specifically, three sets of causal mechanisms have reproduced these historical legacies.

First, the definition of NPC crafted in founding constitutions around the turn of the 20th century became institutionalized within organizations and political discourse, structuring the cohesion of economic classes in nationally distinctive ways. Class cohesion has traditionally been a central determinant of the political contests surrounding the allocation of the tax burden. The exact idioms used for politics or the proper names of political organizations may have changed, but the ideas and myths that hold some groups together and keep others apart have been re-invented and adapted to new circumstances over time. It is simply a lower cost and lower risk strategy to re-apply old political idioms and organizations than to re-invent new ones.

In Brazil, despite some minor challenges by intellectuals and others within society, the myth of racial democracy has persisted, and region has remained the most powerful collective identity. Particularly following the installation of the 1988 constitution, this identity has continued to fragment upper and lower groups. Solutions to the collective action problem of taxation have remained elusive in that country, as state executives have had little bargaining power in the face of multiple and conflicting groups, expressing divergent and narrowly defined interests.

In South Africa, the end of apartheid has clearly provided an opportunity for that society to self-consciously redraw the meaning of both region and

174

race. In fact, in formal terms, the definition of NPC now resembles that of Brazil – it is an officially nonracial federation. Yet, in practice, constitutional change has not immediately restructured the organizational and discursive bonds that generated high levels of class unity during previous decades. The timing and sequencing of defining NPC is critical to how and when identities become truly salient in the political arena. Earlier political patterns of racial exclusion and challenge help to explain the origins of truly national organizations, which continue to be relatively unfettered by regional or linguistic differences, even in a country with eleven official languages. Prior political legacies help account for the relative cohesion of the organizations that link together upper-group interests in that country, including political parties and employer organizations. Within such a polity, the state executive has enormous bargaining power because narrowly based groups are rendered largely powerless within this political context.

Definitions of NPC have also structured the cross-class alliances and moral imperatives that affect the vertical allocation of the tax burden through the creation and interpretation of political identities. While it is true that upper-income, white South Africans generally do not have the same sense of normative obligation toward poor, black South Africans today that they once did with poor whites, the legacy of apartheid provides a clear imperative for redistribution from white to black. It is widely recognized that economic privilege was explicitly crafted out of racial identity and normative claims that the fiscal system *ought to* redress the legacy of institutionalized white supremacy resonate within society. A form of *collective guilt*[1] motivates upper groups to cooperate with redistributive policies and initiatives. Moreover, much like in the 1920s when poor whites demonstrated their political strength with strike activity, wealthier whites in modern South Africa have recognized the strategic importance of making some concessions to black demands for redistribution of resources and opportunities. In Brazil, despite a strong correlation between skin color and socioeconomic status, no analogous political imperative has successfully captured the imagination of upper Brazilians, compelling them to embrace downward redistribution toward blacks or to the poor more generally. On a discursive level, there is no clearly defined perpetrator responsible for the huge inequalities of income and wealth. From a strategic perspective, poor

---

[1] I am grateful to Kimberly Morgan for suggesting this term.

blacks, or the poor in general, are not viewed as politically powerful enough to warrant significant concessions from upper groups.

Finally, the policies and administrative practices constituting the respective tax states are themselves difficult to change. Patterns of engagement and resistance between state and society that were configured during previous periods have shaped the reproduction of the fiscal relationship between state and society in the contemporary period. Particularly from the perspective of revenue-hungry state executives and bureaucracies, operating in the uncertain conditions posed by the processes of democratization and globalization, the perceived costs and risks of change are high. Expectations concerning the behavior of different groups within society based on their prior patterns of challenging policies or complying with collection efforts clearly influence choices concerning new policies and practices in the ongoing process of tax reform. Existing stocks of human and technological capacity within the government bureaucracy and within society continuously favor certain types of reform options over others. As a result, state leaders have opted to retain practices that they believe will continue to generate revenue, irrespective of "ideal" efficiency and/or equity parameters.

Admittedly, it is difficult to test arguments about path dependence. How would we know if the institutional reproduction of politics, as described above, is *really* the best explanation for why these two tax states look so different from one another at the end of the 20th century? Again, various analytical strategies prove useful in making this inference. First, I describe the political and economic conditions and transformations that have affected the two countries in the late 20th century, as a way of considering rival explanations about the determinants of taxation. Similar scores on these variables serve as analytic controls, demonstrating the extent to which one might predict very similar types of tax reform. Second, I provide evidence demonstrating how the salience of racial and regional identities associated with earlier definitions of National Political Community have shaped the organizational and normative bases of politics in the two countries during this period. Third, I investigate the impact of these different identities on class cohesion in the two societies, and the relationship between class cohesion and the bargaining power of the state executive. Finally, the chapter describes how those strategies as well as pre-existing patterns of taxation have affected the development of the tax state. In short, I deploy various strategies for ruling out rival explanations and detail a plausible narrative of path-dependent processes at work at the end of the 20th century.

176

Table 5.1 *Selected economic indicators for Brazil and South Africa, c. 1994*

	Brazil	South Africa
GNP capita ($US), 1994	2,970	3,040
Human development index, 1994	.783	.716
Average annual growth rate, 1985–94	– 0.4	– 1.3
Manufacturing (% of GDP), 1994	25	23
Industrial labor force (% of total), 1994	23	32
GINI index	63.4 (1989)	58.4 (1993)

Sources: World Bank 1998, United Nations Website.

Pressures for Tax Reform from Home and Abroad

During the last two decades of the 20th century, processes of economic development, globalization, and democratization opened up new political avenues for actors to challenge the size and distribution of the tax burden within Brazil and South Africa. In each country, the similar ways in which these processes have unfolded provide a strong basis for expecting that patterns of tax reform should have been more congruent.

Modernization and Uneven Development

First, the two countries continued to experience similar rates of economic growth, implying similar sets of tax "handles," and similar bases for political mobilization (see Table 5.1). At the end of the 20th century, Brazil and South Africa were classified by the World Bank as upper-middle income countries, and based on 1994 data, were ranked 41st and 42nd most developed of the 133 large countries compared in the annual World Development Report (1996). As measured by the GINI coefficient, they were the first and second most *unequal* societies on Earth, with about half the population living below the poverty line in each country. Both countries are characterized by the stark juxtaposition of modern infrastructures and corporate skyscrapers next to unserviced shantytowns. Finally, the sectoral compositions of the economies have continued to be similar: Manufacturing represents about one-fourth of Gross Domestic Product in both countries, and the size of the industrial labor force is also relatively similar.

Globalization

Second, the developments associated with the process of *globalization* have been the source of homogenizing pressures for tax reform in Brazil,

177

South Africa, and elsewhere. The rapid integration of markets for goods, services, and capital across national borders, and exponential increases in the speed with which information can be transmitted to virtually any-where in the world, pose potentially serious threats to the capacity of national states to collect taxes. Of course, countries and economies have been linked together in terms of trade and investment for several centuries, and as discussed in prior chapters, developments in the international econ-omy influenced state development in these two countries during earlier periods in the 20th century. Yet, never before have people been able to move capital and information within and across national borders so effort-lessly, making the state's ability to regulate national markets exceedingly difficult.[2]

Among scholars and policy analysts, there has been significant consen-sus that globalization threatens state extractive capacities, particularly the capacity to tax upper groups. While there does remain some important dis-agreement about the *extent* to which such pressures hamstring state policy, at the very least, the logic is fairly well accepted: If the state's extractive capacity is a function of its ability to monitor and to regulate various stocks and flows of capital, then globalization poses a significant new challenge to that capacity by providing unprecedented opportunities for erosion of the tax base and revenue leakage. As the director of Fiscal Affairs at the International Monetary Fund (IMF) Vito Tanzi points out, governments are increasingly affected by the actions of other governments in most im-portant aspects of tax policy, and that, "In no other area of taxation can the effect of deepening economic integration be as unsettling or as im-portant as in the taxation of capital."[3] The high degree of capital mobility afforded by a more globalized international economy implies that holders of capital may enjoy a much higher degree of bargaining power relative to the state than in a more closed economy.[4] Multinational firms can use transfer-pricing mechanisms to minimize tax payments on a worldwide basis by concentrating profits in lower-tax jurisdictions and can bargain with national and local governments for lower tax burdens as a prerequi-site for investment. As has by now become common wisdom, these trends have been predicted to lead to flatter tax systems, as governments attempt to protect revenues by shifting increasingly to consumption taxes, and by

[2] "Disappearing Taxes," 1997.
[3] Tanzi 1995: 65.
[4] Bates and Lien 1985: 53–70; Frieden 1991; and Goodman and Pauly 1993.

taxing capital at proportional as opposed to progressive rates.[5] New policy norms associated with the leadership of Ronald Reagan in the United States, and Margaret Thatcher in the United Kingdom, reinforced these global pressures by advocating a smaller role for the state and by espousing the benefits of lower and flatter tax burdens.[6] The 1980s was a decade of profound tax reform in these countries, and around the world, and the ideas associated with Reagan-Thatcherism and globalization pervaded the policy debates in many countries.

Although globalization is a worldwide phenomenon, it is important to recognize that important cross-national differences in levels of market integration may mediate the effects of changes in the global economy.[7] What is relevant to the analysis here is that if Brazil and South Africa were characterized by very *different* levels of market integration, that factor itself might account for differences in tax policy and administration. Nevertheless, more careful scrutiny suggests that even the nature and timing of market integration in these two countries has been quite similar. Both are cases of *delayed* and *partial* integration.

Both economies became more open only after previously successful protected industrialization strategies finally stalled out. As shown in Figure 5.1, throughout the 1980s, both economies underperformed when compared with world averages, and the 1980s is known as the "lost decade" for development in Brazil and South Africa, as well as for the larger Latin American and African regions in which they are situated. In both Brazil and South Africa, the state was forced to subsidize many uncompetitive industries, placing increasing pressure on the fiscus, and on policy makers to adopt what was emerging as the Washington Consensus. This has included policies promoting privatization and trade liberalization increasingly understood to be important prerequisites to participate in this more global economy. With its large domestic economy and resolve to protect many of the industries within its borders, the Brazilian state resisted pressures to conform throughout most of the 1980s. In the case of South Africa, nonintegration was imposed largely by external forces in the 1980s, as various sanctions and economic boycotts against the apartheid government kept it largely, though not entirely, isolated from the world.

---

[5] Tanzi 1996.
[6] Steinmo 1993.
[7] Garrett 1998.

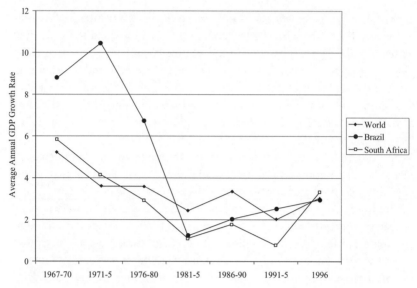

Figure 5.1 International economic growth rates, 1967–1996. *Source:* World Bank 1998.

In the late 1980s and 1990s, national government leaders in both countries made gestures toward accepting many of the new rules of the international economy, even if they did not embrace them with the zealous reforms pursued by certain other middle-income countries such as Chile or Poland. As sanctions lifted following the unbanning of the ANC and the release of Nelson Mandela from prison in 1990, South Africa increasingly joined the international economy. During that decade, Brazil lowered its tariffs, loosened its capital controls, and developed increasing transportation and communication linkages with neighboring countries and with countries of other regions.[8] Ministers of Finance traveled extensively on "road shows" to various financial capitals attempting to lure new investment to their reformed economies. In addition to their linkages with respective regional organizations (Mercosul for Brazil and the Southern African Development Community in South Africa), both countries joined the "Group of 20" (G20), which works together on global economic issues and includes mostly advanced countries such as the United States, France,

---

[8] See Longo 1997.

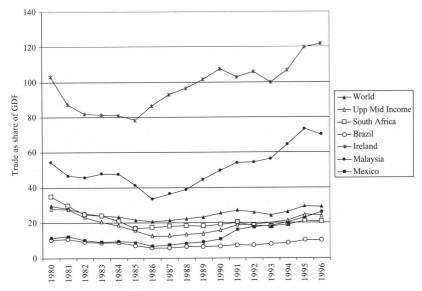

Figure 5.2 World trade, 1980–1996. *Source:* World Bank 1998.

Germany, and Italy, as well as a few other upper-middle income countries such as Argentina, Mexico, and South Korea.[9]

By the mid-1990s, neither country could be described as *highly* integrated into the global economy when compared with other countries at similar levels of development, or when compared with the European countries. As shown in Figure 5.2, employing total trade as share of GDP as an indicator of global integration,[10] we can see that although trade has increased since the mid-1980s in these two countries, neither are exceptional in terms of high levels of trade, and if anything, Brazil is a particular laggard in this area. In 1996, both traded less than the average for upper-middle income countries and the world, and way below countries located close to major Asian or European markets, such as Malaysia and Ireland. Although there has been some liberalization of capital markets, in both countries some controls remained in 1999. Given long histories of protection, political leaders have argued that rapid integration

[9] Trevor Manuel, "Statement Made to the National Assembly, Republic of South Africa, On the Recently-Held Annual Meetings of the International Fund and the World Bank," Cape Town: Ministry of Finance, Republic of South Africa, 1999.
[10] Garrett 1998.

poses substantial risks, including exacerbating already profound problems of unemployment. Policy makers in both countries have tried to moderate the pace at which integration proceeds in order to temper the potentially devastating effects of competition with foreign enterprises, while attempting to stem the flow of capital flight by restricting the amounts that can be taken out of the country. Nevertheless, given the demand for capital and highly skilled professionals abroad, there are limits to the degree to which policy makers are able to control the pace of integration.

The discourse of tax policy debates within both countries during the 1980s and 1990s was centrally concerned with international trends and norms, and the imperative for harmonization. Virtually any tax policy entrepreneur could gain some leverage if he or she could convince others that some aspect of the tax system was out of line with international taxation practices. High-ranking tax officials in both countries explained in interviews that understanding and responding to the pressures of globalization are key priorities. The major macroeconomic plans implemented in the mid-1990s in the respective countries – the Growth, Employment, and Redistribution (GEAR) plan in South Africa, and the Real Plan in Brazil – were both concrete attempts to achieve economic stability and competitiveness by attempting to conform to the new rules of the international economy. Central to the conception of both plans were attempts to control expenditure and to lower budget deficits. More specifically, key documents associated with tax administration and tax reform in both countries paid significant attention to the impact of globalization on taxation. These documents repeatedly made reference to the tax policies and collections of other countries, revealing pressures toward convergence.[11]

Democratization

Third, amidst these patterns of economic change, in the last quarter-century, Brazil and South Africa emerged as two of approximately forty countries that made transitions away from authoritarian rule, part of a

---

[11] In the Brazilian case, see the Ministry of Finance's internal publications, including ESAF 1994, 1995, and 1997, for evidence of important discussions concerning the impact of globalization on tax administration. For the South African case, see discussions in the Reports of the Margo and Katz Commissions of Inquiry into the South African Tax System.

phenomenon generally referred to as the third wave of democratization.[12] Although the implications of democratization for the specific nature of tax reform are more ambiguous, at the very least, this development implies an opening for important tax reforms of *some* kind. Scholars of both Brazil and South Africa have discussed the transition to democracy as *the* critical change in those respective societies in the past several decades, if not the watershed in the history of the past several centuries. The disjuncture with the past is marked with popular political discourse: Contemporary South African society is known as the New South Africa, and the period of the first civilian presidency in Brazil following the military leadership was known as the New Republic (*Nova República*). Democratic transitions have provided openings for the renegotiation of various policies and administrative practices in a range of areas, and tax reform has been a key policy concern in both countries in the 1980s and 1990s. Not surprisingly, a wide range of political actors began to argue that the tax systems should be more fair. The periods surrounding the writing of new constitutions prompted critical debates about what role the state *ought* to play, how it should be financed, and by whom. While democratization on its own does not imply a specific trajectory of tax reform, it does provide a potentially important opening for various political actors and other political and economic pressures to influence tax outcomes, including policies concerned with who should pay, and how much.

In many critical ways, the process of democratization was highly similar across the two countries.[13] Both transitions involved a dialectic mixture of incumbent openings, and intensified pressure for reform from below, and both proceeded at a gradual pace. In Brazil, this opening is widely known by its literal translation, *abertura*, while in South Africa, an analogous, controlled reform process was underway throughout the 1980s. Across the two countries, upper- and working-class actors played similar roles in the process of democratization, in that a combination of elite negotiations from above and popular challenges from below moved the process of political liberalization forward to the point of writing new democratic constitutions.[14]

---

[12] Huntington 1991.

[13] See, for example, Seidman 1994; Munck 1989; Du Toit 1995; Hagopian 1996; Keck 1992; Payne 1995; Sisk 1995; Price 1991; and Sparks 1995.

[14] Some analysts disagree about the degree to which these were "pacted" transitions. See, for example, contributions in Friedman and de Villiers 1996.

As a result of this process, Brazilians in 1989 and South Africans in 1994 of all races and income groups were able to choose their national leaders through relatively free, fair, and competitive elections.[15]

Adding to the remarkable parallels of the two countries, the presidents elected in 1994 came to office offering similar visions of social justice, presumably with similar goals about what would constitute a fair tax burden in their similarly unequal societies.[16] In that year, South Africans and Brazilians both elected leaders who had been banned from political life by earlier authoritarian regimes. Both Nelson Mandela and Fernando Henrique Cardoso had become famous for railing against the authoritarian regimes that ruled their home countries, and each had advocated alternatives to capitalism as a mode of organizing economy and society. Both had also been outspoken concerning the racial inequalities that had been perpetuated since the earliest days of colonialism in their respective societies.

As each became state president, ironically, both would have to confront the particular challenges of a more globalized economy and what that would mean for their ideas for change, particularly for state reform. As Cardoso wrote in a 1996 United Nations publication, "Obviously we cannot return to the ideas of the 1960s. The world has changed."[17] Similarly, Nelson Mandela and his ANC found themselves promoting privatization when they had once authored the Freedom Charter, which had effectively called for nationalization.[18] Each of these leaders promised at the outset of their terms to identify novel solutions to the legacies of inequality that faced their new democracies, including an important role for the state, largely to be financed through taxation.

---

[15] The 1985 election of Tancredo Nevis in Brazil was an indirect election, though most observers of Brazilian politics generally mark the onset of democratization with that election.

[16] Undoubtedly, Brazilian democracy got off to a rocky start as the first civilian president-elect died unexpectedly before he was able to serve his term, installing a leader who had been strongly linked to the military government. The second elected president, also a former military government ally, was removed from office on corruption charges.

[17] United Nations Development Program 1996: 44.

[18] The Freedom Charter, adopted at the Congress of the People, Kliptown, on June 26, 1955, declared, "The national wealth of our country, the heritage of South Africans, shall be restored to the people; The mineral wealth beneath the soil, the Banks and monopoly industry shall be transferred to the ownership of the people as a whole; All other industry and trade shall be controlled to assist the wellbeing of the people . . ."

The Reconstruction of Racial and Regional Identities

Even amidst economic modernization, and more recent processes of democratization and globalization, "old" group identities have remained central to political life in Brazil and South Africa, and have served to structure patterns of conflict and consensus in decision making and in attempts to wield state authority in the late 20th century. Earlier definitions of NPC are largely responsible for the relative salience of certain identities over others, as the political identities that mattered in the past still shape what matters today. As discussed in Chapter 1, the NPC can be redefined at particular moments in time, particularly during moments of disorienting change, but such definitions tend to be a *response* to old definitions, in which previously excluded groups are now included or vice versa. Within the political arena, discussions of contemporary problems and prospects for future change tend to be shaped by a repertoire of existing frameworks developed in the past. Political organization, normative obligations, and commonly accepted ideas about justice and equity evolve with a political vocabulary developed within a country's own national history. As political elites carried out the process of writing *new* democratic constitutions in Brazil and South Africa, they found that racial identity and place of residence or regional identity were important predictors of social and economic inequality. Nevertheless, as summarized in Table 5.2, the political relevance of these identities as bases for political organization and political discourse continued to vary widely.

In both countries, there continue to be significant economic bases for race-based political mobilization, as whites are better educated, have better access to services, and hold better-paying jobs than people of color.[19] In Brazil, a study conducted in 1995 showed that the mortality rate for white infants up to one year old was 37.3 per 1,000 live births, while for infants of color, the rate was 62.3 per 100. Rates of unemployment were 22 percent higher for women of color than for white women, and 14 percent

---

[19] Indeed, there are important demographic differences in the size of the racial populations in the two countries: While whites represent approximately half of the Brazilian population, they comprise less than one-fifth of the South African population. Although one could argue that Brazil's larger white population explains the relative demobilization of race, the political salience of race in the United States, where blacks are an even smaller minority, suggests that this is not necessarily the case. Moreover, using South African criteria about race, many Brazilians who describe themselves as white would not be recognized as such in South Africa. This is not to imply that one definition of racial categories is more correct than the other, but to re-emphasize the socially constructed nature of these categories, and how they shift over time.

Table 5.2 *Racial and regional identities in Brazil and South Africa, 1990s*

	Identity	Brazil	South Africa
Predictor of socioeconomic inequality?	Race	Yes – high Wealth concentrated among whites	Yes – high Wealth concentrated among whites
	Region	Yes – high Wealth concentrated in the South and Southeast	Yes – high Wealth concentrated in Gauteng and Western Cape Provinces
Constitutional provisions for group-based inequalities?	Race	Yes Discrimination expressly forbidden	Yes Discrimination expressly forbidden
	Region	Yes Horizontal redistribution across federal units	Yes Horizontal redistribution across federal units
Political salience of group identity?	Race	Low Very little demarcation of organizations by race group	HIGH Political parties, organizations still along race lines
	Region	HIGH Most organizations and parties are divided along regional lines	Low But increased since federal constitution; Kwaz-Natal exception

higher for men of color than for white men.[20] In South Africa, the racial extremes are greater: In 1987, the infant mortality rate for white infants up to one year old was 13 per 1,000 live births, and 142 for Africans, Coloureds, and Asians.[21] Rates of unemployment in 1990 were approximately 67 percent higher for people of color in South Africa than for whites.[22]

Regional inequalities are also great, providing an additional potential cleavage in both countries. In Brazil, there are enormous disparities in social and economic conditions across the five major regions.[23] In 1992,

---

[20] See "Mortalidade Entre Negros," 1998.

[21] Weir 1992, as cited in MERG 1993. The result for the nonwhite group is a weighted average using population statistics from Central Statistical Service 1995.

[22] This statistic was calculated using actual employment and potential labor force measures from the MERG Macroeconomic model, 1990.

[23] The five regions are comprised of the twenty-six states and the federal district as follows: North: Rondônia, Acre, Amazonas, Roraima, Pará, Amapá, Tocantins; Northeast:

when the national Human Development Index was 0.783 for all of Brazil, in the Southern region, the HDI was calculated at 0.838, while for the much poorer Northeast, it was 0.549.[24] In South Africa, the development gaps are similar. Of South Africa's nine provinces, the Western Cape had an HDI of 0.826 compared with an HDI of 0.470 for the Northern Province.[25] In other words, within these countries there are some regions at the level of development of Portugal while others are at the level of Cameroon.

Cognizant of such inequalities, constitutional architects addressed questions about race explicitly in the constitutions of the two countries. In both documents, racial discrimination has been made illegal. Article 5, section 41 of Brazil's constitution states, "The practice of racism is a non-bailable crime, with no limitation, subject to the penalty of confinement, under the terms of the law." Chapter 2 section 9, of South Africa's 1997 constitution similarly prohibits discrimination by the state or any person on the basis of race. Moreover, both constitutions are explicitly federal arrangements, providing some degree of autonomy and mechanisms for redistribution across federal units. The South African constitution of 1996 constituted the National Council of Provinces (NCOP) in order to represent provincial interests in the Parliament, providing for 10 representatives from each of the nine provinces, regardless of population or income, and allowed for the creation of provincial legislatures which could, among other things, develop their own budgets. The 1988 Brazilian constitution firmly entrenched federalism by providing high levels of representation and autonomy to the twenty-seven federal units in the country. In both countries, the constitutionally defined budget process provides opportunities for the central government to re-allocate revenue in favor of poorer federal units.

Owing to the historical construction of NPC, however, the relative salience of such identities has remained distinctive in the democratic era, generating very different political logics: In Brazil, the central political idioms and organizations are primarily territorially based, and

Maranhão, Piauí, Ceará, Rio Grande do Norte, Paraíba, Pernambuco, Alagoas, Sergipe, Bahia; Southeast: Minas Gerais, Espírito Santo, Rio de Janeiro, São Paulo; South: Paraná, Santa Catarina, Rio Grande do Sul; Central West: Mato Grosso do Sul, Mato Grosso, Goiás, Federal District.

[24] United Nations Development Program 1994.
[25] South African Institute of Race Relations 1997, as cited in James and Levy 1998: 63. See also Whiteford, Posel, and Kelatwang 1995.

racial inequalities are perpetuated in more subtle ways. By contrast, in South Africa, place of residence remains as a marginal political identity, while race has continued to trump all other identities and symbols as the basis for political life. In both countries, the specific meanings of both race and region have shifted over time – as the matching of traits and labels has been reconfigured in various ways – but for now, the relevance of these basic group identities persists into the 21st century.[26] Such differences are highly consequential for the organization of class relations within these societies, a theme that will be taken up in the following section.

The Political Salience of Race

Following a century of very different national government approaches to race in Brazil and South Africa, the political relevance of that category remained radically different across the two countries at the end of the 20th century. Perhaps the clearest evidence of this difference can be seen by comparing the bases for political party support, the foundational mechanism of political participation in the new democracies. As shown in Figure 5.3, one can see that in South Africa, political parties have distinctive racial bases, whereas in Brazil, they do not.

The results of the Institute for Democracy's (Idasa) 1997 national survey in South Africa reveal that support for the victorious African National Congress and for the Inkatha Freedom Party was comprised almost exclusively of blacks/Africans (more than 90 percent for both parties), while fewer than 30 percent of the supporters for the next two parties, the Democratic Party and the National Party, were Black/African.[27] What is particularly interesting about such racial composition is that *none* of the leading parties have mobilized their membership based on explicit racial or ethnic claims, and all of them have attempted to attract supporters across the racial divide. In fact, the parties that did make such

---

[26] See, for example, Lovell 1994, for a discussion of the changing definitions of racial categories in Brazil over time. In South Africa, the state's reshaping of borders at various moments in time in the 20th century has necessarily altered the prospects for regional identification.

[27] The Public Opinion Service unit of the Institute for Democracy in South Africa (IDASA) designed the survey. Research Surveys Pty Ltd. conducted the fieldwork during June and July 1997. The universe for the survey was all South Africans, 18 years and older; 3,500 interviews were conducted. Results based on the total national sample have a margin of error of plus/minus three percentage points.

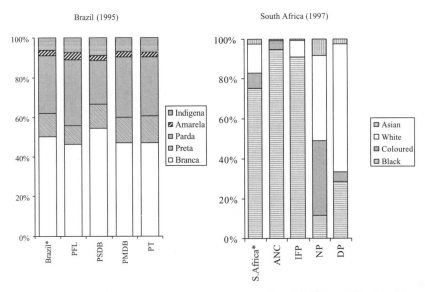

Figure 5.3   Racial composition of party support in Brazil (1995) and South Africa (1997). Asterisk (*) denotes racial composition of national sample. *Sources:* Author analyses of Datafolha survey (1995); IDASA survey (1997).

calls – the Pan African Congress (PAC) and the Freedom Front (FF) – suffered dismal electoral returns.[28] Nevertheless, the historical legacy of apartheid politics, which pitted white "insiders" against explicitly excluded black "outsiders," shaped the dynamics of this post-apartheid party system.[29] By contrast, in Brazil, there is no evidence of direct or indirect relationships between race and political party support, as the racial basis of support across four leading political parties is virtually identical, revealing the legacy of that country's official nonracialism. Based on a 1995 national survey, the PMDB, PT, PSDB, and PFL could all claim that approximately half their supporters were white (*branca*) and that the other half were people of color.[30]

[28] Price 1997.
[29] And "Coloureds" – as a "middle" group in the South African system of racial stratification – were split in their support for the National Party (NP) and the African National Congress (ANC).
[30] The newspaper company, *Folha de S. Paulo*, designed the "300 *Anos de Zumbi*" survey. The research unit, *Datafolha*, conducted the fieldwork during April 4–6, 1995. The universe for the survey was all Brazilians, 16 years and older; 5,081 interviews were conducted. Results

In recent years, scholars and political leaders have attempted to better understand the seeming contradictions of the absence of racial political mobilization in Brazil and its myth of a racial democracy, in light of findings of race-based inequalities and evidence of racial discrimination. Even President Fernando Henrique Cardoso has spoken publicly about the problems of racial discrimination in Brazil, and has called for Brazilians to reflect upon patterns of discrimination that continue to persist within their society.[31] And yet, the legacy of policies of "whitening" and official nondiscrimination have dulled the points of protest around such differences. The subtle contradictions of contemporary Brazilian race relations only become evident when one compares interactions across various settings within that society. On the one hand, in terms of public recreational spaces, such as the streets and beaches of a city like Rio de Janeiro, people of all colors intermingle freely with one another with seemingly little hostility. Yet below the surface, racial divisions become more evident. For example, obvious racial divisions are apparent when one enters the gates of one of the most prestigious universities such as the University of São Paulo or the Catholic University of Rio de Janeiro, or the headquarters of a large corporation. In such places, one finds that students and executives are virtually all light skinned, while the janitors and unskilled workers are virtually all dark skinned. This phenomenon, aptly described as *Racismo Cordial*, is the product of Brazil's unique history of race politics.[32] On the one hand, Brazilians are more willing to associate across the color line in casual settings, and they like the *idea* of a society built around nondiscrimination to a greater extent than in other multiracial societies.[33] On the other hand, white and mulatto Brazilians hold many negative stereotypes about Afro-Brazilians, and they

based on the total national sample have a margin of error of plus/minus two percentage points. For more information, see Turra and Venturi 1995.

[31] See, for example, the speech delivered by Fernando Henrique Cardoso, Seminário Internacional "Multiculturalismo e Racismo: O Papel da Ação Afirmativa nos Estados Democráticos Contemporâneos," Palácio do Planalto, July 2, 1996. In interviews with the author, several respondents pointed out that Cardoso had once commented that he "had one foot in the kitchen, too," to describe his partial black ancestry. The comment further highlights an important line of debate concerning the real roots of racism in Brazil – specifically, whether or not it is simply a manifestation of class differences. See, for example, Lovell 1994. Also, see the lyrics of a song by Gilberto Gil and Caetano Veloso, entitled, "Haiti," in which they refer to "whites so poor they're almost black."

[32] See Turra and Venturi 1995.

[33] As Pereira (1996: 75–79) argues, it is considered "impolite" to be overtly racist in modern Brazilian society.

practice race-based discrimination in various aspects of their personal and professional lives.[34] As Carlos Hasenbalg points out, race-based inequality is *not* merely a socioeconomic legacy from slavery, but also a product of persistent discrimination and cultural stereotyping.[35] The result has been that Brazil has managed to maintain a racially unequal distribution of power and money, but no significant race-based challenge has been made to this order.

The contrast with South Africa is striking because at the end of the 20th century in that country, few political issues have been discussed without some direct or indirect attention to race-based inequalities. Questions about poverty, health, education, violence, land, and basic infrastructure, for example, must inevitably deal with the racial divide that was made so profound and overt, particularly during the apartheid era. While the 1994 election of Nelson Mandela signaled the end of the apartheid era, no sound analyst would have expected racial fault lines to disappear overnight – and they have not. Many of the country's political leaders have tried to promote racial reconciliation following more than three centuries of institutionalized white supremacy by promoting the notion of a "rainbow nation," a nation comprised of and fully tolerant of South Africa's various racial and language groups. Yet even this concept is rooted in a sense of racial difference because the very notion of "rainbow," from the South African perspective, involves an *explicit* attention to race.

Most observers would agree that the democratic transition in South Africa has been peaceful, and since 1994, people of all colors and language groups have participated jointly in the decision-making processes of that society. This must be seen as truly remarkable in light of the country's history and predictions of violent ethnic conflict.[36] On the other hand, the reality of racial antagonism and inequality still stood in conflict with the ideal of the rainbow nation on the eve of the 21st century. After four years of post-apartheid government, the ANC leadership elected to highlight the persistence of racial disparities, and Thabo Mbeki speaking as Deputy President in 1998 (prior to being elected State President in 1999) made a

---

[34] The popular news magazine, *Veja*, reported an incident of a television program systematically manipulating shots of live audiences in order to show only white children on the air. The writer described the incident as evidence of an "apartheid not declared." *Veja*, May 13, 1992.

[35] Hasenbalg and Silva 1987: 80.

[36] See, for example, discussions of the possibilities for conflict advanced by Horowitz 1991.

speech raising the idea that South Africa consists of two nations, divided along racial lines:

A major component part of the issue of reconciliation and nation building is defined by and derives from the material conditions in our society which have divided our country into two nations, the one black and the other white. . . . One of these nations is white, relatively prosperous, regardless of gender or geographic dispersal. It has ready access to a developed economic, physical, educational, communication and other infrastructure. . . . The second and larger nation of South Africa is black and poor.[37]

Few political issues in South Africa escape racial scrutiny. When it comes to national sports teams, observers consistently evaluate the racial composition of the team. Race is the optic through which South Africans consider questions about equity, collective interest, and decisions about the future. While there exist important differences within South African society regarding the extent to which members of one race group have positive or negative feelings about the other group, no South African can avoid being highly race conscious. In other words, the definition of NPC constructed in the 1909 South Africa Act – rooted in racial exclusion – continues to structure the organization of South African politics and society.

The Political Salience of Region

The relevance of place or region as a political idiom and basis for organization has also varied across the two cases during the last two decades. Despite regional inequalities and federal constitutions in both countries, only in Brazil do state and regional identities form the basis of persistent competition, acting as central idioms of political life. In that country, regional and/or *estado* identities are widely used as metrics for evaluating questions about equity and fairness. By contrast, South Africans rarely articulate their interests or preferences in regional terms. Given the reconfiguration of NPC in the new constitution as a federal polity, this may change in the future, but since 1994, provincial borders have not served as particularly important political boundaries in organizational or discursive terms.

In Brazil, political competition is waged primarily in terms of subnational spatial units – as municipalities, states, or regions. If there is any agreement

---

[37] Statement of Deputy President Thabo Mbeki at the Opening of the Debate in the National Assembly on "Reconciliation and Nation Building," National Assembly, Cape Town, May 29, 1998.

across these units, it is a common repudiation of the authoritarian past in terms of the centralizing tendencies of military rule, which provides political space to mobilize at the local, state, and regional levels.[38] Such a shift represents yet another swing of the centralization/decentralization pendulum that has moved back and forth for centuries in Brazil's history. The constitution produced in 1988 after a year of work by a constituent assembly firmly entrenched autonomy for states and municipalities, as the struggle for democracy in Brazil took on a distinctly local flavor. Governors and mayors are highly influential political figures, not simply as autonomous leaders of their own constituencies, but as stakeholders in national politics. As Abrucio points out, the 1988 constitution effectively gave the governors veto power over critical decisions made at the national level with a variety of tools: control over federal deputies and senators; a political institution, the *Conselho de Política Fazendária* (CONFAZ), which decides various fiscal incentives; and an influential role in various regional development organizations.[39] Many state governors are recognized as having significantly more power than members of Congress, who rely upon the governors to be voted into office.[40]

The strength of state governors and state rights has engendered two types of federal competition – among states and regions; and between states, regions, and municipalities on one side, and the federal government on the other.[41] The degree to which there are disparities in income, wealth, and/or development across regions is the standard framework for evaluating

---

[38] See Hagopian 1996, for a discussion of the persistent power of regional elites in the democratic era.

[39] Abrucio 1998: 170–71.

[40] Gordon 1998.

[41] A critical demonstration of the relative power of state leadership came in 1998, when President Fernando Henrique Cardoso found himself at the mercy of a renegade state leader, Itamar Franco (who, incidentally, had previously been president and who Cardoso had served under as Minister of Finance) who flaunted his power by declaring a moratorium on his debt to the central government during a critical period when the central government was negotiating a financial package with the IMF. Drawing on historical memory, Cardoso referred to this action as reminiscent of the Joaquim Silvério dos Reis, a hero from the historical challenge to the Brazilian nation during the *Inconfidência Mineira* (see Chapter 3) – a statement that touched a sharp nerve among other political leaders in the country, and was condemned in congress. During the course of his standoff with the federal government, Franco visited several other states to explain why he was "at war" with the central government, and Cardoso was forced to meet repeatedly with various other state governors to negotiate a settlement. That episode revealed the political strength of the governors within Brazil.

distributive justice, and few national statistics are reported in the media or in other reports without regional breakdowns.

For people living in the South and Southeast of the country, inequalities are often rationalized with expressions of cultural chauvinism. In particular the notion of the *Nordestino* is a powerful idiom with which white, upper-income Southerners interpret the social and economic problems of the country, particularly as they identify the *favela* populations in their cities as immigrants from the North. In discussing questions about regionalism, several respondents referred to a "murmuring" of secessionist sentiment in the Southern states. In 1995, secessionist leader Irton Marx went on television in Brazil with the heretic proposal of creating a Republic of the Pampas, arguing that the three Southernmost states would do better by declaring independence and ridding themselves of the obligation to pay taxes to a central state that makes large and wasteful financial transfers to the poorer regions of the North and Northeast. Underscoring the racial underpinnings of the regional differences in the country, Marx was widely labeled as a racist for his proposal.[42] While few sober observers would predict a rupture of the Brazilian federation, the discourse of difference makes the lines of regional or spatial competition politically emotive.

By contrast, in South Africa, where land has traditionally been demarcated in terms of racial identities, the notion of regional competition or conflict has been rendered largely meaningless. Regional identity, per se, is not intrinsically important in the political arena. Even in the post-apartheid context, the physical territory of the country has again been defined in terms of strategies for *redressing* racial policies, making race more important than space. The new constitution has redrawn the political landscape into a unified, multiracial territory. Former homelands and self-governing territories have been incorporated with the four provinces of the old South Africa into a new set of nine provinces. Each of these joins areas formerly designated for different race groups. Similarly, former black and white local authorities have been deliberately joined to create new multiracial local government districts within those provinces.

Although the new constitution is expressly federal, provincial identities are still less politically meaningful than the racial identities that cut across provinces and local authorities. Historically, both supporters of and challengers to the apartheid regime – including the most important political,

---

[42] Brooke 1993.

business, and labor organizations – have not developed distinctively regional personalities.[43] To the extent that there are regional offices for various organizations, these tend to exist merely at functional units within a larger division of labor, but still hierarchically below the national headquarters, which tends to fall in one of the national centers of either Johannesburg, Cape Town, Pretoria, or Durban. Regional identities continue to have little meaning from either an idiomatic perspective – that is, as a way of differentiating people or political systems – or from an organizational perspective. For example, the National Council of Provinces has been a particularly irrelevant institution of the South African parliament, to the extent that its chairperson, Patrick Lekota, publicly chastised nine cabinet ministers for failing to bother to make scheduled presentations to that house of the legislature.[44] There is very little political space for provincial leaders to flex their muscles, and to politicize the horizontal distribution of revenue allocated to the provinces. Provincial leadership in all nine provinces is determined by national organizations, and particularly for the ANC, which controlled seven of the nine provinces following the 1994 election, national leadership has exercised tight control over those appointments.

Class Relations and Political Strategies

The relative political salience of racial and regional group identities has continued to structure the organizations, interests, and strategies of class actors in these two societies, in turn shaping the relative ability of the state executive to command authority over these groups and to demand taxes from them (Table 5.3). The relative bargaining power or authority of the state executive is inversely proportional to the number of competing

[43] One important exception to the characterization of South Africa as devoid of regional conflict is the case of KwaZulu-Natal, where a particular political party, the Inkatha Freedom Party (IFP), has mobilized around a shared ethnic (Zulu) identity within this particular region. Over the past decade, much of the political violence in the country can be related to clashes between this group and other predominantly black groups, identified in political (ANC) or sometimes ethnic (Xhosa) terms. Indeed, during the negotiations for a new constitution, IFP leader Mangosuthu Buthelezi took a firm stand for stronger federal powers. The federal constitution that was eventually adopted was a compromise that resulted from such pressures, and associated threats of instability. Yet, in practice, the dynamic of political competition could hardly be said to take place across regions in the country, and Buthelezi has been consistently wooed by the first two ANC presidents with recognition and opportunities to serve as acting president in their absence. As a result, the one potential powder keg of provincial competition in the near term was doused, at least temporarily.

[44] "Truant Cabinet Minsters," 1998.

Table 5.3 *Collective actors, strategies, and bargaining power in Brazil and South Africa in the 1990s*

Collective Actor	Political Characteristics	**Brazil**	**South Africa**
UPPER GROUPS	Level of cohesion	Low	High
	Political strategies with respect to tax policy	Challenge proposals in favor of narrowly defined interests	Broad demands for simplification and general distribution downward
LOWER GROUPS	Level of cohesion	Low	High
	Political strategies with respect to tax policy	Various, weak, mixed strategies	Maintain pressure for progressive burden, particularly with normative imperatives
		↓	↓
STATE EXECUTIVE	Bargaining power with respect to societal actors	Weak Multiple, competing societal actors derail identification of acceptable tax solutions	Strong Easier to strike bargains with fewer actors, certainty of support. Little political space for narrow groups to challenge executive

groups that must be satisfied within the political arena,[45] implying that relative levels of class cohesion are critical to the nature of the strategic interaction. The comparative historical analysis presented in this section highlights the ways in which individual and collective actors with similar sets of *economic* interests have pursued very different strategies in terms of making demands, forming political partnerships, and accepting demands for sacrifice.

In South Africa, the political salience of race, and the influence of racial politics in previous years on contemporary organizations, has helped to produce political cohesion among groups with similar economic means. Lower

[45] Hardin 1982, 1985.

groups have been able to make strong political demands for redistribution, because the history of opposition to the white regime has provided very strong bases for organizational unity, and shared demands for white-to-black redistribution in the post-apartheid context. Meanwhile, upper groups have expressed desires to shift the tax burden downward, but the normative order of post-apartheid South Africa has provided compelling reasons for the rich to pony up to their tax obligations. Moreover, in the absence of regional and sectoral divisions, upper-group actors have found few opportunities to make more narrowly defined claims for special tax treatment. Rather, well-organized and broad-based political actors in South Africa have tended to politicize only "big" questions, such as the degree to which the tax burden should be distributed between direct and indirect taxes, while generally agreeing that questions of horizontal equity should be left to technocrats. In such an environment, the state executive has not needed to bargain with special interest groups to create a winning coalition in the legislature or to gain consensus among organized collective actors, making the reform dynamic fairly smooth and productive.

In Brazil, the dynamic has been quite different. At the end of the 20th century, upper and lower groups remained divided along regional lines. The absence of horizontal camaraderie within classes, and of normative idioms compelling distribution from top-to-bottom, provided little incentive for collective sacrifice. The lack of a coherent set of national organizations and/or interests has made the bargaining process quite unstable, with little certainty about what will comprise a winning coalition. This has created strong incentives for narrowly organized groups to articulate very particular demands, forcing others to address their concerns in order to gain sufficient support for a larger reform package. As a result, the executive's bargaining power, and control over the reform process, has been weak. Such a dynamic – analogous to American-style pork-barrel politics – has led to high degrees of compromise and/or stalemate in the political process.

By comparing the words and deeds of collective actors across the two countries during the recent period of tax reform, it is possible to observe how definitions of NPC shape the dynamic of political power.[46] Using the results of structured, open-ended interviews, survey research, as well as printed primary and secondary sources, I identify the different perspectives

---

[46] For a more general discussion of the relationship between institutions and political power, see Immergut 1998.

of these otherwise similar actors, and trace the impact of their interactions on the development and implementation of tax policy.

Upper Groups

Upper groups have always been highly influential over tax issues, and the integration of markets across national borders in the late 20th century has provided them even greater leverage for influencing this set of policies by using new strategies for voice and for exit. Business leaders have found they can lobby for lowered tax rates under the banner of globalization, identifying competitiveness and the need for harmonization as key rationales for lowering their tax burden. In recent years, they have enjoyed greater options to avoid and to evade the tax burden, using transfer pricing mechanisms, portfolio asset allocation strategies, and other strategies. In order to lower or to escape a tax burden, many high-income individuals simply move themselves, their families, and/or their businesses to other countries.

Such strategic options cannot be pursued without cost, however, given pre-existing investments and switching costs, and the desire to continue making profits within a given market. The economic elites of Brazil and South Africa have profited tremendously from investment in their own economies, and have a vested interest in continued stability, the provision of basic services, and the security of property rights, all of which presume the financial viability of the state. In both cases, although business sectors benefited from labor-repressive authoritarian regimes, one cannot lose sight of the fact that these sectors played a role in moving the country toward democratic transitions, and as such, have a stake in securing a more stable order to avoid regime or state collapse. Finally, even recognizing the extent to which upper groups have benefited from the unequal and often ruthless histories of their countries, the political arena still demands that they must justify their policy positions with normative rationales, and in this sense, the ability of such actors to pursue narrowly defined self-interests is highly constrained.[47]

Even in a more globalized world, upper groups do not pursue the same sets of strategies in all contexts. By comparing the organization, beliefs,

---

[47] At the extreme, of course, it would be fruitless for any single individual to attempt to secure complete tax exemption while maintaining the tax burden on all others within a given society.

and strategies of business actors across the two countries it is possible to understand why actors with similar economic means behave differently. As Mark Granovetter insightfully points out, there are multiple dimensions of variation that can characterize the organization of business groups across countries,[48] and such variation structures political action. The "axes of solidarity" he identifies as important can be examined from the perspective of racially and regionally defined identities in Brazil and South Africa. These identities have influenced both the formal organizations and the other political and social networks through which business leaders make decisions, develop strategies, and mobilize action.

Upper Groups in Brazil. In Brazil, the process of democratization did not lead to the increased aggregation of business and upper-group interests, but had just the opposite effect, producing increased fragmentation. While there is substantial evidence for the claims that the business sectors were generally supportive of the transition away from the very authoritarian regime that they helped to install in 1964, once the political transition was underway, historical patterns of intra-capital conflict re-appeared.[49] Largely common racial characteristics of the economically privileged never provided any form of organizational or ideological "glue" for upper groups, and this has continued to be true in the democratic era. As a result, the politics of tax reform has lacked a dynamic whereby a large constituency of upper groups accepts the legitimacy of demands for taxation imposed by the central state.

The most important business organizations have continued to be the Vargas-inspired products such as FIESP and FIRJAN, the state industrial associations of São Paulo and Rio de Janeiro. The national confederation of industries (CNI), under which these two state organizations (and the twenty-five others) formally fall under, generally has been regarded as much weaker and does not truly speak for national business. Because of the equal votes given to each state federation, despite the highly unequal size and sophistication of the business sectors in the different states, the leadership of CNI has tended to be captured by Northern business interests, making the organization seem illegitimate in the eyes of Southern industrialists. The CNI itself has engaged in distributive politics across business regions,

[48] See Granovetter 1994.
[49] Payne 1994: 243.

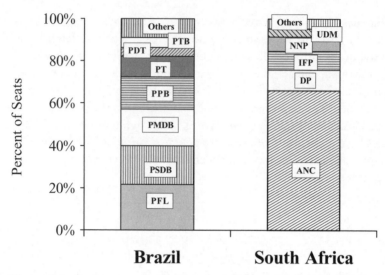

Figure 5.4 Party representation in the lower house of the legislature in Brazil and South Africa, 1999. *Source:* Government Websites.

rather than articulating a shared collective interest of Brazilian business. As a result, the state-level federations have employed their economic clout to articulate their demands directly to the national executive, and indirectly through lobbying efforts via the media.[50]

In a similar manner, political parties have also served to divide rather than to aggregate interests in the democratic era. While the military government under Castello Branco instituted a two-party system in 1965, by 1985 there were eleven parties in the congress and by 1991, there were nineteen, most of which could hardly be considered coherent in national terms.[51] In other words, the post-1988 polity was characterized by a heightened salience of more local political identities, and high levels of political fragmentation. Although the political party system is not the only place where such fragmentation is manifest, it is in this arena that splintering is most easily measured (see Figure 5.4). As of 1994, 17 parties were represented in the 513 seats of congress, 9 of which had less than 30 members, and no party had more than 107 seats.[52] Business interests are divided among a plethora

---

[50] Interviews with FIESP, FIRJAN, and CNI representatives, and other business leaders and political analysts.
[51] Skidmore 1999: 191–2.
[52] Gordon 1998.

of these political organizations, none of which have very strong national organizations or command high levels of loyalty. Of high-income individuals surveyed in 1995 (those earning at least twenty times the minimum salary per month), a full 53 percent did not express a party preference when asked. Of the remainder who did, the most support was actually expressed for the workers' party, the PT (33.5 percent), and no other major party received more than 20 percent of upper-income group support: the PSDB (16.3 percent), the PMDB (15.2 percent), and the PDT (7.0 percent). In other words, there is no single party that truly represents the wealthy.

Moreover, regionally divisive political idioms inhibit interclass empathy. Among wealthy Southerners, the equating of *Nordestinos* with *favelas*, crime, and cultural laziness, when combined with subtle racial prejudice, provides a ready script for protesting the payment of taxes as a waste of useful resources. Alongside the increased economic inequalities in Brazil during the 1980s, there has been an increase in crime, which "reinforced the Brazilian elite's image of the lower classes as threatening," and shifted focus from the working poor to the *marginais* ("mere" criminals and hustlers).[53]

In multiple interviews with participants and observers in the tax policy reform process in Brazil, including with members of the congressional tax reform commission, individuals identified the "complaints" of more developed states that they are forced to finance poorer regions. Such sentiments were re-iterated over and over again in structured interviews and in more casual conversations with upper-income individuals in the Southern regions of the country. An economist with private business interests in São Paulo responded to my question, "Is there a regional issue associated with taxation in this country?" with the following: "(It is) very important. Why is the North so powerful? Well, São Paulo has only 60 deputies. We are under-represented here. We have 40% of GDP and 30% of the votes. The coalition of poor states are more than 50% of the vote.... We don't really care about the northeast down here. Yes, there is a clear rivalry."[54]

An official from the Banco Nacional de Desenvolvimento Econômico e Social (BNDES), whose work focuses on problems of regional development, explained why there was so much controversy over fiscal federalism: "The South and Southeast have a prejudice. Perhaps it is about

---

[53] Skidmore 1999: 200. This characterization was confirmed through structured interviews and more informal conversations in Brazil in 1997, 1998, and 1999.
[54] Interview with economist/entrepreneur in São Paulo, August 18, 1997.

color.... They make jokes about the *Nordestino*. In the North, they resent it."[55] A federal government minister long involved in taxation issues in Brazil explained, "Many down in the South say they are paying taxes for the North. They think that their money is being wasted. There is even a small voice of secession."[56]

Upper groups have not embraced the normative obligation to redistribute income or wealth *downward*. In Brazil, an outspoken PT senator, Eduardo Suplicy, has made repeated calls to develop a tax system that not only is progressive in terms of who pays but acts as a direct agent for cash transfers similar to the American Earned Income Tax Credit system.[57] And yet, the lack of any truly integrating link either organizationally or ideologically between the upper and lower sectors of society makes redistribution in this way seem completely irrational to those with bases available to tax. In an article, Suplicy highlighted the unequal history of Brazil as a rationale for redistributive policies, arguing that: "During the course of our history, we have not succeeded in rescuing the rights of citizenship for those who are descendents of slaves and for all those who constitute a huge part of the Brazilian population, yet don't enjoy the minimum conditions of life."[58]

However, there has been very little serious discussion of Suplicy's proposal in the press or within business circles in Brazil.[59] Without a proximate and widely understood atrocity such as apartheid, there is no similar normative imperative to sacrifice. Rather, the long hiatus since the end of slavery, and the myth of racial democracy, have obscured the source of blame for inequality in that society. The moral imperatives for progressive taxation are far more elusive, and without greater political clout, the prospects for advancing such proposals are far weaker.

Organizational and discursive fragmentation structures more narrow calculations about future returns from the collective goods provided by the national state, in turn making tax payment appear to be a high-cost, low-benefit endeavor. Given incomplete information about the future, the common-sense prediction that has emerged is that "they" will benefit rather

---

[55] Interview with official from the BNDES (Development Bank of Brazil) Rio de Janeiro, August 8, 1997.
[56] Interview with a top government bureaucrat involved in the formulation of tax policy, Brasília, August 13, 1997.
[57] Suplicy 1995.
[58] Suplicy 1995: 24.
[59] Interviews with various deputies and technical advisors on the congressional tax reform commission.

than "us," because "us" is defined in such narrow (local) terms. Upper-income actors have come to view the allocation of the tax burden as a zero-sum game across a diverse range of interests. As a result, the dominant set of strategies of Brazilian upper groups with respect to national taxation has been to lobby for narrow exemptions, to make extreme demands for more favorable treatment, and to avoid or even evade the tax burden altogether. The institutional foundations of Brazilian politics created a situation in which virtually no tax proposal has the possibility of emerging as fair, and the best strategy has been to lobby for narrowly defined incentives, particularly for extreme ones, which provide room for compromise and an incentive for political leaders to make bargains. Neutrality or tacit compliance has provided few rewards in this political environment, given that others are constantly jockeying for better treatment, and as a result, business actors constantly propose new amendments and ideas for tax reform.

Upper Groups in South Africa. The contrast in terms of the salient political idioms and cohesion of upper groups in South Africa is stark. In fact, over the course of the 20th century, business groups and upper-income earners in South Africa became increasingly more cohesive, and this pattern has largely persisted into the post-apartheid era. Unlike in Brazil, where attempts at greater class unity repeatedly splintered into regional and sectional factions, in South Africa, there is remarkably little polarization within the ranks of business and professionals on key policy positions, particularly with respect to taxation. This can be explained by the historical underpinnings of South African society, which privileged race over region, leading to increasing cohesion among national business leaders and economically privileged groups in general – who continued to be almost exclusively white. Moreover, in the 20th century, South Africa carried out one of the most effective affirmative action programs in the world for Afrikaners, effectively wiping out the poor white problem, and providing an overlap for racial and economic interests.

The business community has developed in a relatively hierarchical and encompassing manner, and two truly national business organizations came to represent the vast majority of the mid- to large-sized businesses in South Africa: the South African Chamber of Business (SACOB) and the *Afrikaanse Handelsinstituut* (AHI).[60] These are almost exclusively white organizations, largely English-speaking in the former case, and largely Afrikaans-speaking

---

[60] Where there was once significant intra-white tension, today Afrikaner and English business leaders see their interests as shared. Not a single respondent contradicted this claim.

in the latter. In recent years, both SACOB and AHI have contributed to Business South Africa (BSA), which serves as a single voice on the corporatist National Economic Development and Labour Council (NEDLAC). Within the new political dispensation, these organizations have attempted to bring blacks onto their boards and into their memberships as a way of consolidating their influence in post-apartheid South Africa, whereas the ANC government is less likely to be receptive to exclusively white interests and actors. As part of this strategy, SACOB elected a black president, Humphrey Khoza, in October 1997. Subsequently, SACOB merged with the largely black National African Federated Chamber of Commerce (NAFCOC) to form the South African Federated Chamber of Commerce (SAFCOC) in September 2001.

As in Brazil, there still exist many more narrowly defined business associations, such as the National Association of Automobile Manufacturers in South Africa (NAAMSA), but such groups ultimately view political influence as resting with the larger umbrella organizations.[61] Similarly, on a regional level, the major business organizations have created provincial organizations, but these are still components of a larger organization that is most powerful at the national level. Given the relative lack of independent political clout held by provincial premiers within South Africa, business leaders do not turn to them to represent their interests, particularly in tax matters at the national level. However, there are already signs suggesting that this may change over time. The wealthier provinces have begun to sell themselves to foreign investors as attractive opportunities, especially when compared with other provinces in the region. Such practices suggest the possibility of increased provincial identity in the future, which may spill over to tax issues.

The racial dimension of party politics has also affected how class interests are represented in the legislature. On the one hand, as in Brazil, most high-income individuals were reluctant to express party support in surveys and in structured, in-depth interviews. (In the 1997 IDASA survey, a full 57.8 percent of high-income earners – monthly earnings above R9,000 – did not express a party preference.) On the other hand, among those that did, 30.2 percent said they supported the National Party (NP), while 27.9 percent said they supported the Democratic Party (DP), and both

Moreover, these organizations, as well as other "think tanks" such as the South Africa Foundation, tend to have overlapping memberships.
[61] Interviews with NAAMSA officials.

parties have strongly supported employer interests. With respect to tax policy, a member of Parliament from the Democratic Party (DP) who serves on the finance committee said with respect to the NP, "What they would say doesn't sound terribly different from what we would say."[62] Although the ANC won with solid majorities in both the 1994 and 1999 elections, only 18.6 percent of the high-income group expressed support for that party.

Moreover, the degree to which the media and decision makers recognize the obligation of white, upper groups to pay more is starkly different from in Brazil. For example, as contrasted with the muted response to the redistributive tax policy proposals of Senator Suplicy (described earlier) in Brazil, plans for a wealth tax in South Africa have been discussed more extensively with reference to that country's history of racial oppression. "[The wealth tax] proposal raises the highly uncomfortable issues of guilt, complicity and responsibility. By raising the spectre of a collective responsibility for reparations, it implies a collective responsibility for the past's wrongs."[63]

At least at the rhetorical level, most business leaders agree that there must be some redistribution from the top down, and while white, upper-income individuals may privately (and some, even publicly) resent cross-racial transfers of income and wealth, there is little political room to contest progressive taxation as fundamentally unfair, or to complain that a particular sector or region is being overtaxed at the expense of others. Rather, particularly at the very top of the economic ladder, whites recognize the strategic importance of improving the material conditions of blacks. Several top business executives echoed the observation of the CEO of one of the leading industrial firms who said, "We can't make progress without black empowerment."[64] Moreover, unlike in Brazil, there is no opportunity for reluctant taxpayers to make pleas to individual parliamentarians, hoping to strike deals or special exemptions – as such tactics would be completely ineffectual given the single party dominance and strong party cohesion within the current Parliament. With such overwhelming electoral support for his party in the

---

[62] Interview with member of Parliament from the Democratic Party, Cape Town, February 3, 1998. In 2000, these two largely white parties formed a formal alliance – the Democratic Alliance – which was later dissolved by the National Party, renamed as the New National Party (NNP).

[63] Stephen Laufer, "Critical Reflection on Apartheid and What Sustained It Is Needed," *Business Day*, November 19, 1997.

[64] Interview with chairman of leading industrial corporation in South Africa, Johannesburg July 31, 1998.

National Assembly, the Minister of Finance has had no need to strike individual deals with particular sectors, regions, or opposition parties unless convinced it is in the national interest. As for lobbying, the chairman of the tax committee of AHI explained, "of course, to be successful, you have to get as big a lobby going eventually as possible."[65] As a result, proposals that facilitate more broadly based and evenly applied taxes have tended to be far more effective than proposals that appeal to special needs.

All of this is not intended to suggest that white South Africans have simply opened their hearts and wallets to the new government. Indeed, there remains significant resistance on the part of many white South Africans to the nature of political change and to the reconfiguration of the NPC. Nonetheless, when compared with the Brazilian case, it is clear that a largely well-organized capitalist class can, as a collective actor, envisage the benefits of contributing to the maintenance of the tax state given the role it can play in the longer-term transformation of the South African economy and society.

The framing and aggregation of upper-group interests in this manner has affected the ways in which individuals, firms, and organizations lobby for tax reform. Unlike in Brazil, South African business organizations do not attempt to propose their own full-blown tax reform packages or even attempt to be seen as the lead player in the tax reform process. Rather, the central government clearly has the power to articulate tax proposals and to get them passed. As a result, the best interests of business are pursued by lobbying the Minister of Finance or the director of the national tax bureaucracy through appeals to broad-based national interests. Generally speaking, this happens in one of three ways: First, throughout the year, business leaders from the major business organizations such as SACOB and AHI, or from the largest national companies, may meet with the Minister of Finance or the director of the revenue service to discuss plans and proposals. Second, businesses may participate by making written and oral contributions to the tax reform commission, which is comprised of members of the private sector, and vested with the authority of the government to review the tax system, to listen to the inputs of broad sectors of society, and to make recommendations in the form of a series of reports. Third, the two major white political parties, the DP and the NP, articulate the concerns of the business sectors in parliamentary speeches, committee meetings, and direct

---

[65] Interview with representative of the AHI tax commission, Johannesburg, June 1, 1998.

appeals to the Minister of Finance or SARS officials responsible for writing tax proposals. Although few powerful business leaders view this option as a very viable one for advancing their interests through an ANC-controlled legislature, DP and NP party platforms have helped to shape the tax reform agenda of big business.

Lower Groups/Organized Labor

Lower groups have had much less direct influence over the development of tax policies and administration in both countries over the course of the 20th century. Industrial workers, peasants, and the unemployed possess many fewer taxable resources, and they have also tended to lack the technical capacity to become involved in the often-critical intricacies of tax policy. When it comes to budgets, lower groups in both countries have tended to be much more concerned with the expenditure side than with the revenue side. It tends to be more difficult for lower-income individuals to avoid or evade the consumption taxes or the taxes that may be withheld by their employers at source, limiting the exit option. Moreover, in recent years, the political vocabulary for demanding progressive taxation has been narrowed around the world. In both countries, the left and social movements that had been guided by socialist and communist ideologies were in many ways deflated by the collapse of the Soviet Union. Unions and political parties representing the poor have been forced to temper their strategies and demands to a level closer to that being espoused by domestic and international business interests.

Nonetheless, the political openings implied by democratization in Brazil and South Africa have offered truly unique opportunities for lower groups and organized labor to play a more active role in the contest over how the tax burden should be allocated. One might predict that given such profound inequalities, and the common overlap of race and class, the working classes would unite and push for higher taxes on the wealthy in both countries. Particularly under less repressive, democratic regimes, lower groups are provided opportunities to express their political interests more openly through the media, with representations to the legislature and the executive, and most importantly through political parties and through strike action. In the early 1990s, union density was higher in Brazil (32.1 percent of the nonagricultural work force were union members) than in South Africa (21.8 percent), but as shown in Figure 5.5, both countries had typical rates of unionization among upper-middle income countries.

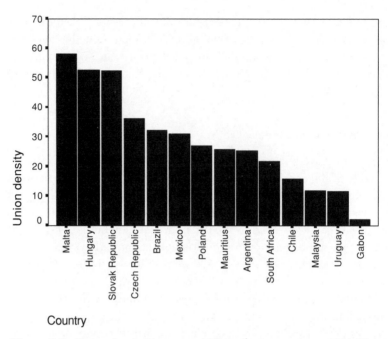

Figure 5.5   Union density in upper-middle income countries, c. 1994. Union density is the percent of the nonagricultural work force belonging to a labor union. *Source:* ILO 1997.

And yet, the varied salience of region and race as political idioms and organizational strategies has strongly shaped the coherence of organized labor and other lower groups, as well as their political linkages to upper groups. As a result, democratization has implied that the organization, interests, and strategies of workers and other lower groups have been very different across the two countries. In South Africa, despite the plurality of linguistic and ethnic differences among the black or African population, workers and the poor in general became very strongly organized and cohesive within the political arena, particularly after the mid-1970s. The history of race-based oppression has provided a strong basis for collective solidarity and the making of moral demands concerning the unjust allocation of resources.[66] The situation for the poor in Brazil has been much less clear: Even with the wide-ranging evidence of racial inequality within the country, the more subtle mechanisms for perpetuating such disparities provide very

[66] Marx 1998: 264, makes this point nicely.

little basis for building organizations or making strong claims. Although Brazilians are very conscious of class in a social sense, class solidarity is weak, particularly at the national level. Given the prevalence of regional organizations and the locally based political power, most lower- (and zero-) income individuals tie their future interests much more closely to their regions and/or sectors than to the working class or poor in general.

Lower Groups in South Africa. Lower groups in post-apartheid South Africa are well organized, well represented, and politically strong, largely because they have rallied around the banner of the anti-apartheid struggle for decades, and have faced the specter of institutionalized white supremacy for more than three centuries. In the 1990s, two organizations played a critical role in representing the interests of lower groups: First is the ANC, a political organization founded in 1912 in response to the proposal for the Native Land Act, and which gained international recognition as it operated underground challenging the apartheid regime while formally banned between 1960 and 1990. After its unbanning in 1990, the ANC emerged as a political party, and has been the governing party since 1994. Second, the Congress of South African Trade Unions (COSATU), built in the 1970s as an umbrella organization of unions, is today the largest labor federation in the country. While both of these organizations have been committed to nonracialism, and individuals from all race groups are represented as members and in positions of leadership, both gained political support as direct challengers to the white regime. Both are truly national organizations, in which regional and sectoral interests are relegated as secondary to the more universal interests of workers, the poor, and those disadvantaged by the apartheid system. Of those individuals with household incomes of less than R3,000/month in 1997 (the bottom three-fourths of the survey sample), a full 78.3 percent said they supported the ANC.[67]

Since 1994, COSATU (along with the South African Communist Party[68]) has been in a formal governing alliance with the ANC, placing organized labor in a strategically strong position to advance its interests on a broad range of distributive policies such as taxation. On the other hand,

[67] Author analysis of 1997 IDASA survey data.
[68] Despite its name, the South African Communist Party (SACP) is not really a political party in the traditional sense. It organizes workers and individuals committed to socialist ideals, but has only sought out political power in the state through its relationship with the ANC and has not stood for elections at any level of government.

the ANC, in its capacity as governing party, has been forced to develop policies subject to the constraints of capital and other constituencies, generating
some tension within the alliance regarding the types of policies that have
been enacted. In particular, macroeconomic questions about the equity-
efficiency trade-off and the role government should play in attaining these
goals through fiscal (and monetary) policy have been divisive ones between
the ANC leadership on the one hand, and its tripartite alliance partners
and the rank-and-file on the other. Nonetheless, in the first six years of
government, the alliance remained strong, commanded two-thirds of the
vote in the 1999 elections, and was relatively undivided by regional, ethnic,
or sectoral interests.[69]

With respect to national tax policy, the main challenge for organized
labor – dominated by unions and political organizations with mostly black
memberships – has been to hold back pressures to shift the tax burden from
capital to labor with higher levels of indirect taxation. The main strategies for achieving this objective have included demonstrating the collective
solidarity of workers, exerting influence on government leaders through
formal policy submissions arguing that capital has not been overtaxed, and
maintaining strong appeals to the moral imperative of redistribution within
a highly unequal society. Within a number of forums, including through
the Truth and Reconciliation Commission (TRC),[70] South Africans have
reflected extensively upon the legacy of apartheid, and the various ways in
which whites have benefited unfairly from the exploitation of other groups.
The tax system has become one of several institutions targeted for righting
past wrongs. By equating corporate taxation with the taxation of whites,
and VAT payment with the taxation of blacks, union and community leaders have managed to create a bulwark against the logic of globalization with
a nationally distinctive interpretation of democratization that emphasized
equitable development.

Lower Groups in Brazil. The union movement also played an important
role in the democratization process in Brazil,[71] but the class unity of low-
income groups has been comparatively weak, and political influence over

---

[69] Price 1997.
[70] Among its functions to promote fact-finding and reconciliation with respect to South
Africa's apartheid past, the TRC receives submissions for amnesty from individuals who may
have committed various crimes, including crimes against humanity, for political motives.
[71] See Seidman 1994; Keck 1989, 1992.

tax reform has been modest. Despite the persistence of severe race-based inequalities, the perception of a racial democracy in Brazil has militated against organization along racial lines. Beyond ideology and organization, it is important to recognize that black Brazilians were not segregated in the way black South Africans (and black Americans) were,[72] further contributing to the lack of mobilization around race. Meanwhile, regional- and state-based organizational fragmentation, created under the corporatist arrangements of the Vargas era, continue to hamstring the unity of workers and lower groups in Brazil more generally. Two important organizations did emerge during the process of democratization that promised to achieve greater national labor unity: the Central Única dos Trabalhadores (CUT), or Central Workers' Organization, was founded in 1983 as a labor federation essentially analogous to COSATU, and the Partido dos Trabalhadores (PT) or Workers' Party, formed in 1979 under the charismatic leadership of Luís Inácio "Lula" da Silva.

In practice, however, the PT has not been nearly as effective in gaining political support as the ANC has been in South Africa. After several showings as a remarkably competitive presidential candidate, "Lula" finally succeeded in winning an election in 2002. His PT is generally recognized as the most programmatic and nationally coherent of any of Brazil's political parties, but in 1999 it was ranked fifth in terms of number of seats in the legislature, and of its sixty-one seats in the lower house, 50 percent were from three states in the industrial South-Southeast (São Paulo, Minas Gerais, and Rio Grande do Sul). After the 2002 elections, the PT secured the most seats of any party (91), but this still represents less than one-fifth of the total seats (513). While this may be changing, there has been very little party identification among the poor: in a 1995 survey, 50.6 percent of individuals with household income amounting to 10 minimum salaries per month or less (the bottom three-fifths of the survey sample) said they had no party preference. The PT received support from only 10.5 percent of low-income respondents, second to the PMDB, a long-existing left party that commanded support from 16.2 percent of the lower-income group.[73] Although the PT may articulate the most coherent policy platforms that favor the poor, it does not represent a national underclass the way the ANC does in South Africa.

[72] Skidmore 1999: 209.
[73] Author analysis of 1995 Datafolha survey.

Similarly, when considering the role of organized labor, there is no clear analog to COSATU in Brazil. Rather, the CUT faces multiple, competing labor organizations, including rural union organizations and a rival confederation, the *Confederação Geral dos Trabalhadores* (CGT). Although workers were highly constrained in their ability to participate in decision-making processes prior to the democratic period, national government efforts at co-optation through highly constrained corporatist arrangements (which included the provision of state-collected resources for union leaders) were not rejected as illegitimate with the same fervor as state attempts to co-opt blacks through homeland and other apartheid strategies in South Africa. As a result, many different groups compete for the support of lower groups in Brazil, none with the hegemonic political resources of COSATU. In Brazil, political entrepreneurs have more space to mobilize lower groups into narrower groupings, often in terms of regional or sectoral identities as opposed to class ones, and almost never in terms of race. Multiple organizations claim the political loyalties of lower groups, including peasant organizations, and local political bosses who engage the poor in clientelist ties.[74] For example, an unemployed Afro-Brazilian in the state of Bahia is generally less likely to view his or her fortunes as tied to the black auto worker in São Paulo than to the conservative sugar planter in his own state.

Lower groups in Brazil have no ready-made political idiom such as apartheid with which to make collective claims for redistribution. Although upper-income groups benefited from the period of military rule, they have managed to disassociate themselves from the military in the democratic era. As a result, within the popular discourse of the country, upper groups are not charged with having *perpetrated* direct injustices against lower groups, or with having benefited in an *unfair* way from that country's history. While the military may be to blame for the excesses of the authoritarian period, there is no redistributive tax strategy available as a form of recourse.

The ambiguities of political life in Brazil imply that organized lower groups vary widely in terms of how they make calculations about costs and benefits, and the strategies they pursue for various political concerns, including the question of tax policy. To the extent that people make calculations about equity in terms of regional inequality, regional incentives for industry have often emerged as more important than policies that would affect the vertical redistribution of resources across the board.

---

[74] Weyland 1996: 66–74. See also Hagopian 1996.

While the PT and the CUT are the most broadly based organizations representing workers, they have tended to articulate the regional and sectoral interests of their constituents, creating important contradictions that must be understood from the perspective of Brazilian federalism. A PT representative in São Paulo highlighted the central concern of regional equity: "We want a better distribution of power. The problem now is that (the Northern and Northeastern) states have a better representation in Congress. They are this way because of pacts. We need to re-discuss the representation of the country. . . . We want more decentralization – a new federalist arrangement in the country."[75]

In practice, the labor movement has remained tied to the Brazilian political idiom of regionalism, and questions of equity tend to be considered from a local, not a national, perspective. The result is that like upper groups, lower groups in Brazil present no coherent set of demands for tax reform, and the impact of multiple, conflicting pressures is the further weakening of the central state in its ability to impose uniform authority in the form of tax collection.

Patterns of Tax Reform Compared

In the context of similar structural pressures, and varying political dynamics, the process of late 20th century tax reform in Brazil and South Africa produced very different outcomes (Table 5.4). High levels of class solidarity and strong cross-class linkages in South Africa have generated a highly stable reform environment, which is controlled by the state executive and is largely supported through partnerships with various class actors. In such a context, the state executive has been mostly successful in simplifying the overall tax system, in maintaining a policy framework in which upper-income actors pay the lion's share of the tax burden, and in enforcing relatively high levels of compliance. By contrast in Brazil, fragmentation within and across classes has led to a serious diffusion of political power, and an inability on the part of the state executive to achieve such goals. Rather, the tax burden has remained largely regressive, efforts to simplify the tax system have been rebuffed with additional proposals and compromises that have effectively brought greater complexity to that system, and already poor compliance has gotten worse. In short, South Africa's tax state continues to be characterized

---

[75] Interview with senior PT policy analyst, São Paulo, Brazil, November 20, 1998.

Table 5.4 *Tax state reforms during periods of democratization and globalization in Brazil and South Africa, 1985–1999*

Reform area	Trends	
	Brazil	South Africa
Policy		
Reform dynamics	Stalemated, centrifugal	Active, ongoing, centripetal
Use of tax system for downward redistribution	Very little	Significant
Simplification of tax system	Minor; additional complexity	Extensive
Compliance	Higher levels of avoidance and evasion (from already poor base)	Generally improved compliance (some decline among whites, improvement among blacks)
Collections of income and property tax (% GDP)*		
1985	5.4	12.1
1990	4.2	13.7
1995	4.8	14.2
1997	5.3	15.7
Tax State	ADVERSARIAL	COOPERATIVE

* Does not include mining revenues; central state tax collections only.

by cooperative relations with upper groups, and Brazil's tax state continues to be characterized by adversarial relations.

In evaluating the impact of the political factors described earlier on these qualities of the tax state, it is important to recall that the pre-existing legacy of the tax state, and its institutionalized relationship with society, have served as important constraints on the development of new policies and collection practices. Though a central argument of this book has been that the organization of society helped shape the tax system, once the system was well institutionalized, it acted to shape the organization of politics and society.[76] In this manner, early choices have been self-reinforcing. The respective state bureaucracies developed tools to collect certain types of taxes and

---

[76] As Schumpeter (1954: 17) writes, "tax . . . becomes a formative factor in the very organism which has developed it."

not others, and members of society became accustomed to either paying or avoiding them. Patterns of participation in both the reform and collections processes became routinized. Pre-existing patterns of compliance, and the ways in which taxpayers share information with tax collectors, are also highly "sticky," as personal relationships, standard practices, and even market operations have tended to be reinforcing. Variations in the quality of the taxpayers' databases, in the relationships between taxpayers and collectors, and in the sources of unevenness in administrative capacity are specific products of the past that are particularly difficult to change. As such, this section also attempts to identify aspects of the contemporary tax systems that can best be understood as holdovers from the past, when patterns got locked in. Such factors explain why these countries have maintained nationally distinctive patterns of taxation even in the wake of strong external pressures toward convergence.

Tax Policy Reform

Tax policies are ultimately made into law by state executives and legislatures, who are themselves heavily influenced by public opinion, and by the lobbying of interest groups, particularly of business organizations. Comparative analysis reveals that even amidst similar domestic and international economic conditions, choices about which tax policies to adopt, reject, and/or revise have varied widely because of the very different configurations of actors in these countries. The relative strength of different groups and the ways in which they frame their interests and demands, as discussed in earlier sections, has affected how and where tax policies have been crafted.

In South Africa, the election of Nelson Mandela in 1994 provided a significant opening to reform the country's tax system, perceived to be somewhat outdated by technical experts within the bureaucracy.[77] The state executive, particularly the Minister of Finance, has enjoyed significant power to craft tax policy in conjunction with the bureaucracy without the need to make significant compromises. South Africa's reform dynamic has been

---

[77] According to the former Minister of Finance, Barend du Plessis, and a top Ministry of Finance official, technical experts within the tax commission, the finance ministry, and the revenue service had been considering reforming the tax system throughout the 1980s. However, during that period, which was still prior to the democratic transition, there was insufficient political stability and support for the state to actually carry out such a reform. These informants argued that any major tax reforms carried out by the white government during this period would have been viewed as illegitimate, and were avoided.

more centripetal – that is, various social forces have come together rather than spread apart – as actors within society have recognized the state as lead player in the reform process, and the benefits of cooperation as opposed to conflict. Both business organizations and labor unions have articulated their demands and concerns with respect to particular proposals, but since the executive enjoys the ability to pass any set of tax policies through the budget, there are much greater incentives for societal actors to contribute suggestions with broad appeal and likely to be of national benefit. Societal actors have tended to engage the state through participation in national forums, such as by making submissions to the tax reform commission, or to the parliamentary committee on finance, but none of these groups have attempted to take the lead in this process, as they have recognized the state's undisputed power to control the outcome.

By contrast, particularly following the enactment of the 1988 constitution, the process of tax reform in Brazil has been highly centrifugal, reducing the bargaining power of the state executive, who has been forced to make compromises with multiple actors in order to secure acceptance of any major reform proposal. Well trained technical experts from various corners of the federal bureaucracy had also long proposed sweeping reforms of the Brazilian tax system, hoping to rid themselves of the multitude of complex taxes that had crept in during the second half of the military period.[78] Yet, the democratic era engendered a different dynamic than in South Africa. Tax proposals have been easily defeated in the congress, where the state executive has not even enjoyed solid support from his own party, let alone the many others necessary for approving major policy changes. Despite consensus that the tax system is in great need of reform, the policy-making process has been largely stalemated. Powerful local and sectoral political interests have blocked attempts to introduce thoroughgoing reform efforts in this very complex tax system, and a congressional committee charged with introducing a sweeping tax reform proposal has been stalled since 1995. Regional and business interests are divided organizationally, and express widely conflicting interests, constraining the ability of any actor – including the president – to emerge as a clear authority in the reform process.

Recent economic history in Brazil also helps to rule out a different, highly popular explanation for the state's inability to collect taxes efficiently or effectively, namely the problem of inflation for the calculation and payment of taxes. As shown graphically in Figure 5.6, the 1994 Real Plan provided

---

[78] Varsano 1984; Rezende 1996b.

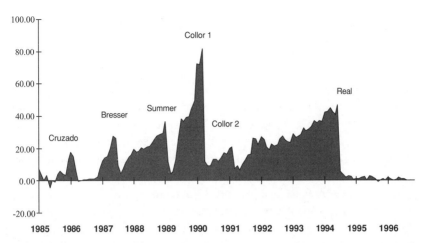

Figure 5.6 Monthly inflation in Brazil, 1985–1996. Names of stabilization plans indicated. *Source:* Central Bank of Brazil, Website, 1998.

a dramatic, and to date lasting, solution to the problem of hyper-inflation. Nevertheless, there has not been radical change in the tax structure – though there have been some improvements in income tax collections at the margins. These findings imply that inflation, per se, is not *the* reason for poor and inefficient collections in that country.

Vertical Redistribution. The impact of different political patterns on the redistributive aspects of the policy framework has been significant. Policymakers in both countries have been well aware of international trends to flatten tax systems, and to make lower groups pay a larger share of the burden. Meanwhile, they have also been aware of the profound socioeconomic inequalities within their respective societies. Given the stated goals of national executives in both countries to address such inequalities through social policy, including through the tax system, the relative ability of the state to enact such policies has depended upon the degree to which the state enjoys greater relative bargaining power with respect to upper groups. Clearly, this has been the case in South Africa to a much greater extent than in Brazil. While tax incidence is extraordinarily difficult to measure, virtually all Brazilian analysts agree that their tax system is largely regressive.[79] By contrast, in

[79] See, for example, Varsano, 1996; ESAF 1997; Gutierres, Merege, and Batista 1995; Weyland 1996; Rezende 1996a, 1996b.

217

South Africa, an already very progressive tax system has largely remained so in the democratic era.

International trends associated with globalization inspired policy makers to consider lowering tax rates on capital in both countries. Indeed, corporate and top income tax rates did come down, but dramatically in Brazil, and only marginally in South Africa. In 1986, the top individual income tax rate in both countries was 50 percent, and had been higher in both countries in earlier years. By 1998, the rate structure in South Africa had become much more progressive: In terms of individual income taxes, there were six brackets, ranging from 0 percent to 45 percent, whereas in Brazil, there were only three brackets – 0 percent, 15 percent, and 27.5 percent. In both cases, the top marginal rate was effective for income above approximately US $20,000. In 1998, the basic corporate tax rate in Brazil was 15 percent, or 25 percent for corporate entities with taxable income above R$240,000, while in South Africa it was 35 percent.

In Brazil, both the salience of regionalism and the political fragmentation described above have made initiatives for progressive taxation a nonstarter on the political agenda of virtually all parties to the debate about tax reform. First, the Minister of Finance and the Brazilian federal tax bureaucracy (SRF) have not placed very much emphasis on income tax. Because the constitution mandates a revenue-sharing formula for income tax collections between the central government (which collects the tax) and the states and provinces, the central government has chosen to pursue additional revenue needs with social contributions. These are not shared with the other tiers of government and tend to be less visible.[80] Moreover, in the late 20th century, feelings of difference across classes, regions, and sectors reinforced a sense of division within society, as did the fragmented political system, leading upper-income individuals to believe that centrally collected revenues would wind up benefiting "them," not "us." Even in the wake of a true fiscal crisis following the collapse of the Asian economies in 1997, the congress did not rally around the center for a presidential initiative requiring sacrifice. Senate leader Antônio Carlos Magalhães – supposedly a partner in the Cardoso government – effectively blocked executive initiatives for increased taxes to meet budget deficits.[81]

Even when organized workers in Brazil have successfully campaigned for tax reform, the debate has been framed in ways that emphasize the

---

[80] Interviews with SRF and IPEA representatives.
[81] "Brazil Near the Edge," *The Economist*, November 22, 1997.

importance of regions over race or class, relegating the goal of vertical equity to the sidelines. This is best demonstrated in the case of negotiations over the taxation of the automotive industry in the 1990s. In this case, the CUT and various unions associated with the auto industry participated in a series of strikes against the high rates of taxation on the automotive sector. As a result, in 1992, twenty-eight union factions along with various industry representatives and government ministries agreed to various tax cuts, and unions agreed to refrain from further strike activity.[82] Such action was ultimately successful in restraining the national government's desire to tax this industry, and ultimately benefited workers in the automotive sectors and its downstream industry partners. Similarly in 1999, President Cardoso agreed to reduce the federal consumption tax on the automotive sector after meetings with industry leaders in the state of São Paulo, in order to address the problem of growing unemployment. In these cases, the associated beneficiaries were the automotive manufacturers themselves, and the upper-income groups from those industries – particularly within the state of São Paulo – not the working class and unemployed from other sectors, and from states without automotive industries. Representatives from other sectors still point to those tax cuts as examples of unfair treatment in the zero-sum game of Brazilian tax politics.

By contrast, owing to the moral imperatives associated with post-apartheid South African development and the broad-based organization of business interests in that country, privileged economic actors in South Africa have not challenged progressive taxation to the same extent as their counterparts in Brazil. Following the 1994 election of Nelson Mandela, the budget continued to be financed largely through income taxes. The state even managed to collect a transition levy of 5 percent of taxable income exceeding R50,000 during the tax years 1994–5 and 1995–6, to help fund the expenses of the new election and to finance deficits that had been accumulating amidst a tumultuous political transition. In the climate of reconciliation that surrounded the 1994 elections, and the moral imperative to redress the legacy of apartheid, the tax was paid without significant resentment from any quarter challenging its appropriateness or legitimacy. Although the transition levy was only a temporary one of two years, it reflected the state's ability to look to upper-income groups for additional finance at critical moments.

---

[82] Nicole Sierra, "The Americas: A Supply-Side Jump Start for Brazil's Stalled Economy," *Wall Street Journal*, January 28, 1994, A14.

Moreover, lower groups have managed to hold firm against further broadening of the South African tax base. Together, the ANC and COSATU held a strong line against the trend to increase the level of taxation on consumers, which began in the mid-1970s as company income tax receipts began to decline. In 1991, the state's General Sales Tax (GST) was converted into a Value Added Tax (VAT), and set at a rate of 10 percent. Barend Du Plessis, the Minister of Finance at the time, recalled in an interview that as part of the process of negotiating the political transition, the top ANC economic advisors (including COSATU's leader, Jay Naidoo, and the man who would become Reserve Bank Governor, Tito Mboweni) held firm that there should be no increase in the VAT rates and that income tax should continue to be the primary revenue source for the fiscus.[83] Responding to the government's persistence in levying the regressive tax, COSATU led the largest general strike in the country's history (in terms of numbers of participants) on November 4–5, 1991, in which millions of South Africans stayed away from work to protest the enactment of the VAT, challenging its legitimacy – particularly because it was enacted without consultation with labor groups during the period of political negotiations. The challenge, reminiscent of South Africa's much earlier Rand Revolt in demonstrating the potential power of organized labor, led to the government exclusion of several basic foods from the tax base.

In subsequent years, despite significant pressure from business and international policy experts, the VAT rate has increased only marginally. Amidst very strong budgetary pressures, the rate was increased in 1993 to 14 percent but with an increased list of exempt items, softening the blow to low-income households. Moreover, by international standards, 14 percent is not a particularly high rate of VAT – the top rate in Brazil is 25 percent (note that the main Brazilian consumption tax is collected at the *estado* level), and in several European countries the top rate is well over 20 percent. Since the ANC took power in 1994 in partnership with COSATU, there has been no increase in the VAT rate, and no attempts to differentiate rates across regions or sectors, as has been the case in Brazil.

In Figure 5.7, important differences in the redistributive effects of the respective tax systems are demonstrated clearly through a comparison of the ratio of posttax to pretax incomes between low-income workers and high-income professionals. A ratio of one to one would indicate a neutral tax

---

[83] Interview with former top official from the Ministry of Finance, Johannesburg, South Africa, June 2, 1998.

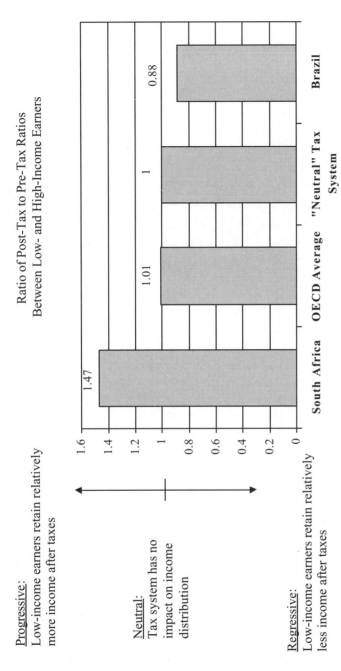

Figure 5.7 Income redistribution through taxation, c. 1994. *Sources*: Escola de Administração Fazendaria 1994; Department of Finance South Africa, *Budget Review 1998*.

system – that is, a tax system that does not affect the distribution of income within society. On average, OECD countries have only slightly progressive tax systems, as the mix of progressive and regressive taxes winds up being relatively flat in those countries. However, in the case of South Africa, the tax system increases the relative income of low-income workers by about 47 percent, making it one of the most progressive tax systems in the world.[84] In Brazil, the tax system actually *lowers* the relative income of workers by 12 percent, making it highly regressive.[85]

Simplification. Efforts to simplify the tax system have also met varied levels of success. By simplicity, I mean the degree to which the taxes received by the state are well recognized and transparent to the society that is paying them. When the state collects from multiple tax bases, or introduces various exemptions and incentives to the tax policy framework, this makes the tax system more complex. In recent years, international trends have involved the increasing simplification of national tax systems, as part of the process of harmonizing tax systems and reducing administrative costs. At first blush, both citizens and the state would seem to prefer a more simple tax system, because people ought to know how much they are paying over to the state, and because economic inefficiencies often result from overly cumbersome tax policies. On the other hand, states may use special taxes and/or incentives to induce certain types of social and economic outcomes. Whatever the merits of simplification, the task of carrying out such reforms can have high political costs because it often requires that the state remove favorable tax treatment and/or reduce earmarked benefits for certain groups. Again, the strong relative power of the South African central state has facilitated such reform in a way that has been impossible in Brazil.

In South Africa, many low-yielding taxes have been abolished since 1994, and many parts of the tax system streamlined, including the harmonization of the tax systems of the former "homelands," the abolition of nonresident shareholders tax, a levy on financial services, and the withdrawal of the tax-exempt status of various bodies and institutions.

---

[84] The South African data are from the South African *Budget Review* 1998. Similar findings were reported for the incidence of the South African tax burden in 1990. See Fourie and Owen 1993.

[85] The Brazilian and OECD data are from ESAF 1994: 54. See also the discussions in Gutierres et al. 1995. More detailed estimates of the regressive tax burden in Brazil are available for earlier periods. See Maddison 1992: 108.

Extensive and cooperative discussions between the South African Revenue Service (SARS), the Ministry of Finance, and private-sector representatives, deliberating both in open forums and behind closed doors, have provided opportunities to gain consensus on tax proposals and to learn about how the tax system could be improved.[86] Of course, during this process, some individuals and groups have *tried* to make their case for special treatment and exemptions,[87] and some Cabinet Ministers have proposed special levies and surcharges as ways of generating extra revenue for their own portfolios. However, the ANC leadership has felt no need to cater to such interests, and has proceeded with its program of creating a tax system that is more evenly applied and perceived as more fair within society-at-large. Even potentially strong critics of the ANC government – members of Parliament from rival political parties – said during interviews in 1998 that they were impressed with the streamlining and efficiency gains that had been made in the South African Revenue Service and in the tax system at large since 1994. In each of the 1998, 1999, and 2000 budget speeches, the Minister of Finance identified revenue gains, even as certain old taxes were abolished. Given the centripetal nature of the reform process and the inability of legislators to introduce amendments to money bills, technically "clean" tax proposals have been enacted without political log-rolling.

In Brazil, despite vague commitments to modernize the tax system, the post-1988 tax system has grown ever more complex and cumbersome.[88]

---

[86] Interview with NP Member of Parliament, who is also a former Department of Finance official, Cape Town, South Africa, February 11, 1998.

[87] Interview with Professor Michael Katz, Johannesburg, South Africa, November 12, 1997.

[88] The frustrations associated with Brazil's stalemated reform process and that country's complex tax system have provided inspiration for the formulation of unconventional new policy proposals. For example, one popular proposal that was afforded significant attention in the Brazilian media was the idea of the *Imposto Único* or "Single Tax," proposed by Marcos Cintra de Albuquerque in a July 14, 1990 edition of *Folha de São Paulo*, and was meant to solve the problems of complexity and perceived unfairness in the tax system by imposing a single transactions tax within the economy that would be very difficult to evade. Ultimately, however, the dynamic that doomed the tax was not merely its imperfections in terms of its potential to demonetize the economy or the fact that it was regressive. In practice, it is unlikely that it would have been worse for the economy than the existing regime. Rather, in its simplicity, the tax provides no opportunity to strike political bargains or accommodations, and the manner in which private resources would be reallocated would be potentially *too* transparent for conflicting social forces. A São Paulo finance official argued that the battles that would have emerged from trying to assign the revenues "would result in a North-South rupture." Interview with top tax official from the government of the state of São Paulo, November 17, 1998.

The state continues to use a host of regionally and sectorally based incentives and exemptions with the goal of promoting horizontal equity. In order to make up for lost revenues, a host of new taxes have been adopted, often with reference to a specific expenditure need, but quickly used for other purposes. Many federal tax revenues tend to be highly regressive and complex, and many of these are cascading taxes,[89] which are quite inefficient and make many Brazilian products noncompetitive. A long list of surcharges, social security, and other contributions create the impression among citizens of being overtaxed, even as no single tax generates significant revenue and the vast majority of the resources are earmarked, providing little in the way of discretionary expenditure for the central state.

For example, in April 1996, the congress approved a temporary contribution on financial movements (CPMF)[90] to be levied in 1997 with the specific purpose of raising funds to upgrade the public health system. Because it was officially defined as a social contribution, the federal government was able to implement it without sharing the revenues with subnational tiers of government and without constitutional amendment. The tax is collected from financial institutions on virtually all transactions, including the writing of checks and the use of bank machines, and as such, is a nondeclaratory tax, withheld at source. As many have noted, the funds generated by the tax are no longer used for health, and its re-enactment suggests that it is hardly temporary. Analysts have argued that it will lead to financial de-intermediation, as firms will attempt higher levels of vertical integration in order to avoid the tax, and business analysts say the tax makes Brazil even less attractive as an investment location.[91] Nonetheless, the CPMF has proved remarkably attractive to government officials because citizens have little opportunity to avoid or evade the highly hidden tax which is collected directly from Brazil's relatively sophisticated banking system. Following the Asian currency crisis and the $40Bn bailout from the IMF, the state opted to raise the rate of this tax from 0.20 percent to 0.38 percent, rather than, for example, increasing the rates of income tax, because the central state had no desire to share revenues with other tiers of government, and because it needed a tax that was immune to Brazilian exit strategies.

---

[89] A tax that grows with increasing transactions such that individuals wind up paying tax on earlier taxes. This differs from a Value Added Tax, in which, by definition, taxes increase only on additional value added to a particular good or service.

[90] This tax was previously enacted in 1994 as a "normal" tax (IMPF), but was re-implemented as a contributions tax (CPMF) beginning in 1997.

[91] Wisnefski 1999.

The expenditure obligations associated with the respective revenue structures further exacerbated the different prospects for redistribution within the two country cases. In the mid-1990s in South Africa, less than 2 percent of total tax revenue collected at all levels of government was specifically earmarked with respect to those who actually paid the taxes themselves, whereas in Brazil, at least one-third of total revenues entered the fiscus earmarked for expenditure directly to those taxpayers who represented only a small fraction of the whole population. Such earmarking constrains the central government's ability to redistribute from richer households to poorer ones, as significant resources are used to provide security to those with jobs, and since the level of payout is often commensurate with employment classification, the impact is regressive. Given the high correlation between race and class in the two countries, this also implies less redistribution from white to black in Brazil than in South Africa.

Tax Compliance

The influence of old as well as more recent political dynamics on the respective tax states can also be seen in the area of tax administration, and particularly in terms of levels of tax compliance on the part of upper groups. In South Africa, despite common wisdom (among high-income individuals) to the contrary, tax compliance is excellent, while in Brazil, the practices of aggressive avoidance and evasion are extensive. Upper-income South Africans have continued to cooperate much more actively with the bureaucracy than have their Brazilian counterparts. Such differences are largely due to inherited patterns from the past, as white South Africans traditionally viewed the state as furthering their collective goals, while upper-income Brazilians challenged a central state that they saw as redistributing private resources to "other" groups. Within the context of these recently democratic polities, old patterns are in many ways locked in, and there is not significant room for citizens to alter their behavior to a significant degree. In the Brazilian case, the political dynamic of inter-regional competition continues to delegitimate the central state, and in this sense, patterns of noncompliance and/or noncooperation are reinforced. In the South African case, the influence of more recent political change on the willingness of upper groups to pay and to comply is more complex as there is greater variation with respect to the legitimating qualities of post-apartheid transition on the country's (still mostly white) upper-income individuals and firms. Nevertheless, absent a broad campaign to challenge the legitimacy of the tax system on

225

the part of upper groups, the South African state continues to benefit from what amounts to a strategic partnership with those groups in the collections process.

A rival explanation for the relative degree of compliance is that the quality of the bureaucracies differs, but if anything, the Brazilian bureaucracy is more advanced, and certainly spends more for each dollar-equivalent of revenue collected. During the 1990s, collection costs as share of total tax revenue have ranged from 1.19 percent to 1.74 percent in Brazil, while in South Africa, the range for the same period was between 0.50 percent and 0.90 percent. In the 1980s and 1990s, with loans from Inter-American Development Bank (IADB), the Brazilian tax administrations upgraded computer technology significantly – both at the federal level and in the states.[92] Moreover, the training programs required of tax officials are extensive. But even with the aid of sophisticated technology, deceptive practices on the part of taxpayers, involving reporting inaccurate data, rendered such technology ineffective in the fight against tax evasion. Indeed, the modern tax ledger is large and in 1997, the administration received 77 million returns,[93] but poor information remains problematic. Leading international tax experts familiar with the technical capacity of tax administrations around the world confirm that Brazil's is among the most sophisticated for countries at its level of development, suggesting that the inability to monitor and to assess properly more likely stems from poor information provided by taxpayers.[94] There is nothing remarkable about the internal organization or training of South Africa's tax bureaucracy that could account for its phenomenal success in collecting income tax. It is thus reasonable to conclude that the professional or technical qualities of the state bureaucracy do not explain differences in collections – rather, it is key differences in societal responses to state demands for the tax that have profoundly influenced collections.

A second rival explanation concerns the role of the credibility and trustworthiness of the state. In interviews with business and economic elites in both countries, most respondents said they received "nothing" in return for "heavy" tax burdens and that problems of corruption within the state and among taxpayers were "rampant." News of various "scandals" and

---

[92] ESAF 1995, and interviews with Inter-American Development Bank, SRF, and State of São Paulo officials in 1997.

[93] Interview with senior policy analyst in the Brazilian Federal Tax Administration (SRF), August 13, 1997.

[94] Interviews with World Bank and IMF tax experts.

"corruption" within both the South African and Brazilian states have been the source of headlines throughout the respective democratic eras.[95] Deeper probing in both countries revealed important differences in tax morality, however, with much more extreme forms of avoidance and evasion in Brazil. Although it is difficult to assess the actual quality of all government services provided, since a much greater portion of Brazilian expenditure is earmarked for contributors, Brazilian wage-earners have tended to receive more directly from the state than have South African wage-earners. More generally, the structure of expenditure in the two countries has been remarkably similar in recent years, further suggesting that tax compliance is not merely a material quid pro quo with the state.

Patterns of Compliance in South Africa. While the South African state was viewed as illegitimate in the eyes of the majority of the country's inhabitants for most of the 20th century, the minority of people who did view the state as legitimate were actually the ones controlling the vast majority of income and wealth. As a result, the fiscus benefits from patterns of interaction that are particularly favorable for collections, including the possession of good quality information, and regular, productive contact between collectors and upper-income payers. As black entrepreneurs have begun to prosper in the post-apartheid business climate, they have been increasingly integrated into the tax system.[96] Those whites rejecting the new political order have only minimal opportunities to alter their behavior, and the norm continues to be relatively high levels of compliance and cooperation.[97]

---

[95] To date, there has been no scandal in South Africa that has been widely recognized as evidence of corruption that can equal the 1992 resignation of Brazilian President Fernando Collor de Melo in the wake of impeachment proceedings prompted by corrupt behavior. On the other hand, that event had some legitimating qualities as it was largely hailed as a triumph of democracy because of the demonstrated ability of a system of due process to weed out such behavior. In South Africa, the Truth and Reconciliation Commission has uncovered examples of massive abuse of power during the apartheid era, in which various state actions constituted crimes against humanity. Other recent research suggests that between 1948 and 1990, government contracts were regularly awarded on a nepotistic basis, rather than on the basis of merit. See Heymans and Lipiez 1999.

[96] Interviews with SARS officials.

[97] Of course one option – that many have taken – has been to emigrate. Unfortunately, there are no reliable statistics on emigration or "white flight" in South Africa, particularly because many wealthy South Africans, like many wealthy Brazilians, have held multiple passports.

Indeed, many white South African business leaders and high-income individuals have complained in private and in the media about taxes, and have practiced tax avoidance and evasion, but a more accurate characterization of business participation in the development and implementation of tax policy reflects continued engagement with the state rather than conflict. In interviews with top officials at the revenue bureaucracy, with various tax intermediaries, and with business group leaders, there was consensus that although these upper groups had become somewhat more aggressive in their tax avoidance strategies, tax morality was still quite high in the country in the late 1990s, and the majority of business noncompliance was in the small- and medium-sized business sectors. Even there, rates of evasion were estimated to be on the order of 30 percent, implying that a much smaller percentage of the tax bill is evaded overall.[98] While there is certainly a range of variation within the white community concerning its evaluations of their obligations to pay taxes,[99] and this variation is likely to affect compliance patterns at the margins, within the institutional framework there are few clear opportunities to translate such sentiment into a lobbying strategy or even to alter individual patterns of compliance. Prominent business leaders or upper-income individuals have not publicly challenged the legitimacy of the tax system to nearly the degree as in Brazil, because at least in the 1990s, the post-apartheid political transition has provided a strong normative idiom for compliance with state demands.

Large businesses and high-income individuals have long provided excellent, well-audited information about their activities, and have withheld large sums of tax from employees. The result is that today, most South Africans who are liable for income tax have little opportunity to do anything *but* pay. It is much more difficult to alter one's economic behavior, and to report substantially lower earnings or wealth, once prior patterns have been established and alterations can be easily detected. In both informal conversations and structured interviews with upper-income South Africans, it became apparent that actual evasion and highly aggressive avoidance schemes were rare, and what dishonesty has taken place tends to be exaggerated. A Johannesburg tax consultant from a major multinational accounting firm "confessed" in an interview that he himself was actively engaged in malevolent tax avoidance, pointing out that he took unnecessary

[98] Interviews with SARS officials.
[99] Lieberman 2002.

228

delays in paying his taxes because the rate of penalty was less severe than the interest payments on his mortgage.[100] When seen in light of the Brazilian experiences, such practices can hardly be described as aggressively evasive. The same South African tax consultant pointed out that virtually all of his high-income clients pay some tax, whereas a tax consultant in São Paulo, Brazil with the same position, also from an American-based Big-Six accounting firm, highlighted that most of his clients pay no income taxes at all.[101] "Widespread tax avoidance and evasion" clearly means different things in the two country contexts.

Various tax intermediaries and those responsible for tax matters at large firms in South Africa described a relatively cooperative relationship between themselves and the tax bureaucracy in terms of exchanging information and interpreting tax law on an ongoing basis. As contrasted with the comments from the Brazilian tax bureaucracy, a high-ranking SARS official commented, "Normally, I would say we experience very good co-operation, especially from the accountancy profession . . ."[102] Tax consultants from the major firms echoed one another in explaining that they enjoy relatively open and consistent communications with individuals from SARS, which helps them to arrive at interpretations of the tax law that both parties agree are fair.

These patterns of compliance and capacity are largely unique to the privileged white minority in South Africa. By contrast, a notable lack of tax capacity in South Africa is evident in the heavily populated areas mostly inhabited by black South Africans, who are being integrated into a new relationship with the state. For the key taxes levied by the national government – income tax and consumption tax – the illegitimate quality of the apartheid government provided a rationale for avoiding the tax collector. Moreover, the low level of economic activity meant that there was no significant financial incentive for the state to act to rectify this situation. As a result, in the late 1990s, a large portion of the black community was off the register, and the national bureaucracy was attempting to bring them in through tax amnesties, education programs, and increased auditing. According to tax collectors and close observers, these tasks have been particularly difficult to accomplish because the largely white, and largely Afrikaans-speaking,

---

[100] Interview with tax partner, Big-Six accounting firm, Johannesburg, South Africa, November 19, 1997.

[101] Interview with tax partner, Big-Six accounting firm, São Paulo, Brazil, August 19, 1997.

[102] Interview with senior SARS bureaucrat, Pretoria, South Africa, June 5, 1998.

tax bureaucracy has perceived an inability to go into black areas.[103] An investigations officer in the tax bureaucracy said, "I can't see an auditor going out to Soweto or Khayelitsha"[104] (two of the largest, mostly black-inhabited townships in the country). Similarly, in the former homeland areas, which were developed with puppet governments and administrative functions intended to model those of functioning modern states, the quality of tax administration was very poor. The problem is a double-edged sword as many white taxpayers argue that the lack of collections in black areas is unfair, while tax administration officials concede that the level of economic activity in these areas is still highly depressed, and that the amount of tax not being collected relative to the entire budget is probably quite minimal.

Patterns of Compliance in Brazil. By contrast, the collection of taxes among upper groups in contemporary Brazil continues to be a very difficult task. A long history of upper-group challenges to the central state's attempts to collect has created patterns of economic behavior that reflect presumed noncompliance with the tax authorities. As alluded to earlier, because the economically privileged sectors in Brazil have for so long escaped direct payment, the state has had incentives to develop a battery of more regressive and indirect taxes as sources of revenue. This has produced much different types of capacities and expectations about normal levels of compliance.

Today, Brazilians speak openly about the widespread practices of tax avoidance and evasion that they engage in, and most argue that they feel justified in such action, complaining of waste and unfairness in the public sector. Systems of *caixa dois* and *caixa quatro* – dual and even four bookkeeping systems – are long established in Brazil, as are a wide range of other avoidance and evasion schemes. A representative from FIRJAN, one of the leading business associations, explained:

Few people pay income taxes. There are many ways to avoid it. Firms may, for example, give salary as a pension.... (Often) the people who escape are not formal employees – physicians, dentists, etc. – they don't give out receipts. Firms, companies, etc. usually have two accounts. Some companies have one very correct one with income, output and profit. But, there is another one with the same information,

---

[103] While the black portion of the staff is growing, it is largely inexperienced. In April 1992, a full 95 percent of the SARS staff was white, but by February 1998 that figure had dropped to 67 percent, with 21 percent of the staff being black. Internal SARS mimeo, Human Resources Department.

[104] Interview with mid-level bureaucrat in the South African Revenue Service, June 7, 1996.

reported differently. But, that's not mentioned. This happens more in small and medium enterprises, but the big ones are also experienced in taxes.[105]

In 1995, it was estimated that among Brazilians with assets of $90MM to $800MM, 30 percent pay no direct taxes, and the rest pay amazingly small sums.[106] In 1992, the 460 wealthiest people, who earned eighty times what the average taxpayer did, paid only eleven times more in taxes. Though this group has a net worth of almost $27 billion, they paid a mere $33 million in federal taxes.[107]

Adversarial relations between state and society are manifest in various tactics: Some individuals evade simply through outright nonreporting of earned income. Others take an exceptionally aggressive approach to the reporting of costs within firms, placing personal family expenses such as vacations, education, and medical expenses on the debit side of the books. Many create firms with no productive purposes, establishing tax avoidance shelters. Moreover, high-income taxpayers with their paid consultants have continued to engage in bitter arguments with the bureaucracy over the interpretation of tax liabilities in this complex system. "People complain, but this is not participatory,"[108] explained a top official at SRF when asked about whether democracy had improved the legitimacy and functioning of the tax system. In the absence of closer ties between collector and payer, the prospects for improving compliance and gathering information are low. Such practices are so widespread that Brazilians have come to accept them as a fact of economic life.

Even for those Brazilian citizens who might feel that they *ought* to pay their full tax obligations, in such an environment, the costs of compliance are particularly high. While there are obvious financial incentives for shirking one's tax obligation, many Brazilian business leaders explain that existing policies and administrative procedures are so burdensome, that businesses would not survive if they complied fully. Moreover, markets have adjusted to such behavior. In order to address noncompliance in the past, the state has levied multiple overlapping taxes to the extent that if one were to be fully compliant to the letter of the law, it would be virtually impossible to be profitable or to have an after-tax take. The FIRJAN representative

---

[105] Interview with policy analyst, FIRJAN, Rio de Janeiro, Brazil, November 12, 1998.

[106] Mariana Crespo, "Reform from Ipanema," *Financial World*, May 23 1995.

[107] Mendes 1995.

[108] Interview with senior policy analyst in the Brazilian Federal Tax Administration (SRF), August 13, 1997.

Table 5.5 *Government receipts in Brazil and South Africa, 1998*

Sphere of government	Tax	Brazil (1998)		South Africa (1997/8)	
		Percent of GDP	Share of total collections (%)	Percent of GDP	Share of total collections (%)
NATIONAL	TOTAL NATIONAL	20.7	69.4	27.5	94.5
	Ordinary Taxes	*8.3*	*27.7*	*27.0*	*92.8*
	Income and property tax	5.3	17.7	16.0	55.0
	Individuals	4.0	13.2	11.5	39.5
	Companies	1.3	4.5	4.5	15.5
	Property tax	0.0	0.0	0.0	0.0
	Consumption tax	3.0	10.1	11.0	37.8
	Main consumption tax	1.8	6.0	6.7	23.0
	Other consumption taxes (includes taxes on trade)	1.2	4.0	4.3	14.8
	Security/Earmarked Taxes	*9.9*	*33.2*	*0.5*	*1.7*
	Social Security	5.2	17.3	0.5	1.7
	Other social contributions (CPMF, COFINS, PIS, etc.)	4.7	15.8	0.0	0.0
	Other Federal Taxes	*2.5*	*8.4*	*0.0*	*0.0*
PROVINCIAL/ ESTADO*	TOTAL PROVINCIAL	7.9	26.4	0.2	0.7
MUNICIPAL	TOTAL MUNICIPAL	1.3	4.3	1.4	4.8
ALL LEVELS	TOTAL TAXATION	29.8	100.0	29.1	100.0

* Indirect taxation only

Sources: Department of Finance, *Budget Review*; SRF Website; World Bank 1998.

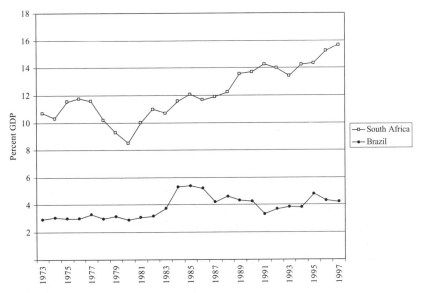

Figure 5.8   Income tax collections in Brazil and South Africa, 1973–1997. *Sources:* Department of Finance, RSA various; Escola de Administração Fazendaria 1997; World Bank 1998.

explained, "I am usually told by company owners that if they paid all the taxes that were due, that they couldn't go on. But, we do see that many of them are very wealthy."[109] A Brazilian dentist in São Paulo, for example, claimed that she would lose clients if she did not charge a "cash" price.[110] It is clear that in order to be competitive in many markets in Brazil, tax avoidance and evasion must be practiced at several levels.

Collections Compared

Ultimately, cross-national differences in the relationship between state and society are manifest in the structure of tax collections. By 1997, total tax collections for all spheres of government in both countries amounted to just under 30 percent of GDP, suggesting that the size of the public sector was very similar in the two countries. Yet, the *manner* in which such taxes were collected was radically different. There was a very high concentration of progressive income taxes in South Africa (16 percent of GDP) compared with Brazil (5.3 percent of GDP) in 1997 (see Table 5.5 and Figure 5.8).

[109] Interview with policy analyst, FIRJAN, Rio de Janeiro, Brazil, November 12, 1998.
[110] Interview with dentist in private practice, São Paulo, Brazil, November 1998.

233

Both in terms of individual income tax collections and corporate income taxes, South Africa was collecting approximately three times as much as a share of GDP at the end of the 20th century.[111] Meanwhile, the concentration of tax collections varies widely. In South Africa, just two taxes – federal income tax and the Value Added Tax – accounted for 78 percent of all tax revenues, or 83 percent of federal tax revenues in 1997. In Brazil, those two revenue sources – which were also the most important ones – accounted for only 24 percent of total tax revenues or 34 percent of federal tax revenues. Instead, the Brazilian state collects a host of earmarked taxes and earmarked social contributions, many of which are used to fund expenses other than those for which they were explicitly intended.[112] From an historical perspective one can find that to a large extent, national patterns were developed during earlier periods. In South Africa, in 1973, the main income tax and consumption tax accounted for 76 percent of all federal taxes, while in Brazil, income taxes and consumption taxes accounted for about 39 percent of all federal taxes. Yet, since democratization, the trend has been toward greater concentration and rationalization of revenue sources in South Africa and just the opposite in Brazil.

The qualities of the respective tax states strongly influence the prospects for balancing regional inequalities, and again, South Africa's tax structure provides a firmer foundation for regional equalization. The central state's ability to redistribute resources through the fiscus is a function of the share of total taxes it collects from wealthier regions. In South Africa in the late 1990s, more than 90 percent of provincial-level financial resources came in the form of transfers from the central government. In Brazil, only about one-fourth of the total financial resources of the provincial (*estado*) level of government were in the form of such transfer grants, with the rest coming from taxes and fees collected by the *estados* themselves, largely in the form of regressive taxes. Because the taxable base of regions varies widely, this implies that the available revenue shares also vary widely within Brazil.

---

[111] Increased individual income tax revenues in the 1980s were largely due to fiscal drag – that is, the noncorrection of marginal bracket thresholds in an inflationary environment, which acts to push income-earners into higher brackets without commensurate gains in real income. This phenomenon of "bracket creep" was partially adjusted in the late 1990s with new rate schedules, which provided some relief for lower-income earners who were still in the income tax system.

[112] Including a social contributions tax, a tax on financial operations (IOF), a social integration tax (PIS), a social security financing contribution (COFINS), other social security contributions, and a contribution to the unemployment severance pay indemnity fund (FGTS).

The impact for these two countries where there are huge regional inequalities of resources is that in Brazil, poor regions wind up having relatively much smaller shares of the total revenue pie than do their poor region counterparts in South Africa. Such systems of intergovernmental finance serve to reproduce regional inequalities. Given the greater concentration of blacks in the poorer regions of the two countries, this outcome again implies that the South African tax state is better equipped to redistribute from whites to blacks than is the Brazilian tax state.

Although much of this variation was already well established by the end of the 1970s, what is remarkable is that national differences became *more* exaggerated during a period of international reform, just at a time when most would have expected greater convergence. South Africa's tax system became *more* progressive relative to Brazil's, and Brazil's became *more* complex and inefficient, compared to South Africa's. Such differences reflect the state's varied authority over upper groups and the varied constructions of distributive justice that developed out of very different types of political dynamics.

Conclusion

What is the effect of an increasingly integrated international economy? This chapter has demonstrated the resilience of national patterns of politics and taxation in two countries undergoing largely similar processes of political and economic change. As a result, South Africa has entered the 21st century with a *cooperative* tax state, and Brazil with an *adversarial* one. Beyond simply identifying key differences in contemporary tax policy and tax administration, the chapter has explained *how* patterns were reproduced during otherwise quite similar political openings. Different forms of inclusion and exclusion articulated in constitutions written around the turn of the 20th century influenced the idioms and organization of politics in the contemporary societies, in turn affecting the calculations, strategies, and behavior of collective actors. Powerful institutional legacies made state-society relations highly resistant to change. In South Africa, the organizations and idioms produced by a history of explicit racial exclusion still provide a political "glue," keeping economic interests largely cohesive and crowding out more particularistic demands even as racial discrimination has become illegal, effectively changing the definition of NPC in a quite dramatic way. In Brazil, expressions of regional difference have remained symbolically very important, reinforcing organizational fragmentation and centrifugal political dynamics. Race acts to reinforce a sense of regional difference, rather than to overcome those differences, as is the case in South Africa. By demonstrating how these different symbols and frameworks structured politics, the analysis has highlighted the enduring influence of definitions of National Political Community on patterns of state-building.

More generally, the analyses presented in this chapter point to the value of an historical perspective on contemporary politics. The process of tax reform, and struggles over the national state's authority within society more generally, are dynamic interactions with longstanding origins. The parameters of fundamental political questions tend to be so deeply embedded in institutions in society that central actors within the political process would not likely be able to identify them as the explanation for nationally distinctive taxation outputs. From the more distant vantage point of broad, comparative-historical analysis, however, it is possible to observe the influence of path-dependent processes at work.

And what about change? The creation of a nonracial, federal constitution in South Africa in the 1990s *has* had some influence on the calculations and strategies of political actors. Many upper-income South Africans now see the state as serving "them," not "us," and would prefer to avoid and to evade payment. But such institutional change did not cause a wholesale reversal of the effects of a century of identity and state construction within a very different institutional context. Moreover, the transformation to a more "Brazilian" definition of NPC, taking place at the end of the 20th century, occurred in a very much changed domestic and international environment in which expressly racist bases for citizenship have been widely discredited and condemned. In Brazil, the end of authoritarian rule provided an *opportunity* for change, but the parameters for specifying the NPC in the 1988 constitution were largely similar to those of the 1891 constitution. As a result, in both cases, taxation outcomes have been "sticky" across time.

Timing and sequencing matter, and convergence in institutional forms at the end of the 20th century continued to be mediated by the legacies of the past. Yet, change – even dramatic change – is very possible, and a speculative discussion of how such change could unfold is the subject of Chapter 7. Before engaging in such a forward-looking discussion, however, I turn sideways, to examine the extent to which the ideas explored in this and previous chapters may help to explain variation in patterns of taxation and state-building in other parts of the world.

6

Political Community and Taxation Beyond Brazil and South Africa

To what extent have the politics of race and regionalism influenced the development of the tax state in countries other than Brazil and South Africa? Extending the geographic scope of the analysis to countries around the world provides opportunities to explore the general applicability of the political community model, and to gain additional analytic leverage over the comparison between these two countries. While it is not possible to carry out the type of detailed historical analysis presented in the previous chapters for additional country cases, we can estimate statistical relationships between key independent variables and various taxation measures in order to assess the theoretical reach of the arguments advanced above. This return to the "large-N" analysis, which originally helped to frame the central puzzles of this book, represents an attempt to deploy a nested research design, taking advantage of multiple research strategies. It reflects a belief in the multiple purposes of social science research, which includes both the development of general theories and the elucidation of historically specific places and time periods that are of particular interest. Every approach has its limitations, and the use of multiple methods helps to compensate for the shortcomings of any single approach used in isolation.

Before proceeding with such analysis, however, it is useful to review the main conclusion from the previous chapters. Comparative historical analysis revealed that early definitions of National Political Community (NPC), varying in terms of the manner of incorporation of racial and regional identities, affected patterns of tax state development during the course of the 20th century. Varied approaches to racial and regional cleavages produced different sets of class relations, which in turn structured the adoption and implementation of tax policy in the wake of common pressures toward the expansion of the national state. The early construction of a racially

237

exclusive union in South Africa helped to generate a cross-class coalition among whites and a politics of collective sacrifice among the economically privileged, and led to the development of a more efficient and progressive tax state. That case was contrasted with the record of tax state construction in Brazil, where an officially nonracial federation exacerbated problematic political divisions, particularly among high-income/wealth actors, leading to lower levels of willingness to pay progressive taxes. Although informally practiced race chauvinism has persisted in Brazil – a holdover from the legacy of slavery and centuries of racial thinking – deliberate political strategies to deny any political salience to race impeded the formation of cross-class coalitions that might have used race as a unifying idiom.

It was possible to make causal inferences with only two country cases because the remarkable similarity of Brazil and South Africa in terms of level of development, demographic patterns, international influences, and social structure provided a set of controls for a host of otherwise potentially important rival explanations. Analytic comparisons of historical processes provided insights into the determinants of varied state-building patterns.

In this chapter, Brazil and South Africa are used as ideal type cases that provide a backdrop for classifying additional country cases and for conducting comparative analyses with the cross-national dataset introduced in Chapters 1 and 2. I conduct statistical analyses to assess the impact of definitions of NPC on taxation, and to evaluate a host of alternative explanations, including those emphasizing the influence of labor union density, regime type, and culture. Because it was not possible to carry out more extensive qualitative assessments of the tax policies and tax administration in each of the countries under analysis, I rely exclusively on collections data for measuring the quality of the tax state.

Case Selection

A key component of theory building and model testing is the specification of a universe of cases to which the theory ought to apply. While my argument attempts to account for differences in the development of modern national states, it does not easily apply to all the polities generally recognized as national states because some of the concepts and measures are not infinitely portable. I have excluded all cases with populations of fewer than one million people because in such societies, the very need for public goods, as well as the nature of the collective action and administrative problems involved in collecting revenues, are so different from those of larger countries, that it is unlikely that similar types of factors would affect state development in similar ways. Second, because of the very unique histories of state development in Communist countries, particularly the nature of taxation (as discussed in Chapter 2), I have excluded all current and former Communist states from the analysis. Third, because oil-rich countries tend to rely so heavily on oil-related revenues to finance government activities, and because such revenues are so different from normal taxation on members of society, I have excluded the main oil exporting countries from the analysis.[1] Finally, I have been forced to exclude all cases for which good taxation data are not available, a move that introduces very little bias into the estimates because these are largely the poorest countries, for which we have sufficient cases to conduct sound analysis. As a result of these exclusions, seventy-one countries remain for comparison.

Estimating the Impact of National Political Community on Taxation

In order to estimate the political community model with these additional cases, the variable, National Political Community, must be specified in a manner that makes sense for a wider range of contexts. Whereas other areas of cross-national analysis benefit from accumulated research on conceptualization and classification – for example, scholars have extensively debated the best ways to classify country regime types as either democracies or dictatorships[2] – there has been little explicit discussion of the variables considered here, and this classification process does not benefit from the

---

[1] In particular, see the argument made in Karl 1997. The group of oil exporters includes the members of the Organization of Petroleum Exporting Countries (OPEC) and the countries in which oil exports account for at least 40 percent of total exports. See Przeworski, Alvarez, Cheibub, and Limongi 2000. I have not excluded other mineral-exporting countries, however, because other minerals have not tended to provide the same types of consistent rewards as oil, and because South Africa clearly has a large mineral industry. It is worth noting that Botswana's high level of income tax collections is largely from its mineral industry, as distinct from South Africa, where income taxes on mining firms represent only a very small share of total receipts.

[2] See, for example, Collier and Adcock 1999; Przeworski et al. 2000.

same body of accumulated research. As a result, it is necessary to explicate a set of rules and justifications for classifying individual country cases that is largely without precedent.

The comparative historical analysis presented in the previous chapters relied on the sustained interpretation of historical facts in order to assess their analytical significance. In comparing and contrasting the definitions of NPC specified in Brazil and South Africa, I have benefited from a relatively extensive secondary literature on race policies in those countries, including important comparative work such as Marx's (1998) study. In order to explore the argument more broadly, within the context of a larger cross-national statistical analysis, I must rely on information gleaned from a much thinner collection of secondary sources and consultations with other scholars about classification of countries, without the opportunities to verify these classifications with other forms of data including field research. As a result, my ability to classify these cases properly is weaker, and it is more likely that future research may suggest the need to reconsider how some cases are scored. Beyond the problem of measuring definitions of National Political Community, there are also inferential limitations associated with this statistical analysis. The political community model attempts to take time, timing, and history quite seriously by giving analytical weight to the notion of a critical juncture. However, in the absence of appropriate data for long periods of time for several countries, it is simply not possible to fully evaluate the theoretical model as specified in Chapter 1 with a relatively simple, cross-sectional dataset.

Notwithstanding these analytical constraints, I still attempt to investigate the generalizability of my argument by examining statistical relationships between various explanatory variables and measures of tax collection. In order to conclude that the argument has some broader theoretical purchase beyond Brazil and South Africa, we should be able to observe a causal effect that resonates with the predictions associated with the political community model.

Definitions of National Political Community

While the definition of NPC is treated here as a politically constructed variable – and not a structural or genetic given – it does not make sense to assume that virtually *any* definition of NPC has been feasible everywhere. Rather, the model is concerned with the impact of *different* solutions to otherwise *similar*, pre-existing social and political cleavages. Thus, in order to proceed in a manner that is analytically tractable, and does not lead to infinite historical regress, I limit the analysis of variation in definitions of NPC to the dimensions of race and region, as discussed in the cases of Brazil and South Africa. From this starting point, we can investigate the extent to which other country cases faced similar social and political cleavages, and when they did, assess the extent to which institutional resolutions of such cleavages approximated one or another ideal type. Although Brazil and South Africa were cases of extreme opposite solutions to the dual cleavage of race and regionalism – a federation with an officially nonracial approach to race, and a unitary state with an explicitly exclusionary approach to race – the analysis in this chapter allows for mixed approaches by considering the dimensions of race and regionalism separately without regard to how they interact with one another. Moreover, although definitions of NPC tend to become altered through political contests over time, I am concerned with the impact of enduring historical legacies, and as such, I do not attempt to account for variation over time. This simplification must obscure changing understandings of racial categories and changes in policy. Nonetheless, I believe we gain analytical power by accepting such simplifications as a preliminary step. My coding scheme reflects the most substantial articulation of the National Political Community evident during the first three-quarters of the 20th century, and following independence for countries not already independent and autonomous at the turn of the 20th century (see Table 6.1).

Race. Because race itself is a widely used concept with different meanings and interpretations in both scholarly and general usage, it is necessary to specify the nature of the racial conflict being addressed. Specifically, I limit the problem of race to a relatively narrow subset of cases, which Louis Hartz described as "European fragment societies."[3] Theoretically, this group is of interest because it is defined in terms of a common set of core political cleavages. In all of these cases, political and intellectual elites were forced to choose from a menu of contested definitions of nationhood in the face of real and perceived social heterogeneity. These fragment societies share a common history in that groups of Europeans settled decades and even centuries prior to the Second World War, and these settlers confronted indigenous populations' African-descended populations brought to

[3] Hartz 1964.

Table 6.1 *Classification of countries according to early definitions of National Political Community. Excludes countries with a Communist legacy, with populations less than one million, that are members of OPEC or with oil exports > 50 percent of total exports*

		Federal	Unitary		
Fragment Societies	Race Exclusionary	Australia Canada United States	South Africa New Zealand Namibia (previously South West Africa) Zimbabwe (previously Rhodesia)		
	Race Inclusionary	Argentina Brazil	Bolivia Chile Colombia Costa Rica Dominican Republic El Salvador Guatemala Nicaragua Panama Paraguay Peru Uruguay		
Not Fragment Societies		Austria Ethiopia Germany India Malaysia Pakistan Switzerland	Belgium Botswana Burkina Faso Burundi Chad Congo, Dem. Rep. Denmark Egypt, Arab Rep. Finland France Gambia, The Ghana Greece Guinea Ireland	Israel Italy Japan Jordan Kenya Korea, Rep. Lesotho Madagascar Malawi Mauritius Mongolia Morocco Netherlands Norway Pap. New Guinea	Philippines Portugal Rwanda Sierra Leone Singapore Spain Sri Lanka Sweden Syria Thailand Tunisia Turkey United Kingdom Zambia

the countries through the slave trade, and/or immigrants from other parts of the world. In such societies, the European fragments, which helped to create new, autonomous national states, were instrumental in the construction of new national identities, as political elites defined the criteria for citizenship. Within all of these heterogeneous societies, prejudice has defined intra-societal relations, and where there has been race, there has also been racial prejudice. According to Hartz, the group of fragment societies includes all of the Americas, from Canada to Chile, as well as South Africa and Australia. I also include New Zealand, Zimbabwe, and Namibia, because of obvious similarities in terms of shared histories of white settlement and contact with Africans and indigenous groups.

Although there are other cases of settler colonialism elsewhere in Africa – for example, in Kenya, Botswana, Zambia, and Malawi – in none of these cases did a substantial white or European population remain in the country following independence. Black Africans immediately took control of government, implying a very different type of political backdrop to questions of taxation and state-building more generally, because white economic elites would no longer perceive the state as serving their interests as a racial group. And while there have been many cases of post-independence ascriptive political tension in other parts of the world which have been described as racial conflicts – for example in Indonesia, Malaysia, and Algeria – the terms of such political battles have been so different that a quite distinctive analytical framework would be necessary to incorporate those cases into the analysis. What the fragment societies share, that other former colonies including other countries in sub-Saharan Africa do not, are political traditions in which a European-descended group retained political, economic, and administrative control of territories simultaneously inhabited by themselves and other groups understood as belonging to different, interior races. They have also shared a set of pseudo-scientific claims and myths about racial difference that have been used to legitimate patterns of white or European racial domination. Such a backdrop has created similar underlying political conflicts about if and how class privilege overlapping with a shared racial identity might be mobilized, and if so, how a white working and/or underclass might be incorporated into the political arena.

For this analysis, it is necessary to identify how the various fragment societies addressed the race question – namely, in the face of widespread feelings of race chauvinism among white or European insiders, what would be done about those people residing in the same territory who were understood to be from inferior race groups? How would they be either included in or excluded from membership in the National Political Community, and on what terms?

In the cases of Brazil and South Africa it was possible to focus on decisions made in reference to this question within the context of a specific constitutional moment and its immediate legacy. However, because of wide-ranging differences in the form and timing of constitutions in other countries, particularly in relation to statements about race policies, I must take a more broad view of the institutional choices that were made to define the NPC. That is, I consider the various legislative, policy, and other official actions taken by governments toward nonwhite groups. Given the theoretical expectations generated in previous chapters, I am most interested in distinguishing among the countries in terms of their resemblance to either Brazil or South Africa, varying in terms of the state's explicit use of racial categories as a means of exclusion, particularly during the first three-quarters of the century – which in some cases included holdovers from the late 19th century. Why this period? Certainly in more recent decades, international norms weighing against ethnic- and race-based discrimination have become much more widespread and ethnic- and race-based groups have made claims for new rights and some restitution. I provide a more speculative assessment of the impact of such changing patterns of identity mobilization on the tax state in Chapter 7. In the meantime, the most relevant insight is that the political community model emphasizes the stickiness of tax collections after the initial patterns of modern tax state-building get set in motion. Empirically, this seems to hold true: For the 45 countries for which tax collection data were available for the years 1975 and 1995, a measure of income and profits taxes as share of GDP was extremely highly correlated between those two time points,[4] implying that the relative ranking of countries in terms of tax collections has barely changed at all in two decades! This suggests that the best place to look for explanations of cross-national variation in tax systems at the end of the 20th century is during the period prior to 1975.

In attempting to classify country cases in terms of similarity to either Brazil or South Africa, I found that several countries displayed some traits evident in *both* countries. Given the complex nature of the large-scale social phenomenon being investigated, this should not come as a surprise. For example, any attempt to classify countries according to political regime type would reveal that some countries simultaneously possess traits evident in democracies and dictatorships. Nonetheless, based on the data available, it was possible to classify countries according to one or the other type of approach to the race question, and I express my reservations about the classification of individual cases below. I should point out that I was not

[4] Pearson's R = .86, significant at the .01 level.

concerned with the actual intentions of the actors involved in deciding these approaches – for example, reservation systems were often established with a rhetorical justification that this was meant to protect those groups, and there is evidence suggesting that policies of nonracialism were the product of deliberate calculations that this would be the surest way to maintain a socioeconomic hierarchy. Rather, I was only interested in distinguishing among the countries in terms of how government leaders and bureaucrats used explicitly racial and ethnic labels as forms of social control, attempting to distinguish access to the rights and responsibilities of citizenship between those who were white and those who were not.

Of the two approaches to the question of race, the South African approach was notable for the explicit exclusion of people of color, which helped to make a shared white or European identity an important aspect of politics throughout society. The dominant features of this exclusion strategy included that the relevant nonwhite "other" was made highly visible with explicit terms for participation in political life, such as voting for Europeans only and creating a separate administration for Native Affairs. As a result, whiteness took on very high social and political salience. In looking for cases with similar features, I tried to find evidence within country histories in which there were distinctive facilities, representation, benefits, and/or obligations for nonwhite groups, including differential access to property. In order to classify a country as a case of an exclusionary strategy, these distinctions had to be based explicitly on ethnic or racial identity, not socioeconomic status.

Certain countries are relatively easy to classify as having had relatively similar strategies for defining the NPC: The United States prior to the civil rights legislation of the 1960s, with its "Jim Crow" laws and maintenance of segregation, both of African Americans and indigenous groups; and Rhodesia/Zimbabwe prior to 1980 and Southwest Africa/Namibia prior to 1989 both maintained apartheid-like systems of government.[5] To a lesser degree, but clearly within the same category, Australia is a case where differentiation from the aboriginal community and other nonwhites produced a high salience for whiteness, and a white labor movement. Its first parliament passed Act 12, which mandated that the country would be party to no mail contract that did not commit itself to a white labor policy on its vessels.[6] The Aborigines Protection Acts maintained a system of institutionalized

---

[5] See, for example, Carton 2000; and Herbst 1989.
[6] Huttenback 1976: 279.

white supremacy,[7] and aborigines have been denied many civil rights such as being able to manage their own finances, access to certain government benefits such as pensions, less protection of property rights, and not being able to pass other privileges on to children.[8]

Canada and New Zealand are slightly more problematic for classification. These countries maintained more extensive rhetoric concerned with the fair treatment of indigenous and other nonwhite groups during the late 19th and early 20th centuries, and people within those societies have tended to take pride in having better or less conflictual race relations than in the countries mentioned above. Some historical facts seem more reminiscent of the Brazilian case: For example, there were various Canadian initiatives to "civilize" the Indian population in the mid- to late 19th century, extending various rights and responsibilities of citizenship onto this indigenous group. In New Zealand, there also appears to be more evidence of deliberate attempts to assimilate the Maori population into the European society through education and other strategies, which would *not* be in line with the South African ideal-type.

Nonetheless, I concluded that Canada and New Zealand are best described as examples of the exclusionary strategy because sufficient evidence points to deliberate state strategies for differentiating white from nonwhite groups within the territory. While political leaders and citizens from these countries have advanced notions of racial *harmony*, particularly when compared with countries such as the United States and South Africa, in practice this tended to take on a more patronizing tone, and racial distinctions were simultaneously reinforced. In turn, this helped to generate high degrees of social and political salience for a white or European identity that could be mobilized in response to perceived threats. Indeed, much of the scholarship on identity politics in those countries has tended to draw strong parallels between the strategies for race relations in these countries with those practiced in South Africa, the United States, and Australia.[9]

In Canada, several pieces of legislation imply an exclusionary approach. The late 19th century Indian Acts made Indians "children in the eyes of the law,"[10] and "status Indians" did not have the right to vote until 1959.

---

[7] Blackburn 1999: 161.
[8] Haskins 1998: fn1.
[9] Huttenback 1976: 317. See also Lunt, Spoonley, and Mataira 2002; Roberts 2002; Haskins 1998; Knowles 1996; Markey 1996; Baker 1992; Mungazi 1981; Bull 1967; and Price 1950.
[10] Harring 1998: 263.

During the decades surrounding the turn of the 20th century, the government even enacted a pass system restricting the movement of Indians in Western Canada, although it was not effectively implemented.[11] Meanwhile, blacks in Canada in the late 19th century faced segregated schools, churches, and voluntary associations.[12] Particularly in Western Canada, Asians faced extreme discrimination, with various exclusion leagues, and social movements advocating a White Canada.[13] At the federal level, most discriminatory legislation concerned immigration policy – which for our purposes cannot be used to distinguish among inclusionary and exclusionary approaches to the race question, because both types preferred white immigrants. However, various provinces enacted their own discriminatory legislation concerning voting and workplace regulations, such as in 1875, when a bill was introduced in the British Columbian legislature disenfranchising Chinese from provincial elections, even if Canadian-born.[14]

In New Zealand, while it is true that Maori representatives were included in the national parliament from early on, and officially enjoyed equal recognition under the 1840 Treaty of Waitangi,[15] their representation was *as* Maoris – distinctively as a racial group in which the qualifications for office and for voting were based on "blood." Adding to the distinction, voting took place at different times for the two race groups.[16] Pearson (1990: 54) points out that this system has often raised comparisons with the South African apartheid system, and that the " 'special' place of Maori in parliament effectively marginalizes their input," and has reinforced the salience of racial categories. A speech given by New Zealand's Governor-General in 1934 to a gathering of Maori and Europeans on the anniversary of the Treaty of Waitangi reveals evidence of a clear differentiation strategy:

On the part of those of us who belong to the British people this gathering affords an opportunity of renewing our obligations to the Maori people – obligations which have become all the greater since, during the intervening years, our race has become the dominant partner in the possession and enjoyment of this country, the sovereignty of which we still hold as a sacred and inviolable trust.[17]

---

[11] Barron 1996: 184–5.
[12] Roberts 2002: 19.
[13] For an account of policy and attitudes toward Asians in British Columbia, see Ward 1978.
[14] Huttenback 1976: 262.
[15] Lunt, Spoonley, and Mataira 2002: 143.
[16] Pearson 1990: 152.
[17] Bledisloe, Bathurst, and Buick 1940: 140.

Moreover, in 1909, adoption of European children by Maori was made illegal,[18] and in 1959, Maori members of the New Zealand Rugby Union were excluded from the team due to visit South Africa[19] – a move that would have been unthinkable in a place like Brazil. As in Canada, fear of Asian immigration also fueled explicit racist doctrines and quite overt calls for a "white New Zealand" during the first decades of the 20th century.[20]

In these countries, as in South Africa, race provided an important discursive-ideational category for political organization and for the development of normative frameworks within which questions about equity and collective goods could be interpreted. The hypothesis generated from the political community model is that such exclusion promoted inter- and intra-class solidarity among racial "insiders," facilitating the state's ability to collect progressive income taxes in such societies. The proximity of a highly visible and excluded group helped to cement the necessary bonds of cooperation and a shared, long-term time horizon, which would make quasi-voluntary tax payment a widely practiced behavior.

As contrasted with the South African case, Brazil was a fragment society in which an inclusionary strategy was adopted for dealing with the race question in the late 19th century and for most of the 20th century. The Brazilian government and political elites pursued various strategies of integration and assimilation, in which the stated aim was to homogenize the population. As compared with South Africa, the nonwhite other was made much less prominent and relevant as a basis for political life and mobilization within society. The state acted to remove nonwhites from the national imagination through the adoption of official nonracialism, including the promotion of racial mixing within society and prohibitions on the use of racial categories in the administration of government. As I have tried to make clear, this in no way implied a benign attitude about race: Whiteness was clearly preferred. By using the term inclusion, I do not mean to imply a normative evaluation; I simply intend to provide a contrast to a deliberately exclusionary approach. Indeed, there is substantial evidence suggesting the persistence of negative racial stereotypes within Brazilian society, as well as informal barriers to progress, and legal barriers specified in nonracial terms. Notwithstanding, nonwhites have not been excluded from membership in the NPC explicitly along racial lines during the 20th century. Nonwhite

[18] Ballara 1986: 98.
[19] Ballara 1986: 116.
[20] O'Connor 1968.

groups have not made truly substantial political claims as members of disadvantaged ethnic or racial groups until quite late in the 20th century in Brazil, and neither lower nor upper groups have defined themselves as explicitly "white" groups in the political arena.

In attempting to identify other fragment societies with similar approaches to race, it became clear that in fact the Brazilian case was a relatively extreme case of a more general approach evident throughout Latin America. When comparing the groups of fragment societies, Hartz (1964: 14) explains, "Latin-American treatment of slave and Indian was harsh, but it was far freer from a sense of property and race, far more involved in distinctions of status, than was the treatment of the non-Westerner by the British and the Dutch." In an introduction to an edited volume on race and ethnicity in Latin America, Jorge Dominguez (1994: vii) argues, "In nearly all racially and ethnically heterogeneous societies, there is overt national conflict among parties and social movements organized on the basis of race and ethnicity. Such conflict has been much less evident in Latin America." In a similar vein, Merrick (1998: 27) writes, "Latin America is rich in ethnic and cultural diversity, with a history of assimilation and mixing of racial and ethnic groups in many of its populations."

Although scholars have recently unearthed more subtle tensions among racial and ethnic groups that have interacted in complex ways with class tensions, the very fact that scholars have had to *convince* others that race and ethnicity are indeed relevant categories in these countries suggests just how different these cases are from the countries described above. While Brazil may represent an extreme example of an integrationist whitening strategy, varying degrees of such a strategy can be found throughout Latin America, particularly between the 1920s and the 1940s with a set of government policies that came to be known as *indigenismo*.[21] In Latin America, unlike in cases such as the United States, South Africa, or the other explicitly exclusionary fragment societies, skin color has not been the basis for a rigid classification system into which rights and privileges were clearly specified.[22]

When considering the two modal strategies for dealing with the problem of race, what was ultimately common to all of the Latin American cases during the early to mid-20th century was that the relevant, proximate "other" was effectively eliminated from the national imagination, either through

---

[21] Graham 1992; Stavenhagen 1994: 336.
[22] Pitt-Rivers 1994: 60. See also Morse 1964: 124–5.

actual extermination, through "whitening," or through assimilation. As a result, there was not a highly visible, explicit exclusion comparable to that in South Africa that could form the basis of political claims and calculations among the white insiders "proving" that they were collectively different and somehow threatened by a proximate, nonwhite outsider.

Certain cases can be easily recognized as similar to the Brazilian approach to the definition of NPC given their strategies of *indigenismo*.[23] While describing such trends more generally throughout Latin America, Yashar (1996: 89) points out,

policy was designed in places like Mexico, Guatemala, Peru and Bolivia to incorporate people perceived as backward into the ranks of a new, presumably more civilized nation. States encouraged indigenous men and women to discard any display of indigenous identity, encouraged the adoption of a mestizo identity, and thus publicly encouraged miscegenation to "whiten" the population.

Safford (1991) points out that in Colombia, between 1750 and 1870, several pieces of legislation made Indians official citizens of the state, while Arocha (1998) argues that Afro-Colombians were largely ignored and the working class in particular sought out strategies of whitening. In the Dominican Republic one finds evidence of a whitening project combined with race chauvinism as in Brazil.[24] Despite the influence of American ideas about race in Panama, and rampant racial chauvinism, the strategy for defining the NPC in that country has involved neither segregation nor formal discrimination.[25]

In several of the Latin American cases there is fairly well documented evidence of violence against indigenous groups, and it is necessary to square this type of violence with my classification of these countries as cases of *less* explicit exclusion. Here it is helpful to think about the concept of the NPC in terms of the causal theory that relates such political strategies to the outcomes under investigation. Because violence tended to be carried out quickly, and generally without explicit reference to a racially based "us-them" dynamic, subsequent opportunities to mobilize race within society in a visible way were greatly reduced. For example, in El Salvador, after the 1932 brutal killings of peasants – comprised largely of Indians – elites in

---

[23] Zulawski 2000; Degregori 1998; Brysk and Wise 1997; Elton 1998; Gott 1999.

[24] See Howard 2001. Gaffney (1994) also points out that citizenship and distinctions within society tend not to be very racialized or understood in color terms, as citizens are self-affirmingly "mixed."

[25] Pitt-Rivers 1994: 550; Biesanz and Smith 1951: 9.

that country came to believe that a substantial "Indian question" no longer existed. While some Indians did remain, their visibility remained low, particularly as leftist movements opted against identifying with or championing this identity during the middle decades of the 20th century.[26] Similar patterns are evident in the history of Nicaragua.[27] In other words, despite truly insidious motives and actions toward lower groups, in which class tensions took on ethnic overtones, the enduring political legacy in these countries was more consistent with the Brazilian case, where patterns of discrimination were less visible, and ethnic and racial identities were more fluid.

Cases such as Argentina, Chile, and Uruguay appear at first blush to be distinctive because they tend to be recognized today as truly "white" countries, suggesting either that they were not fragment societies to begin with, or that the pattern of exclusion in these countries was even more extreme than in the South African case. In fact, all of these countries faced analogous race questions, and very recent claims of minority groups have helped to shed light on these histories. Upon further inspection, the political histories of race and definitions of NPC in these countries appear much closer to the Brazilian model than the South African strategy of exclusion, and thus it is reasonable to hypothesize that such approaches to race had similar effects on class relations within these societies. Again, while large populations of blacks and mestizos were killed off in these countries, at least partially through wars, these groups were also assimilated by various waves of European immigration during the late 19th and 20th centuries.[28] In the first decades of the 20th century, many Afro-Argentineans maintained professions requiring Argentinean citizenship, implying a less rigid approach. While people of color may have been discriminated against in practice, no explicit restrictions on access to equal citizenship, or other explicit race-based policies, served this end.[29] By 1910, an Argentinean nationalist myth included the idea of the "Indian Soul" – a rhetorical strategy of *indigenismo* analogous to Brazil's.[30] In the case of Chile, discrimination against the Mapuche became a private affair beginning in the 1920s, and indigenous groups were generally not acknowledged as problematic by the government

---

[26] Ching and Tilley 1998: 156.
[27] Gould 1993.
[28] See Wagley 1994: 15; Pitt-Rivers 1994; Safford 1991; Arocha 1998; Howard 2001; and Gaffney 1994.
[29] Helg 1992: 43–4.
[30] Helg 1992: 46.

or by society more generally.[31] Commenting on a recent report on race relations in Uruguay, the director of that country's National Statistics Institute concluded that "racial discrimination in Uruguay did exist, although it had been hidden until now."[32] In sum, for the cases of Argentina, Chile, and Uruguay, existing scholarship suggests that in the wake of strong race chauvinism, combined with an increasingly less visible other, state leaders did not pursue the type of explicit exclusion or differentiation strategies found in places such as South Africa or the United States.

Several additional features of the Latin American cases suggest their appropriateness for classification along with the Brazilian case. First, lower-income, illiterate whites could expect no particular special privileges when compared with individuals from other racial groups who shared a similar economic status. Moreover, given the particular institutional choices about how to define the NPC, people of color could plausibly rise to positions of political power in these countries and achieve a high socioeconomic status. In such environments, people of color have not had much political room to challenge their economic and social marginalization as stemming from racial prejudice. The hypothesis associated with the political community model is that in the absence of such challenges – real or perceived – whites have not had a common political "glue" to hold together class interests, either from above or below. In turn, the associated prediction is that when controlling for other factors, the national government of these countries will collect less in progressive taxation.

While the statistical analyses do not assess the internal dynamics of causal mechanisms, there is some evidence suggesting that the relationship between race, class, and social policy extends beyond Brazil. For example, in the case of the Dominican Republic, scholars and other observers have pointed out the combination of an anti-Haitian ideology with an image of racial harmony has been used "as an ideological weapon of control and manipulation of the Dominican people – specifically the dark-skinned lower classes – for it diffuses class tensions and moves the political agenda away from the issue of equitable redistribution of wealth in Dominican Society."[33]

Because I realize that my classifications demand a fair bit of interpretation of country histories, I attempted to identify an alternative source of

---

[31] Cantoni 1977: 302, 307.
[32] Ronzoni 1998.
[33] Sagás 2000: 122.

data, which might provide some independent corroboration of my scorings. The Minorities at Risk (MAR) dataset[34] was not designed to answer the question of how countries defined the NPC as explored in this book, but it does provide important clues that help to distinguish among the cases of interest. First, it identifies minority groups at risk for discrimination and bias,[35] and of the fragment societies considered here, every country except Uruguay contains at least one such group. This finding is in line with my assessment that in virtually none of the fragment societies did the nation-building project successfully homogenize the population. Both overt and more subtle forms of chauvinism helped to generate patterns of political, social, and/or economic inequality along ethnic and/or racial lines.

Moreover, the dataset provides some insights into how the NPC was defined in terms of the race question in each country. For each at-risk minority group, the dataset identifies an antagonist group for which one might have anticipated communal conflict during the period 1945–1998, regardless of the extent to which actual violence was observed. By definition, all of the at-risk minority groups are ethnic or racial groups. However, it is interesting to note that while many of the minorities are classified as being in potential conflict with an ethnically or racially defined antagonist group, in many other cases there is no specific group identified or the antagonist group is defined in terms of class or ideology. Given the hypotheses associated with the political community model, I would expect ethnic and racial group labels to be especially salient and obvious in the countries that carried out explicit racial exclusion strategies, and just the opposite in the countries that carried out inclusionary strategies.

Indeed, an analysis of the MAR dataset largely confirms my classification of the definitions of NPC in the fragment society countries. In South Africa, Australia, Namibia, the United States, and Zimbabwe, the antagonist communal group labels are all racial or ethnic – white, European, or Anglo settler – suggesting the appropriateness of the explicit exclusion category for those cases. However, there is no specific antagonist communal group identified either for the indigenous peoples of Canada or for the Maori of New Zealand, suggesting that these cases might be alternatively classified as having had less explicit strategies of

---

[34] Minorities at Risk 1999 dataset, available from the Center for International Development and Conflict Management, University of Maryland.
[35] In some cases, the minority groups are identified in the dataset as advantaged minorities, such as Europeans in Namibia and Zimbabwe.

racial exclusion, which would gibe with some of my reservations expressed above.

Meanwhile, in almost every Latin American country considered here and in the MAR dataset, for each ethnic minority, there was either no antagonist communal group label, or the label was not explicitly ethnic or racial. For example, in Argentina and Brazil, indigenous groups are said to be pitted against Ranchers/Miners; in Colombia, blacks and indigenous groups are potentially in conflict with FARC rebels; in Paraguay, the indigenous groups are juxtaposed with landowners; and in Peru, these groups are potentially in conflict with Shining Path rebels. In such cases, the dominant group labels provide little basis for broad class coherence, let alone cross-class coalitions, as is possible with ethnic and racial labels. Where no antagonist group could be identified, I interpret this as signifying the absence of a clear in-group identified in terms of its reference to the ethnic or racial minority, which I would expect to find in countries that had adopted inclusionary strategies. Of the Latin American cases, only in Panama[36] did the MAR dataset identify ethnic antagonist groups in conjunction with at-risk minority group – blacks were said to be in conflict with mestizos, and indigenous groups in conflict with mestizo farmers. On the one hand, this may suggest that in the face of an inclusionary strategy, racial or ethnic labels sometimes become politically salient, and that this case is simply not well predicted by the political community model. Alternatively, it may suggest that Panama should be classified as a case of an exclusionary strategy – an exception to the Latin American pattern.

Region. The second dimension of variation in the definition of NPC concerns the ways in which regionally based claims to political autonomy have been addressed through different national institutions. Specifically, have countries adopted federal or unitary models for the organization of government? Federal systems are characterized by a significant devolution of central government power and authority to subnational units.[37] In the history of the development of national states, the question of whether or not to adopt a federal constitution has often ignited a high-stakes political game. Spatial proximity can generate political solidarity through ease of communication, propensity to share public "goods" and "bads," similar and/or

---

[36] Also in Guyana, but that case was excluded from my analysis because of its small population size and lack of current data.

[37] Derbyshire and Derbyshire 1999: 17.

interdependent economic activities, and likelihood of shared historical experiences among the individuals and groups within a particular region. Regionally based claims for political voice and/or autonomy within a national state can be particularly powerful because these multiple and overlapping commonalities can cement together collective actors, who may be unwilling to evaluate policies in terms of a larger, national good.

Except for in very small polities, physical space almost always presents a political problem for the consolidation of national state authority. When the goal of political elites is to maintain the integrity of the national state, there are basically two key options for addressing the demands of regionally based political cleavages: One option is to establish a federal constitution and/or system of government. Federalism "represents the principle of the separation of power among levels of government based on separate agencies with mutual vetoes."[38] Such a solution effectively grants the wishes of subnational elites to enjoy greater autonomy and power, while maintaining consensus around the need for a larger national government and national market. Federalism can constrain decision making and sow the seeds of regionally based political conflict by providing institutional backing to the myth of a regional identity. Alternatively, a second option is to create a unitary political structure. From the perspective of national elites, such a strategy can help to promote a larger sense of collective solidarity and unity while closing out opportunities for regionally based political entrepreneurs to advance narrowly defined political interests. The risk is that in closing off demands for regional autonomy and/or voice in national decision making, the political reactions can prove devastating in the form of policy gridlock, rebellion, secession, and/or civil war.

Distinguishing among cases of unitary and federal systems is not as straightforward as it might initially appear because, in practice, there are many shades of gray in the manner in which government power is devolved. Many unitary countries maintain regional units, and even provide some limited institutional voice for these units. In the case of South Africa, for example, four provinces were maintained as administrative units and a second chamber was established for provincial administration, despite the fact that the state was clearly established and functioned as a unitary state between 1910 and 1994. My argument is that in most, but not all, cases, the constitutional decision about the sovereignty of subnational units strongly influences the degree to which space or region becomes a salient

[38] Crepaz 1998: 69.

dimension of political life.[39] Alternatively, a federal system is one in which "separate regional and political units (often referred to as states or provinces) are combined for limited, specified purposes under an overarching administration, but in such a way that the government of each separate regional unit maintains its integrity and substantial autonomy."[40]

As shown in Table 6.1, of the seventy-one countries considered, thirteen have been classified as federal, and the remainder as unitary states. Several federal systems, such as Nigeria and Russia, have been omitted for reasons described above. Of those listed, only a few present some difficulties for classification. Only Malaysia and Austria stand out as countries classified as federal, for which an argument could be made that they should be classified as unitary. Similar to the case of Mexico, Malaysia is a country in which the federal system in practice is weak because of the strength of the national party leadership; and in the case of Austria, the policy-making powers of the subnational governments are relatively weak.[41] Of the larger number of cases of unitary states, Bolivia, Denmark, Dominican Republic, France, Israel, Italy, Netherlands, Philippines, Portugal, Spain, the United Kingdom, and Zambia all have important decentralized features.[42] Nonetheless, these countries are classified here as unitary states because the constitutions and foundational policies of these countries do not explicitly describe the respective countries as federal, nor do they protect the sovereignty of subnational governments, implying that they are ultimately unitary states. As of 1993, Belgium amended its constitution to become a true federal system, but because the outcomes under investigation are for the period 1990–4, the prior institutional incarnation as a unitary state is used for classification purposes. In any case, given the institutional nature of the political community model, we would not expect recent constitutional changes to have an *immediate* impact on the quality of the tax state.

The causal link between the institution of federalism and the development of the tax state is primarily through its divisive impact on national politics. I am *not* making the point that revenues tend to be more decentralized and as a result, the overall level of financial resources of the

---

[39] A notable exception would be Mexico, where, despite an explicitly federal constitution, decision making has been highly centralized for most of the 20th century.
[40] Hawkesworth and Kogan 1992: 336.
[41] Derbyshire and Derbyshire 1999: 18–19.
[42] Derbyshire and Derbyshire 1999: 23. In his essay on federalism, Stepan (1999) classifies Spain as a federal country.

central government are less than in unitary states. Indeed, in many cases that is the very objective of federalism, and the fact that this is true in practice is not particularly startling. Rather, the political community model makes the point that the *political* ramifications of the institution of federalism result in much more regressive tax structures throughout society. The fragmentation of economic classes that becomes reinforced when the NPC is defined as a federation makes the direct taxation of upper groups much more difficult because upper groups in wealthier regions tend to perceive the imposition of taxation as an attempt to divert resources to "them" rather than to be used for one of "us." (Of course, to the extent that there is perfect economic equality across regions, this would be less of a problem, but this is virtually never the case in either federal or unitary systems.) Given this argument, one might expect higher levels of tax compliance and taxation at the subnational level, ultimately washing out the difference in total income tax collections when compared with all revenues collected in unitary states. However, the problem of subnational government income tax collection is that provinces or states tend to compete for a tax base by promising lower tax rates and/or special incentives, creating the perverse effect of producing lower and lower income tax rates over time. Because the barriers to cross-province or cross-state residency have been negligible in virtually all federal countries, the threats of individuals and firms to leave in search of cheaper tax pastures may be credible. Subnational government income tax rates and collections are hard to maintain at high levels unless uniformity is maintained by the central government – a strategy that would fly in the face of a truly federal system.

Statistical Analysis

In order to estimate the influence of definitions of NPC on the development of the tax state, I use Ordinary Least Squares (OLS) regression analysis with several measures of tax collections, varying in terms of types of taxes collected and the level of government responsible for collections, as reported in Table 6.2.[43] The statistical analysis is conducted from a static cross-sectional perspective, analyzing the 1990–4 period, using data on

---

[43] Taxation data from World Bank 1998; IMF 1998, 1999, and 2000; British colony, Catholic, GDP/capita, and regime variables from Cheibub 1998 (replication dataset provided by the author); Population from World Bank 1998; Union density from ILO 1997.

Table 6.2 OLS estimates of the determinants of tax collections by level of government, 1990–1994

Independent Variables	(A) Income and property tax/GDP (National only)	(B) Income and property tax/GDP (Subnational only)	(C) Income and property tax/GDP (All levels)	(D) Consumption, social security, and other tax/ GDP (National only)	(E) Consumption, social security, and other tax/ GDP (Subnational only)	(F) Consumption, social security, and other tax/ GDP (All levels)
(Constant)	4.81**	−.890	3.92**	6.04**	−.01	6.14**
	(.65)	(.62)	(.76)	(1.04)	(.20)	(1.16)
GDP/capita (thousands $PPP)	.39**	.45**	.83**	1.11**	.03	1.14**
	(.08)	(.08)	(.09)	(.13)	(.02)	(.14)
Race inclusionary fragment societies	−2.89**	−.21	−3.10*	1.39	.64*	2.63
	(1.03)	(.97)	(1.19)	(1.61)	(.32)	(1.84)
Race exclusionary fragment societies	6.50**	−2.21	4.29**	−6.72**	.35	−6.57**
	(1.38)	(1.31)	(1.61)	(2.16)	(.40)	(2.32)
Federal countries	−3.54**	−.00	−3.54**	−4.29*	2.94**	−2.36
	(1.17)	(1.11)	(1.36)	(1.83)	(.35)	(2.06)
Adj. R-squared	.51	.34	.64	.53	.61	.51
SEE	3.29	3.11	3.82	5.13	.93	5.46
N	71	71	71	70	65	65
F (Sig.)	19.51**	10.03**	31.87**	20.07**	26.20*	17.92**

Note: unstandardized coefficients; standard errors in parentheses.
* $p \leq .05$; ** $p \leq .01$; two-tailed tests

institutional legacies as described above as explanatory variables.[44] Because the theoretical argument under examination emphasizes the *stickiness* of institutions and the enduring impact of critical junctures, the institutional explanatory variables are not time-varying, and as such, the model does not attempt to account for over-time variation within countries. Nonetheless, the availability of time-varying taxation data (1975–94) and some other economic and political data provided opportunities for two analytic moves that helped to rule out the possibility that my findings are spuriously relevant only for a single moment in time: First, in conducting the cross-sectional regression analysis, five years of data were averaged for each country, providing a more accurate picture of overall state capacities by smoothing out the influence of "odd" years and random events on the analysis. Second, I repeated the cross-sectional analysis for different periods between 1975 and 1994, and concluded that the findings were not unique to the 1990–4 period – the most recent period for which sufficient taxation data are available across a large group of countries. This suggests that even in the wake of various types of external shocks in the international political economy, the relationships found between variables during the 1990–4 period have persisted for several decades.

The primary dependent variable of interest is the state's ability to collect income and property taxes, because of the properties that these taxes are the least requited (that is, they are paid with the least expectation of being repaid with something specific in return), paid in the most direct manner from citizen to state, and are the most progressive. Income and property taxes as share of GDP are the dependent variable in models A, B, and C. It is useful to compare the results of these analyses to estimates of the determinants of all other types of domestic taxes, which are reported in models D, E, and F.

---

[44] Although scholars are increasingly using pooled timed series cross-sectional (TSCS) models to analyze taxation and other budgetary data – see, for example, Cheibub 1998 and Garrett 1998 – this is not the correct model for evaluating the theoretical claims of this book. The TSCS model must control for "fixed" unit-effects through the construction of country and/or regional dummy variables. That technique is useful for studies in which a central goal is to identify the factors that influence *within-country* change, over time, and in which a central assumption is that the same factors influence both longitudinal and cross-sectional variation, and in a similar manner. By contrast, the central question of this book concerns unpacking what is behind the "fixed" country effects that produce varied trajectories of over-time development. Country dummy variables would filter out from the analyses the very variation that needs to be explained here.

Although this book has largely been concerned with the development of national states, and thus with the tax collections of the national state, it would be problematic to ignore the tax collections of middle and lower tiers of government. Whether through cooperative decentralization or through competition within and across spheres of government, taxes collected at lower levels of government certainly influence what the center collects and vice versa. In the cases of Brazil and South Africa, it was possible to speak of income tax collections only at the national level because in those two countries, through constitutional mandates, only the national government has been responsible for that tax base – a fact that is not true in all countries. There are important instances of both federal (the United States) and unitary (Sweden) states with significant subnational income tax collections. Without specific information about the competitive or cooperative nature of the distribution of tax revenues across spheres of government, it is necessary to estimate models of the determinants of taxation using various units of analysis. I consider national government collections only (models A and D), subnational government collections only (models B and E), and all levels of government combined (models C and F).[45]

We can estimate various models of tax collection as a function of level of development (measured as GDP per capita in 1990 international dollars),[46]

---

[45] I am grateful to an anonymous reviewer at Cambridge University Press and to Margaret Levi for encouraging me to include subnational taxation data in my analysis after the original manuscript was completed.

[46] Levels of economic development or modernization can be measured in a variety of ways, but the best measure is GDP per capita (in purchasing power parity units). That variable is highly correlated with several other modernization variables, including urbanization rates, agriculture as share of value added, and industry as share of value added. All of these variables are also correlated with various measure of tax collections. In all cases, because GDP is used as a standardizing variable with the various taxation indicators, and is also a measure of level of economic development, some additional explication is necessary as one could mistakenly assume that the same variable was appearing on both sides of the regression equation. The specification of a model employing ratio variables is a practice with extensive precedent, but is worthy of some explication as its usage raises the specter of finding spurious relationships. The "ratio-variable" problem arises when two ratio variables are constructed out of three, independent random variables (A, B, and C) in the following manner. If a sample of observations is drawn for all three variables and two ratio variables are constructed in the following manner:

$$D_i = A_i/B_i \quad E_i = B_i/C_i$$

the expectation of the sample covariance of D_i and E_i will not equal zero. In the analysis presented in this chapter, the dependent variable is measured as a ratio-variable with GDP in the denominator while a central independent variable is GDP divided by population.

dummy variables for federalism, and the two dummy variables which code for different approaches to the racial dimension of National Political Community. The results of the statistical analyses with respect to the political community model are highly robust, and suggest the strong relationship between definitions of NPC and the structures and levels of government tax collections.

As reported in model A, countries with legacies of explicit racial exclusion similar to South Africa's have, on average, collected much more in progressive taxation, collecting 6.50 percent of GDP more in income tax, and 6.72 percent of GDP less in other types of taxes at the national level than other countries. Also, as predicted, fragment societies that did not carry out such projects, adopting inclusionary approaches, collected 2.89 percent of GDP less in income taxes at the national level than in other countries. The differences remain important even when taxes at all levels of government are included, as reported in models C and E: In the explicitly exclusionary countries, on average, almost 4 percent of GDP in income taxes was collected above what was typically collected in other countries. Meanwhile, in the other fragment societies, not only were income tax revenues lower overall, by more than 3 GDP percentage points, but other types of tax revenues, which tend to be more requited and regressive, were slightly higher in subnational government accounts. In short, fragment societies with legacies of explicit racial exclusion today have more progressive tax structures, while other fragment societies now have more regressive tax systems, with higher levels of fiscal illusion.

There are clearly inferential problems associated with classifying all of the Latin American countries (or almost all, when reclassifying a few difficult cases) as cases of the inclusionary race strategy, particularly because no cases of this type are identified outside of Latin America. Specifically,

The question is, what is the impact of having this term on both sides of the equation, and should the equation be re-written to avoid this problem altogether? As Kritzer (1990) points out, the problem is actually mathematically nontractable, and must be decided on theoretical groups. Firebaugh and Gibbs argue that the choice of whether to use component or ratio variables should be based upon which term is less likely to violate the assumption of homoskedastic error terms. In both cases, the ratio-variable is more appropriate than a model estimating the component of income taxes alone (in local or international dollar units). Theoretically, the constructed ratio-variables should not necessarily covary. As a further test, Berry (1986) points out that the ratio variable problem should be evaluated with simulations. Simulations suggest that the estimate of the impact of GDP per capita on the dependent variable will be only slightly biased downward. For further discussion, see also Firebaugh and Gibbs 1985.

we must be suspicious that perhaps there is something else that is common to the Latin American cases that could be influencing tax outcomes in a similar manner. If we were to expand the domain of relevant cases for addressing the race question beyond the fragment societies, we would likely find other examples, but this would imply a great loss in analytic power: The cases would no longer share the experience of European settlement, a common ideology of white supremacy, and an ordered racial hierarchy in which lighter implied better. In the face of the empirical limitations, I would argue that it is quite reasonable to hypothesize that this common mode of defining the NPC has profoundly affected the development of state, society, and economy throughout Latin America. The prior question of why this particular approach to addressing the question of race was taken throughout Latin America is an important one, but it is not the question considered here. Rather, the concern is with the impact of political institutions on patterns of state-building. Countries that adopted inclusionary strategies were predicted to collect less taxes from upper groups, and this account is consistent with the statistical results.

Although I only present the statistical results using the classifications that I think are most appropriate (as shown in Table 6.1), the results remain robust even when some of the more difficult cases such as Canada, New Zealand, Panama, and Uruguay are recoded. The reclassification of Panama as an exclusionary case had the effect of lowering the size of the parameter estimate for the race exclusionary dummy variable, but it is worth noting that of all of the Latin American cases considered here, Panama was ranked second in terms of income and property tax collections. This suggests that future research might fruitfully consider the impact of more subtle variations in definitions of NPC within and across regions.

As for federal countries, given the propensity for decentralization of government activity, it is not very surprising that at the national level, both income and other types of taxes are significantly lower than in unitary states. What is more surprising, however, is that at the subnational level, a substantive and statistically significant compensation for this revenue loss is evident only for the more regressive and indirect group of taxes. As a result, overall collections of income and property taxes, even when calculated as an aggregate across levels of government, are on average 3.54 percentage points of GDP lower than in unitary states. In the case of other types of taxes collected for all levels of government combined, the coefficient is also negative, but of lesser magnitude and with a very high standard error. In federal countries, poor people in poor regions are doubly worse off than their counterparts in unitary countries when it comes to the tax system: Not only is the overall tax system likely to be more regressive, but less revenue flows to the central government, providing fewer resources for cross-regional redistribution.

One could raise the question, why not control for ethnic heterogeneity, particularly in a study that makes identity politics so central? A central tenet of this book has been that notions of ethnic and racial heterogeneity are political constructions. Any given proxy for the racial or ethnic composition of a population would merely be the product of the types of political processes of inclusion and exclusion discussed herein. How would one code racial heterogeneity in South Africa, for example? At the beginning of the 20th century, an English-speaking citizen in that country would have described Afrikaners, Jews, Natives, and Coloureds as all belonging to different races. Today, alternative notions of race would be used for reasons wholly unrelated to actual changes in demographic patterns. It is difficult to imagine a very useful, objective measure of social heterogeneity. By comparing fragment societies, I have attempted to control for patterns of perceived difference between Europeans and non-Europeans at an initial point of contact, taking for granted that the exact demographics for each group would be very influential. Indeed, in South Africa, whites were a small minority, while in the United States, whites were in the majority, and yet in both countries, the state developed and reinforced patterns of exclusion. Similarly, in terms of federalism, the cases of South Africa and Brazil revealed that the choice to adopt a federal system was contingent, not predetermined by existing ethno-regional conflicts. In other cases, we may be able to find evidence of pre-existing conflict that tended to lead to the adoption of federal systems. Alternatively, as was the case in South Africa, other countries may have adopted a unitary model because they wanted to address such conflicts. I will have to leave it for future research to determine if the choice to adopt a federal system is endogenous to some other process, but for now, I assume it to be contingent.

Finally, as predicted, level of economic development was an important determinant of tax collections virtually across the board, with wealthier countries collecting more income and other types of taxes. Only in the case of subnational consumption taxes was no relationship evident. For overall government revenues, for every (PPP) $1,000 of GDP per capita, one could expect that income taxes would increase more than proportionately by 0.83 percent of GDP and other types of taxes by 1.14 percent of GDP. Skeletal tax states with very little authority are more likely to be found in poorer and less modern economies, while cooperative tax states, in which states and societies enjoy close and regularized relations, are more likely to be found in wealthier and more advanced ones. Wealthier economies have more resources to tax, the tax bases tend to be more visible because of the higher degree of monetization of the economy,[47] and modernization itself presents greater needs for specialization and the provision of public goods, requiring higher levels of taxation.[48]

Alternative Explanations

Beyond providing an opportunity to estimate the impact of the variables associated with the political community model, cross-national statistical analysis provides an avenue for considering the influence of several other rival explanatory factors. Using model C as a baseline, I consider the extent to which these factors exhibit important relationships with general government collections of income and property taxes (results are reported in Table 6.3, with all variables included in the regression in model L). Not only does such analysis help to widen our understanding of state development more generally, but it helps to answer questions about the puzzle of variation between Brazil and South Africa which could not be addressed through the two-country comparison alone.

Labor Union Density

The political community model relates definitions of NPC to taxation outcomes via an argument about class relations that unfold during the processes of modernization and industrialization. The model hypothesizes that income tax collections, particularly as collected by the central state, are likely to be higher when economic classes are more cohesive and when there are political idioms that link upper to lower groups, and that the reverse is likely to be true when certain political idioms and/or identities serve to fragment classes. A potential rival explanation might be that this is simply a story about class organization, independent of the influence of identity politics. To test this argument, I consider the influence of a measure of union density (percent of the work force that is a member of a labor union).[49] Of course,

---

[47] Cheibub 1998.
[48] This is a corollary of Wagner's Law (1883), which posits that government expenditure will increase exponentially with rises in national income.
[49] This measure is used by Rothstein 1995.

Table 6.3 *OLS estimates of the determinants of income and property tax collections for all levels of government, 1990–1994*

Independent Variables	(G)	(H)	(I)	(J)	(K)	(L)
(Constant)	2.35*	3.34**	12.57*	4.21**	3.81**	−.57
	(.90)	(.98)	(6.12)	(1.31)	(.82)	(6.30)
GDP/capita	.44**	.87**	.83**	.81**	.87**	.46**
(thousands $PPP)	(.10)	(.10)	(.09)	(.12)	(.09)	(.11)
Race inclusionary	−3.56**	−2.59*	−3.26**	−3.26*	−1.85	−2.68*
fragment societies	(1.03)	(1.32)	(1.19)	(1.32)	(1.49)	(1.33)
Race exclusionary	4.75**	3.71*	4.11*	4.32**	4.46**	6.20**
fragment societies	(1.28)	(1.73)	(1.60)	(1.62)	(1.69)	(1.51)
Federal countries	−2.42*	−3.86**	−2.62$^{\#}$	−3.57*	−3.54**	−2.52*
	(1.08)	(1.41)	(1.50)	(1.38)	(1.31)	(1.16)
Union density	.21**					.22**
	(.03)					(.03)
British colonies		1.09				−1.11
		(1.19)				(1.26)
Log population			−.54			.16
			(.38)			(.34)
Dictatorships				−.35		.70
				(1.36)		(1.08)
Percent Catholic					−.01	−.01
					(.02)	(.01)
Adj. *R*-squared	.80	.64	.64	.63	.68	.85
SEE	3.01	3.82	3.79	3.84	3.65	2.64
N	56	71	71	71	68	54
F (Sig.)	44.36**	25.60**	26.30**	25.16**	28.81**	33.03**

Note: unstandardized coefficients; standard errors in parentheses.
$^{\#}p \leq .10$; $^{*}p \leq .05$; $^{**}p \leq .01$; two-tailed tests

this is an imperfect measure of class solidarity because unions themselves may be at odds with one another, but it is a reasonable proxy of the political organization of lower groups.

As shown in model G, this variable proves to be substantively and statistically significant, and helps to produce a good-fitting model.[50] As compared with model C, the direction and relative magnitude of the other explanatory

---

[50] Because of a lack of cross-national data on union density, the number of cases drops from seventy-one to fifty-six. However, when those fifty-six cases are analyzed using the specification in model C, the parameter estimates are largely unchanged, suggesting that these results are comparable.

variables remains similar, but we also learn that for every 10 percent of the work force that is unionized, we can expect an additional 2.1 percent of GDP to be collected in income tax revenue. Using the same model specification for other types of taxes (not reported), I found that union density had no effect. Although these results are certainly relevant for understanding broader patterns of cross-national variation, they shed little additional light on the Brazil–South Africa comparison, as union density is actually higher in Brazil (32 percent) than in South Africa (22 percent). More generally, the variables associated with the political community model remain significant even when we control for union density.

Colonial Legacy

As discussed in the earlier chapters, the claim that differences in Brazilian and South African tax structures were the product of some holdover from the colonial past was rendered implausible by an historical analysis of colonial taxation in the two countries. Nonetheless, in the broader cross-national analysis, it is important to note that of the fragment societies historically characterized by an explicitly *exclusionary* approach to race in the definition of the NPC, almost all were former British colonies, and of the fragments that pursued an inclusionary strategy, not one was previously a British colony. Such a finding clearly merits some closer scrutiny.

In order to assess the possible influence of some more general "British" or "Anglo" colonial legacy on levels and structures of tax collection, I inserted a dummy variable for British colonial legacy into the regression equation (H), and found that this factor has no statistically significant independent effect on income tax collections. As it turns out, many former British colonies such as Ghana, India, and Sierra Leone are not very effective at collecting progressive income taxes, which explains why the statistical results lead to a rejection of this hypothesis. Nonetheless, it remains highly plausible that some aspect of British colonialism likely predisposed certain settler societies toward a particular model of defining the NPC as compared with Spanish, Portuguese, and other colonial legacies. Such an observation should provide a launching pad for future research.

Population Size

Reflecting upon the comparison between Brazil and South Africa, one potentially important difference is that the population size of the former is three times as large as the latter, and while all of the preceding analyses take into account economic data on a per capita basis, there are at least two plausible explanations that could relate this difference in total population size to variations in income tax collections. The first is an administrative one: It might stand to reason that the administrative costs of collecting in countries where there are more people are higher. On the other hand, arguments about scale economies could suggest exactly the opposite approach. Second, the types of political cohesion hypothesized as necessary to produce a politics of collective sacrifice may be more difficult to achieve when there are more people in the country.

The statistical analysis does not reveal population size to be a clear determinant of tax collections. As shown in model I, when the log of population size is inserted in the regression equation, there is no statistically significant effect. However, the insertion of this variable has the effect of decreasing the absolute value of the parameter estimate for the federalism dummy variable, and increasing the standard error such that the estimate is closer to the threshold of statistical significance. It is important to note that there is a moderately strong correlation ($R = .43$) between population size and federalism – nine of the twelve federal countries were in the top quartile for population, and none of the federal countries were from the bottom quartile – and this constrains our ability to estimate the independent effect of these factors simultaneously. Although population size does influence the likelihood that a country will adopt a federal system (of course the reverse causal order is not theoretically plausible), it seems to be the institution of federalism, not population size, which ultimately influences taxation outcomes.

Regime Type

Analysts have identified many possible causal relationships between regime type and the state's ability to tax upper groups. On the one hand, democracies may provide greater opportunities to legitimate the state and openings for lower groups to apply pressure on government leaders to extract higher levels of taxation from upper groups. On the other hand, more repressive regimes may have greater opportunities to serve the interests of upper groups, legitimating the central state in the eyes of this group, while possessing greater coercive pressures to extract taxes. As a result, dictatorships could also be expected to collect more income taxes.[51] In order to

---

[51] See Cheibub 1998. See also Shapiro 1999.

explore this relationship empirically, as reported in model J, I investigated the influence of a dummy variable coded as 0 for democracies and 1 for dictatorships in the year 1990,[52] and found no important statistical relationship with the measure of taxation.[53] Because the statistical analysis has been strictly cross-sectional, it is not possible to answer the question of the likely impact of regime *change* on any given country. Yet, it is possible to conclude from this analysis that a democratic government alone is not a powerful determinant of a strong and authoritative state or of a progressive tax system.

Religion as Culture, Values

As discussed in Chapter 1, there are severe theoretical and empirical impediments to evaluating if and how cultural factors serve as independent causal influences on social and political phenomena. It is simply too easy to conflate the outcome under investigation with the cultural variable, making the argument tautological. Perceptions of trust within societies as reported in surveys are just as likely to be the product of perceptions of the functioning of the national tax system as they are to be truly independent attitudinal dispositions that affect the functioning of government institutions. The only viable way in which we could assess the influence of culture on taxation would be if we could measure or classify countries according to a pre-established conceptual category that is theoretically distant from taxation. Clearly, religion, and the values and orientations that go along with religion, is an example of such a category.

Indeed, one "folk theorem" of Brazilian state development relates the religious orientation of its population to "low quality" citizenship.[54] This might be described as a corollary to Max Weber's argument about the positive impact of Protestantism, which he presented in the

---

[52] Using a dichotomous variable to measure regime type advantages and disadvantages. For example, both Brazil and South Africa are coded as dictatorships during periods when elections were held. One could argue that such regimes were *partial* democracies, or that, at times, they were *oligarchic* democracies. The challenge of constructing valid measures for a large sample of cases presents serious trade-offs between reliability and validity. For further discussion of dichotomous and other conceptualizations of democracy, see Collier and Adcock 1999.

[53] Although there is a moderately strong correlation between regime type and GDP per capita ($R = .59$), even when the latter variable was removed from the regression equation, regime type did not emerge as a statistically significant predictor of tax collections.

[54] Author interviews with various Brazilian scholars, tax collectors, and taxpayers.

Protestant Ethic.[55] Yet, as shown in models K and L, no systematic relationship exists between the percent of the population that is Catholic and income tax collections.

A strong correlation between Catholic membership and the classification of Race inclusionary fragment societies, (Pearson's $R = .59$) makes it somewhat difficult to assess the independent effect of each within a multivariate regression analysis. When the Catholic membership variable is inserted into various models, the Race inclusionary variable is not as consistently robust, as demonstrated in model K. This is not surprising because all of the race inclusionary countries are in Latin America, where rates of Catholic membership are extremely high. However, on balance, the Catholic membership variable does far less well as a predictor of various taxation outcomes when subject to various robustness checks, suggesting that the Race inclusionary variable has a stronger and more consistent relationship with the taxation outcomes under investigation here. It is certainly possible that the Catholic Church may have influenced the particular adoption of more inclusionary approaches to the race question in Latin America. The degree to which there is evidence to support this claim is a question that I leave for future research. Nonetheless, the historical record in Brazil revealed the various options for defining NPC were available during key critical junctures, highlighting the autonomous role of political decisions and that the strategy of racial inclusion was not already determined by the cultural/doctrinaire influences of the Catholic Church. Limited evidence outside of Latin America provides the strongest case against the autonomous influence of the Church on taxation outcomes. In other words, although the two-country comparative analysis could not rule out national religious orientation as a possible determinant of taxation, the cross-national statistical analysis provides the evidence needed to reject this hypothesis.

Conclusion

The findings presented in this chapter complement the comparative historical analysis presented in the earlier chapters: First, the chapter showed that the political community model is generalizable beyond Brazil and South Africa. Substantial statistical evidence supported the claim that in

---

[55] Weber 1991. Absent good data on Protestant membership, I explored this hypothesis from the perspective of Catholic membership only.

addition to modernization factors, the construction of National Political Community likely influenced the development of the tax state in other countries. In particular, this chapter has demonstrated that political responses to the problems of race and regionalism have a measurable influence on that outcome. Undoubtedly, the historically specific ways in which these sets of political identities emerged within other country cases were distinctive along numerous dimensions from the cases of Brazil and South Africa, but the robust statistical findings suggest that modal differences in the definition of NPC ultimately served as a powerful predictor of tax state characteristics across a wider group of countries. In particular, the countries most like South Africa all have enjoyed tax collections far above average for countries at their respective levels of economic development.

Second, the chapter considered several other factors that might account for the varied development of the Brazilian and South African tax states. While there are limits to what can actually be measured and systematically evaluated in cross-national research, particularly beyond a small set of highly comparable cases, none of the plausible hypotheses had any strong statistical support. Differences between Brazil and South Africa in terms of religious value orientations, population size, and colonial legacy were not associated with cross-national differences in taxation in the larger sample, suggesting that it is unlikely that these factors can explain differences across this pair of countries. Although union membership is higher in Brazil than in South Africa, the statistical analysis revealed that union membership tends to predict higher tax collections in a *positive* manner, implying that this variable could not explain differences between the two countries.

Methodologically, this chapter has revealed the benefits to be gained by combining statistical analysis with structured comparisons. Additional data provided opportunities for more hypothesis testing, providing higher levels of confidence in the findings overall. Conceptualization and measurement benefited from the iterative process of classifying cases in terms of their similarities and differences with respect to the ideal type cases from the structured comparison. Finally, the parsimonious statement of the political community model in regression form invites a look back at the more detailed historical analysis of South Africa and Brazil, and more in-depth investigation of additional country cases in future research.

7

Conclusion

As George Tsebelis points out, the value of social scientific explanations may best be measured by the degree to which they force us to re-evaluate our prior beliefs.[1] On this score, scholars of South African politics could reasonably argue that it is hardly surprising to discover that race was central to understanding political dynamics in that country. Similarly, most scholars of Brazilian politics would immediately recognize federalism as a defining feature of political life in Brazil. So what aspects of the analysis and evidence presented in the previous chapters stand in the face of conventional wisdom about politics in these two countries, let alone at a more general, theoretical level? What new understanding have we gained with respect to the process of state-building, and particularly the development of national tax systems, by exploring the implications of the political community model? In fact, many of the conclusions drawn from the analysis and evidence presented above *do* imply the need to re-evaluate prior beliefs about a number of relationships. With these insights, we can explore the implications – albeit in a highly speculative manner – for the future of these two countries, and a range of additional questions and concerns relevant to other political and policy problems and in other world areas.

More than anything, the explanation of tax state building presented in this book revealed the surprising causal relationship between the politics of race and regionalism on the one hand, and the development of tax policy and tax administration on the other. First, we found that policies of deliberate racial *exclusion* were responsible for a legacy of a much more effective and progressive tax system, such that black South Africans today benefit from that legacy to a much greater extent than their counterparts in Brazil.

[1] Tsebelis 1997.

In other words, race mattered, but not with the distributive consequences we ordinarily would have expected – that those previously excluded would ultimately benefit *least* from any set of social and/or economic policy legacies. As it turned out, insiders were more likely to cooperate with the state, and to make sacrifices in material terms, when outsiders were excluded in an explicit manner. The outsiders inadvertently captured some of the benefits of such sacrifices.

And in Brazil, where most observers have played down the role of the politics of race in shaping outcomes, it turned out that race *did* matter, just in a very different way than in South Africa. Brazil has long been characterized by a high degree of racial heterogeneity and pervasive race chauvinism. When these factors were combined with deliberate attempts to "whiten" the population and with legal prohibitions against racial discrimination in the 20th century, the product was social and political fragmentation. Indeed, the upside of state prohibitions on explicit race chauvinism has been that life chances in Brazil today are less strongly correlated with race than in South Africa, there is much greater mixing and intermingling of race groups, and there has been much less race-based conflict. It is safe to say that during the 20th century, even in the wake of pervasive discrimination, Afro-Brazilians did not suffer the types of injustices and humiliation leveled against black South Africans. But the news for black Brazilians has not been all positive. Absent the class coherence produced by exclusionary politics, progressive tax collection has been extremely difficult to achieve, and as a result, race-based (and other) inequalities of income have been reinforced by the fiscus. More hidden forms of racial discrimination have weighed heavily against people of color, and the poor more generally, and the myth of racial equality is easily dispelled when measured in socioeconomic terms.

In terms of the politics of regionalism, Brazilian federalism revealed the political shortcomings of a constitutional form that economists and policy makers often hail as optimal for producing "efficient" outcomes, and that can afford some protections for minority groups. Federalism reinforced a sense of regional conflict in the Brazilian political arena, and in so doing, reified deep political fault lines, across which cooperation and collective sacrifice have proved impossible at the national level. As a result, the tax system has not been an effective instrument for addressing regional inequalities in income and wealth, despite the efforts of national political leaders. By contrast, in South Africa, despite expectations for a federal constitution, a unitary political system was installed early in the 20th century. Narrowly based, ethno-regional demands for special tax treatment were highly constrained in this unitary system, effectively saving the tax state from multiple loop-holes and leakages. The decision to opt *against* a federal constitution was an important determinant of the relative success of the South African tax state building project. Of course, there are other potentially compelling reasons for adopting a federal constitution, but this book has suggested some of the problems from a fiscal and distributive perspective.

The impact of class politics also emerged in novel ways. Following the insights of Karl Marx, most scholars and other analysts have tended to assume that the better organized and more coherent a set of class actors, the better able it will be to act in its own "best" interests, pushing the tax burden onto members of the other economic class. In fact, the implications of the political community model are just the opposite. Strong class cohesion of upper groups actually helped to *overcome* the free rider problem of taxation, and the state executive was better able to strike more extractive fiscal bargains with upper groups because of organizational and idiomatic cohesion. It is true that when lower groups were well organized – in the case of white South African labor in the early part of the 20th century, and in the case of largely black South African labor at the end of the century – they were able to press for more favorable tax treatment than could fragmented labor in Brazil during either of these periods. Yet in both country cases, lower groups could not wrest resources from the rich through brute force alone. Rather, through compelling normative appeals, they have managed to pressure upper-income actors to perceive a sense of *obligation* to pay.

Contrary to conventional wisdom, Brazil and South Africa did not emerge as simply "strange" or "unique" cases.[2] Although they may be extreme variants of differing approaches to the questions of dealing with race and region in the definition of National Political Community, the relationship between definitions of NPC and patterns of taxation has more general application. In broad comparative perspective, these differences proved to be more important than several other "standard" political variables such as regime type, culture, and union density. Where there is racial heterogeneity, patterns of incorporation of various race group appears to have mattered for politics and policy outcomes. Hartz's category of the European fragment society proved analytically useful. And everywhere, variation in

---

[2] Certainly, Brazil has been used in many important comparative analyses, but generally for comparisons within Latin America or across the newly industrialized countries. South Africa has been much less prominent in the comparative politics and comparative political economy literatures.

the solutions to the potential problem of regional conflict – specifically, the question of whether or not to adopt a federal political system – has proved highly influential over the development of the tax state. This is not to deny that historically specific contexts of politics and of state-building clearly vary from country to country. Nonetheless, the two-country comparison helped to generate important hypotheses, which continue to appear plausible in light of cross-national analyses of levels and structures of taxation.

Finally, by considering a host of rival and partial explanations, we found that some conventional wisdom is either less useful than we might have thought, or just plain wrong. Economic and international factors surely influence the politics of taxation, but these factors are far from determinative. There is no natural condition for the taxation system of a developing or middle-income country, for example. When we looked at deep-seated cultural factors, such as religious orientations and value systems, these factors proved to be uncorrelated with tax outcomes. Colonial legacies of pre-20th century state-building provided little predictive power for understanding the future, suggesting that such legacies do not constrain future successes or failures for governments in the taxation arena. While it would be hard to dispute the common wisdom that a better-trained and better-educated bureaucracy is likely to produce more efficient collections, *ceteris paribus*, we found that despite Brazil's relatively better-trained tax administration, tax collection has been easier and more efficient in South Africa.

To what extent can the insights gleaned from the various comparative analyses of tax state development be "exported" to other questions? In the remainder of this concluding chapter, I consider several predictions and hypotheses that should follow from these results and the theoretical relationships that we have observed. First, I identify the potential relevance of these findings for other cases, and for other political and policy questions. Next, I look toward the future of politics and policy-making in Brazil and South Africa.

The Influence of Identity Politics and Political Community

My analyses of the development of the tax state confirm what others have found at a more general level: Institutions structure politics by influencing individuals' subjective models of the world, by making the development of certain types of organizations and coalitions more likely than others, and by shaping patterns of politics through self-enforcing mechanisms for long periods of time.[3] In this book, I have demonstrated that the construction of political community through constitutional and other formal and informal rules of membership has had a major influence within a key policy area, affecting the quality of state authority. It is quite reasonable to hypothesize that identities and definitions of political community would have a big effect in other policy areas.

While I have focused on the racial and regional dimensions of NPC, these need not be the only dimensions of identity for which sets of political rules get defined. In other countries and during other periods, other identity-based cleavages are relevant and have had an analogous influence on inter- and intra-class relations. The myths that underpin affective bonds provide an organizing logic for groups of individuals to emerge as collective actors and to articulate shared interests and agendas, even when underlying material conditions might suggest a wide range of possibilities for how interests can aggregate. Commonly held beliefs about common interest and about which groups are likely to share fortunes and calamities tend to structure the fault lines of political competition with both normative and strategic imperatives.

Although I have argued that taxation is distinctive from other types of public policies, there is good reason to believe that many of the core causal mechanisms identified in the political community model could be at work in other aspects of the relationship between states and societies. The most obvious choice would be to consider the other area of state extraction from society: conscription for military service.[4] Other key research areas would include the influence of definitions of NPC on the expenditure side of the welfare state. For example, the varied configuration of social security and health insurance systems across countries could fruitfully be explored with an approach similar to the one carried out in this book. Although the expenditure side of the budget does not involve a demand for "sacrifice," the challenge of allocating scarce community resources also involves questions about distributive justice and collective identity that are central to the model.[5]

---

[3] Thanks to an anonymous reviewer from Cambridge University Press for suggesting I be more explicit about these points. Although he/she attributes such theoretical insights to the "new institutionalism" in economics, I maintain that such findings are also largely associated with historical institutionalism in political science.

[4] Levi 1997.

[5] See, for example, Baldwin 1990.

By inserting the definition of the NPC into the institutional repertoire, it becomes possible to compare the organization and operation of
politics in a much broader group of countries, beyond the rich, industrial
democracies. In much of the developing world, formal and informal rules
of decision making are much farther apart. Moreover, particularly in new
democracies, institutional variation with respect to electoral rules and legislative procedures tends to be a direct response to underlying variations
in prior definitions of NPC, suggesting that regime change may not radically redistribute the sources of political power within society. For example,
the choices about whether or not to adopt a federal constitution, various
consociational models, and parliamentary or presidential systems are rarely
the product of some abstract decision about which model will promote
efficiency or stability. Rather, such choices tend to result from pressures to
reproduce existing and commonly recognized distributions of power, and
often such choices are the product of violent conflict in which the victor
establishes the rules.[6] If a certain group is recognized as important, the
new rules are often designed to provide a voice and a veto point to that
group. Of course, the long-term influence of formal institutional choices
may produce results other than those intended, but that very tension is
worthy of investigation. Moreover, in much of the postcolonial world, the
formal rules of decision making may say little about the actual rules of the
various political processes that allocate financial and other resources within
a society. Understanding how and where collective consciousness is reproduced is a prerequisite for applying the historical institutional model within
such settings.

The attempt to extend the political community model, which was presented in Chapter 6, could provide a launching pad for considering a series
of other country cases, and groups of cases, particularly with more nuanced
conceptualizations of political community. In terms of regional politics, the
dichotomous characterization of federalism could surely be refined to capture different forms of federalism. For example, Alfred Stepan makes useful
distinctions between the various reasons for and manifestations of federal
constitutions.[7] Similarly, the question of how racial and ethnic groups are
variously included and excluded from political and economic life could also
be conceptualized to recognize more subtle variations than those presented
in this book.

[6] This is a central point made by Chaudhry 1997: 14–16.
[7] Stepan 1999.

A further critical area of research concerns the development of the tax state in post-Soviet successor states. Attempts to understand the disintegration of various federal polities and the varied success with tax collections within the post-Soviet space could profit from the framework developed in the political community model. However, in applying the model to such cases it is critical to recognize that the process of tax state building in recent years has been one in which the state is being *removed* from a position of being in virtual control of the economy, quite different from the process of tax state building where the private economy was previously autonomous from the state. As shown in this book, other economic and international factors surely influence the outcomes, but the task of analytically untangling the dimensions of relevant ascriptive group identities, and the ways in which groups are variously included and excluded by the national state, should provide an opportunity to generate insights into the varied construction of the tax state in this part of the world.

Variations in institutional design and in the salience of group identities strongly influence patterns of cooperation and exchange, and ultimately, these factors affect the production and distribution of material resources within society. While others have argued that "institutions matter," this book has demonstrated that the causal influence of institutions on group identities, and class relations, can have a more lasting and potentially more powerful causal influence than more formal decision-making procedures. Further analysis of the interstices between the politics of identity, class, and the political economy of development is likely to be a promising avenue for future investigation. A key implication is that policy makers attempting to influence outcomes through efforts at institutional reform should consider the intermediating role of political community and identity politics.

Implications for Brazil and South Africa in the 21st Century

Looking forward, the politics of the past have important distributive implications for the 21st century. For South Africa, the legacy of the tax state provides some promising prospects. Though absolute and per capita expenditure on whites was always significantly greater than on blacks in apartheid South Africa, within this highly unequal society, blacks still received more on the expenditure side than they contributed in the form of taxes on the revenue side.[8] In the fiscal year 1990–91, the "independent" homelands

---

[8] McGrath 1979.

and Self-Governing Territories received transfers from the central government amounting to 58.1 percent of their own revenues.[9] Indeed, these findings are at odds with what most observers commonly expect given the structure of the apartheid state and its prior incarnations, which appear to be at the very root of race-based inequality. In fact, inequalities between race groups were maintained with far more hideous strategies, including segregation of housing and labor markets, and an educational system designed to limit the skills and thus the opportunities of the black population. There is good reason to believe that with the eradication of such racial engineering, the post-apartheid state has better-than-average capacities to ameliorate income and wealth disparities, particularly given the tax state it inherited. The inclinations of the current South African government to equalize expenditure across groups provides outstanding opportunities for redressing the past. Of course, in an economy where rates of unemployment are sometimes estimated as high as 40 percent, and where one in four adults is HIV-positive, the obstacles to success are clearly great.

The legacy of the Brazilian tax state is much more of a burden than a boon to equitable development. As it turns out, the contradictory machinations of racial democracy have proved ill-fated, and the Brazilian fiscal system has tended to exacerbate inequalities during the first years of the 21st century. The historical failure of the state to collect income taxes has left a heavy debt burden, and when combined with massive social security obligations, the maneuvering room for redistribution is miniscule. Meanwhile the educational, health, and other backlogs in Brazil remain as troubling as in South Africa. Without resources for publicly provided services, life chances in Brazil will be more closely tied to current levels of income and wealth than in South Africa, serving to reproduce inequality. Given the much greater loyalty of citizens to municipalities and states (*estados*), equity enhancing policies and practices may be more forthcoming at these more local levels of government. In particular, income taxes might be more easily collected at these lower levels of government, but at the moment, this is a constitutional impossibility. Moreover, the politics of regionalism have created new, within-region political conflicts that could further block redistributive appeals. For example, in the cities of São Paulo and Rio de Janeiro, wealthy Brazilians have tended to blame the problems of crime and poverty on the *favela* dwellers, who they describe as immigrants from the Northeast.

[9] Ahmad 1998: 240.

For Brazilians and South Africans, the analysis of the past presented in this book will be most useful if it can shed some light on the future, specifically with regard to the possibilities and prospects for change. Critics of institutional arguments have tended to berate their limited scope for identifying mechanisms of over-time change.[10] Admittedly, the analysis presented in this book *has* emphasized the consistency of cross-national patterns to a greater degree than longitudinal variation. As was discussed in Chapter 5, legacies of path-dependent development tend to be reinforced through multiple mechanisms. Nonetheless, the findings provide significant analytic leverage for thinking about the future.

There is no reason to believe that South Africa will continue to be a cooperative tax state or that Brazil will continue to be an adversarial one in perpetuity, or that the associated distributive implications will necessarily persist. In fact, the very system of national states that undergirds the typology of tax states in Chapter 2 should not be taken for granted as a permanent fixture in the world order. At the very least, the impact of the early critical juncture can be expected to diminish over time, and there are good reasons to believe that change in the tax relationship between the state and upper groups is both possible and likely in these two societies. Specifically, the Brazilian state *could* be restructured to be more efficient and more equitable, and South Africa's tax state *could* some day come to resemble that of Brazil. Indeed, each of the key sets of explanatory variables identified within the political community model, including economic factors, the international environment, and the definition of NPC, are likely to affect reform and restructuring in the years to come. Perhaps more than anything, technology will provide openings for change, while the content of political community will structure the manifestation of such change.

First, ongoing changes in the structure of the international political economy are likely to continue to impede the efficacy of the modern tax state. As discussed in Chapter 5, there are good reasons to believe that the pressures of globalization will constrain the policies and administrative practices of national states, particularly in semi-peripheral countries such as Brazil and South Africa. Tax competition with other countries, combined with the ever-increasing mobility of skills and capital, will continue to make it difficult for the central state to tax upper groups. Moreover, very recent technological changes are literally displacing markets for certain goods and

---

[10] These arguments and some rebuttals are summarized in Steinmo, Thelen, and Longstreth 1995: 16–26.

services from the physical world. As described in Chapter 2, tax liabilities are calculated with respect to particular sets of economic stocks and flows, and to the extent that the very nature of those tax handles change, we should anticipate change in the state's ability to tax. Throughout the 20th century, the processes of urbanization and industrialization provided increasing scope for collecting additional tax revenues as the costs of monitoring and enforcement declined with higher levels of monetization of economies, concentration of resources, and needs for public goods. By contrast, the increasing proliferation of economic activity in an electronic world may prove increasingly difficult to tax. Already, the United States and other governments have elected to let certain aspects of Internet commerce evolve on a "tax-free" basis, and as demonstrated in this book, once certain precedents become established in the relationship between state and society, they are difficult to change. Moreover, new technologies may create greater scope for barter, and the prospects for demonetization of economies could prove fatal for taxation.

The current international environment is far from peaceful, and as discussed in Chapter 4, no moment in the 20th century was more critical for the development of national tax systems than the waging of the Second World War. Transnational conflicts could certainly raise the need for new taxes, introducing new forms and/or levels of taxation. Moreover, further conflict could increase the proliferation of new states, as has been the trend over the past decade.

While international and economic factors may create openings for new demands for and/or resistance to taxation, the definition and resonance of political community is likely to have a very strong influence on the legislation and implementation of tax policy around the world and certainly in Brazil and South Africa. Perhaps more than at any time during the 20th century, national states will come to rely upon the political community as a basis for raising tax revenues, as the opportunities to shirk one's tax obligations increase. In other words, the voluntary aspect of tax systems will be critical for the financial solvency of modern states. The willingness of upper groups to sacrifice will depend upon their ability to see themselves as strategically and morally aligned with larger groups of people with both similar and lesser economic means.

The future configuration of national political community is likely to emerge as a combination of re-invention and pure novelty. The definitions of NPC identified in this book, which have varied in terms of their constructions of racial and regional identities, certainly provide a starting point for thinking about the future. One of the more dismal conclusions from this study is that the mobilization of *difference* has been a particularly strong solvent for cementing political community, as was the case in the mobilization of whiteness through the explicit exclusion of black South Africans. Nonetheless, the possibilities for imagination and the configuration of new identities are vast, and more positive specifications of political community could also form the basis for eliciting collective sacrifice. For example, in South Africa, it is not inconceivable that the invention of the "rainbow nation" could succeed, and that chauvinism based on racial stereotyping could be eliminated in favor of some common, civic, national identity. If indeed exclusion is the most powerful agent for cementing group identities, potentially less corrosive forms of exclusion could be mobilized, such as a rejection of the past, or a rejection of intolerance.

On the other hand, there is good reason to speculate that South Africa's social experiment will fail, that white South Africans, controlling the lion's share of skills and resources, will reject the new South African nation and head for other corners of the globe. Many have already done so, and many more speak of such possibilities on a regular basis. Since the end of apartheid, many white South Africans have complained loudly about the taxes they owe at the national level, and have begun to hold back on paying their *local* taxes in recently reconstituted local government districts.[11] Particularly for those whites with low levels of racial tolerance, they have bemoaned the ramifications of political transition as tax bases have been only modestly extended – given the extremely low incomes of black citizens – while the need to provide services to members of all race groups has implied a relative loss of public services for whites.

If the configurations of racial and regional identities are important determinants of levels of political cohesion and the politics of taxation, there are several possibilities for how these identities might be redrawn in future years. As discussed in Chapter 5, there are certainly multiple avenues for re-interpreting, mobilizing, and/or demobilizing existing identities and constructions of political community in both cases. And as other scholars have pointed out, these labels are often highly malleable and can be re-invented to include different groups over time.[12] Depending upon the ways

---

[11] Most notable was the 1996 "boycott" of local rates by affluent whites in the Johannesburg suburb of Sandton in response to rate increases proposed in order to extend services to township residents.

[12] Jung 2000; Munro 1995; Manzo 1996.

in which these groups are mobilized or demobilized, new forms of economic conflict could surely promote different types of tax outcomes. Similarly, in Brazil, where racially based political claims have been few and far between, there are indeed currents suggesting that this could change. In recent years, it has become increasingly common to find people in schools, offices, and in the media, subjecting the myths of a racial democracy to scrutiny and challenge. Such intellectual currents in that country could eventually lead to a greater political salience for race than is currently the case. Ironically, the availability of American and South African-based ideas and images around the political relevance of race-based resistance has helped to inspire political entrepreneurs to mobilize race, an outcome that would reverse a century's history of attempting to eradicate the category of race altogether.[13] The territorial fault lines specified in federal constitutions always provide opportunities for distributive conflict, particularly when they overlap with other ethnic and/or cultural differences. Now that South Africa has a federal constitution, and one in which the provincial boundaries overlap with certain ethnic and cultural groups as well as economic differences, it is certainly possible to imagine regionalism taking on increased political salience, in turn impeding the national state's ability to govern.

Such axes hardly exhaust the possibilities for defining political community in the 21st century, where physical proximity is perhaps less meaningful than during any time in history. New forms of communication and new ideas are creating unprecedented opportunities for novel configurations of community and solidarity, particularly in ways that may transcend the borders of the national state. Quite clearly, high-income individuals within urban centers in these countries have much greater opportunities to interact with individuals in other countries via the Internet and/or through global satellite communications than they do with low-income individuals in their own cities, let alone in outlying areas within their own countries. This new "space" in which new communities of people can transcend physical boundaries may prove to undermine the loyalties and social cohesion necessary for the stable functioning of the national state as we know it today, as the structural possibilities for new types of "imagined communities" are vastly expanded. Clearly it is too early to predict how such identities will manifest themselves, but the powerful new tools that exist for communication and coordination will likely be central to the future development of collective consciousness in much of the world.

[13] See Marx 1998.

For as long as the national state remains the dominant form of political authority around the world, definitions of National Political Community will have a strong influence on public policy and human development. The rules concerning who may become a citizen, and on what basis, will continue to have important political ramifications. When new states are constructed, or when opportunities arise to alter definitions of NPC within existing states, political elites must choose among inclusionary and exclusionary approaches. The very rules that establish barriers to the acquisition of citizenship create value for membership in the political community and may help to constitute shared political identities. In turn, such identities may facilitate collective action and help to overcome free rider problems. On the other hand, if political community is defined as a collection of distinct groups, each with some degree of autonomy, these identities may create enduring political divisions, impeding the state's ability to implement uniform public policies within its domain. Moreover, if the barriers to full citizenship are overly restrictive and fail to respect the human rights of individuals and groups, this may provoke rebellion from within or condemnation from the international community. These difficult political dilemmas are fundamental problems of contemporary politics.

APPENDIX

Comparative-Historical Analysis

The findings presented in Chapters 3 through 5 are based on analyses of an historical database developed for this research project. The database was designed to make comparisons with respect to over-time political, economic, and social processes across countries. It integrates historical observations from secondary sources, and from a host of primary sources, including newspaper articles, in-depth interviews, and analysis of survey data. The analysis was carried out by organizing this eclectic set of data into an analyzable electronic format, largely through Microsoft Access software. That software provided significant flexibility in sorting records by place, time, variable, and/or on key words, facilitating the development of qualitative comparisons. Ultimately, the analyses still required interpretation and discussion, as presented in the book chapters, but the organization of the data in this format greatly simplified the task of creating historical narratives, and this technique may be useful for other scholars.

Analysis

The database was designed to facilitate comparative-historical analysis – that is, the making of comparisons of outcomes and processes simultaneously across time and space. The main challenge in designing the database was that the historical record of countries does not neatly fit into a grid of time series cross-sectional data. That is, there is sufficient incongruence between the units of observation (real events and outcomes) and the units of analysis (periods) that it was necessary to develop a tool for analysis that would allow me to retrieve data in a variety of different formats, allowing me to quickly assess the historical order of various outcomes and processes and to compare those outcomes across countries.

284

Database Records and Fields

As in any database, the historical database is a collection of discrete records. Each record in the database describes some aspect of political, social, or economic life within the respective countries, and was coded in terms of lower and upper time boundaries – or "start" and "end" years, an analytic variable, and a "score" or set of notes relating a fact or set of facts relevant to the research project.

Thus, each record in the database represents a distinctive "fact," observation, or relationship characterizing a particular country during a particular period in time. Each record was coded in terms of the following fields:

Case (Brazil, South Africa, and other countries)
Subregion/sector (coded when a record did not apply uniformly within the country)
Year start (range 1500–2000)
Year end (range 1500–2000)
Variable (see list below)
Notes
Analysis
Source (bibliographic or other information)

Variables

Each record was intended to provide insight into a particular dimension of social, political, or economic life, and as such, the database was defined in terms of a series of grouping variables. In particular, this was useful for analyzing the extent to which changes in outcome (taxation) variables covaried with other factors. The database incorporates approximately fifty variables, including the following categories, which were most useful for the analysis:

Economic policy
Income distribution
International factors
Industrial policy
Political institutions (including NPC)
Politics – class
Politics – cleavages
Politics – crisis

Politics – identity
Politics – party system
Politics – regime
Politics – tax
Tax administration
Tax compliance
Tax incidence
Tax policy – indirect
Tax policy – income
Tax revenues

Data Sources

The records for the database were generated from a variety of sources. Where historical accounts and interpretations varied, I attempted to gather additional information in order to make the most accurate characterizations possible. Ultimately, certain judgment calls were required, but I have tried to identify these disputes where appropriate in the text.

Printed Materials

Printed primary and secondary sources provided the foundation for the majority of the records in the database. The goal was *not* to create an original history of either country, for which excellent secondary sources already exist. However, it was often necessary to look at key primary sources to examine specific outcomes, intentions, and political discourse centrally relevant to the outcome under investigation. All of the materials consulted can be found in the bibliography and in the footnotes of the text of the book.

Interviews

In addition to the printed materials, the comparative historical analysis draws heavily from a series of in-depth interviews conducted over the course of two years of field work in the respective countries. The goal of these interviews was to complement the printed materials, filling in gaps where data could not be found, and to verify characterizations made by other authors. I was attempting to understand how the tax states worked *in practice*,

Comparative-Historical Analysis

Table A.1 *Summary of in-depth interviews conducted*

	Brazil	South Africa
Government (executives, bureaucrats)	22	31
Organized interests (business, labor, political parties)	12	21
Taxpayers (business owners/executives, tax intermediaries)	12	25
Analysts (academics, NGOs, international organizations)	20	18
Total interviews*	62	91

* Total interviews conducted is less than sum because some respondents have held multiple positions and were counted for their various roles.

and to be able to distinguish theoretical from actual application of the tax policies.

Number of Interviews

Approximately 150 formal interviews were conducted and transcribed (see Table A.1). These were supplemented with many more informal conversations with people in my daily life, conducting field work in these countries. More interviews were conducted in South Africa than in Brazil for two key reasons: I carried out my research there first, and came to learn what information was and was not relevant to the analysis; and there exists a much richer secondary literature on Brazilian business and political interests and their relationship to taxation than on the South African case.

Time of Interviews

The interviews lasted from thirty minutes to four hours, and several individuals were interviewed more than once. Approximately one-half the interviews were tape recorded and then transcribed. Transcripts from the remaining interviews are based on written notes and impressions following the interview.

Confidentiality

Almost all of the interviews were conducted on a confidential basis. A few high-profile individuals, whose opinions and attitudes are a matter of public record, were asked if they would be willing to have their comments identified by name, and their names are identified in the text.

287

Language

In South Africa, all interviews were conducted in English. In Brazil, the interviews were conducted in Portuguese, English, and often, a mix of the two languages.

Format/Interview Guides

The interviews were conducted in a loosely structured, open-ended format. Virtually all of the respondents/informants were highly educated professionals who were reluctant to follow the rigid constraints of an interview guide. It was often difficult to know ahead of time whether a respondent would provide twenty minutes or two hours for our meeting. Since the goal of these interviews was to gain information about larger processes and historical events, not to make inferences about individuals, I found it more productive to adapt my style to the respondent when necessary. Depending upon the age and career background of the respondent, I asked questions concerning reflections about over-time change.

I entered each interview with a prepared outline of questions, organized by subheadings, allowing me to move on to different aspects of the research when possible and/or necessary in the conversation. Over time, I prioritized some questions over others depending upon data needs.

The following are standard questions asked in most of the interviews. Certain questions were omitted and others added, depending upon the respondent's position, time available, and own introduction of other issue areas for discussion.

Background

- Please describe position, history with the organization, etc.
- Political background/other special?

Attitudes about Tax System

- What are your general impressions of your tax system? Is it fair? Why or why not? Do you think your views reflect those of most others in your organization? Or do you think your views are somewhat unique? How so?
- Who benefits most? Least?
- Has this gotten better or worse in the past few years? Why?

Interaction with the State

- How do you/your organization influence tax policy? Through a business/labor organization? Political party? Public opinion? Direct contact with government?
- How successful are you?
- How does tax policy get made? Who are the most important actors in this process?
- How would you describe the country's tax compliance? Who complies most/least? Do your clients pay *any* taxes? How do they lower their tax burdens?
- Do people get in trouble for not paying? What happens to them?

Functioning of the Tax System

- Please explain the background/policy/administration of (a particular) tax.
- Who pays for (a particular) tax?
- How does it get collected?
- Are there differences across regions? Sectors? Income groups? Other?
- Is this a progressive or regressive tax system? How has that changed over time?
- What are the costs of administration/compliance?

Politics/Identity

- What do you think about the changes that have been taking place in your country in recent years? Do you think (members of) your organization feel they benefit from these changes? (If they ask, "which changes," refer to end of apartheid or end of military rule/ onset of democracy.)
- Do you think the current government does a good job in serving your interests? Those of the organization? How has this changed?
- Do you think the state spends money in a fair manner? More or less so than in prior years?
- Which groups do you think benefit most from state spending? Is this a change from the past?
- From your perspective, what are the most important political divides in the country?

References

Abrucio, Fernando Luiz. *Os Barões da Federação: Os Governadores e a Redemocratização Brasileira*. São Paulo: Editora Hucitec, 1998.

Ahmad, Junaid K. "South Africa: An Intergovernmental Fiscal System in Transition." In *Fiscal Decentralization in Developing Countries*, edited by Richard Miller Bird and François Vaillancourt, 239–70. Cambridge and New York: Cambridge University Press, 1998.

Alden, Dauril. *Royal Government in Colonial Brazil*. Berkeley and Los Angeles: University of California Press, 1968.

Almond, Gabriel Abraham, and Sidney Verba. *The Civic Culture: Political Attitudes and Democracy in Five Nations*. Princeton, NJ: Princeton University Press, 1963.

Altman, Daniel. "Reviving Argentina: The Trouble with Taxes." *New York Times*, January 1, 2002, C1.

Ames, Edward, and Richard T. Rapp. "The Birth and Death of Taxes." *Journal of Economic History* 37, no. 1 (1977): 161–78.

Anderson, Benedict. *Imagined Communities: Reflections on the Origin and Spread of Nationalism*. London: Verso, 1996.

Andrews, George Reid. *Blacks and Whites in São Paulo, Brazil, 1888–1988*. Madison: University of Wisconsin Press, 1991.

Andrews, George Reid. "Black Political Protest in Sao Paulo, 1888–1988." *Journal of Latin American Studies* 24 (1992): 147–71.

Ardant, Gabriel. "Financial Policy and the Economic Infrastructure of Modern States and Nations." In *The Formation of National States in Western Europe*, edited by Charles Tilly. Princeton, NJ: Princeton University Press, 1975.

Arendt, Hannah. *The Origins of Totalitarianism*. San Diego, CA: Harcourt, Brace, Jovanovich, 1979.

Arocha, Jaime. "Inclusion of Afro-Colombians." *Latin American Perspectives* 25, no. 3 (1998): 70–90.

"Associaçao Comercial de São Paulo." *O Estado de São Paulo*, January 6, 1944, 2.

Association of Chambers of Commerce (ASSOCOM). *Annual report*. Various years.

Association of Chambers of Commerce of South Africa. *Submission to the Margo Commission*. Johannesburg: ASSOCOM, 1985.

References

Baer, Werner. *The Brazilian Economy: Growth and Development*. Westport, CT: Praeger, 1995.

Baker, Donald G. "Review Article, Race and Ethnic Studies: The New Zealand Case." *Ethnic and Racial Studies* 15, no. 1 (1992): 137–45.

Baldwin, Peter. *The Politics of Social Solidarity: Class Bases in the European Welfare State, 1875–1975*. New York: Cambridge University Press, 1990.

Ballara, Angela. *Proud To Be White?: A Survey of Pakeha Prejudice in New Zealand*. Auckland, NZ: Heinemann, 1986.

Banton, Michael. *Racial Theories*. Cambridge: Cambridge University Press, 1992.

Barkey, Karen, and Sunita Parikh. "Comparative Perspectives on the State." *Annual Review of Sociology* 17 (1991): 523–49.

Barman, Roderick J. *Brazil: The Forging of a Nation 1798–1852*. Stanford, CA: Stanford University Press, 1988.

Barron, F. Laurie. "The Indian Pass System in the Canadian West, 1882–1935." In *The Native Imprint: The Contribution of First Peoples to Canada's Character*, edited by Olive Patricia Dickason, 184–204. Athabasca, Alta: Athabasca University Educational Enterprises, 1996.

Bates, Robert, H. "A Political Scientist Looks at Tax Reform." In *Tax Reform in Developing Countries*, edited by Malcolm Gillis, 473–91. Durham: Duke University Press, 1989.

Bates, Robert, H., Rui J. P. de Figueiredo, and Barry R. Weingast. "The Politics of Interpretation: Rationality, Culture, and Transition." *Politics and Society* 26, no. 4 (1998): 603–42.

Bates, Robert H., Avner Greif, Margaret Levi, Jean-Laurent Rosenthal, and Barry R. Weingast. *Analytic Narratives*. Princeton, NJ: Princeton University Press, 1998.

Bates, Robert H., and Donald Da-Hsiang Lien. "A Note on Taxation, Development and Representative Government." *Politics and Society* 14, no. 1 (1985): 53–70.

Bendix, Reinhard. *Nation Building and Citizenship: Studies of Our Changing Social Order*. New York: Wiley, 1964.

Berry, William Dale. "Testing Budgetary Theories with Budgetary Data: Assessing the Risks." *American Journal of Political Science* 30, no. 3 (1986): 597–627.

Biesanz, John, and Luke M. Smith. "Race Relations in Panama and the Canal Zone." *American Journal of Sociology* 57, no. 1 (1951): 7–14.

Blackburn, Kevin. "White Agitation for an Aboriginal State in Australia (1925–1929)." *Australian Journal of Politics and History* 45, no. 2 (1999): 157–80.

Bledisloe, Charles Bathurst, and Thomas Lindsay Buick. *Ideals of Nationhood: A Selection of Addresses Delivered in New Zealand by the Right Hon. Lord Bledisloe During His Governor-Generalship of the Dominion*. New Zealand Centennial ed. New Plymouth, NZ: Thomas Avery & Sons, 1940.

Boskin, Michael J., and Charles E. McLure. *World Tax Reform: Case Studies of Developed and Developing Countries*. San Francisco and Lanham, MD: ICS Press, 1990.

Bouças, Valentim F. "Os Tributos e sua Arrecadação em Face da Constituição." *Boletim do Conselho Técnico de Economia e Finanças*, no. 68–9 (1946): 4–6.

Braithwaite, V. A., and Margaret Levi. *Trust and Governance*. The Russell Sage Foundation series on trust; v. 1. New York: Russell Sage Foundation, 1998.

292

References

Brooke, James. "White Flight in Brazil? Secessionist Cauldron Boils." *New York Times*, May 12, 1993, A4.

Brownlee, W. Elliot. *Federal Taxation in America: A Short History*. New York: Cambridge University Press, 1996.

Brysk, Alison, and Carol Wise. "Liberalization and Ethnic Conflict in Latin America." *Studies in Comparative International Development* 32, no. 2 (1997): 76–105.

Bulhões, Augusto de. "A Reforma da Legislação do Impôsto de Renda de 1947." *Revista do Serviço Público* 3, no. 3–4 (1948): 5–12.

Bull, Theodore, ed. *Rhodesia: Crisis of Color*. Chicago: Quadrangle Books, 1967.

Bulmer-Thomas, Victor. *The Economic History of Latin America Since Independence*. Edited by Simon Collier, *Cambridge Latin American Studies*. New York: Cambridge University Press, 1994.

Bunting, Brian. *The Rise of the South African Reich*. London: International Defence and Aid Fund for Southern Africa, 1986.

Bureau of Census and Statistics South Africa. *Uniestatistieke oor vyftig jaar. Union Statistics for Fifty Years. Jubilee Issue, 1910–1960*. Pretoria, South Africa, 1960.

Burgess, Robin, and Nicholas Stern. "Taxation and Development." *Journal of Economic Literature* 31, no. 2 (1993): 762–830.

Burns, E. Bradfurd. *A History of Brazil*. New York: Columbia University Press, 1993.

Campbell, John L. "The State and Fiscal Sociology." *Annual Review of Sociology* 19 (1993): 163–85.

Canto, Gilberto de Ulhôa. "Brazilian Taxation Alterations During and After the War." *Bulletin for International Fiscal Documentation* 2 (1948): 66–72.

Canto, Gilberto de Ulhôa. "Study of the Brazilian Tax System in View of the Federal Regime." *Bulletin for International Fiscal Documentation* 3, no. 49 (1949): 72–104.

Cantoni, Wilson. "Chile: Relations between the Mapuche and Chilean National Society." In *Race and Class in Post-Colonial Society: A Study of Ethnic Group Relations in the English-Speaking Caribbean, Bolivia, Chile and Mexico*, 458. Paris: Unesco, 1977.

Cardoso, Fernando Henrique. "On the Characterization of Authoritarian Regimes in Latin America." In *The New Authoritarianism in Latin America*, edited by David Collier, 33–57. Princeton, NJ: Princeton University Press, 1979.

Cardoso, Fernando Henrique, and Enzo Faletto. *Dependency and Development in Latin America*. Berkeley: University of California Press, 1979.

Carnegie Commission. "Report of the Carnegie Commission: The Poor White Problem in South Africa." Stellenbosch, South Africa: Pro-Ecclesia-drukkery, 1932.

Carone, Edgar. *O Pensamento Industrial No Brasil*. Rio de Janeiro: DIFEL, 1978.

Carton, Ben. "Unfinished Exorcism: The Legacy of Apartheid in Democratic Southern Africa." *Social Justice* 27, no. 1 (2000): 116–28.

Cell, John. *The Highest Stage of White Supremacy: The Origins of Segregation in South Africa and the American South*. Cambridge and New York: Cambridge University Press, 1982.

Central Statistical Service. *South African Statistics*. Pretoria, South Africa: Central Statistical Service, 1995.

References

Chamber of Mines/ Transvaal Chamber of Mines. *Annual Reports and Presidential Addresses.* Various years.

Chaudhry, Kiren Aziz. *The Price of Wealth: Economies and Institutions in the Middle East.* Ithaca, NY: Cornell University Press, 1997.

Cheibub, José Antonio. "Political Regimes and the Extractive Capacity of Governments: Taxation in Democracies and Dictatorships." *World Politics* 50 (1998): 349–76.

Ching, Erik, and Virginia Tilley. "Indians, the Military and the Rebellion of 1932 in El Salvador." *Journal of Latin American Studies* 30 (1998): 121–56.

Collier, David, and Robert Adcock. "Democracy and Dichotomies: A Pragmatic Approach to Choices About Concepts." *Annual Review of Political Science* 2 (1999): 537–65.

Collier, Ruth Berins, and David Collier. *Shaping the Political Arena.* Princeton, NJ: Princeton University Press, 1991.

Comissão de Finanças e Orçamento. *República dos Estados Unidos do Brasil.* Rio de Janeiro: Câmara dos Deputados, 1936.

Commissioner of Inland Revenue, Union of South Africa. *Annual Reports.* Pretoria: Government Printers, 1910–1966. (Also listed as Secretary for Inland Revenue.)

Conjuntura Econômica. Fundação Getúlio Vargas, various years.

Costa, Alcides Jorge. "História do Direito Tributário." *Revista Especial do Tribunal Regional Federal (3a região)* (1995): 15–54.

Crepaz, Markus M. L. "Inclusion Versus Exclusion: Political Institutions and Welfare Expenditures." *Comparative Politics* 31, no. 1 (1998): 61–80.

Crespo, Mariana. "Reform from Ipanema." *Financial World,* May 23, 1995.

Davenport, T. R. H. *South Africa: A Modern History.* Toronto: University of Toronto Press, 1991.

Davies, Robert. "The White Working Class in South Africa." *New Left Review* 82, Nov.–Dec. (1973): 40–59.

Davies, Robert, David Kaplan, Mike Morris, and Dan O'Meara. "Class Struggle and the Periodisation of the State in South Africa." *Review of African Political Economy* 7, Sept.–Dec. (1976): 4–30.

Degler, Carl N. *Neither Black Nor White: Slavery and Race Relations in Brazil and the United States.* Madison: University of Wisconsin Press, 1971.

Degregori, Carlos Iván. "Ethnicity and Democratic Governability in Latin America: Reflections from Two Central Andean Countries." In *Fault Lines of Democracy in Post-Transition Latin America,* edited by Felipe Agüero and Jeffrey Stark, 203–34. Miami: North-South Center Press, 1998.

Department of Finance, Republic of South Africa. *Inland Revenue Statistical Bulletin.* Pretoria, South Africa: Government Printer, 1983–90.

Department of Finance, South Africa. *Budget Review.* Cape Town, South Africa: Government Printer, 1991–2000.

Derbyshire, J. Denis, and Ian Derbyshire. *Political Systems of the World.* New York: St. Martin's Press, 1999.

Diederichs Commission. *First and Final Report of the Income Tax Commission, 1953.* Pretoria, 1954.

References

"Disappearing Taxes: The Tap Runs Dry." *The Economist*, May 31, 1997.

Domínguez, Jorge I. *Race and Ethnicity in Latin America, Essays on Mexico, Central and South America; V. 7.* New York: Garland Publishers, 1994.

Durand, Francisco, and Eduardo Silva, editors. *Organized Business, Economic Change, and Democracy in Latin America.* Coral Gables, FL: North-South Center Press, 1998.

Du Toit, Pierre. *State-Building and Democracy in Southern Africa.* Pretoria: Human Sciences Research Council, 1995.

Ellis, Howard S. *The Economy of Brazil.* Berkeley: University of California Press, 1969.

Elphick, Richard, and Hermann Giliomee, eds. *The Shaping of South African Society, 1652–1820.* Middletown, CT: Wesleyan University Press, 1989.

Elton, Catherine. "Not Letting Skin Shade Color Life." *Christian Science Monitor*, November 3, 1998, 1.

Ertman, Thomas. *Birth of the Leviathan: Building States and Regimes in Medieval and Early Modern Europe.* New York: Cambridge University Press, 1997.

Escola de Administração Fazendaria (ESAF). *Sistema Tributário: Características Gerais, Tendências Internacionais e Administração.* Brasília: Secretaria da Receita Federal, 1994.

Escola de Administração Fazendaria (ESAF). *Um Perfil da Administração Tributária Brasileira.* Brasília: Secretaria da Receita Federal, 1995.

Escola de Administração Fazendaria (ESAF). *Disciplina: Sistema Tributário Nacional Evolução e Tendências.* Brasília: Ministério da Fazenda, 1997.

Esman, Milton J. *Ethnic Politics.* Ithaca, NY: Cornell University Press, 1994.

Esping-Andersen, Gosta. *The Three Worlds of Welfare Capitalism.* Princeton, NJ: Princeton University Press, 1990.

Evans, Peter. *Embedded Autonomy: States and Industrial Transformation.* Princeton, NJ: Princeton University Press, 1995.

Evans, Peter, Dietrich Rueschemeyer, and Theda Skocpol, eds. *Bringing the State Back In.* Cambridge and New York: Cambridge University Press, 1985.

Fausto, Boris. "Brazil: The Social and Political Structure of the First Republic." In Leslie Bethell, ed. *The Cambridge History of Latin America*, 779–829. Cambridge and New York: Cambridge University Press, 1986.

Fausto, Boris. *A Concise History of Brazil.* Cambridge and New York: Cambridge University Press, 1999.

Ferreira, Benedito. *Legislação Tributária: A Historia da Tributação no Brasil.* Brasília: Senado Federal, Centro Grafico, 1986.

Firebaugh, Glenn, and Jack P. Gibbs. "User's Guide to Ratio Variables." *American Sociological Review* 50, no. 5 (1985): 713–22.

Fontaine, Pierre-Michel, ed. *Race, Class and Power in Brazil.* Los Angeles: Center for Afro-American Studies, University of California, Los Angeles, 1985.

Fourie, F.C.v.N., and A. Owen. "Value-Added Tax and Regressivity in South Africa." *South African Journal of Economics* 61, no. 4 (1993): 281–300.

Fredrickson, George M. *White Supremacy: A Comparative Study in American and South African History.* New York: Oxford University Press, 1982.

References

Freyre, Gilberto. *The Mansions and the Shanties: The Making of Modern Brazil.* Berkeley: University of California Press, 1986.

Freyre, Gilberto, and Rod William Horton. *Order and Progress: Brazil from Monarchy to Republic.* Berkeley: University of California Press, 1986.

Freyre, Gilberto, and Samuel Putnam. *The Masters and the Slaves.* New York: Knopf, 1946.

Frieden, Jeffrey. "Invested Interests: The Politics of National Economic Policies in a World of Global Finance." *International Organization* 45, no. 4 (1991): 425–51.

Friedman, Steven, and Riaan de Villiers, eds. *Comparing Brazil and South Africa: Two Transitional States in Political and Economic Perspective.* Johannesburg: Center for Policy Studies, 1996.

Fundação Getúlio Vargas, Commisão de Reforma do Ministério da Fazenda. *Evolução do Impôsto de Renda no Brasil.* Rio de Janeiro: Ministério da Fazenda, 1966.

Gaffney, James. "Race and Politics Where America Began." *America* 170, no. 18 (1994): 10–13.

Garrett, Geoffrey. *Partisan Politics in the Global Economy.* Cambridge and New York: Cambridge University Press, 1998.

Gillis, Malcolm, ed. *Tax Reform in Developing Countries, Fiscal Reform in the Developing World.* Durham, NC: Duke University Press, 1989.

Goldscheid, Rudolf. "A Sociological Approach to Problems of Public Finance." In *Classics in the Theory of Public Finance,* edited by Richard Musgrave and Alan T. Peacock, 202–13. London: Macmillan, 1964.

Goldstone, Jack A. "Initial Conditions, General Laws, Path Dependence, and Explanations in Historical Sociology." *American Journal of Sociology* 104, no. 3 (1998): 829–45.

Goodman, J. B., and L. W. Pauly. "The Obsolescence of Capital Control – Economic Management in an Age of Global Markets." *World Politics* 46, no. 1 (1993): 50–82.

Gordon, Lincoln. "Assessing Brazil's Political Modernization." *Current History* (1998): 76–81.

Gott, Richard. "A Question of Black and White." *New Statesman*, April 2, 1999, 22–3.

Gould, Jeffrey L. "¡Vana Ilusión! The Highlands Indians and the Myth of the Nicaragua Mestiza 1880–1925." *The Hispanic American Historical Review* 73, no. 3 (1993): 393–429.

Graham, Richard, ed. *The Idea of Race in Latin America, 1870–1940.* Austin: University of Texas Press, 1992.

Granovetter, Mark. "Business Groups." In *The Handbook of Economic Sociology,* edited by Neil J. Smelser and Richard Swedberg, 453–75. Princeton, NJ: Princeton University Press; New York: Russell Sage Foundation, 1994.

Greenberg, Stanley. *Race and State in Capitalist Development: South Africa in Comparative Perspective.* Johannesburg: Ravan Press, 1980.

Greenberg, Stanley B. *Legitimating the Illegitimate: State, Markets, and Resistance in South Africa.* Berkeley: University of California Press, 1987.

References

Gutierres, Lourdes, Luiz Carlos Merege, and Jr. Paulo Nogueira Batista. *Aspectos da Questão Tributária no Brasil*. São Paulo: Folha de São Paulo, 1995.

Haas, Ernst B. "What Is Nationalism and Why Should We Study It?" *International Organization* 40, no. 3 (1986): 701–43.

Hagopian, Frances. *Traditional Politics and Regime Change in Brazil. Cambridge Studies in Comparative Politics*. Cambridge and New York: Cambridge University Press, 1996.

Hardin, Russell. *Collective Action*. Baltimore: Published for Resources for the Future by the Johns Hopkins University Press, 1982.

Hardin, Russell. *One for All: The Logic of Group Conflict*. Princeton, NJ: Princeton University Press, 1995.

Harring, Sidney L. *White Man's Law: Native People in Nineteenth-Century Canadian Jurisprudence*. Toronto; Buffalo: Osgoode Society for Canadian Legal History by University of Toronto Press, 1998.

Hartz, Louis. *The Founding of New Societies; Studies in the History of the United States, Latin America, South Africa, Canada, and Australia*. 1st ed. New York: Harcourt Brace & World, 1964.

Hasenbalg, Carlos A. "Desigualdades Raçiais no Brasil." *Dados*, no. 14 (1977): 7–33.

Hasenbalg, Carlos A., and Nelson do Valle Silva. "Industrialization, Employment and Stratification in Brazil." In *State and Society in Brazil: Continuity and Change*, edited by John D. Wirth, Edson de Oliveira Nunes, and Thomas E. Bogenschild. Boulder, CO: Westview Press, 1987.

Haskins, Victoria. "'Lovable Natives' and 'Tribal Sisters': Feminism, Maternalism, and the Campaign for Aboriginal Citizenship in New South Wales in the Late 1930s." *Hecate* 24, no. 2 (1998): 8–22.

Hawkesworth, Mary, and Maurice Kogan. *Encyclopedia of Government and Politics*. London and New York: Routledge, 1992.

Helg, Aline. "Race in Argentina and Cuba, 1880–1930: Theory, Policies, and Popular Reaction." In *The Idea of Race in Latin America, 1870–1940*, edited by Richard Graham, 37–69. Austin: University of Texas Press, 1992.

Hellmann, Ellen. *Handbook on Race Relations in South Africa*. Cape Town: Oxford University Press for the South African Institute of Race Relations, 1949.

Herbst, Jeffrey. "Racial Reconciliation in Southern Africa." *International Affairs* 65, no. 1 (1989): 43–55.

Herbst, Jeffrey Ira. *States and Power in Africa: Comparative Lessons in Authority and Control*. Princeton, NJ: Princeton University Press, 2000.

Heston, Alan, and Richard Summers. *Penn World Table*. Philadelphia: Center for International Comparisons, University of Pennsylvania, <http://www.pwt.econ.upenn.edu/home.html>, 2000.

Heymans, Chris, and Barbara Lipiez. "Corruption and Development: Some Perspectives." *Institute for Security Studies Monograph no. 40*, 1999.

Hinrichs, Harley H., and Harvard University International Program in Taxation. *A General Theory of Tax Structure Change During Economic Development*. Cambridge, MA: Law School of Harvard University, 1966.

References

Horowitz, Donald. *A Democratic South Africa? Constitutional Engineering in a Divided Society*. Berkeley: University of California Press, 1991.

Howard, David. "Coloring the Nation." *Hempisphere* 9, no. 3 (2001): 21–4.

Huntington, Samuel P. *The Third Wave: Democratization in the Late Twentieth Century*. The Julian J. Rothbaum distinguished lecture series; v. 4. Norman: University of Oklahoma Press, 1991.

Huttenback, Robert A. *Racism and Empire: White Settlers and Colored Immigrants in the British Self-Governing Colonies, 1830–1910*. Ithaca: Cornell University Press, 1976.

IBGE – Fundação Instituto Brasileiro de Geografia e Estatísticas. *Estatísticas Históricas do Brasil: Series Econômicas, Demográficas e Sociais de 1550 a 1988*. Rio de Janeiro, Brasil: IBGE, 1990.

IBOPE – Instituto Brasileiro de Pesquisa e Estatística. "Quatro Diferentes Graus de Relações do Carioca com o Negro." 1,32 June 10–16 (1951).

ILO – International Labour Office. *World Labour Report 1997–98: Industrial Relations, Democracy and Social Stability*. Geneva: International Labour Office, 1997.

IMF – International Monetary Fund. *Government Finance Statistics Yearbook*. Washington, DC: International Monetary Fund, 1998, 1999, and 2000.

Immergut, Ellen M. *Health Politics: Interests and Institutions in Western Europe, Cambridge Studies in Comparative Politics*. Cambridge and New York: Cambridge University Press, 1992.

Immergut, Ellen M. "The Theoretical Core of the New Institutionalism." *Politics and Society* 26, no. 1 (1998): 5–34.

Inglehart, Ronald. *Culture Shift in Advanced Industrial Society*. Princeton, NJ: Princeton University Press, 1990.

Inglehart, Ronald. *Modernization and Postmodernization: Cultural, Economic, and Political Change in 43 Societies*. Princeton, NJ: Princeton University Press, 1997.

Inglehart, Ronald, and Marita Carballo. "Does Latin America Exist? (And Is There a Confucian Culture?): A Global Analysis of Cross-Cultural Differences." *PS: Political Science and Politics*, no. March (1997): 34–47.

James, Herman G. *The Constitutional System of Brazil*. Washington, DC: The Carnegie Institution of Washington, 1923.

James, Wilmot Godfrey, and Moira Levy. *Pulse: Passages in Democracy-Building: Assessing South Africa's Transition*. Cape Town, South Africa: Idasa, 1998.

Jones, Stuart, and Andre Muller. *South African Economy, 1910–90*. New York: St. Martin's Press, 1992.

Jowitt, Ken. *New World Disorder: The Leninist Extinction*. Berkeley: University of California Press, 1991.

Jung, Courtney. *Then I Was Black*. New Haven, CT: Yale University Press, 2000.

Karl, Terry Lynn. *The Paradox of Plenty: Oil Booms and Petro-States*. Berkeley: University of California Press, 1997.

Katz, M. M. *Interim Report of the Commission of Inquiry into Certain Aspects of the Tax Structure of South Africa*. Johannesburg: Commission of Inquiry, Republic of South Africa, Various years.

298

References

Keck, Margaret. "The New Unionism in the Brazilian Transition." In *Democratizing Brazil: Problems of Transition and Consolidation*, edited by Alfred C. Stepan, 252–96. New York: Oxford University Press, 1989.

Keck, Margaret E. *The Workers' Party and Democratization in Brazil*. New Haven, CT: Yale University Press, 1992.

Kiser, Edgar. "Markets and Hierarchies in Early Modern Tax Systems: A Principal-Agent Analysis." *Politics and Society* 22, no. 3 (1994): 284–315.

Kiser, Edgar, and April Linton. "Determinants of the Growth of the State: War and Taxation in Early Modern France and England." *Social Forces* 80, no. 2 (2001): 411–48.

Knowles, Caroline. "The Symbolic Empire and the History of Racial Inequality." *Ethnic and Racial Studies* 19, no. 4 (1996).

Kritzer, Herbert M. "Substance and Method in the Use of Ratio Variables, or the Spurious Nature of Spurious Correlation?" *Journal of Politics* 52, no. 1 (1990): 243–54.

Laitin, David. *Hegemony and Culture: Politics and Religious Change Among the Yoruba*. Chicago: University of Chicago Press, 1986.

Lambert, Francis. "Trends in Administrative Reform in Brazil." *Journal of Latin American Studies* 1, no. 2 (1969): 167–88.

Leff, Nathaniel. *Economic Policy Making and Development in Brazil 1947–64*. New York: Wiley, 1968.

Leite, Dante Moreira. *O Caráter Nacional Brasileiro: História de Uma Ideologia*. São Paulo: Editora Atica, 1992.

Levi, Margaret. *Of Rule and Revenue*. Berkeley: University of California Press, 1988.

Levi, Margaret. *Consent, Dissent, and Patriotism*. New York: Cambridge University Press, 1997.

Levi, Margaret, and Margaret Stoker. "Political Trust and Trustworthiness." *Annual Review of Political Science* 3 (2000): 475–507.

Lieberman, Evan. "Causal Inference in Historical Institutional Analysis: A Specification of Periodization Strategies." *Comparative Political Studies* 34, no. 9 (2001a): 1011–35.

Lieberman, Evan. "National Political Community and the Politics of Income Taxation in Brazil and South Africa in the 20th Century." *Politics and Society* 29, no. 4 (2001b): 515–55.

Lieberman, Evan. "Taxation Data as Indicators of State-Society Relations: Possibilities and Pitfalls in Cross-National Research." *Studies in Comparative International Development* 36, no. 4 (2001c): 89–115.

Lieberman, Evan. "How South African Citizens Evaluate Their Economic Obligations to the State." *Journal of Development Studies* 38, no. 3 (2002): 37–62.

Longo, Carlos Alberto. "The State and the Liberalization of the Brazilian Economy." In *The Brazilian Economy: Structure and Performance in Recent Decades*, edited by Maria Jose Fernandes Willumsen and Eduardo Giannetti da Fonseca, 25–43. Coral Gables, FL, Boulder, CO: North-South Center Press University of Miami; distributed by Lynne Rienner Publishers, 1997.

Lovell, Peggy A. "Race, Gender, and Development in Brazil." *Latin American Research Review* 29, no. 3, Summer (1994).

Ludwig, Armin K. *Brazil: A Handbook of Historical Statistics.* Boston: G. K. Hall, 1985.

Luebbert, Gregory M. *Liberalism, Fascism and Social Democracy.* London: Oxford University Press, 1991.

Lunt, Neil, Paul Spoonley, and Peter Mataira. "Past and Present: Reflections on Citizenship within New Zealand." *Social Policy and Administration* 36, no. 4 (2002): 346–62.

MacCrone, I. D. *Race Attitudes in South Africa: Historical, Experimental and Psychological Studies.* Johannesburg: Oxford University Press, 1937.

Macedo, Roberto, and Fábio Barbosa. "Brazil: Instability and Macroeconomic Policies." In *The Brazilian Economy: Structure and Performance in Recent Decades*, edited by Maria Jose Fernandes Willumsen and Eduardo Giannetti da Fonseca, 1–23. Coral Gables, FL, Boulder, CO: North-South Center Press University of Miami, 1997.

Macroeconomic Research Group, MERG. *Making Democracy Work: A Framework for Macroeconomic Policy in South Africa.* Cape Town: Centre for Development Studies, 1993.

Maddison, Angus. *Brazil and Mexico.* Oxford, UK, and New York: Published for the World Bank by Oxford University Press, 1992.

Mahar, Dennis J. "Fiscal Incentives and the Economic Development of the Western Amazonia." *Brazilian Economic Studies* 2 (1975): 147–74.

Mahoney, James. "Uses of Path Dependence in Historical Sociology." Paper presented at the American Political Science Association, Atlanta, GA, September, 1999.

Manzo, Kathryn A. *Creating Boundaries: The Politics of Race and Nation.* Boulder, CO: L. Rienner, 1996.

Margo, C. S. *Report of the Commission of Inquiry into the Tax Structure of the Republic of South Africa.* Pretoria: Commission of Inquiry into the Tax Structure of the Republic of South Africa, 1987.

Markey, Raymond. "Race and Organized Labor in Australia, 1850–1901." *Historian* 58, no. 2 (1996): 343–61.

Marx, Anthony. *Making Race and Nation.* Cambridge: Cambridge University Press, 1998.

McGrath, M. D. "The Racial Distribution of Taxes and State Expenditures." Durban: Department of Economics, University of Natal, 1979.

Mendes, Daniela. "The Taxers Go for the Gold." *World Press Review* 1995, 16–17.

Merrick, Thomas. "The Population of Latin America, 1930–1990." In *Latin America: Economy and Society Since 1930*, edited by Leslie Bethell, 3–61. Cambridge, UK: Cambridge University Press, 1998.

Migdal, Joel. "The State in Society: An Approach to Struggles for Domination." In *State Power and Social Forces*, edited by Joel Migdal, Atul Kohli, and Vivienne Shue, 7–36. Cambridge: Cambridge University Press, 1994.

Migdal, Joel. "Studying the State." In *Comparative Politics*, edited by Marc Lichbach and Alan Zuckerman, 208–35. Cambridge: Cambridge University Press, 1997.

References

Migdal, Joel S. *State in Society: Studying How States and Societies Transform and Constitute One Another.* New York: Cambridge University Press, 2001.

Migdal, Joel S., Atul Kohli, and Vivienne Shue, eds. *State Power and Social Forces: Domination and Transformation in the Third World.* New York: Cambridge University Press, 1994.

Minister of Finance, South Africa. *Budget Speech.* Pretoria: Government Printer, 1991–2000.

Ministério da Fazenda. *Imposto de Renda: 60 Anos No Desenvolvimento.* Rio de Janeiro: Ministério da Fazenda, 1982.

Mitchell, B. R. *International Historical Statistics: The Americas 1750–1988.* New York: Stockton Press, 1993.

Moffat, J. B. *Report on the Working of the Income Tax Act, 1914, for the Year Ended 30th June, 1915.* Pretoria: Union of South Africa, 1915.

Moll, Terence. "Did the Apartheid Economy 'Fail?'" *Journal of Southern African Studies* 17, no. 2 (1991): 271–91.

Moore, Barrington. *Social Origins of Dictatorship and Democracy.* Boston: Beacon, 1966.

Moraes, Antonio Carlos Robert. "Notas Sobre Identidade Nacional E Institutionalização da Geografia no Brasil." *Estudos Históricos* 4, no. 8 (1991): 166–76.

Morse, Richard M. "The Heritage of Latin America." In *The Founding of New Societies; Studies in the History of the United States, Latin America, South Africa, Canada, and Australia,* edited by Louis Hartz. New York: Harcourt Brace & World, 1964, 123–77.

"Mortalidade Entre Negros no País Supera a da África." *Folha de S. Paulo,* November 15, 1998, 2.

Munck, Ronaldo. *Latin America: The Transition to Democracy.* London: Zed Books, 1989.

Mungazi, Dickson. *The Cross Between Rhodesia and Zimbabwe: Racial Conflict in Rhodesia 1962–1979.* New York: Vantage Press, 1981.

Munro, William A. "Revisiting Tradition, Reconstructing Identity? Afrikaner Nationalism and Political Transition in South Africa." *Politikon* 22, no. 2 (1995): 5–33.

Nattrass, Nicoli, and Elisabeth Ardington, eds. *The Political Economy of South Africa.* Cape Town: Oxford University Press, 1990.

Newbery, David. "Taxation and Development." In David Newbery and Nicholas Stern, eds., *The Theory of Taxation for Developing Countries,* 165–204. New York: Oxford University Press, 1987.

Newbery, David, and Nicholas Stern, eds. *The Theory of Taxation for Developing Countries.* New York: Oxford University Press, 1987.

Newcomer, Mabel. "Reconciling Conflicting Taxes in Federal Governments: A Summary of the Tax Systems of the Argentine, Australia, Brazil, Canada, Germany, Mexico, Switzerland, and the Union of South Africa." Washington, DC: Treasury Department, 1942.

Nobles, Melissa. *Shades of Citizenship: Race and the Census in Modern Politics.* Stanford, CA: Stanford University Press, 2000.

References

North, Douglass. *Structure and Change in Economic History*. New York: Norton, 1981.

North, Douglass. *Institutions, Institutional Change, and Economic Performance*. New York and Cambridge: Cambridge University Press, 1990.

Oates, Wallace. "On the Nature and Measurement of Fiscal Illusion: A Survey." In *Taxation and Fiscal Federalism: Essays in Honour of Russell Mathews*, edited by Bhajan S. Grewal, Peter D. Groenewegen, Russell L. Mathews, and Geoffrey Brennan, 65–82. Sydney and New York: Australian National University Press, 1988.

O'Connor, P.S. "Keeping New Zealand White. 1908–1920." *New Zealand Journal of History* 2, no. 1 (1968): 41–5.

O'Donnell, Guillermo. "The State, Democratization, and Some Conceptual Problems (A Latin American View with Glances at Some Post-Communist Countries)." In *Latin American Political Economy in the Age of Neoliberal Reform: Theoretical and Comparative Perspectives for the 1990s*, edited by William C. Smith, Carlos Acuña, and Eduardo Gamarra, 157–80. Coral Gables, FL: North-South Center University of Miami, 1994.

O'Meara, Dan. "Analyzing Afrikaner Nationalism: The 'Christian-National' Assault on White Trade Unionism in South Africa, 1934–48." *African Affairs* 77, no. 306 (1978).

O'Meara, Dan. *Volkskaapitalisme: Class, Capital and Ideology in the Development of Afrikaner Nationalism, 1934–1948*. Johannesburg: Ravan Press, 1983.

O'Meara, Dan. *Forty Lost Years: The Apartheid State and the Politics of the National Party, 1948–1994*. Randburg, South Africa; Athens: Ravan Press; Ohio University Press, 1996.

Pakenham, Thomas. *The Boer War*. London: Futura, 1988.

Payne, Leigh A. *Brazilian Industrialists and Democratic Change*. Baltimore, MD: Johns Hopkins University Press, 1994.

Payne, Leigh A. "Brazilian Business and the Democratic Transition: New Attitudes and Influence." In *Business and Democracy in Latin America*, edited by Ernest J. Bartell and Leigh A. Payne, 217–56. Pittsburgh: University of Pittsburgh Press, 1995.

Pearson, David G. *A Dream Deferred: The Origins of Ethnic Conflict in New Zealand*. Wellington, NZ and Boston: Allen & Unwin, 1990.

Penna, Maria Valeria Junho. "The Formation of the Tax State in Brazil: The Genesis of Income Tax." Rio de Janeiro: Instituto de Economia Industrial, Universidade Federal do Rio de Janeiro, 1992.

Pereira, João Baptista Borges. "Racismo á Brasileira." In *Estratégias e Políticas de Combate á Discriminação Racial*, edited by Kabengele Munanga, 75–9. São Paulo: Universidade de São Paulo, 1996.

Peters, B. Guy. *The Politics of Taxation: A Comparative Perspective*. Cambridge, MA: Blackwell, 1991.

Pierson, Paul. *Dismantling the Welfare State?: Reagan, Thatcher, and the Politics of Retrenchment*. New York: Cambridge University Press, 1994.

Pierson, Paul. "Increasing Returns, Path Dependence, and the Study of Politics." *American Political Science Review* 94, no. 2 (2000): 251–67.

References

Pierson, Paul, and Theda Skocpol. "Why History Matters." *APSA-CP Newsletter* 10, no. 1 (1999): 29–31.

Pitt-Rivers, Julian. "Race, Color, and Class in Central America and the Andes." In *Race and Ethnicity in Latin America*, edited by Jorge I. Dominguez, 56–74. New York: Garland, 1994.

Polanyi, Karl. *The Great Transformation*. Boston: Beacon Press, 1944.

Price, A. Grenfell. *White Settlers and Native Peoples: An Historical Study of Racial Contacts between English-Speaking Whites and Aboriginal Peoples in the United States, Canada, Australia and New Zealand*. Cambridge: Cambridge University Press, 1950.

Price, Robert M. *The Apartheid State in Crisis: Political Transformation in South Africa 1975–1990*. New York: Oxford University Press, 1991.

Price, Robert. "Race and Reconciliation in the New South Africa." *Politics and Society* 25, no. 2 (1997): 149–78.

Przeworski, Adam, Michael E. Alvarez, José Antonio Cheibub, and Fernando Limongi. *Democracy and Development: Political Institutions and Material Well-Being in the World, 1950–1990*. Cambridge: Cambridge University Press, 2000.

Przeworski, Adam, and Michael Wallerstein. "Structural Dependence of the State on Capital." *The American Political Science Review* 82, no. 1 (1988): 11–29.

Putnam, Robert. *Making Democracy Work: Civic Traditions in Modern Italy*. Princeton, NJ: Princeton University Press, 1993.

Putnam, Robert D. *Bowling Alone: The Collapse and Revival of American Community*. New York: Simon & Schuster, 2000.

Rezende, Fernando. "Income Taxation and Fiscal Equity." *Brazilian Economic Studies* 2 (1975): 105–45.

Rezende, Fernando. *O Processo da Reforma Tributária*. Brasília: IPEA, 1996a.

Rezende, Fernando. *Propostas de Reforma no Sistema Tributária Nacional*. Brasília: IPEA, 1996b.

Ribeiro, Darcy. *O Povo Brasileiro*. São Paulo: Companhia das Letras, 1995.

Ritschl, Hans. "Communal Economy and Market Economy." In *Classics in the Theory of Public Finance*, edited by Richard Musgrave and Alan T. Peacock, 233–41. London: Macmillan, 1964.

Roberts, Julia. "'A Mixed Assemblage of Persons': Race and Tavern Space in Upper Canada." *The Canadian Historical Review* 83, no. 1 (2002): 1–28.

Ronzoni, Raul. "Uruguay: Afro-Uruguayans Face Discrimination, Says Report." Inter-Press Service. June 1998. Available at: www.oneworld.net.

Rothstein, Bo. "Labor-Market Institutions and Working-Class Strength." In *Structuring Politics: Historical Institutionalism in Comparative Analysis*, edited by Sven Steinmo, Kathleen Thelen, and Frank Longstreth, 33–56. New York: Cambridge University Press, 1995.

Safford, F. "Race, Integration, and Progress: Elite Attitudes and the Indian in Colombia, 1750–1870." *Hispanic American Historical Review* 71, no. 1 (1991): 1–34.

Sagás, Ernesto. *Race and Politics in the Dominican Republic*. Gainesville: University Press of Florida, 2000.

Schmitter, Philippe. *Interest Conflict and Political Change in Brazil*. Stanford, CA: Stanford University Press, 1971.

Scholz, John T., and Neil Pinney. "Duty, Fear, and Tax Compliance: The Heuristic Basis of Citizenship." *American Journal of Political Science* 39, no. 2 (1995): 490–512.

Schumpeter, Joseph A. "The Crisis of the Tax State." In *International Economic Papers, Number 4*, edited by Alan T. Peacock et al., 5–38. London: Macmillan, 1954.

Scott, James C. *Seeing Like a State: How Certain Schemes to Improve the Human Condition Have Failed*. New Haven, CT; London: Yale University Press, 1998.

Seidman, Gay. *Manufacturing Militance: Workers' Movements in Brazil and South Africa 1970–85*. Berkeley University of California Press, 1994.

Shah, Anwar, and John Whalley. "The Redistributive Impact of Taxation in Developing Countries." In *Tax Policy in Developing Countries*, edited by Javad Khalilzadeh-Shirazi and Anwar Shah, 166–87. Washington, DC: World Bank, 1991.

Shapiro, Ian. "Why the Poor Don't Soak the Rich: Notes on Democracy and Distribution." Paper presented at the the the Conference on Democracy and Distribution, Yale University, October, 1999.

Shoup, Carl S. *The Tax System of Brazil*. Rio de Janeiro: Fundação Getúlio Vargas, Commisão de Reforma de Ministério da Fazenda, 1965.

Sierra, Nicole. "The Americas: A Supply-Side Jump Start for Brazil's Stalled Economy." *Wall Street Journal*, January 28, 1994, A14.

Simson, Howard. "The Myth of the White Working Class in South Africa." *African Review* 4, no. 2 (1974).

Sisk, Timothy D. *Democratization in South Africa: The Elusive Social Contract*. Princeton, NJ: Princeton University Press, 1995.

Skidmore, Thomas. *Politics in Brazil, 1930–1964*. New York: Oxford University Press, 1967.

Skidmore, Thomas. "Politics and Economic Policy Making in Authoritarian Brazil, 1937–1971." In *Authoritarian Brazil: Origins, Policies, and Future*, edited by Alfred Stepan, 3–46. New Haven, CT: Yale University Press, 1973.

Skidmore, Thomas E. *Black into White: Race and Nationality in Brazilian Thought*. Durham, NC: Duke University Press, 1995.

Skidmore, Thomas E. *Brazil: Five Centuries of Change, Latin American Histories*. New York: Oxford University Press, 1999.

Skocpol, Theda, ed. *Vision and Method in Historical Sociology*. New York: Cambridge University Press, 1984.

Skocpol, Theda, and Margaret Somers. "The Uses of Comparative History in Macrosocial Inquiry." *Comparative Studies in Society and History* 22, no. 2 (1980): 174–97.

Slemrod, Joel. "On Voluntary Compliance, Voluntary Taxes, and Social Capital." *National Tax Journal* 51, September (1998): 485–91.

Social and Economic Planning Council. *Report No. 7 of the Social and Economic Planning Council into the Tax System*, 1946.

South African Reserve Bank. *Public Finance Statistics of South Africa 1946–1993*. Pretoria: South African Reserve Bank, 1994.

References

Sparks, Allister Haddon. *Tomorrow Is Another Country: The Inside Story of South Africa's Road to Change.* New York: Hill and Wang, 1995.

Stavenhagen, Rodolfo. "Challenging the Nation-State in Latin America." In *Race and Ethnicity in Latin America*, edited by Jorge I. Dominguez, 329–48. New York: Garland, 1994.

Steinmo, Sven. *Taxation and Democracy.* New Haven, CT: Yale University Press, 1993.

Steinmo, Sven, Kathleen Thelen, and Frank Longstreth. *Structuring Politics: Historical Institutionalism in Comparative Analysis.* New York: Cambridge University Press, 1995.

Steinmo, Sven, and Caroline J. Tolbert. "Do Institutions Really Matter? Taxation in Industrialized Democracies." *Comparative Political Studies* 31, no. 2 (1998): 165–87.

Stepan, Alfred. "Federalism and Democracy: Beyond the U.S. Model." *Journal of Democracy* 10, no. 4 (1999): 19–34.

Suplicy, Eduardo Matarazzo. "O Programa de Renda Mínima." In *Seminario: Aspetos da Questão Tributária no Brasil*, edited by Lourdes Gutierres, Luiz Carlos Merege, and Paulo Nogueira Batista, 23–30. Sao Paulo, Brazil: Folha de São Paulo, 1995.

Surtees, Peter Geoffrey. "An Historical Perspective on Income Tax Legislation in South Africa." Masters thesis, Rhodes University, Grahamstown, South Africa, 1985.

Swank, Duane. "Culture, Institutions, and Economic Growth: Theory, Recent Evidence, and the Role of Communitarian Polities." *American Political Science Review* 40, no. 3 (1996): 660–79.

Tanzi, Vito. "Quantitative Characteristics of the Tax Systems of Developing Countries." In *The Theory of Taxation for Developing Countries*, edited by David Newberry and Nicholas Stern, 205–41. Washington, DC: Oxford University Press, 1987.

Tanzi, Vito. *Taxation in an Integrating World.* Washington, DC: The Brookings Institution, 1995.

Tanzi, Vito. "Globalization, Tax Competition and the Future of Tax Systems." In *Steuersysteme der Zukunft.* Berlin: Duncker & Humblot, 1996.

Terreblanche, Sampie J. "Testimony Before the TRC During the Special Hearing on the Role of the Business Sector." Johannesburg, November 11, 1997.

Thelen, Kathleen. "The Politics of Flexibility in the German Metalworking Industries." In *Bargaining for Change*, edited by Miriam Golden and Jonas Pontusson, 215–46. Ithaca, NY: Cornell University Press, 1992.

Thelen, Kathleen. "Beyond Corporatism: Toward a New Framework for the Study of Labor in Advanced Capitalism." *Comparative Politics* 27, no. 1 (1994): 107–24.

Thelen, Kathleen. "Historical Institutionalism in Comparative Politics." *Annual Review of Political Science* 2 (1999): 369–404.

Thompson, Leonard. *The Unification of South Africa 1902–1910.* London: Oxford University Press, 1960.

Thompson, Leonard. *A History of South Africa.* New Haven, CT: Yale University Press, 1990.

References

Tilly, Charles, ed. *The Formation of National States in Western Europe*. Princeton, NJ: Princeton University Press, 1975.

Tilly, Charles. *Coercion, Capital, and European States, AD 990–1992*. Malden, MA: Blackwell, 1992.

"Truant Cabinet Ministers to be Called to Account." *Business Day*, March 4, 1998.

Tsebelis, George. "Rational Choice and Culture." *APSA-CP Newsletter* 8, no. 2 (1997): 15–18.

Turra, Cleusa, and Gustavo Venturi, eds. *Racismo Cordial*. São Paulo: Editora Ática, 1995.

United Nations Development Program. *Human Development Report*. Vol. 1990. New York: Oxford University Press, 1990.

United Nations Development Program. *Human Development Report*. Vol. 1994. New York: Oxford University Press, 1994.

United Nations Development Program. *Human Development Report*. Vol. 1996. New York: Oxford University Press, 1996.

Van Blerck, Marius Cloete. *Mining Tax in South Africa*. Rivonia, South Africa: Taxfax CC, 1992.

Varsano, Ricardo. "The Tax System of 1967: Is It Still Adequate for Brazil in the 1980s." In *Brazilian Economic Studies*, 327–65. Rio de Janeiro: Instituto de Planejamento Econômico e Social, 1984.

Varsano, Ricardo. "A Evolução do Sistema Tributário Brasileiro ao Longo do Século: Anotações e Reflexões para Futura Reformas." Rio de Janeiro: Instituto de Pesquisa Econômica Aplicada, 1996.

Villela, Annibal V., and Wilson Suzigan. "Government Policy and the Economic Growth of Brazil, 1889–1945." Rio de Janeiro: Instituto de Planejamento Economico e Social/Instituto de Pesquisas (INPES), 1977.

Von Stein, Lorenz. "On Taxation." In *Classics in the Theory of Public Finance*, edited by Richard Musgrave and Alan T. Peacock, 28–36. London: Macmillan, 1964.

Wagley, Charles. *An Introduction to Brazil*. New York: Columbia University Press, 1971.

Wagley, Charles. On the Concept of the Social Race in the Americas. In *Race and Ethnicity in Latin America*, edited by J. I. Dominguez, 13–27. New York: Garland, 1994.

Wainer, Graham D. "An Enquiry into the Factors Affecting the Development of the South African Tax Structure (1946/7–1985/6)." Masters, University of Cape Town, 1987.

Ward, W. Peter. *White Canada Forever: Popular Attitudes and Public Policy Toward Orientals in British Columbia*. Montreal: McGill-Queen's University Press, 1978.

Webber, Carolyn, and Aaron B. Wildavsky. *A History of Taxation and Expenditure in the Western World*. New York: Simon and Schuster, 1986.

Weber, Max. *Economy and Society*. New York: Bedminster Press, 1968.

Weber, Max. *The Protestant Ethic and the Spirit of Capitalism*. Hammersmith, London, UK: Harper Collins Academic, 1991.

Weyland, Kurt. *Democracy Without Equity: Failures of Reform in Brazil*. Pittsburgh: University of Pittsburgh Press, 1996.

References

Weyland, Kurt. "The Fragmentation of Business in Brazil." In *Organized Business, Economic Change, and Democracy in Latin America*, edited by Francisco Durand and Eduardo Silva, 73–97. Coral Gables, FL: North-South Center Press, 1998a.

Weyland, Kurt. "From Leviathan to Gulliver? The Decline of the Developmental State in Brazil." *Governance: An International Journal of Policy and Administration* 11, no. 1 (1998b): 51–75.

Whiteford, Andrew, Dori Posel, and Teresa Kelatwang. *A Profile of Poverty, Inequality and Human Development*. Pretoria: Human Sciences Research Council, 1995.

Widner, Jennifer. "States and Statelessness in Late Twentieth Century Africa." *Daedalus* 124, no. 3 (1995).

Wilson, Monica, and Leonard Monteath Thompson. *The Oxford History of South Africa*. New York: Oxford University Press, 1969.

Wisnefski, Stephen. "Brazil's Tax on Financial Transactions Helps Turn Bovespa Into Sleepier Place." *Wall Street Journal*, August 9, 1999, A9.

World Bank. *World Development Report: Opportunities and Risks in Managing the World Economy/Public Finance in Development*. Washington, DC: Oxford University Press, 1988.

World Bank. *World Development Report: From Plan to Market*. Washington, DC: Oxford University Press, 1996.

World Bank. *World Development Indicators on CD-ROM 1998*. Washington, DC: World Bank, 1998.

Wyman, Donald L., and Gary Gereffi. *Manufacturing Miracles: Paths of Industrialization in Latin America and East Asia*. Princeton, NJ: Princeton University Press, 1990.

Yashar, Deborah J. "Indigenous Protest and Democracy in Latin America." In *Constructing Democratic Governance: Latin America and the Carribean in the 1990s: Themes and Issues*, edited by Jorge I. Dominquez and Abraham F. Lowenthal, 87–105. Baltimore: Johns Hopkins University Press, 1996.

Young, Crawford. *The Politics of Cultural Pluralism*. Palo Alto, CA: Stanford University Press, 1976.

Young, Crawford, and Thomas Turner. *The Rise and Decline of the Zairean State*. Madison: University of Wisconsin Press, 1985.

Yudelman, David. *The Emergence of Modern South Africa: State, Capital, and the Incorporation of Organized Labor on the South African Gold Fields, 1902–1939*. Westport, CT: Greenwood Press, 1983.

Zulawski, Ann. "Hygiene and the 'Indian Problem': Ethnicity and Medicine in Bolivia, 1910–1920." *Latin American Research Review* 35, no. 2 (2000): 107–30.

Zysman, John. *Governments, Markets and Growth*. Ithaca, NY: Cornell University Press, 1983.

Zysman, John. "How Institutions Create Historically Rooted Trajectories of Growth." *Industrial and Corporate Change* 3, no. 1 (1994): 243–83.

Index

abertura, 183
Aborigines Protection Acts, in
    Australia, 245
Abrucio, Fernando Luiz, 85, 163, 192
African National Congress (ANC), in
    South Africa, 95, 180, 188, 204,
    205, 209, 210, 211, 220, 223
Afrikaanse Handelsinstituut (AHI), in
    South Africa, 203, 204
Afrikaners, in South Africa, 80, 83, 151,
    155
Afro-Argentineans, 251
Afro-Colombians, 250
AHI. *See* Afrikaanse Handelsinstituut
    (AHI)
Algeria, 243
American State Department, dispatch
    to, 135
ANC. *See* African National Congress
    (ANC)
Anderson, Benedict, 69
Anderson, P. M., 142
Anglo–Boer War, 13, 35, 69, 74, 76
    Africans in, 73
anti-Communism, 155
    apartheid and, 158–9
    Brazil and, 163
apartheid, in South Africa, 79, 151, 174
    anti-Communism and, 158–9
    end of, 191
    legislation of, 159

race and, 79–80
tax compliance and, 229
apartheid-like government, in Rhodesia
    and Southwest Africa, 245
Arendt, Hannah, 97
Argentina, 60, 251, 254
Asian economic crisis, 2, 218, 224
Asians, discrimination against, in
    Canada, 247
Associação Industrial, in Brazil, 133
Association of Chambers of Commerce
    (ASSOCOM), in South Africa,
    91, 128
Australia, 81, 243, 245, 253
Austria, 256
automotive industry strike, in Brazil,
    219

Bahia capitania, 77
Banco Nacional de Desenvolvimento
    Econômico e Social (BNDES),
    in Brazil, 201
Barbosa, Rui, 85, 131, 132
Belgium, 256
Bendix, Reinhard, 78
black business, in South Africa, 205,
    227
Black Guard, in Brazil, 88
black markets, 58
Bloemfontein Convention, in South
    Africa, 75

BNDES. *See* Banco Nacional de
  Desenvolvimento Econômico e
  Social (BNDES)
Boer War. *See* Anglo–Boer War
Bolivia, 250, 256
Botha, Louis, 80, 125, 159
Branco, Rio, 87
Branco, Castello, 200
Brazil
  Brazilian empire, 76–7, 85, 111
  class relations in, 97–104, 134,
    149–50, 197, 213
  colonial taxation in, 71, 108–10,
    112
  constitution of, 35, 69–70, 74, 84–5,
    101, 124, 187
  corruption in, 26
  coup d'etat in, 146
  developmentalism in, 151
  Dutch empire in, 77
  federalism in, 4, 19, 79, 84–5, 98,
    132, 187, 242, 271–3
  immigration policy of, 87
  industrialization in, 98
  lower groups in, 102–3, 134, 147–9,
    166, 196, 210–13, 218–9
  National Political Community
    (NPC) in, 4–5, 9, 19, 35–6, 79t,
    84–9, 98, 105, 122, 161, 164,
    172, 174, 185, 235–8, 241–2,
    250
  political community model in,
    18–19
  provincial revolts in, 77
  race in, 4–5, 11, 19, 35–6, 71, 73,
    84–8, 97–104, 125, 134, 145,
    161, 163, 172–5, 185–94, 201,
    211, 225, 238, 242, 246–9, 272,
    281
  regionalism in, 4, 76–8, 84, 97–101,
    103, 122, 144–51, 161–2, 164–6,
    192–4, 197, 201, 208, 212, 272
  republican movement in, 69
  South Africa, similarities with, 8–9,
    34, 238

  tax administration in, 109–10, 124t,
    134–6, 139t, 147, 150, 156–8,
    163, 226
  tax compliance in, 110, 112, 131,
    133, 135–6, 139t, 148–51, 156–7,
    164, 166, 203, 214, 225, 227,
    229–33
  tax policy in, 110–1, 122–4, 131–6,
    139t, 144–50, 156–7, 166, 202,
    218, 222, 224, 234–5
  tax reform in, 144–8, 150, 153–4,
    156t, 161–6, 212–9, 222–4,
    235
  tax revenues in, 2, 63, 65t, 110–11,
    118–20, 124–5, 132, 137–9, 144,
    146, 150–1, 155–6, 162, 166–8,
    214, 229–35
  tax state in, 7, 11, 39, 57t, 108, 117,
    137–9, 156t, 162, 165, 171–4,
    214, 234–5, 278–9
  upper groups in, 101, 133–7,
    147–50, 155–7, 161–6,
    199–203
  whitening strategy in, 86–7, 100,
    134, 190, 250
Bretton Woods organizations, 116
bribery, in Brazil, 26
bureaucracy, tax collection and, 31–2
Business South Africa, 204

Café com Leite, in Brazil, 99
Campbell-Bannerman, Sir Henry, 81
Canada, 81, 243, 246, 253, 262
Cape Colony, 75, 111
  taxation in, 112
Cape Province, black vote in, 81
captaincy system. *See* capitanias
capital mobility, 178
capitalists. *See* upper groups
capitanias, in Brazil 76–7
Cardoso, Fernando Henrique, 1, 2,
  184, 190
Catholic University of Rio De Janeiro,
  190
Central South African Railways, 108

Index

Central Única dos Trabalhadores
(CUT), in Brazil, 211, 212, 213,
219
Centro Industrial do Brasil, 133, 135
Centro Industrial do Rio de Janeiro,
135
CGT. See Confederação Geral dos
Trabalhadores (CGT)
Chamber of Mines, in South Africa, 91,
128, 142
Cheibub, José Antonio, 31
Chile, 180, 243, 251
civil rights legislation, in the United
States, 245
class relations, 3–4, 14–18, 89–104,
155, 174–5, 257
in Brazil, 97–104, 134, 149–50, 197,
213
cohesion in, 3, 16, 90, 155, 174
cross-class, 15, 17, 95–7, 103–4, 175
fragmentation in, 15, 97, 213, 257
National Political Community
(NPC) and, 15, 89
organizations and, 15
political strategies and, 195–213
social norms and 15
in South Africa, 90–7, 140–1, 155,
175, 196–7
class solidarity, labor union density as
measure of, 264–5
clientelism, in Brazil, 97
CNI. See National Confederation of
Industries (CNI)
coercion, in tax collection, 40
coffee industry, in Brazil, 77, 113, 146
Cold War, 116, 123, 155
Brazilian taxation during, 161,166
South African taxation during,
158–61
influence on the development of tax
states, 152–8
taxation during, 152–66
colonial legacies, impact on taxation,
30, 106, 171, 266
Colombia, 250, 254

Communist parties, 116. See also
anti-Communism
Communist states, 54–5, 58, 62, 239.
comparative historical analysis, 196,
240
National Political Community
(NPC) and, 35–6
nested approach to, 32–5
CONFAZ. See Conselho de Política
Fazendária (CONFAZ)
Confederação Geral dos Trabalhadores
(CGT), 212
Congress of South African Trade
Unions (COSATU), 209, 212,
220
Conselho de Política Fazendária
(CONFAZ), 193
constitution(s)
of Brazil (1891), 35, 69–70, 79,
84–5, 124
of Brazil (1946), 101
of Brazil (1988), 187
conventions, 13, 78–9
critical junctures and, 68–70, 104–5
National Political Community
(NPC) and, 69, 106
of South Africa (1909). See South
Africa Act
of South Africa (1997), 35,
69–70,187, 236
of the United States, 85
consumption taxes, 46, 49, 54, 163,
179, 207
in Brazil/South Africa, 137f
contribution on financial movements
(CPMF), in Brazil, 224
coronelismo, in Brazil, 99
corporate taxation, 49, 210, 218
corruption. See trustworthiness of the
state
COSATU. See Congress of South
African Trade Unions
(COSATU)
Council of State, in Brazil, 111
coup d'etat, in Brazil, 146

CPMF. *See* contribution on financial
    movements (CPMF)
critical junctures
    in Brazil/South Africa 35, 68–105,
        172
    cleavages, 70–8, 185–95
    defined, 12–14
    mechanisms of reproduction in
        relation to, 19–23, 174–6, 185,
        187, 214–5, 225–30, 235–6
Cuba, 58
culture, taxation and, 28–30, 268–9
CUT. *See* Central Única dos
    Trabalhadores (CUT)

de Souza, Tomé, 77
Degler, Carl, 104
Delagoa Bay, 109
democracy. *See also* regime type(s)
    relationship to taxes, 30–1,
        234
Democratic Party, in South Africa, 188,
        204–5, 206
democratization, 182–4
    in Brazil, 173, 199
    lower groups and, 183, 208
    in South Africa, 173
    tax collection and, 234
Denmark, 60, 256
Department of Inland Revenue, Data
    Processing Section of, 161
Department of Social Welfare, of
    South Africa, 143
developmentalism, in Brazil, 151
diamonds, in South Africa, 76
dictatorship. *See also* regime type(s)
    in Brazil, 146
    tax collection under, 31
direct taxation, 48, 118–19, 132, 146
    in Brazil, 146
do Patrocínio, José, 88
D'Oliveira, João Daudt, 148
Dominguez, Jorge, 249
Dominican Republic, 250, 252,
        256
Dom Pedro I, 111

duties/tariffs. *See* trade taxes
Dutch East India Company, 72
Dutch empire, in Brazil, 77
Dutch settlement, of South Africa,
        75

Earned Income Tax Credit system, in
    the United States, 202
economic boycotts, against South
    Africa, 179
economic crises, 167–71
economic development
    National Political Community
        (NPC) and, 9, 10–12
    post-War, 2
    taxation and, 10–11, 113–4, 263–4
economic growth, 177, 180*f*
    in Brazil/South Africa, 154–5
Ehrlich, W., 91
El Salvador, 250
Ellis, Alfredo, 100
Estado Novo, in Brazil, 144, 150
estados, 84, 131, 145, 165, 278
ethnicity, 74, 263
ethno-regionalism. *See*
    region/regionalism
excess profits tax, 129
extermination policies, of indigenous
    peoples, 250–1

FARC rebels, in Colombia, 254
favelas, in Brazil, 194, 201, 278
fazendeiros, in Brazil 85
Federação Industrial do Estado de São
    Paulo (FIESP), 147, 199
Federação Industrial do Estado do Rio
    De Janeiro (FIRJAN), 133, 147,
        199, 230
federalism, 187, 256. *See also*
    constitutions; regionalism
    in Brazil, 4, 19, 79, 84–5, 98, 132,
        187, 242, 271–3
    country classification and, 242*t*,
        254–7
    National Political Community
        (NPC) and, 14

political community model and, 14,
256
regional identity and, 255
in South Africa, 187, 194–5, 236
tax state development and, 256,
268t, 265t
FF. *See* Freedom Front (FF)
FIESP. *See* Federação Industrial do
Estado de São Paulo (FIESP)
FIRJAN. *See* Federação Industrial do
Rio De Janeiro (FIRJAN)
First World War. *See* World War I
fiscal illusion, 48
Folha, 135, 148
fragment societies, 242–9, 261
National Political Community
(NPC) and, 244
race and, 243, 248–9
France, 60, 256
free rider problem, and taxation, 8, 40
Freedom Charter, in South Africa, 152,
184
Freedom Front (FF), South Africa,
189
Frente Negra Brasileira, Brazil, 104
Freyre, Gilberto, 163

Gandhi, Mohandas, 95
GDP. *See* Gross Domestic Product
(GDP)
General Sales Tax (GST), 220
generalized least squares (GLS)
regression, of annual tax in
South Africa, 121t
Ghana, 55, 266
GINI coefficient, 177
globalization, and tax reform, 173,
177–82, 198–9, 235
gold
in Brazil, 77
in South Africa, 76, 142
tax on, 111
Golden Law, in Brazil, 86
Goldscheid, Rudolph, 2
Goulart, João, 153
Gouvêa de Bulhões, Octâvio, 147

government receipts. *See* tax revenues
Granovetter, Mark, 199
Greenberg, Stanley, 159
Gross Domestic Product (GDP)
in Brazil, 119, 154t, 167t
income tax, ratio of, 61
per capita, as function of tax
collection, 11f
in South Africa, 119, 154t, 167t
tax state and, 61
Group of 20 (G20), 180
GST. *See* General Sales Tax (GST)
Guatemala, 250

Hagopian, Frances, 163
Hartz, Louis, 241, 249
Hasenbalg, Carlos, 191
HDI. *See* Human Development Index
(HDI)
head tax, 46
historical institutional (HI) approach,
22, 60–2, 279
HIV/AIDS, 278
homelands, in South Africa, 222
House of Assembly, in South Africa,
83
Hull, H. C., 125
Human Development Index (HDI),
187

IDASA. *See* Institute for Democracy in
South Africa (IDASA)
IFP. *See* Inkatha Freedom Party (IFP)
IMF. *See* International Monetary Fund
(IMF)
immigration
to Brazil, 71–2
Brazilian policy of, 87
policy, as an indicator of political
exclusion, 247
Immorality Act, in South Africa,
82
imperialism, 71
import substitution industrialization
(ISI), 113
Inácio da Silva, Luís "Lula," 211

income disparity, in post–apartheid
  South Africa, 278
income redistribution, through
  taxation, 221*f*
Income Tax Act, in South Africa, 125,
  141
income taxes, 48, 111, 122–37
  in Brazil, 1, 2, 112, 118, 125, 131–7,
    150
  collections, 13*f*, 63*t*, 118*f*, 129, 233*f*,
    265*t*
  enactment of, 123–4
  Gross Domestic Product (GDP)
    and, 61, 119
  paths to, 124*t*
  progressive, 48–9
  in South Africa, 1, 111–12, 118,
    125–31
  war and, 149
incorporation of labor, 15, 172
India, 60, 266
Indian Acts, of Canada, 246
Indians
  Latin American treatment of,
    249
indigenismo, 249–51
indigenous groups, 254
  treatment of, 246
indirect taxes, 48, 54, 127
  in Brazil, 150
Industrial Center of Brazil, 133
industrialization, 98, 113–4
infant mortality, 185–6
inflation, 137–8
  in Brazil, 148, 170, 170*f*, 216–17,
    217*f*
  in South Africa, 170, 170*f*
Inkatha Freedom Party (IFP), in South
  Africa, 188
Institute for Democracy in South
  Africa (IDASA), 188, 204
interest payments, in Brazil/South
  Africa, 169*f*
international economic growth rates,
  180*f*

International Monetary Fund (IMF), 2,
  61*n*, 116, 178
Internet commerce, taxation and, 280
Ireland, 181
Isabella, Princess, 86
ISI. *See* import substitution
  industrialization (ISI)
Israel, 256
Italy, 256

Jim Crow laws, 245
João III, 76
Jornal do Brasil, 165

Keynesianism, 116, 147
Khoza, Humphrey, 204
Kubitschek, Juscelino, 151
Kuwait, 58

labor, organized. *See* labor unions;
  lower groups
labor union(s)
  density of 264–5
  in Brazil, 102, 103, 213
  strikes, 93, 127
  in South Africa, 95–6
Lands Act, in South Africa, 95
language problem, in South Africa, 83
Latin American countries
  National Political Community
    (NPC) in, 250
  racial conflict in, 249–50
  slave/Indian treatment by, 249
League of Nations, 115
Leff, Nathaniel, 101
Levi, Margaret, 23
Liberia, 55
Lindblom, Charles, 7
Lourenço Marquez, 109
lower groups, 42. *See also* labor unions
  African National Congress and, 209
  in Brazil, 102–3, 134, 147–9, 166,
    196, 210–13, 218–9
  collective solidarity of, 208
  democratization and, 183, 208

organizations of, 42, 93,102
race and, 93
redistribution demands of, 196–7
regional interests of, 209
in South Africa, 93–7, 127–8, 141,
   209–10, 212, 220
strategies of, 208
strikes and, 93, 127, 141
tax policy and, 207–9
"Lula." *See* Inácio da Silva, Luís "Lula"
luxury taxes, 48

MacCrone, I. D., 93
macroeconomic policy, in Brazil, 168
Madagascar, slaves from, 72
Magalhães, Antônio Carlos, 218
Malawi, 243
Malaysia, 181, 243, 256
Mali, 55
Mandela, Nelson, 1, 2, 180, 184, 191,
   215
Maoris, in New Zealand, 246, 247, 253
Mapuche, discrimination against, 251
MAR dataset. *See* Minorities at Risk
   (MAR) dataset
Maranhão, 77, 109
market integration, 179
Marx, Anthony, 76, 98, 240
Marx, Irton, 194
Marx, Karl, 7, 273
Marxism, 42
Mbeki, Thabo, 191
Mboweni, Tito, 220
mechanisms of reproduction, following
   critical junctures, 19–23, 174–6,
   185, 187, 214–5, 225–30, 235–6
Mercosul, 180
Merrick, Thomas, 249
mestizo, 100
Mexico, 250
middle class, 42
Migdal, Joel, 40, 41
military rule, in Brazil, 212
Milner, Lord, 81
Minas Gerais, 77, 99

mining revenues, in South Africa,
   120–1
Minister of Finance
   of Brazil, 162, 164–5, 218
   of South Africa, 126, 141–2, 160,
      206, 207
Minorities at Risk (MAR) dataset, 253,
   254
miscegenation, 72
   policy of, 250
Mobutu, Sese Seko, 26
modernization
   in Brazil/South Africa, 177
   influence on the tax state, 10–11
Mozambique, slaves from, 72
multinational firms, 178

NAAMSA. *See* National Association of
   Automobile Manufacturers in
   South Africa (NAAMSA)
NAFCOC. *See* National African
   Federated Chamber of
   Commerce (NAFCOC)
Naidoo, Jay, 220
Namibia, 243, 245, 253
Napoleonic Wars, 75
Natal, 75, 82, 109, 111
National African Federated Chamber
   of Commerce (NAFCOC), 204
National Association of Automobile
   Manufacturers in South Africa
   (NAAMSA), 204
National Confederation of Industries
   (CNI), in Brazil, 101, 199
National Council of Provinces
   (NCOP), in South Africa, 187
National Economic Development and
   Labour Council (NEDLAC), in
   South Africa, 204
National Party (NP), in South Africa,
   151, 159, 160, 188, 204–5, 206
National Political Community (NPC),
   3, 12–14, 35, 68–105, 106, 122,
   172, 174, 176, 185, 187, 206,
   235–7, 262, 269

National Political Community (*cont.*)
in Brazil, 4–5, 9, 19, 35–6, 79t,
84–9, 98, 105, 122, 161, 164,
172, 174, 185, 235–8, 241–2, 250
class relations and, 15, 89
comparative analysis and, 35–6
constitutions and,15, 69, 89, 106
constitutional definitions of, 79t
country, classification by, 242t
critical junctures and, 68
definitions of, 3–5, 9, 12, 69, 240–1
economic development and, 9,
10–12
fragment societies and, 244
future configuration of, 280–1
identity formation and, 3, 14
institutionalization of, 20
in Latin America, 250
political community model and, 89
predatory rule model and, 25
race and, 69, 87
in South Africa, 4–5, 9, 18–9, 78–84,
92, 105, 122, 125, 172–4, 185,
235–8, 241–2
statistical analysis and, 257
strategies of, 245
tax administration and, 5
tax compliance and, 236
tax policies and, 5
tax reform and, 174–6
taxation and, 9, 239–240, 273
whiteness and, 19
National Statistics Institute in
Uruguay, 252
nationalization, 184
nationhood, 69
Native Land Act, in South Africa, 82
NCOP. *See* National Council of
Provinces (NCOP)
NEDLAC. *See* National Economic
Development and Labour
Council (NEDLAC)
nested research design, 32–5
Netherlands, 256
Netto, Delfim, 162, 164

New Deal, 116
"New" South Africa, 183
New Zealand, 81, 243, 246, 253, 262
Nicaragua, 251
Nigeria, 256
nonracialism, 245, 248
Nordestino, 194, 202
North Korea, 58
Nova República, 183
NP. *See* National Party (NP)
NPC. *See* National Political
Community (NPC)

OECD. *See* Organization for
Economic Co-operation and
Development (OECD)
oil-rich states, 239
Old Republic, of Brazil, 99
Orange Free State, 75
ordinary least squares (OLS),
regression analysis of tax
collections, 257–8, 258t
Organization for Economic
Co-operation and Development
(OECD), 61n
organized labor. See labor unions;
lower groups

Pakenham, Thomas, 76
Pan African Congress (PAC), in South
Africa, 189
Panama, 250, 254, 262
Paraguay, 254
Paraguayan War, 69, 73
Partido dos Trabalhadores (PT), in
Brazil, 211, 213
Passos, Oliveira, 135
path dependency. *See* mechanisms of
reproduction
pay-as-you-earn (PAYE) system, of tax
collection, 161
Personal and Savings Fund Levy, in
South Africa, 141
Peru, 250
Peters, B. Guy, 115

Philippines, 256
PIS. *See* Program for Social Integration (PIS)
PMDB, 201, 211
Poland, 180
political cleavage, 14, 70–1
political community model of tax state development, 5, 9–18, 11*f*, 13*f*, 23, 30, 32, 174, 240, 274–5
    Brazil and, 18–19
    extension of, 276–7
    federalism and, 14, 256
    South Africa and, 18–19
    tax collections and, 244
    taxation and, 20
political crises, 69, 167, 169
political culture, 20
political fragmentation, 16, 18, 98
    among Brazilian workers, 102, 200
political parties, representation in national legislatures compared, 90–2, 188–9, 200
political strategies
    in Brazil/South Africa, 196*t*
    class relations and, 195–213
Pombal government, 109
"Poor White Problem in South Africa" (Carnegie Commission), 97
poor-whites, in South Africa, 140–1
population size, tax collection and, 266–7
Portugal, 109, 256
Portuguese colonization, 76
pre-modern taxation, legacies of, 107–13
predatory rule model, 23
    National Political Community (NPC) and, 25
    bargaining power, 235
privatization, 179, 184
Program for Social Integration (PIS), 166
progressive taxation, 48, 205, 207, 219
property taxes, 48
Protestant Ethic, 269

Przeworski, Adam, 42
PSDB, 201
PT. *See* Partido dos Trabalhadores (PT)
Putnam, Robert, 26

race. *See also* racial democracy; whitening strategy; slavery
    apartheid and, 79–80
    in Brazil, 4–5, 11, 19, 35–6, 71, 73, 84–8, 97–104, 125, 134, 145, 161, 163, 172–5, 185–94, 201, 211, 225, 238, 242, 246–9, 272, 281
    definition of, 71, 241
    in fragment societies, 241–54
    Latin America and, 249–50
    legacies of, 73
    National Political Community (NPC) and, 14, 69, 87
    politics of, 182–92, 196, 272
    problem of, 71–4
    regional cleavages and, 71
    in South Africa, 4–5, 11, 18–9, 35–6, 69–76, 80–4, 90–3, 97, 102–3, 125–8, 138, 140–3, 155, 158–60, 172–5, 185–96, 203–9, 212, 225–30, 237–8, 242, 245, 248, 253, 263, 271–3, 278–81
    state and, 241–54
    white supremacy and, 72, 73, 81, 90, 95, 246
    whitening strategy and, 68–87, 100, 134, 190, 250
racial democracy, in Brazil, 86, 163–4, 174, 201, 282
racial whitening. *See* whitening
racial/regional identities, compared in Brazil/South Africa, 186*t*
racismo cordial, in Brazil, 190
rainbow nation, in South Africa, 281
Ranchers/Miners, in Brazil/Argentina, 254
Rand Daily Mail, 142
Rand Revolt, in South Africa, 93, 141
rational choice approach, 21–2

Reagan, Ronald, 179
Real Plan, in Brazil, 216
recession, 167
redistribution, 225
of wealth, 197
regime type(s), 267–8
authoritarian states and, 30–1
tax collection and, 267–8
and taxation, 30–1
region/regionalism, 14, 164, 185–88,
192–5, 237. *See also* federalism
in Brazil, 4, 76–8, 84, 97–101, 103,
122, 144–51, 161–2, 164–6,
192–4, 197, 201, 208, 212, 272
cleavages, 71, 164, 185–8
inequalities in, 186–7, 191, 194–5,
212, 234–5
National Political Community
(NPC) and, 155, 254
politics of, 4, 192–5, 272–3
problem of, defined, 74
reconstruction of, 183–7
in South Africa, 4–5, 35, 75–6, 83–4,
174–5, 192, 204, 272, 282
state and, 254–7
regressive taxation, 48
religion, tax collection and, 268–9
rentier states, 58, 62
Republic of the Pampas, 194
republican model, in Brazil, 131–2
revenue collection, cost of, 2
Revolution of 1930, in Brazil, 145
Revolution of 1964, in Brazil, 162
Rhodesia. *See* Zimbabwe
Ritschl, Hans, 38
Russia, 256

SACOB. *See* South African Chamber of
Business (SACOB)
SAFCOC. *See* South African Federated
Chamber of Commerce
(SAFCOC)
Safford, F., 250
Sand River Convention, 75
São Paulo, 78, 99, 102

SARS. *See* South African Revenue
Service (SARS)
Saudi Arabia, 58
Scholz, John, T., 26
Schumpeter, Joseph, 1, 5
Second World War. *See* World War II
Secretaria da Receita Federal (SRF), 163,
218
segregation, 245
in Canada, 247
Seidman, Gay, 167
settler colonialism, 243
Sharpeville, 153, 159
Shepstone, Lord, 112
Shining Path rebels, 254
Sierra Leone, 266
skeletal state, 54, 55, 62, 107–8
slave trade, 80, 86
slavery, 71, 72
abolition of, 86
in Brazil, 72, 86
in Latin America, 249
in South Africa, 72
Slemrod, Joel, 26
Smuts, Jan, 80, 138, 140
social capital, 26
social heterogeneity, 263
social security taxes/withholdings, 49,
120*f*
Somalia, 55
South Africa. *See also* apartheid
Brazil, similarities with, 8–9, 34,
238
class relations in, 90–7, 140–1, 155,
175, 196–7
collective guilt about apartheid, 175,
205
colonial taxation in, 110–3
constitution of, 35, 69–70,187, 236
creation of (Union of South Africa)
80–4, 108
diamonds in, 76
federalism in, 187, 194–5, 236
first government of, 125–6
gold in, 76, 142

lower groups in, 93–7, 127–8, 141,
    209–10, 212, 220
National Party in, 151
National Political Community
    (NPC) in, 4–5, 9, 18–9, 78–84,
    92, 105, 122, 125, 172–4, 185,
    235–8, 241–2
political community model in,
    18–19
political party strength in, 92f
race in, 4–5, 11, 18–9, 35–6, 69–76,
    80–4, 90–3, 97, 102–3, 125–8,
    138, 140–3, 155, 158–60, 172–5,
    185–96, 203–9, 212, 225–30,
    237–8, 242, 245, 248, 253, 263,
    271–3, 278–81
regionalism in, 4–5, 35, 75–6, 83–4,
    174–5, 192, 204, 272, 282
tax administration in, 111, 124t,
    129–31, 139t, 143–4, 156–8, 161,
    223, 226, 229–30
tax compliance in, 111–2, 130–1,
    139t, 142, 156–8, 160–1, 169,
    206, 214, 225, 227–9
tax policy in, 111–2, 122–31, 139t,
    141, 142, 143, 156t, 157, 160,
    205, 210, 215, 218, 219, 220,
    222
tax reform in, 153–4, 156t, 159–61,
    205–7, 210–19, 222–3, 235, 273
tax revenues in, 1, 63–4, 111,
    118–21, 124–5, 128, 129, 137–9,
    141, 143–4, 151, 155–6, 168–9,
    214, 220, 232–5
tax state in, 7, 11, 39, 57t, 108, 117,
    121, 137–9, 156t, 171–4, 214,
    234–5, 272–9
upper groups in, 91–3, 140–4,
    156–60, 203–7, 219
South Africa Act, 69, 79, 80–1, 90, 96,
    192
South African Chamber of Business
    (SACOB), 203, 204, 206
South African Communist Party
    (SACP), 209

South African Customs Union, 109
South African Federated Chamber of
    Commerce (SAFCOC), 204
South African Native National
    Congress, 95
South African Party (SAP), 125, 139
South African Revenue Service (SARS),
    223, 229
Southern African Development
    Community, 180
Southwest Africa. See Namibia
Soviet Union, 58
    collapse of, 207
Spain, 256
Special Taxation Act, No. 40, 141
SRF. See Secretaria da Receita Ferderal
    (SRF)
state. See also tax state
    definition of, 6, 40–2
    executives of, 41
    model of predatory rule and, 23–5
    modern developmental differences
        in, 238
    pyramid structure of, 41
    race and, 241–54
    region/regionalism and, 254–7
    tax administration and, 6, 7
    as tax collector, 40–2
    tax revenue and, 6, 117
    taxation and, 7, 30, 39
    trustworthiness of, 25–8
    upper groups and, 7
state-building, 6, 113–17
    international factors in, 114–17
    path dependency and, 19–23
    taxation and, 39, 117–23
    war and, 115
state incorporation, 103
state rights, 193
state-society relations, taxation and, 40,
    49, 231
Steinmo, Sven, 19
subnational income tax collection, 257,
    259–60
    in federal v. unitary states, 262

Suplicy, Eduardo Matarazzo, 202, 204
Sweden, 60, 260

Tanzi, Vito, 178
Tanzi effect, 170
tariffs, in Brazil, 180
tax
  on gold, 110–111
  on mining, 129
tax administration, 2, 5, 6, 50–53, 118–19, 226
  auditors, 52
  in Brazil, 109–10, 124t, 134–6, 139t, 147, 150, 156–8, 163, 226
  Brazilian reforms in, 63
  bureaucracy and, 31–2
  challenge of, 53–4
  coercion in, 40, 157
  collection capacity and, 7–8
  colonial legacies and, 108–10, 266
  compared collections in, 233–5
  compliance with, 16–17, 130–1, 166
  computer technology and, 157
  costs of, 157, 157f, 226
  efficiency in, 274
  inclusionary strategies of, 262
  leakage, 52–3
  liability, calculation of, 52
  National Political Community (NPC) and, 5
  pay-as-you-earn (PAYE) system of, 161
  process of, 51f
  record keeping and, 6
  in South Africa, 111, 124t, 129–31, 139t, 143–4, 156–8, 161, 223, 226, 229–30
  South Africa's cost of, 157f
  state and, 6, 7
  tax state and, 39, 40–1
tax base, 46, 48
tax burden
  allocation of, 207, 221f
  regressive, 213

tax collection. *See* tax administration; tax revenues
tax competition, 279–80
tax compliance, 225–7
  avoidance, 229, 231
  in Brazil, 110, 112, 131, 133, 135–6, 139t, 148–51, 156–7, 164, 166, 203, 214, 225, 227, 229–33
  bureaucracy and, 226
  corruption and, 226
  in South Africa, 111–2, 130–1, 139t, 142, 156–8, 160–1, 169, 206, 214, 225, 227–9
  state credibility and, 226
tax corruption. *See* tax compliance
tax evasion. *See* tax compliance
tax incidence, measurement of, 217
tax liability, collection of, 53
tax offices, 130
tax paying cultures, 29, 171
tax policy, 45–9, 122, 182
  in Brazil, 110–1, 122–4, 131–6, 139t, 144–50, 156–7, 166, 202, 218, 222, 224, 234–5
  business engagement and, 228
  debates on, 182
  development of, 19
  hypothetical framework of, 47f
  individual influence on, 6
  lower groups and, 207–13
  National Political Community (NPC) and, 5
  modern, 19
  progressive, 218
  reform of, 214–17
  simplification of, 222–5
  in South Africa, 111–2, 122–31, 139t, 141, 142, 143, 156t, 157, 160, 205, 210, 215, 218, 219, 220, 222
  tax base and, 46, 48
  tax exemptions and, 50
  tax expenditures in, 50
  tax handles in, 46, 177
  tax holidays and, 50

tax incentives in, 50
tax rates in, 49–50
upper groups and, 198–207
vertical redistribution of, 217–22
tax reform, 154, 156*t*, 164, 173–6, 207,
    213–35
  in Brazil, 144–8, 150, 153–4, 156*t*,
    161–6, 212–9, 222–4, 235
  cost of, 176
  democratization and, 183
  globalization and, 177–82
  lobbying for, 206
  modernization and, 177
  National Political Community
    (NPC) and, 174–6
  organized workers for, 218–19
  pressures for, 177
  simplification, 222–5
  in South Africa, 153–4, 156t,
    159–61, 205–7, 210–19, 222–3,
    235, 273
tax revenues, 2, 44. *See also* income
    taxes; consumption taxes
  around the world, 64*t*–66*t*
  in Brazil, 2, 63, 65t, 110–11,
    118–20, 124–5, 132, 137–9, 144,
    146, 150–1, 155–6, 162, 166–8,
    214, 229–35
  as function of GDP/capita, 13*f*
  potential/actual, 50
  in South Africa, 1, 63–4, 111,
    118–21, 124–5, 128, 129, 137–9,
    141, 143–4, 151, 155–6, 168–9,
    214, 220, 232–5
  state power and, 6
tax state(s), 5
  adversarial, 7, 39, 55, 58, 59, 122,
    138, 161–2, 214
  in Brazil, 7, 11, 39, 57t, 108, 117,
    137–9, 156t, 162, 165, 171–4,
    214, 234–5, 278–9
  Communist, 55, 58, 62
  conceptualization of, 40
  cooperative, 7, 39, 58, 59, 122, 138
  definition of, 39–40

development of, 7–8, 39
economic performance and, 170
federalism and, 256–7
fiscal illusion and, 48, 59
Gross Domestic Product (GDP)
    and, 61
growth patterns, 113
in post-War period, 151
inflation and, 170, 170*f*
late 19th-century, 108*t*
legacy of, 107
lower groups in, 42
measurement/classification of, 60–3
modern, 40
political community model of, 11*f*,
    12–13, 13*f*
qualities of, 173
reforms of. *See* tax reform
rentier, 58, 62
rise of, 106–72
during Second World War, 139*t*
skeletal, 58, 62
in South Africa, 7, 11, 39, 57t, 108,
    117, 121, 137–9, 156t, 171–4,
    214, 234–5, 272–9
study of, 7–8
tax administration and, 39, 40–1
trajectories of development,
    117–121, 167
typology of, 43, 54–60, 56–7*t*
upper groups in, 42–3, 59
during war on Communism, 156*t*
taxation. *See also* income taxes;
    consumption taxes; tax state
  on capital, 178, 221*f*
  compliance, 157
  consumption, 49
  culture and, 28–30, 268–9
  definition of, 43–5
  democracy and, 30–1, 234
  dictatorship and, 31
  direct, 48, 118–19, 132, 146
  duties/tariffs as, 45
  economic development and, 10–11,
    113–4, 263–4

taxation (*cont.*)
  free rider problem and, 8, 40
  history of, 6
  indirect, 48, 54, 127, 150
  international influences on, 1–12,
    114–7
  Internet commerce and, 280
  National Political Community
    (NPC) and, 9, 239–240, 273
  path dependency and, 21
  political community model and, 20
  politics of, 1–37, 67
  population size and, 266–7
  post–War, 120
  pre-modern legacies, 107–13
  progressive, 17, 48, 205, 207, 219
  as public policy, 275
  regime types and, 267–8
  regional equalization and, 234–5
  regressive, 48, 217
  religion and, 268–9
  state and, 7, 140
  state development and, 39, 117–23
  tax state and, 38–9
  trends, international, 218
  upper groups and, 17–18, 39
  war and, 11–12, 137–50
  war on communism and, 152–66
  whiteness and, 3
Taxation and Democracy (Steinmo), 19
taxpayers, 50
  registration of, 52
  tax liability of, 52
  upper groups as, 42
Thatcher, Margaret, 179
Tito de Souza Reis, Francisco, 134
trade liberalization, 179
trade taxes, 45
  revenues, in Brazil and South Africa,
    116, 117*f*
trade unions, in South Africa. *See*
  Congress of South African Trade
  Unions (CONSATU)
transition levy, 219
Transvaal Province, 111, 112

Transvaal Republic, 75
TRC. *See* Truth and Reconciliation
  Commission (TRC)
Treaty of Vereeniging, in South Africa,
  69, 80, 108
Treaty of Waitangi, in New Zealand,
  247
Tribunal of the National Treasury, in
  Brazil, 110
trustworthiness of the state, 25–8
Truth and Reconciliation Commission
  (TRC), 210
Tsebelis, George, 271

Umgeni, taxation in, 112
unemployment, 182, 185–6
unequal societies, Brazil/South Africa
  as, 177
union density. *See also* labor unions
  in Brazil, 207
  as measure of class solidarity, 264–5
  in South Africa, 207
  in upper–middle income countries,
    208*f*
Union of South Africa. *See* South Africa
unitary states, 79, 82, 122, 254–7, 262
United Kingdom, 60, 256
United Nations, 41, 115, 116
United Party, of South Africa, 139
United States, 81, 85, 245, 253, 260
  end of slavery in, 74
United States constitution, 85
University of São Paulo, 190
upper groups, 15
  in Brazil, 101, 133–7, 147–50,
    155-7, 161–6, 199–203
  calculations/strategies of, 16–18,
    198–9
  collective guilt in, 175
  defined, 42–3
  democratization and, 183
  organizations of, 91, 101
  political influence of, 198
  in South Africa, 91–3,
    140–4,156–60, 203–7, 219

state and, 7
as tax payers, 42
tax policies and, 198–207
tax resistance of, 136
in tax state, 42–3, 59
tax support from, 160
taxation and, 17–18, 39
war and, 12
whiteness and, 18
Uruguay, 251, 262

Value Added Tax (VAT), 54, 163, 210,
220
Van Riebeeck, Jan, 72
Vargas, Gétulio, 98, 101, 144, 148, 172,
211
centralized administration of, 145
Venezuela, 58
vertical redistribution, 217–22
Von Stein, Lorenz, 44

Wagner's Law, 113
Wallerstein, Michael, 42
war
on Communism, 163. *See also* Cold
War
taxation and, 11–12, 137–50
Washington Consensus, 179
Weber, Max, 29, 268
Weyland, Kurt, 172

white supremacy, 72, 73, 81, 90, 95,
246, 262
white tolerance, of other South African
groups, 94*f*
white unions, 95, 96
whiteness, 4, 245
idiom of, 96
National Political Community
(NPC) and, 19
taxation and, 3
upper groups and, 18
whitening strategy, in Brazil, 68–87,
100, 134, 190, 250
Wildavsky, Aaron, 29, 49
worker's party (PT), in Brazil, 200–1
World Bank, 61*n*, 116, 177
World Development Report, 177
world trade, 181*f*
World War I, 123, 124, 131, 132
World War II, 115, 123
Brazil and, 144–50
South Africa and, 142–3
special taxation for, 137–8
taxes during, 149

Yashar, Deborah, J., 250
Yudelman, David, 171

Zambia, 243, 256
Zimbabwe, 243, 245, 253

Other Books in the Series (continued from page iii)

Gerald Easter, *Reconstructing the State: Personal Networks and Elite Identity*

Robert F. Franzese, *Macroeconomic Policies of Developed Democracies*

Roberto Franzosi, *The Puzzle of Strikes: Class and State Strategies in Postwar Italy*

Geoffrey Garrett, *Partisan Politics in the Global Economy*

Miriam Golden, *Heroic Defeats: The Politics of Job Loss*

Merilee Serrill Grindle, *Challenging the State*

Anna Gryzymala-Busse, *Redeeming the Communist Past: The Regeneration of Communist Parties in East Central Europe*

Frances Hagopian, *Traditional Politics and Regime Change in Brazil*

J. Rogers Hollingsworth and Robert Boyer, eds., *Contemporary Capitalism: The Embeddedness of Institutions*

Ellen Immergut, *Health Politics: Interests and Institutions in Western Europe*

Torben Iversen, *Contested Economic Institutions*

Torben Iversen, Jonas Pontusson, and David Soskice, eds., *Unions, Employers, and Central Banks: Macroeconomic Coordination and Institutional Change in Social Market Economies*

Thomas Janoski and Alexander M. Hicks, eds., *The Comparative Political Economy of the Welfare State*

David C. Kang, *Crony Capitalism: Corruption and Capitalism in South Korea and Philippines*

Robert O. Keohane and Helen B. Milner, eds., *Internationalization and Domestic Politics*

Herbert Kitschelt, *The Transformation of European Social Democracy*

Herbert Kitschelt, Peter Lange, Gary Marks, and John D. Stephens, eds., *Continuity and Change in Contemporary Capitalism*

Herbert Kitschelt, Zdenka Mansfeldova, Radek Markowski, and Gabor Toka, *Post-Communist Party Systems*

David Knoke, Franz Urban Pappi, Jeffrey Broadbent, and Yutaka Tsujinaka, eds., *Comparing Policy Networks*

Allan Kornberg and Harold D. Clarke, *Citizens and Community: Political Support in a Representative Democracy*

Amie Kreppel, *The European Parliament and the Supranational Party System*

David D. Laitin, *Language Repertories and State Construction in Africa*

Fabrice E. Lehoucq and Ivan Molina, *Stuffing the Ballot Box: Fraud, Electoral Reform, and Democratization in Costa Rica*

Mark Irving Lichbach and Alan S. Zuckerman, eds., *Comparative Politics: Rationality, Culture, and Structure*

Pauline Jones Luong, *Institutional Change and Political Continuity in Post-Soviet Central Asia*

Doug McAdam, John McCarthy, and Mayer Zald, eds., *Comparative Perspectives on Social Movements*

Scott Mainwaring and Matthew Soberg Shugart, eds., *Presidentialism and Democracy in Latin America*

Anthony W. Marx, *Making Race, Making Nations: A Comparison of South Africa, the United States, and Brazil*

Joel S. Migdal, *State in Society: Studying How States and Societies Constitute One Another*

Joel S. Migdal, Atul Kohli, and Vivienne Shue, eds., *State Power and Social Forces: Domination and Transformation in the Third World*

Scott Morgenstern and Benito Nacif, eds., *Legislative Politics in Latin America*

Wolfgang C. Muller and Kaare Strom, *Policy, Office, or Votes?*

Ton Notermans, *Money, Markets, and the State: Social Democratic Economic Policies Since 1918*

Paul Pierson, *Dismantling the Welfare State?: Reagan, Thatcher, and the Politics of Retrenchment*

Marino Regini, *Uncertain Boundaries: The Social and Political Construction of European Economies*

Jefferey M. Sellers, *Governing from Below: Urban Regions and the Global Economy*

Yossi Shain and Juan Linz, eds., *Interim Governments and Democratic Transitions*

Theda Skocpol, *Social Revolutions in the Modern World*

Richard Snyder, *Politics after Neoliberalism: Reregulation in Mexico*

David Stark and László Bruszt, *Postsocialist Pathways: Transforming Politics and Property in East Central Europe*

Sven Steinmo, Kathleen Thelen, and Frank Longstreth, eds., *Structuring Politics: Historical Institutionalism in Comparative Analysis*

Duane Swank, *Global Capital, Political Institutions, and Policy Change in Developed Welfare States*

Sidney Tarrow, *Power in Movement: Social Movements and Contentious Politics*

Ashutosh Varshney, *Democracy, Development, and the Countryside*